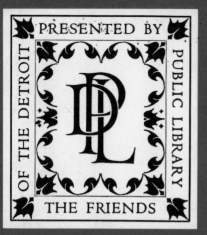

PARNASSUS ON MAIN STREET

PARNASSUS
ON MAIN STREET

A History of the Detroit Public Library

by FRANK B. WOODFORD

With a Foreword by
Ralph R. Shaw

Illustrated by
Donald G. Blaney

Wayne State University Press, Detroit 1965

CONTENTS

ILLUSTRATIONS

Contents

7

Grateful acknowledgment for illustrative materials and suggestions is made
to Ralph A. Ulveling and Charles Mohrhardt (Director and Associate Di-
rector), Catharine Haughey (Publications & Exhibits), Bernice Sprenger and
James Babcock (Burton Historical Collection), James Bradley (Automotive
History Collection), Florence Tucker (Technology & Science), and Jack
Cuthill (Printing), all of the Library staff, and to Helen Reisdorf, Robert
Shaftoe and The Detroit News

8

FOREWORD

THE HISTORY of the Detroit Public Library is the history of a very special part of the American dream.

The concept of a public library was pioneered in Detroit which continues to provide leadership in its development as a people's university. More than a hundred and fifty years ago Father Gabriel Richard proposed establishment of a public library in Detroit. Then in 1864, before the library opened its doors, the library committee showed the vision that was destined to guide the Detroit Public Library. The condensed extract below drawn from the committee's 1863 report may serve even today as a model for public libraries throughout the country.

> The library should be capable of use by the largest number of readers. While it may accumulate great resources, its capability of usefulness to the majority of the people must be its essential and ruling idea.
>
> While it should be a popular library, it must not be thought of as one that provides books for pastime or amusement only. It should furnish the means of genuine instruction and culture; books of real value and authority in all branches of human knowledge. It should be a repository of the best learning upon every subject of intellectual inquiry, and of the best literature of our own and other languages and times; distinguished rather for the excellence than the extent of its treasures.

The Detroit Public Library picked up the thread of history just as our nation was moving from the concept of libraries as storehouses of books—considered as precious physical objects for the use of the few—to the conception of books and libraries as people.

9

The ultimate magic of the American Public Library rests upon recognition of the fact that books are people. A book, or a pamphlet, or a magazine article, or a film, is really a person in recorded form. In this form, if we want to know what Matthew Arnold thought about predestination, we can ask him—long gone though he is—by consulting what he told us in *Sohrab and Rustum*. At another end of the scale, if we want to know how to line a blast furnace or how to grease a Stanley Steamer, we can, at our convenience and our will, consult the experts in these fields through their writings. Where else can any of us, whenever we wish to do so, command the great French chefs to tell us how to prepare their favorite dishes or, for that matter, how else could we get John F. Kennedy to tell us of his concern for the people living in areas of poverty within this country?

The Detroit Public Library had its beginnings just as the industrial revolution was getting into full stride; when we had begun to think of using conveyors and lifting devices for handling materials instead of using man as a beast of burden. This freed man to use his mind instead of his back. But minds needed nurture if they were to be used effectively. So the concept of man as an intellectual being grew, and with it grew greater need for understanding and compassion and wisdom, and for opportunities for continued intellectual growth for every man. Here the free public library provided a unique medium for supporting the growth of each literate human being. It provided opportunity for him to develop in any direction he chose, at his own pace. He was free to have intimate contact with all the people who could help to contribute to his aspirations and his achievement—whether or not they lived in his town or in his time.

There is another facet of the concept of books as people speaking to people. It is the idea of librarians as people who recognize the need to bring the people of books and the people of the community together. It is this factor—this catalyst that has been supplied—that has made the Detroit Public Library a great exemplar. The dream needs dreaming—but it also needs doing.

Practically from its inception, Detroit looked to its librarian for leadership. That leadership was forthcoming is attested by the fact that every chief librarian of Detroit in the last seventy-five

10

years has been a nationally recognized leader in the profession at large. Henry M. Utley, Adam Strohm and Ralph A. Ulveling, each in turn, were sought out by the profession to provide leadership on the highest level. Each has served as president of the American Library Association. Continuously over the years professional distinction has not been limited to the head of the organization but has extended out through the staff. The heads of many of the country's greatest libraries have been recruited from the people who had their training as staff members of the Detroit Public Library: Harvard University Library, General Motors Research Library, Cincinnati Public Library, and many others.

The Detroit Public Library has long provided leadership in selection and training of its staff for high professional ideals and service. It was one of the first libraries in the country to have a full-time personnel officer, to provide for high standards of personnel selection, and to develop an in-service training program.

As Americans assumed responsibility in the world at large, it is not surprising that our government turned to Charles M. Mohrhardt, Associate Director, to help in designing our Window-on-the-East—The American Memorial Library in Berlin—or that Mr. Ulveling has been asked to advise on library development abroad. Detroit has become recognized as one of the outstanding sources of imaginative librarianship.

In the early part of the century Mr. Utley started the great work carrying books to people by developing relationships with the schools that helped to enrich their curricula and produce a generation that knew books as part of their heritage. Mr. Strohm, the great idealist and builder, carried the library's facilities out to the neighborhood. Mr. Ulveling went a long step farther in making the library a part of the fiber and conscience of community living, with the library accepting responsibility for participation in community affairs.

Scientific management is now just beginning to come into its own in the library world. The Detroit Public Library, however, has pioneered this area for thirty years. As a result, simplified procedures were developed and many of the basic principles which were evolved at Detroit—the use of identification cards, pre-dated date-due cards—have become a fundamental part of all major book-charging systems in the country, including the photographic systems and the IBM-punched-card system. However, the staff of the Detroit Public Library was not interested in scientific management for its own sake. They were interested in management of operations to free more staff time for effective program development.

The great contribution of the Detroit Public Library in the current generation has not been single-shot spectaculars; nor has it been simply that the library has participated in community affairs that are in the news. Its contribution has been in the intellectual resources it has made a part of every man's way of life. Where other libraries were content to have readers' advisory service (if they had it at all) as a small and very special privilege for a few people at the main library, Detroit designed it into all of its branch outlets. Where most libraries have been content to hide their books under conventional classification schemes which librarians understand but the public does not, Detroit has pioneered in reader-interest classification to organize books in a system which would encourage people to use them and use them most fully. While other libraries have provided group services and have turned out booklists, in Detroit the library's involvement with people, singly or in groups, is a way of life.

With the evolving patterns in our complex society the Detroit Public Library has realized that it must not only spread general reader services of high quality throughout the city and provide stimulation and reading motivation in every level of society and to every type of citizen, but also it has realized that it must develop subject literature in depth. During the last two generations we have seen man change from a beast of burden to a controller of machines. We are now seeing changes which further reduce the necessity for routine work on the part of human beings and require higher orders of knowledge and ability by people who design and operate an automated, mechanized civilization. These people require access to specialized information to meet the needs of our society and of the people living in a great metropolitan complex such as Detroit. The development of subject departments with collections in depth and a staff capable of evaluating and servicing specialized materials is a modern contribution in public libraries which bids fair to set an example for the rest of the country.

What the automobile has done for the economic and physical life of the people of Detroit and the country, its library has done for its cultural and intellectual life.

As we turn to new times and new problems, the history of the Detroit Public Library and its splendid leadership makes us confident that we may continue to look to Detroit, not only for its contribution to the economic and physical life of the country, but also for continued, enlightened and dynamic leadership in the things of the human spirit and the human intellect.

—RALPH R. SHAW

Rutgers University
New Brunswick, N.J.
June 26, 1964

PREFACE

ABOUT THE TIME that an author completes the manuscript of a book and before it is published, he receives a questionnaire from his publisher. He is asked to give biographical information and explain how, why and under what circumstances he undertook to write the book. His replies, of course, are intended for the guidance of the sales or promotion department in helping trap the public into buying one or more copies when it appears in print.

One of the standard questions on the form, phrased in different ways, but always with the same meaning, is "When did the idea of writing this book first occur to you?" It is a fair question and deserves a fair answer which, unfortunately, often cannot be given. Many books, like the elephant's child, are the products of such long periods of gestation that it is impossible to mark with any hope of accuracy the day of conception. This is such a book, and the sales department will simply have to do the best it can with vague and indeterminate information.

I would like to think—and there may be much substance in the thought—that this book had its genesis more than fifty years ago when the Detroit Public Library, like the author, was much younger.

Saturday, in that era, was library day. From the home grounds on Seward Avenue to Woodward and Grand Boulevard was not considered a long walk for short legs, particularly when the destination was the branch library in what had been built as a store or commercial structure. The price of admittance was a library card, and the application for one required the signature

15

of an adult. That was easily obtained by going next door to the North End Post Office. The superintendent, James Horan, knew everybody, young or old, and was quite willing to stand sponsor; perhaps in the belief that attendance at the library would preclude other less desirable forms of juvenile entertainment. Jim Horan was a wise man with sons of his own.

Once the requirements had been met, one had become initiated into the select circle and was entitled to participate in the tribal rites. These usually began with the story hour in which some young lady, facing a half circle of youthful seekers after the truth, opened the door to wonderland with stories of Hiawatha, King Arthur, Robin Hood or the Water Babies. From there it was but a short step in distance and time to the bookshelves and such comfortable companions as the Henty books, the Tom Swift series and, through the progressive processes, Bulwer-Lytton, Washington Irving, Charles Dickens, Mark Twain—and who can remember all the others! To use a modern expression, we were "hooked."

If, then, a genesis is required, let that be it. And before more is said, let the reader rest in relaxed assurance that this book is not a personal memoir, or a sentimental tribute to the "good old days." It was not until this book was well begun that the author, despite a lifetime of exposure to the Public Library, realized what a truly complex institution the modern big-city library is. Like most users, he took a great deal for granted. Had he been asked, a few months ago, to describe a public library, he might have pronounced it a big place containing a lot of books, with the ones desired having been previously withdrawn by somebody else. Librarians, by the same definition, are amiable people who disappear into the secret recesses of the library building with a call slip in hand, and return with the sorry news that the desired book is "out." Ah, well! Life is full of disappointments and frustrations, but they can be ameliorated by a detour to the browsing room which results in being late for dinner.

A look behind the scenes, however, produces a decidedly different impression. The biographer of a library is quickly struck by the complexity of its organization and the diffusiveness of its services. Yet, upon reflection, that is not strange because modern

16

civilization is both complex and diffuse, and the library contains the record of civilization. In order, then, for the non-professional to understand the Detroit Public Library, it became necessary to seek the knowledge and experience of experts, along with records which are not ordinarily found on open shelves. And where does one turn for the necessary guidance? Why, to the library, naturally.

This, then, becomes an acknowledgment and an expression of gratitude to the staff of the Detroit Public Library for aid and services above and beyond the call of duty. Without that help, this book could not have been written.

I was patiently and sympathetically counseled by many members of the staff, particularly the director, Ralph A. Ulveling, who met every demand I made upon him. Every resource of the library was placed at my disposal. Others of the staff were equally interested and cooperative, but space limitations prevent the effusive thanks to which they are entitled. Bernice Sprenger and George Southworth, of the Burton Historical Collection, not only dug out all sorts of records for me, but also permitted me to cart them away for use off the premises. Both are dedicated librarians—and good ones. Others who allowed me to infringe upon their time, and who never failed to give me whatever help I called for were Charles M. Mohrhardt, associate director; Arthur Yabroff, business manager; Marian C. Young, chief of Children's Services; Katharine Harris, Reference Services director; Kenneth E. King, Home Reading Services director; Robert Runser, chief, Technology Department; and Frances Brewer, in charge of Gifts and Rare Books. Once a librarian, always a librarian, as I discovered from helpful and productive interviews with two retired staff members. They were Mable Conat, former director of Reference Services, and Ruth Rutzen, former Home Reading Services director. Miss Conat, after completing a distinguished career as a librarian, served as secretary of the Friends of the Detroit Public Library, Inc. She was most helpful in supplying information in that area, as was her successor, Evelyn Tintera. Walter Kaiser, director of the Wayne County Library, was, as always, most cooperative. Others upon whom I called with the happiest of results were Dr. Russell E. Bidlack, associate professor, Department of Library Science, the University of Michigan. He furnished me with materials and suggestions of primary value. Miss Florence Anderson, secretary, Carnegie Corporation of New York, made available to me the records and correspondence pertaining to Andrew Carnegie's gift to the Detroit Public Library, and also furnished me with biographical material on James Bertram, Carnegie's secretary. J S Gray, editor of the *Monroe Evening News* also kindly supplied me with some data on Edward D. Ellis and his role in the first Michigan constitutional convention. Nancy W. Stirling, senior librarian, the New York State Library, gave me some background material on the origin of the penal fines provision for the support of libraries.

There is, I feel, no need for a protracted bibliographical essay. From the list of acknowledgments—which is by no means complete—it will be apparent that the greater part of the source material employed came directly from the library. This falls into three principal categories: the proceedings or minutes of meetings of the Library Commission; the annual reports of the Commission and its predecessor, the Committee on Library of the Detroit Board of Education, and the voluminous correspondence and files of reports of the librarians. The Detroit newspapers were frequently referred to as were the more or less standard history and reference materials relating to Detroit, and to personalities, which are available in the Burton Historical Collection. Various issues of professional journals were examined for specific information. The citations in the table of references indicate the range of the source material and, in most instances, its location.

A final word of acknowledgment is in order. I am grateful for the assistance of Helen Ruth Howell who helped in the research, Christine Colditz who copyread the manuscript, and Mary Anne Harrison and Vivian Sledge who typed it.

F. B. W.

CHAPTER 1

Detroit Gets a Public Library

ON THE AFTERNOON of March 25, 1865, the people of Detroit dedicated their first public library. The event attracted a group of civic dignitaries and, as one newspaper reported, "a large number of citizens." The dedication had been well publicized in advance. The Detroit *Advertiser and Tribune* had carried notices in both its news and advertising columns.

"The public are informed . . ." the *Tribune* announced under the caption "Opening of the Public Library,"

> that the Library will be formally opened on Saturday at 4:00 P.M. It is, indeed, an event worthy of being publicly recognized as of the highest importance to our city. The establishment of a free public institution such as this, opening with over five thousand well-selected books, and with the promise of a rapid, constant, and permanent increase, cannot be too highly appreciated.[1]

There was more, but the public really didn't need much persuasion to exhibit their interest and assure their attendance. This sort of gathering was a welcome change from what they had

19

been accustomed to attending. For four long dreary years, public meetings had been mostly patriotic gatherings, color presentations to a succession of front-bound regiments, recruiting rallies and soldiers' aid fairs. Now, to the relief of everyone, the Civil War blood bath was almost at its end and the citizens of Detroit, like their fellow Americans everywhere, were looking forward to building something solid and lasting in a dawning era of peace and progress. In a sense, Detroit's first free public library was its first war memorial.

True, the war between the states was not yet over, but it was running rapidly toward its end. Appomattox was only fifteen days away; in twenty days would come the tragic climax—the assassination of Abraham Lincoln. But close as the end was, victory could not quite be celebrated on March 25. On that same day, thirteen men in the city's Fifth Ward had been drafted. The New York *Tribune* reported, a little prematurely, the evacuation of Richmond. A bulletin picked up from the Petersburg (Virginia) *Express* of six days earlier said: "Grant's trains were moving all Saturday night with troops toward the left of his line," and a home-grown correspondent with the 10th Michigan Infantry had mailed back a dispatch from Fayetteville, North Carolina, which tempered its jubilation with a stern tone: "Now we have been wreaking vengeance upon South Carolina, the mother of secessia. Woe is upon her, and she has no relief. If she repents, it avails her naught, for it comes too late." [2]

Nevertheless, in spite of war bulletins and casualty lists which, while growing shorter, still were being received daily, Detroiters were in a more relaxed mood and their attention was being diverted to more normal matters. That evening of March 25 at the Athenaeum on Congress Street, Miss Rachel Johnson was appearing as Lady Macbeth, and a full house was assured. The Detroit *Tribune* was whooping it up for the candidacies of Isaac P. Christiancy, for associate justice of the State Supreme Court, and for Edward C. Walker and George Willard for regents of the University of Michigan at the forthcoming spring election. The *Tribune,* being staunchly pro-administration, naturally offered a Republican ticket.

If politics failed to attract the individual interest, there were

20

other things going on which could be relied upon to win attention and cause comment. The Police Commission, for instance, was offering a reward of $500 "for the conviction of the person or persons who murdered S. B. Smith of this city on the night of March 17." Alonzo Rolfe was promising one of the biggest horse auctions the town had seen on the following Tuesday on Monroe Street near the City Hall. Navigation was open, at least on the lower lakes, and there was a column of notices of vessel schedules. Captain John Pridgeon, however, had apparently decided to swallow the anchor. He was offering to sell his brig "Lucy J. Clark," an "A-1 vessel," capable of carrying 21,000 bushels of grain. George Truax listed a bargain, too. He had a house and lot for sale at 83 Miami (now Broadway). It was worth $3500, he said, but he would sacrifice it for less than $3000. Perhaps, he had to sell cheap in the downtown area. Since the horse drawn streetcar lines had been established two years earlier, folks were buying lots and building homes farther out Woodward in the new subdivisions being opened as far north as Adelaide and Sibley streets, or along East Jefferson, beyond Dubois, all the way to Elmwood. A business card announced that L. Black, at Jefferson and Bates, carried complete optical and photographic stocks. Like the Detroit Public Library, L. Black was a Detroit institution which is still thriving one hundred years later.

If anyone wondered whether a public library would be a useful civic adornment, his doubts should have been allayed by the offerings of at least twenty-one bookstores listed in the 1865 city directory. Detroit was a reading town. Aside from the law books, and the old standbys such as Shakespeare, Webster's Dictionary, and the *New American Cyclopedia,* there were such titillating new titles as *Wild Nell the Spy,* and *Dora Darling, The Daughter of the Regiment*—the latter "a story of much interest, and in it are depicted many thrilling scenes of army life both in the hospital and on the battlefield." Or, if the reader of light fiction was surfeited with war stories, the publishing house of Street and Smith was offering diversion with something fluffy entitled *Twice Deceived, or the Frozen Heart.* There was, in fact, something for everybody in the bookshops.[3]

But it was the attainment of the ideal of a free public library

21

which drew people to the Capitol High School at State and Griswold streets that Saturday afternoon. After all, the institution which they assembled to dedicate had been a long time coming. As far back as 1859, the Board of Education in which the law vested the responsibility for a library, created its own Permanent Committee on Library and Library Funds. In 1861, acting upon this committee's recommendation, the Board directed that a room in the Capitol School be fitted up as a library, but this was intended only for the use of teachers and students.[4] In the 1862 annual report, establishment of a "general library" in "the old Capitol building" was recommended, and in 1863 the Board was told that the founding of a free public library was assured.

But the public involvement in the war and the uncertainty about finances caused plans to proceed slowly. In 1864, books had been acquired, a catalog was ordered prepared, and "steps were taken to open the library to the public." Progress was still slow, as the Detroit *Free Press* noted on March 2, 1865, when it stated:

> Some delay has occurred in preparing the room and cases for the reception of the books of the Public School Library in the Capitol Union Building, and the formal opening, which was to have taken place today, has been postponed about a week. The room is a fine one and the library is an honor to our city. It is designed that the opening shall be celebrated by public exercise of some sort.[5]

Citizens in stovepipe hats and hoopskirts who turned out to take part in the Library dedication actually numbered about one hundred. That was really an impressive assemblage for a town whose population in 1865 was only 55,000. Unfortunately, no register was kept of those who attended, but it can be assumed that there was at least a majority of the twenty school inspectors from the town's ten wards. And probably there was a fair sprinkling of teachers on hand, mingling with various civic dignitaries. For after all, the Library was pretty much a Board of Education enterprise.

The Library room where the dedication ceremonies were held, comprised roughly the north half of the ground floor of the school. Years before, when the building was the Capitol, first of Michigan Territory and then the state, the space had been occupied by the single-house Territorial Council and then by the House of Representatives. Until the Library moved in, it was given over to lower grades of the union school. The room had been extensively remodeled, furnished with tables, chairs and lamps, and fitted with shelves which held most of the six thousand volumes that had been acquired. These, it was stated, had all been "properly arranged and classified." [6]

The greater part of the collection had been purchased in 1864 by Professor Henry Chaney, principal of the high school. Acting as agent for the school board's library committee under fairly specific instructions, Chaney made two trips east, first in April and again during the summer vacation, on book buying tours. With about $7000 in accumulated Library funds at his disposal, he visited publishers and dealers in Boston, New York and Philadelphia. He discovered that he could do best at the secondhand bookstores. One purchase of five hundred volumes consisted of the private library of a New York collector. It included a complete set of standard works known as the Bohn Libraries, published in England. Having made his selections and purchases "with great diligence and circumspection," the Library could point on opening day to a collection "selected with admirable care and discrimination." [7] The reporter for the Detroit *Free Press,* marveled at what he termed "a rare collection."

Among the acquisitions were treasures to bring a gleam to the eye of any bibliophile. Classics and rarities were included, along with such standard fare as Scott, Dickens, Charlotte Bronte, and James Fenimore Cooper. It is worth noting that a hundred years later, almost two thousand of the five thousand books he purchased are still treasured possessions of the Detroit Public Library. So well had Chaney carried out his assignment that he was given $100 for his efforts. His continued service was regarded as "a necessity," and it was recommended to the school board "that he be appointed Superintendent of the Library, at such salary payable from the Library Fund, as may be determined by the Board." The salary for his services totaled $400 in 1865, but the following year, when he was on a regular permanent basis as librarian, he was paid $620.[8]

In general, Chaney followed the classification and selection policies set by the Library Committee in 1863. It had been decided then, as stated in that year's annual report, that

> after due regard to the views . . . as expressed as to the character, purposes, and probable future growth of the library, the following plan of classification should be adopted: I. Theology; II. Philosophy; III. History; IV. Politics, Law, and Commerce; V. Sciences and Arts; VI. Literature.

In line with this classification, it was recommended that the initial purchases should be within the following classifications: "1. General Literature; 2. Works of Reference; 3. History (other than American); 4. American History; 5. Biography; 6. Poetry and the Drama; 7. Science and Art."

The choice of the original statehouse, now converted to a high school, as the location for the Library over which Chaney was to preside was a fortuitous one. The building had a long tradition of service to both education and enlightened government, and the Library was the offspring as well as the servant of each. Its situation provided a symbol of its source and obligation.

The Capitol building, or court house as early Detroiters called it, was a two-story building, built along classic Greek revival lines, with a Greek portico supported by six lofty Doric columns across its front. Above the main structure was a tall, graceful tower, rising in four stages and surmounted by a pepper-box top. The tower reached 140 feet above the ground. The structure's ground dimensions originally were 60 by 90 feet, on a roughly triangular piece of ground fronting on State Street. The plot resembled a pie-shaped wedge in the middle of Griswold Street, the point toward the north. At that time, the west side of Griswold was called Rowland Street, and it was lined with residences, while Griswold, on the east, contained mostly small business establishments. These two streets formed the legs of a triangle which had its apex at Grand River. Ultimately, after the Capitol and its successor building had vanished, the place was designated as Capitol Park. Modern Detroit converted it to a public transportation loading station, with only a small piece of green lawn and a flower bed remaining on the State Street side. That bit of greenery is adorned with a heroic statue of Stevens Thomson Mason, Michigan's first constitutional governor. The statue also marks the site of Mason's grave.

Like the Library which it ultimately housed, the Capitol had its own difficulties achieving an existence. The land on which it eventually stood was set aside as a park or for public use in the plan drawn up by Augustus B. Woodward, chief justice of the territorial court and a member of the governing body, the Governor and Judges. His was a grand design for a new city to replace the old French-British riverfront settlement which was destroyed by fire in 1805. Woodward conceived a city laid out something like Paris and Washington, with broad streets and boulevards, radiating from a series of connected parks, plazas or "circuses." Across the city, east of Woodward and fronting on East State Street (now Gratiot Avenue) was another green space of almost identical shape and dimensions which later would be closely tied to the destiny of the Library.

North of Capitol Park was the Grand Circus, intended by Woodward and his governmental associates as the location of a court house or territorial building. To finance construction of that and other necessary public buildings, Congress was prevailed upon to donate to the people of Detroit from the public domain, a huge piece of undeveloped land which became known as the Ten Thousand Acre Tract. This was to be sold off in small parcels to private purchasers, the proceeds to be used as the public building fund.

The Grand Circus location was soon found to be impractical. It was much better suited, as Detroit citizens of that era learned, as a place to shoot deer. The open space at the head of Griswold Street looked like a better choice, and in 1815 an act was adopted by the Governor and Judges designating that spot for a building to house the offices and council chamber of the Territory of Michigan.[9]

It was not until September 22, 1823, that the cornerstone was laid. There were troubles with the contractors, and a variety of delays, so that the building, which finally cost $21,000 plus $3500 for "extras," was not ready for occupancy until May 5, 1828. Citizens and officials alike complained at first because Capitol

Park, although closer to the town's center than Grand Circus, was still too far out in the country. Griswold Street was unopened at the time, north of Michigan Avenue, and to reach the Capitol from "downtown," it was necessary to walk out Woodward and go across State Street. That, of course, eventually changed, and before long the Capitol was in an easily-reached location, right in the heart of the city. It was that central location which made it an ideal place for the Library.

The Capitol continued to be the center of government for Michigan for nearly two decades. A roll call of dignitaries who occupied its offices or legislative chairs would have included Lewis Cass, Henry R. Schoolcraft, Father Gabriel Richard, Charles C. Trowbridge, Solomon Sibley and William Wood-bridge, just to mention a few. It was there, in the Convention of 1835 that Michigan's constitution was drafted which was notable, among other reasons, for a unique provision for the financing of libraries. Eventually, however, the building's usefulness as a capitol was outlived. The seat of government was shifted to Lansing, and the last session of the legislature to use the building adjourned on May 17, 1847.

After the state abandoned the Capitol, it stood empty and un-used for several months. Then, by a simple act of appropriation by the Board of Education, the building was taken over and converted into a union school. There was an air of questionable legality in the manner by which the board maneuvered its way into possession. True, the legislature was petitioned several times to donate the property to the school board, but the prayers were ignored. Finally, direct action achieved what petitions could not do. The key to the building happened to be in the possession of D. Bethune Duffield, an eminent lawyer, and a school inspector from the Fifth Ward. What happened is related by George B. Catlin, in his *The Story of Detroit*.

One morning, according to Catlin, people living in the vicinity of the Capitol, noticed that doors and windows were open, and the place inside and out was a-bustle with unusual activity. Loads of lumber were being delivered, and rubbish was being thrown out and carted away.

"Several curious and officious citizens went inside to find a big

26

gang of carpenters clearing away the old desks in the hall of representatives and preparing to erect partitions." The citizens demanded to know what the workmen were doing. "We're hired by the Board of Education and as long as we get our money we don't care a rap for any other authority."

They went on with their work until the interior was completely remodeled into classrooms. Along about that time the school board had some doubts about its high-handedness and asked the state for a lease. No law could be found which empowered anyone to transfer state property. Officials in Lansing suggested that as long as the board was in possession, the best solution would be to forget the whole affair and say nothing more about it.[10]

After a few years, Detroit's educational program grew more sophisticated, and a high school was opened. The first session was held in 1858 in a building on Miami Avenue. The site was long used in later years as the main administrative offices of the Board of Education. But the Miami School soon proved inadequate for high school purposes, and in September, 1863, classes were transferred to the Capitol. The second floor was extensively re-modeled to accommodate the 122 high school students. A news-paper described the preparations and arrangements thus:

> The main room on the second floor is large and commodious, being about fifty-five feet long by forty wide, and will accommodate over one hundred pupils. It is well lighted and neatly finished off. The desks, which are imported from the East, and of the most ap-proved pattern, are well adapted to economize space and give the room a neat and graceful appearance. An additional convenience, secured by the present alterations, and one deserving special notice, is found in the ample recitation rooms, three in number, located in the further end of the building.[11]

When the September, 1863, term opened, it was noted that for the first time all four high school grades were accommodated under one roof. In time, the 1863 quarters were outgrown, and in 1875 a new four-story brick building was erected on the front of the lot. With its construction all vestiges of the venerable Capitol disappeared from view. Generally, it was known as the "High School" or "the Detroit High School." Only the elder citizens referred to it as the "Capitol High School." By whatever

27

name it was called, it served the city as its only public high school until 1893 when it was destroyed by fire. A new school was then located elsewhere and the Capitol site reverted to the city and became a park.[12]

But on March 25, 1865, it was very much in use and the center of educational interest in Detroit. By putting the new public Library under the same roof there was created what might be described as Detroit's first cultural center. At least that is the way the two speakers for the dedication ceremony looked at it. They were Charles Irish Walker and William P. Wells. Born in Butternuts, New York, in 1814, Walker went to Michigan in 1836 and succeeded in making a successful career for himself as a teacher, editor, attorney, judge and law professor at the University of Michigan. In 1865 he was president of the Board of Education. His speech was extemporaneous and consisted of a sketch of the history of education in Michigan.

He was followed to the platform by William P. Wells, who had been a school board member in 1864 when he served as chairman of the Library Committee. He was a native of Vermont, born in 1831, and was a graduate of the University of Vermont and the Harvard Law School. He settled in Detroit in 1856, and became a partner of the distinguished jurist, James Valentine Campbell, whose own interests were closely linked to the Library. Wells, like Walker, became a law professor at the University of Michigan.*

He also spoke without notes, but his remarks must have been eloquent and pointed, because they were taken down in some detail by a reporter in the audience who, if he failed to quote the speaker exactly, at least caught the spirit of his remarks. The newsman jotted down:

> After congratulating our city upon the important acquisition to its attractions of so large and valuable a free library, designed for the benefit of the whole people, he proceeded to speak of the necessity of such a library. Education should be the work of a lifetime, and the man who leaves the halls of learning to engage in the active duties of life, should have the public library, to which he could at all times resort to keep alive his interest and furnish the means for constant

---

* Walker died in Detroit, February 11, 1895. Wells died in 1891.

improvement. Nothing else can supply this want, and the public library is admirably fitted to supply that want.[13]

This idea of the public Library as an adjunct to and extension of the system of free public education had been the thread which ran through the discussions of the school board's Library Committees. In its 1860 report, the committee for that year outlined a policy for a library which it would be difficult to improve upon. It cited eight requisites for the kind of institution which the members, Edmund Hall and D. Bethune Duffield, wanted Detroit to have. These were:

1st. The library must be emphatically a public one. It is a part of our public educational system, and like the schools, is intended for the people at large . . .

2nd. It must be free . . .

3rd. It must be extensive. No library now established, or even likely to be, in this city, can be expected to compare with this in the munificence and permanence of its foundation.

4th. Its location must be central, and its rooms spacious for convenient and systematic arrangement, exchange and circulation of books, as well as for reading rooms and office . . .

5th. As the Libraries were evidently designed for the education of the people, by an agency co-operative with the Common schools, a point of prime importance in the first expenditure of moneys, should be the selection and purchase of such books as may be needed in, or will greatly aid, the regular course of instruction in the schools. This, of course, will include the purchase of such text books as the Board need to buy. But every school that aims at high efficiency, needs, in addition to the simple text books of its classes, works of reference on the topics taught, and collateral branches. Dictionaries, Cyclopedias, and Essays upon various subjects, and upon the modes of instruction therein, are of this class. Such books would not of course be calculated for popular circulation, but should be owned by the Library and located in such places as the necessities and convenience of the schools for which they are purchased might require.*

6th. As our Library is expected to act as a powerful educator of the people, its literature should be as pure as our public schools. Our books should be as carefully selected as our teachers, and no one impure in morals or religion should be tolerated . . .

7th. The preservation and usefulness of the Library will require

---

* In this latter statement, is the first suggestion for a reference library or department.

that it shall be placed under the care of responsible persons. . . . A carefully digested system of regulations or by-laws will be needed for the use and distribution of books . . .

8th. As experience has demonstrated that the funds due for libraries are peculiarly liable to loss and misappropriation, and more care and attention are required at present than any of our standing committees can well give to the subject, it may be well to entrust the subject still to a special committee, whose duty it shall be to attend to the interest of the Library Fund. . . .[14]

As a blueprint for the expression of an ideal, this outline of what a public library should be was complemented in the Library Committee's report for 1863. Signed by William P. Wells, Thomas H. Hartwell and Robert W. King, this report has been described as "a document remarkable for the breadth of vision of its signers. . . ." It stated the following fundamental principles:

It [the Library] fulfills its highest purpose . . . by providing in every department of human knowledge, books adapted to those general intellectual aims and designs which are common to the great mass of readers among the people, and capable of use by the largest number of readers.

Accordingly the library should be "popular" in character, as distinguished from those libraries "useful only to professed scholars." But in being popular, it should not provide books merely for entertainment or "the gratification of desultory tastes."

A just regard for the intellectual advantage and improvement of those who resort to such an institution requires that it should furnish the means of genuine instruction and culture; books of real value and authority in all branches of human knowledge; books not to be read merely, but to be studied. Every public library should, of course, contain a due proportion of the best literature of the day and should provide useful and instructive books for those who read for mere pleasure or recreation. . . .

But to "place our library in the front rank of public libraries," the report continued, it must be made

a repository of the best learning upon every subject of intellectual inquiry, and of the best literature of our own and of other languages and times; distinguished rather for the excellence than the extent of the treasures which it offers to those who seek knowledge and culture within its walls.

30

The committee then recommended that it should be a circulating rather than an exclusively reference library, although it should retain features of the latter. And it concluded if the time ever should come when "it should be thought best to dispense wholly with the free circulation of the books," and necessity makes it a reference library, "even then it cannot cease to be free." [15]

It required, then, about five years of preparation, philosophical and material, before Detroit's first public Library could be made operational in March, 1865. But at last it was ready. On Monday, March 27, the doors were opened, and the library room and the collection were at the disposal of the public. Naturally, a set of rules had been drawn, and attention was called to them in the Detroit *Advertiser and Tribune* of March 28.

> Any inhabitant of the City of Detroit, above the age of 18 years, can borrow books from this library for home use, subject to necessary and reasonable regulations prescribed by the Board of Education of this city, in whose custody and control the library remains. All inhabitants of the city of respectable character and proper behavior, can have free access to the Library for consultation of such books as are not loaned, during all regular hours—that is, from nine o'clock in the morning until two o'clock in the afternoon, and from four o'clock in the afternoon until six o'clock. Persons under eighteen years of age can avail themselves of the privileges of the Library on presenting certificates from parents or guardians that they are proper persons to be entrusted with the custody and perusal of books.

Not mentioned was the ominous recommendation of the committee "that the Police Commissioners be requested to make a regulation, rendering it the duty of policemen (when informed by the Librarian) to demand and return to the Library, books which are retained in violation of the rules of the Library." There were, of course, the usual regulations about the number of books that could be withdrawn. No person was permitted, for home use, to withdraw more than one volume in any one day. The length of time a book could be kept was specified. Also listed were the penalties or fines for books overdue and those lost or damaged.[16]

The penalties were printed on the label pasted in each book. This pointed out that the volume was the property of the people of Detroit and "must be taken special care of, and not allowed to lie around where injury may happen to it." This admonition was followed by the list of fines:

> For each grease spot, 5 cents; for each ink spot, 5 cents; for each leaf torn, 10 cents; for each leaf turned down, 5 cents; for writing in a book, from 5 to 10 or more cents; and for other damage, including soiling the book or injuring the binding, proportionate fines up to the full value of the book where seriously injured. For self-protection, examine the book and report imperfections when drawing a volume from the Library.[17]

Because of a delay in preparing the catalog, the actual circulation of books did not begin until May 2, 1865. On that date, some Detroiter happily withdrew the one book allowed him and trudged homeward, probably unaware of his pathfinding role. It would be interesting to know his name and what his choice of reading matter was. Unfortunately, history can identify him only as the first of many millions.[18]

CHAPTER 2

LAMPS IN THE WILDERNESS

NO ENDURING INSTITUTION is created out of a vacuum. It comes into being and exists as long, and only as long, as it responds to the needs and demands of the people.

The Detroit Public Library came into existence not through the beneficence of one individual or a small group of philanthropic individuals. It was established in response to a universal insistence —because it was needed and wanted to meet a social requirement.

In order to understand the Library, then, it becomes necessary to understand the people for whom and by whom it was established, and their way of life. Its creation and continued existence forms an integral chapter of the social history of Detroit.

As an American community, Detroit's history can be said to have had its beginning after the War of 1812 when a government

33

was formed, providing the people with a measure of economic and political stability, and when, encouraged by prospects for a reasonably secure future, Michigan Territory was opened up to settlement.

The migration of settlers, largely from New England, New York and Ohio, during the two decades from 1820 to 1840, shaped the ultimate destiny and character of this region. There were certain events which encouraged and brought about this immigration. First, the public lands in lower Michigan were placed on the market in 1818, offering homesteads to newcomers, and the promise of an improved economic status over that which they had had in the older regions in the East. Second, the inauguration of steamship service on the Great Lakes in 1818, followed not many years later by the railroads, ended a geographical isolation which long had handicapped the region. Third, in 1825, the Erie Canal was opened, linking the Great Lakes and the Atlantic seaboard, providing the West with easy access to the prosperous eastern and European markets.[1]

With these events as lures, people flocked to Michigan in increasing numbers. In 1810 the population of Michigan Territory (including what is now Wisconsin) was less than five thousand. By 1840, the state of Michigan had close to a quarter of a million souls within its borders.[2]

These new arrivals brought with them more than their precious hoard of dollars with which to buy a few acres of land, and their meager supplies of tools and household furnishings and utensils. Much more important, they brought a settled way of life and progressive ideas, rooted in sound democratic principles. They were able to transplant these in the soil of the western wilderness. Most of them had farm backgrounds, but there was a fair proportion of city people from the professional, mercantile and artisan classes. There was a preponderance of young people, ready to begin raising families—an important fact which resulted in a demand for adequate educational facilities.

These immigrants who put down their roots in Detroit and Michigan were not the Daniel Boone type of pioneer, footloose and with distant prospects always before their eyes. Nor were they, as a class, the rough, uncouth and riotous characters—half

34

man, half alligator—that popular fiction and television delight in depicting. They were, on the contrary, civilized, generally literate and often highly-cultured folk. While a migratory movement of the proportions of that of 1820–40 certainly included its share of misfits, adventurers and ne'er-do-wells, it also brought out sensitive souls, accustomed to the good things of life. It would be difficult, contemplating the scene of frontier life, to imagine men like Solomon Sibley or Charles Trowbridge in coonskin caps, forever toting long rifles. Instead, there were theologians like John Monteith; editors like Edward Ellis; men of science like Henry R. Schoolcraft and Douglass Houghton; medical men like George Russel and Zina Pitcher; lawyers like Elon Farnsworth and Thomas M. Cooley; and literary figures such as Caroline Kirkland and John Trumbull.

The life of the Michigan pioneer may have been crude, but he was not, even though some fresh arrivals thought, as did Mrs. Duane Doty, that the residents of Detroit were "rather dissipated." [3] Mrs. Kirkland, caught up in this westward migratory movement with her schoolmaster husband, found in 1835 upon arriving in Michigan

> that the frontier was already an anachronism . . . civilization had caught up with it. . . . In the late thirties the wealthy and leisured classes were building villas cheek by jowl with the homesteading pioneers. In 1836 the steamboats were bringing a thousand immigrants a day into the port of Detroit. . . .

She and her family were in many respects typical. With four small children, they penetrated the Michigan woods and

> struggled as urban professional people with the exigencies of a one-room "loggery," where a toad, attracted by the free traffic of flies through the open door, lived in a corner by the flour barrel, and rattlesnakes habitually crept under the floor for warmth.[4]

Yet, on the rough pine shelves of the Kirkland cabin was fine imported heirloom china, and books which were read and cherished.

That the settlers were not to be judged by their first rude surroundings was clearly expressed by Alexis de Tocqueville, who looked at American civilization with a discerning eye during his travels in this country in the 1830's. His account of certain aspects of life on the frontier did not apply to Michigan alone, but his general impressions fitted the area around Detroit.

> As soon as the pioneer reaches the place which is to serve him for a retreat, he fells a few trees and builds a log house. Nothing can offer a more miserable aspect than these isolated dwellings. The traveler who approaches one of them towards nightfall sees the flicker of the hearth flame through the chinks in the walls; and at night, if the wind rises, he hears the roof of boughs shake to and fro in the midst of the great forest trees. Who would not suppose that this poor hut is the asylum of rudeness and ignorance? Yet no sort of comparison can be drawn between the pioneer and the dwelling that shelters him. Everything about him is primitive and wild, but he is himself, the result of labor and experience of eighteen centuries. He wears the dress and speaks the language of cities; he is acquainted with the past, curious about the future, and ready for argument about the present; he is, in short, a highly civilized being, who consents for a time to inhabit the backwoods, and who penetrates into the wilds of the New World with the Bible, an axe, and some newspapers. It is difficult to imagine the incredible rapidity with which thought circulates in the midst of these deserts. I do not think so much intellectual activity exists in the most enlightened and populous districts of France.[5]

Of course, the established towns, like Detroit, did not present as rude a picture as the backwoods farms which de Tocqueville described. While the city was, by standards of the day, reasonably modern, its inhabitants were of much the same character as their brethren in the bush.

These people, in town and country alike, had gone to Michigan to improve their lot. That meant not only acquiring material wealth; it meant to those of the old New England tradition, a preservation and enhancement of all that was best of the familiar culture. They were not savages back in Vermont or New York State. They would not be savages in Michigan or Detroit. They knew what was good in life and they wanted it for themselves and their children. High on the list of desired things was the means of education.

It was almost as if the people had no choice but to feel as they did about schools for their children. When the Northwest Territory, including the Michigan area, was established in 1787, the ordinance creating it set the pattern in its third article. Those im-

36

mortal words were: "Religion, morality, and knowledge being necessary to good government, and the happiness of mankind, schools and the means of education shall forever be encouraged." Michigan was most fortunate in that its political leaders accepted that article as a mandate, labored to implement it, and used their personal prestige and influence to crystalize a favorable public opinion as well as a political climate such as to encourage the development of a system of free, universal education. Among those leaders, certain names of men active in the 1820–40 period stand out. There was, first of all, the Reverend Gabriel Richard, rector of St. Anne's Church in Detroit. French born, he was sent to Detroit in 1798, and from that time until his death in 1832 he devoted a great part of life to the cause of education, first to that of the French and Indians, and later to all elements of the population.

After Detroit became an American community, there were others just as interested as Father Richard. The later arrivals were Protestants, but there was little sectarianism evident in their friendship and willingness to work together for a common end. There was Augustus B. Woodward, chief justice of the territorial Supreme Court; Lewis Cass, governor of Michigan Territory from 1813 to 1831; the Reverend John Monteith, who arrived in 1816 to become Detroit's first permanent Protestant minister. Each of these men early in their careers had taught school and were strong advocates of a public school system. Later arrivals, such men as Isaac Crary, Michigan's first representative in Congress, and the Reverend John D. Pierce, who became the state's first superintendent of public instruction, added the weight of their influence. And there were many more. Cass as much as any man expressed the ideal toward which this group was working when he declared:

> As the great mass of mankind is instructed, and public opinion enlightened, a moral force is exerted, which governments dare not resist. The schoolmaster is a more powerful antagonist than the soldier, and the alphabet a more efficient weapon than the bayonet.[6]

The eagerness of these men to start a school system led them to build from the top instead of from the bottom. Before a real public school system was in existence, they founded a university.

Judge Woodward, in 1817, drafted and secured passage of a bill which established the Catholepistemiad or University of Michigania. Monteith was made its president and Richard its vice president, and the two divided between them all of the professorships. Understandably, the university concept was ahead of its time, and soon evolved into a much more needed academy at the elementary and high school levels. Yet it was by no means a failure. It expressed an ideal, and provided some basic legislation which in 1837 enabled it to become the University of Michigan at Ann Arbor.[7]

Progress at the elementary level was slow. Resources of the new territory and state did not permit anything but an evolutionary process in the educational field. But the star shone, and there were those who followed it. In 1809, an act was adopted which set off school districts in settled areas, and provision was made for educational support, even before that year, by reserving one section of each township for the support of common schools. In 1824 Cass reminded the Legislative Council that "a practical and well-digested system, which should extend to all the advantages of education, would be of inestimable value to this young and growing community."

Two years later, he had a definite program for the Council which called for taxation for the support of schools. "The children of the poor," he told the Council, "should be the pupils of the country." Then, in 1829, a department of education was established and the territory, soon to be a state, was committed to a policy and program of free, universal, and in time, compulsory education.[8]

The desire for intellectual improvement was manifested in ways other than the promotion of schools and the university. The western settler had an insatiable hunger for reading matter, and he devoured everything in print that he could get his hands on— newspapers, books and tracts. The familiar picture of a young Abraham Lincoln, trudging miles through the wilderness to borrow a book, and then losing himself in its pages by the light of a pine knot, was an experience shared by many, in Michigan as well as Illinois. This desire for reading matter, particularly newspapers which circulated until they fell apart, was the principal means by which the frontiersman maintained contact with the rest of the world. In the early days of the Michigan Territory, the settlers were starved for newspapers. Importing a printing press in 1809, Father Richard endeavored to start a paper. He was not successful. The *Michigan Essay or Impartial Observer* appeared in 1809, but languished after the first issue. For years thereafter papers from New York, Albany, Pittsburgh and Cincinnati were premium items. Not until 1817, when the New York-New England immigration was beginning, did the Detroit *Gazette* appear, the first successful local publishing venture. Even its press run was so limited that each copy was likely to pass through many hands.

Books, though lacking in numbers, served a dual purpose. They were a means of education, and they provided a form of recreation. Means of satisfying the latter needs of the people were limited. This was particularly so during the ice-bound winter months when Detroit was almost completely isolated from the East. Settlers brought books with them, read them over and over again, and loaned them to their neighbors. No matter how humble a home or cabin may have been, it contained the nucleus of a small library. Visiting one pioneer cabin, which he described as typical, de Tocqueville noted,

> on the right hand of the chimney, a map of the United States, raised and shaken by the wind through the crannies in the wall; near the map, on a shelf formed of a roughly hewn plank, a few volumes of books: a Bible, the first six books of Milton, and two of Shakespeare's plays,

and on a table "some newspapers." [9]

Books and reading matter were common subjects of conversation and correspondence, official as well as private. The measure of true friendship was the willingness of a Detroiter to supply an acquaintance in some remote part or settlement with the latest papers (often months old), books, or, if those were lacking, gossip.

"Do not regret that you have received no news-papers—they contain at present no intelligence," James Duane Doty wrote Schoolcraft at Sault Ste. Marie. "We have no letters or papers this week—I send a few of such as we have." [10]

Others in Detroit were equally solicitous of Schoolcraft. On

June 2, 1829, Henry Whiting wrote him: "I believe the literary world is rather lazy at this time; at least nothing novel, except novels, has reached my eye, and I have not time to read even those." [11]

M. L. Woolsey, reporting a safe journey by ship from the Soo to Detroit, told Schoolcraft:

> And as to beguile the tedious hours of a long evening, we had a motley collection indeed:—a few tracts on materialism, a book of stories by Robert Dale Owen, the drift of which was to ridicule the truths of Christianity—a number of pamphlets and hand bills, the effluvia of the infidel press in New York—together with the *beauties* of Byron, a historical work from the *literary* grist-mill at Hartford, and Goldsmith's *Greece* formed the *tout* of our reading apparatus.[12]

It is no surprise, in light of their hunger for literature, that enterprising Detroit merchants soon opened bookstores. From all indications they did a lively business, and some of the proprietors tried to meet demand by operating circulating libraries. These, it appears, were the first libraries in the city available to the public.

When John Sheldon founded the *Gazette* in 1817, he is said to have opened a bookstore in connection with his publishing enterprise. It was probably Detroit's first. Others followed, and as the town began to grow, it was noted that

> among the new buildings being erected there was, here and there, a bookstore, offering the latest imports from London and the eastern cities. The Detroit Book Store, quite an emporium in 1819, was featuring Thomas Moore's *Irish Melodies,* and a thriller titled *The Scottish Probationer,* a novel in two volumes.[13]

Visitors to the city found shops, a theater, and a great number of taverns and gaming houses. But at the same time, Mrs. Anna Jameson, the English writer who visited Detroit in the summer of 1837, remarked on the fact that "there is also a great number of booksellers' shops, and I read in the papers, long lists of books, newly arrived." [14] Reading tastes, as indicated by the advertisements, were not much different from those of the more cultivated centers of Boston, New York and Philadelphia. There was a constant demand for religious books and for school books. Among the popular choices during the 1820–40 period were

Frankenstein by Mary Shelley; Cooper's *The Last of the Mohicans;* David Crockett's *Autobiography; The Last Days of Pompeii,* by Bulwer-Lytton, and *Two Years Before the Mast,* by Richard Henry Dana. Among the authors most in demand at that time, were William Cullen Bryant, Washington Irving, Poe, Carlyle, Whittier and Hawthorne. Byron, it was said, "was the craze," even if Schoolcraft's friend Woolsey didn't think highly of him.

"Among the other evidences of culture in Detroit," says the historian F. Clever Bald, "in addition to schools, books probably took first place." This was true during the period when the town was under the British flag, as well as later. Many of the more prosperous merchants and professional men had first rate private libraries. Bald tells of the sale of 130 volumes in settling the estate of John Askwith in 1795. William Macomb's widow sold nearly two hundred volumes to a Canadian clergyman. Among them were Swift's *Works,* Plutarch's *Lives,* Lord Chesterfield's *Letters,* Fielding's works, Gibbon's *Decline and Fall of the Roman Empire,* Hume's *England,* and Adam Smith's *Wealth of Nations.*[15] As far as is known, these volumes all remained in the area, although they were probably not at the disposal of the general public. Many of these private collections are believed to have been lost in the fire of 1805 which completely destroyed Detroit, and in the War of 1812.

Many public leaders of the territorial period had personal libraries, some of them of excellent quality. Father Richard had a large collection of books on philosophy and theology. Most of his library was preserved and was eventually turned over to a historical collection at the University of Michigan. It was not at all unusual when merchants sent orders east for goods to include a list of book titles for personal enjoyment. Reverend John Monteith, so it is said, arrived in Detroit in 1816 without even a Bible. The story is that he had to borrow one in order to conduct services. He quickly made friends with Father Richard who presented him with a copy of Thomas à Kempis. Another friend gave him two volumes of Shakespeare. Those contributions really were only to tide him over until his library could be shipped to him from Schenectady. Meanwhile, he sent orders to a Pittsburgh

41

bookseller. In a very short time, Monteith had put together a very respectable library.[16] Judge Woodward was another who got together an impressive collection of books, some being the gift of his friend Thomas Jefferson.

The outstanding private library in Detroit was that of Governor Cass. One room of his spacious house was set aside as a library, and few visitors failed to comment on the profusion of books and papers in evidence. Cass was a fairly prolific writer, for years a regular contributor to the *North American Review*. When the opportunity presented itself, he gathered documents pertaining to the French regime in the Northwest, and in the 1840's, while ambassador to France, he paid for the copying of records relating to Detroit which were in the French archives.

In 1866, a short time after Cass's death, his son-in-law and executor, Henry Ledyard, presented 1081 books, documents and official publications from Cass's private library to the fledgling Detroit Public Library. That was the first major gift to the Library, and many of those books and papers still occupy places of honor on the Library's shelves.[17]

It was inevitable, in view of the interest in schools and books, that a movement would be started in Detroit, looking toward the establishment of a library. Father Richard, in fact, told the Governor and Judges as early as 1808 that a public building should be provided for an academy and which could also be utilized for "framing a Beginning of a public Library." [18] This same thought was incorporated in the Act of 1817 establishing a university which provided for a library.

In 1817 the people of Detroit were ready to do something about it. A meeting was called on March 10, the purpose of which was to organize a "social" proprietary or subscription library. The outcome of the meeting was the formation of the Detroit Library Association which established the City Library of Detroit. The list of promoters included the familiar names which had become identified with civic leadership in Detroit: Cass, Solomon Sibley, Austin Wing, William Woodbridge and Monteith. It has been stated that Monteith was the real organizer of the enterprise, and had his personal library arrived earlier in Detroit, the City Library might never have been founded.[19]

42

Shares in the undertaking were offered at five dollars each. One book could be withdrawn for each share, and in order to get things started, some of the more prosperous supporters bought more than one share. Cass took five, Woodbridge four, and Sibley and Monteith three shares apiece, thus assuring themselves of an adequate supply of reading matter at one time. Altogether, ninety shares were subscribed, and the City Library started off with $450 in its treasury. Monteith took the money to New York where he selected a list of about three hundred volumes, a substantial collection for that time. The books arrived in Detroit in July. The announcement in the Detroit *Gazette* that they had been received, referred to the City Library as the Public Library. In a sense it was a public library, because there were no restrictions on membership in the Library Association, or a limit to the number of shares to be issued. Anyone, regardless of class or station, could become a member and draw books if he had five dollars. On July 30 the membership elected Monteith librarian, and on August 26 the City Library was chartered as a corporation by the Governor and Judges.

As far as can be determined, the City Library had its first quarters in a room in the old Council House which stood on Jefferson Avenue at Randolph Street where Mariners' Church is presently located. Later, in 1818, it occupied space in a building at Jefferson and Griswold. This was a temporary arrangement, pending completion of the Catholepistemiad building on Bates near Congress—a building which, incidentally, never was used for university purposes, but instead as classrooms for an academy and Lancastrian school. Monteith, being president of the Catholepistemiad, arranged to locate the City Library in that building. It was moved into permanent quarters there in February, 1819. During Monteith's administration, and after he left Detroit in 1821, the academy teachers served as librarians.

The City Library was not the success its sponsors hoped it would be, and it fell into a decline within a short time. Several of the founders, men of influence, left Detroit for greener pastures, and interest on the part of others waned. The university or Catholepistemiad building was turned over to the city, and the Library was forced to vacate its quarters. Competition from privately owned circulating libraries, able to offer new, current books, also hurt. The result was that in 1831, the City Library's collection was turned over to a new organization, the Detroit Athenaeum. The latter had been organized by a group of business and professional men, as a literary and debating club. The books were moved to the Athenaeum's quarters in the rear of the Newberry & Kercheval store on Griswold Street, where a reading room also was maintained. The Athenaeum, as far as can be determined, only assumed custody but not title to the City Library collection. In 1832 the Athenaeum also accepted custody of a collection of books and records belonging to the Michigan Historical Society. But the Athenaeum seemed to be the victim of the same adverse circumstances that afflicted the City Library and by the end of 1832 it too had lost its identity, fading into a merger with a new and much more vital organization, the Detroit Young Men's Society.[20]

Toward the end of 1832, a group of young men, mostly clerks in the mercantile houses, met in one of the stores to discuss an association which would provide them the means of recreation and self-improvement. During the winter, when Detroit was cut off from communication with the outside world, business came to a virtual standstill. The young clerks and bookkeepers had little to occupy them. They sought diversion (by necessity genteel, in keeping with their positions) to save them from crushing boredom. The Young Men's Society was the result not only of their own efforts, but had the active approval and cooperation of older men, in many cases their employers. The purpose of the Society was to provide library resources, lectures and decorous social activities. It cost two dollars to join and no one with any claim to respectability was barred from membership. A formal organizational meeting was held in the session rooms of the First Presbyterian Church, on lower Woodward Avenue. A fund raising campaign was launched with contributions solicited from the wealthier citizens, and after January 18, 1833, when a constitution and bylaws were adopted, the Society quickly became established.

For almost fifty years it was to exert a strong influence on nearly every phase of Detroit's civic life. Every citizen of importance became a member. In 1836 it was incorporated by the legislature, and was presented with a lot on Woodward Avenue. That property was sold in 1850 and another purchased on Jefferson, between Bates and Randolph. On it, a hall was erected at a cost of $8500. For years, this was the center of the city's social and political life, and there the library, eventually numbering 16,000 volumes, was housed. The Jefferson Avenue hall was outgrown in time, and a new one costing $24,106 was built on Woodbridge Street in the rear of the Biddle House. This hall seated fifteen hundred persons.

Overextension, together with involvement in politics, ultimately got the Young Men's Society into financial troubles, and in 1875, the building was sold for $16,000. The library moved into rented rooms in the Merrill Block, Woodward at Jefferson. But by this time, the new free Public Library was providing competition, and the day of the Young Men's Society passed.[21]

There was another so-called proprietary library in Detroit which stands in importance alongside the City and Young Men's Society Libraries. That was the library of the Detroit Mechanics' Society, organized by a group of businessmen and skilled craftsmen on June 30, 1818. It was incorporated in 1820 for 20 years, and its charter was renewed in 1857 under a state law expressly providing for mechanics' societies. The Mechanics' Society flourished, and in 1828 the organization was given a lot by the city at the southwest corner of Griswold and Lafayette. It constructed a building consisting of a hall and other quarters for its own use, and a group of stores on Lafayette which were rented. In 1870 the Mechanics' Society had an income of $1000 a year and a membership of two hundred. By setting aside $300 to $400 a year for books, this society soon built up a library of about four thousand volumes. The library was open from 2 to 4:30 P.M. and 7 to 9 P.M. on Wednesdays and Saturdays. The total property—land, buildings and books—was valued in 1873 at $50,000.

Feeling flush, the Society decided to erect a new building, and this proved its undoing. The contractors failed to meet their obligations, tenants did not move in, and in 1876, it being necessary to assign all the property to the creditors, the assets were

45

sold for $112,500. The library, which during construction of the new building had occupied other temporary quarters, was released by the creditors and stored in the Moffat Building which occupied the present site of the Penobscot Building. In 1877 the YMCA, then on Library Street, assumed custody of the books, retaining control until 1881 when the YMCA property was sold to the Detroit Medical College, forerunner of the Wayne State University College of Medicine. The books remained in the building for the time being under control of the Medical College. Title to the library remained vested in the Mechanics' Society which existed, for all practical purposes, as a name only.[22]

Discussing Detroit's library resources in 1866, the *Advertiser and Tribune* pointed out that the Mechanics' Library is "devoted to scientific mechanical works," while the Young Men's Society library, "though possessing a fine collection in almost all departments, is yet stronger in that of fiction than in any other." [23]

From the time the Board of Education's Library Committee began to formulate plans for a free public library, an acquisitive glance was always cast at the proprietary libraries. There were hopes that a consolidation could be affected, bringing the private collections under public control and providing a nucleus for the Public Library. In 1860 the Library Committee stated:

> If either the Young Men's or the Mechanics' Library were destroyed, it would be felt as a public calamity. Their collection of books, the product of years of accumulation, is creditable to those societies and to the city. The former contains something over 4,000 volumes, and the latter about half that number. The amount now due the Library Fund of this city, would, at fair valuation, buy out both those libraries. Neither of those societies is able to expend more than $300 or $400 per year in the purchase of books, while the School Library Fund, with ordinary care in preserving it, can depend upon an income of from ten to fifteen hundred dollars annually, aside from any direct taxes. It is easy to see to what magnificent proportions such annual accumulations would soon swell a library when once established.[24]

In 1863, negotiations were conducted by the Library Committee with the two societies, and also with the Fire Department Society, a social group made up of members of former volunteer fire companies. The purpose of these talks was based on the desire "that the resources available from all sources in the city for library purposes might be concentrated in the establishment and maintenance of a single public library." The committee conceded that this could not be accomplished immediately. But Henry Chaney, purchasing books for the Public Library, was specifically instructed not to duplicate what the private libraries had.[25] In 1865, the committee reminded the Young Men's and Mechanics' societies that they had been the beneficiaries of public assistance, and therefore were obligated to cooperate with the Public Library. Said the committee at that time:

> If the library of the Young Men's Society could be combined with the Public Library, and the means, subject to the control of the Board, could be combined . . . and the whole could be placed under the control of a single organization, properly constituted, it is evident that, within a very few years, Detroit could boast of a free Library of more than a hundred thousand volumes.[26]

Nothing came of this consolidation plan. The private libraries were not ready to lose their identities, and after the Public Library opened in the Capitol, it was seen that there was not enough room to house the consolidated collections. Even the Cass donation in 1866 had to be placed in storage for the time being because of lack of reading room shelf space. Nevertheless, the idea was not forgotten. The *Advertiser and Tribune* noted on June 12, 1866:

> It has several times been attempted to unite the library of the Young Men's Society with that of the Mechanics' Society, and about the time of the opening of the new Public Library, a conference was had between the committee on the library of the Board of Education and a committee of the Young Men's Society and several other gentlemen interested in the Young Men's Society, with the hope that all the collections in the city might be incorporated into one large public library under the management of the Board of Education. No success has yet attended any of these efforts, but the design is surely a praiseworthy one, and may ultimately be carried into execution.

Over the next several years, other such conferences were held. When the Capitol building quarters were outgrown and the Public Library needed a new building, it was proposed that the Mechanics' Society contribute its property on Griswold Street for a site. Nothing came of this plan because, as the *Free Press* pointed out, "the great obstacle to all of this is the dreaded loss of individuality of each association." [27]

Eventually, the consolidations were effected. These were the result, not so much of philanthropic impulses on the part of the proprietary libraries, but because of their financial difficulties. In 1882, the Young Men's Society went out of business, and its collection was put up for sale. The Public Library bought 258 books for $100. What was left of the collection, 4050 volumes, newspapers and other items, were given to the Public Library. The gift included a valuable marble bust of Lewis Cass which thereafter occupied a place of honor in the Main Library buildings. The Mechanics' Society's books which had passed to the control of the Detroit Scientific Association, an offshoot of the College of Medicine, were given to the Library in 1886. This gift comprised 3314 books which were allowed to circulate only on special permit. In the same year, the collection of the Michigan Historical Society, consisting of 611 items, mostly documents relating to Michigan and the Northwest, were deposited in the Public Library. "There is no probability," said the Library Commission, "of their ever being taken away." [28]

CHAPTER 3

FREE BOOKS FOR FREE PEOPLE

IN A VERY REAL SENSE, the Detroit Public Library had its origin in a clause inserted in Michigan's first constitution. Firmly established in the organic law, recognition of and provision for public libraries has remained, with only minor modifications, in succeeding constitutions adopted by the people of Michigan.

How this came about in the first instance is traceable to the New England-New York migration of the 1820–40 period of Michigan's development. The newcomers, while seeking opportunities and a better environment than they had enjoyed in their old homes in the East, still cherished the basic idea of self-government. The town meeting, an almost classic expression of democracy, was strongly inbred in the newcomers' political philosophy. As Justice Cooley stated, the immigrants were people

49

"who valued highly the privilege of choosing their own officers." [1] Having come from established states, and being familiar with the workings of that form of government, they quite naturally had the desire as well as the determination to live in their new surroundings under a system which they knew and understood.

When the settlers began coming to Michigan after the War of 1812, they found a government formed under the territorial system with a Governor and Judges appointed by the President of the United States. As population increased, this system was changed as provided for in the Ordinance of 1787. In 1819 Michigan was permitted to send an elected delegate to Congress. The delegate enjoyed all the privileges of membership in the House of Representatives, except the right to cast a vote. He was, actually, a liaison man linking the people of his territory and Congress. In 1823 Michigan was permitted another forward step toward self-government. Rule by the Governor and Judges was abolished in favor of a governor and council. The council was composed of nine members appointed by the President from a list of eighteen nominated by popular vote. The governor continued to be a presidential appointee. Four years later, in 1827, Michigan progressed to the final stage of territorial government with the popular election of all members of the council. The acts of the latter, however, took effect only upon approval of Congress.

The Yankee immigrants with strongly ingrained ideas about self-government, accepted these various steps, but not with complete satisfaction. They realized they were, in effect, still wards of the federal government; second-class citizens who lacked the same right of self-determination which the citizens of the states possessed. They did not have the right to vote for president, and they were not truly represented in Congress. Nothing short of full statehood would satisfy them, and the movement to attain that status began in the 1820's.[2] By 1831 the stream of migration had become a flood and agitation for a change to state government became increasingly strong. The Ordinance of 1787 promised that a territory would be eligible for statehood when its population reached the 60,000 mark. This minimum requirement was reached early in the 1830 decade. By 1834 Michigan claimed 87,278 people, and the territorial council petitioned Congress for Michigan's admission into the Union.

There was an obstacle however. In defining its boundaries, Michigan claimed a strip of land, seven miles wide running from Lake Erie to Lake Michigan, and including the settlement of Toledo. This "Toledo strip" also was claimed by Ohio which was in the advantageous position of having senators and representatives in Washington as well as possessing a voice in presidential elections. The boundary dispute had to be settled before Michigan could be admitted. Neither the territory nor Ohio would yield.

Nevertheless, Michigan, claiming it had met all the requirements for statehood and without awaiting settlement of the Toledo dispute, proceeded toward the final step—the framing of a constitution. On April 4, 1835, the qualified voters of Michigan went to the polls, and in an acrimonious election picked eighty-nine delegates to a constitutional convention which convened in Detroit May 11. On that day seventy-three delegates, assembled from the far corners of Michigan, walked from the docks, from the riverfront hotels and the boarding houses, to the stately Capitol building on State Street. In the council chamber they were sworn in. Within the next day or two, the remaining delegates joined them; the convention was organized with John Biddle as president; committees were appointed, and the delegates got down to the task of writing a constitution. It took them until June 4—six weeks—to complete their work. One of the great results which they achieved is aptly described by Professor Harold M. Dorr, in his excellent study of the convention:

> The constitution of 1835 carried a complete and enlightened article on public education . . . which laid the foundations for a system of free public schools and has remained the basis of the educational policy of the state for over a century.[3]

And as a corollary to a system of free schools, Section 4 of Article X (the educational article) stated:

> As soon as the circumstances of the state will permit, the legislature shall provide for the establishment of libraries, one at least in each township; and the money which shall be paid by persons as an equivalent for exemption from military duty, and the clear proceeds of all fines assessed in the several counties for any breach of the penal laws, shall be exclusively applied for the support of said libraries.

These constitutional provisions represent political pioneering at its finest. Indeed, the entire educational article, of which it was a part, was far in advance of anything which had been attempted up to that time by any state, giving Michigan an unusual position of leadership in the field of public education. Article X, in fact, was typical of the new constitution's over-all excellence. It has been said that the constitution of 1835 was "the best one Michigan has had." [4] One of the major features of the article was the provision for the office of superintendent of public instruction to be a constitutional, rather than a statutory office. Michigan was the first state to create that post, just as it was the first to assure financial support of libraries by constitutional edict.

What was there in the make-up of the eighty-nine delegates that produced such an enlightened document? One would not have expected that frontiersmen would have been the ones to pioneer in that field. Rather, one would be inclined to expect such a forward-looking document to be the product of one of the old states, with long experience in government and with greater intellectual and legal resources upon which to draw. Declared Justice Cooley:

> If the general education of the people is important to the state, Michigan was fortunate in the persons to whom the destinies of the territory were committed in its early days. In their minds, as we find them expressed in the laws they adopted and the institutions they founded, two ideas appear to have been dominant from the earliest period. These were, that the means of rudimentary education should be placed within the reach of every child in the political society; and that the opportunity for thorough culture should be given as speedily and as completely as the circumstances of the people would permit.[5]

It must be conceded that the delegates to the convention of 1835 were, in their social and political outlook, typical of the great mass of eastern settlers who had but recently come, and were still coming into the territory. Of the 89 delegates, 27 had been born in New York, 15 in New England and 14 in the Middle Atlantic states. They were well instructed in the traditions of the original 13 states and their democratic strivings. They were familiar with the laws of the states from which they had come, and were inclined to retain the best of those laws. At the same time, they were young enough to dare innovation for a community which they were building upon new foundations.

With few exceptions, says Professor Dorr, the social and the educational advantages enjoyed by the delegates were fairly representative of the people who elected them.

> Many had received training in the elementary schools of the older states; some had attended academies and colleges; but for the most part their education was of a more practical nature, acquired outside books and classrooms. Among the delegates who were college graduates were: John Biddle, from Princeton; Edward Mundy, from Rutgers College; Hezekiah Wells, from Kenyon College; Isaac Crary, from Trinity College; Ross Wilkins and Robert McClelland, from Dickinson College; and John Adam, who held a degree conferred in Scotland.[6]

Whatever their backgrounds, they were a remarkably able group of men, and their influence upon the destiny of Michigan extended beyond the convention of 1835. Three of them would become governors of the state; others would represent Michigan in Congress; some would be judges, state and federal; one was destined to occupy a place in the President's cabinet, and still others would serve in appointive and elective office within the framework of the state government and its local subdivisions. To quote Justice Cooley again:

> The founders of a state soon pass away; but in their aims and purposes, and to some extent in their personal characteristics, they build themselves into the structure they create, and give to it a character and individuality of its own. Ages afterwards it may be found that the germinal thoughts which took root under their planting are still growing and expanding, and that the ideas with which they quickened the early polity are dominant in the life of the mature commonwealth, though possibly those who act upon and give effect to them may have lost the recollection of their origin.[7]

Among the delegates, two men are credited with playing major roles in forging Article X, establishing the educational and library systems. They were General Isaac Crary of Marshall, and Edward D. Ellis of Monroe. Each was typical in personal background of the forward-looking young men who shaped the character of Michigan. Crary, whose military title was acquired as a militia officer, was a native of Preston, Connecticut, born October 2, 1804. Raised on a farm, he graduated from Trinity College in Hartford. After studying law he was admitted to practice in Hartford, and combined a legal career with the editorship of a newspaper. Then, like so many young men of his generation, he succumbed to "Michigan fever" and moved west in 1831, at the age of twenty-seven. Upon arriving in Marshall, a thriving city in Calhoun County, he boarded with a Congregationalist minister, the Reverend John Davis Pierce. The latter, a native of New Hampshire, had been orphaned at the age of two, and was raised as an indentured farm boy. But with Yankee determination he obtained an education, first at Brown University, then at Princeton Theological Seminary. He was licensed by the Congregational Association, and also taught school. In 1831 he was sent as a missionary to Michigan. Like so many pioneer ministers, he endeavored to serve not only the spiritual, but also the educational needs of his community. It is told how he and Crary spent hours in the woods, sitting on a log, discussing the necessity for better schools. From those talks, Crary himself developed a deep interest in education, and Pierce helped him to crystallize his ideas. When the Constitutional Convention of 1835 was organized, the chairmanship of the committee on education was given Crary who, it has been stated, "was notable for his report on education which was written into the constitution and was the foundation upon which Michigan's school system was eventually established." [8]

Edward D. Ellis was cut to the same pattern as Crary. He was born at Niles, New York, and learned the printer's trade at Auburn. In 1825, when he was about twenty-four years old, he went west, carrying with him a press and type, and settled in Monroe where he founded a newspaper, the *Sentinel,* one of the earliest journals in the territory, and one which survives to this day as the Monroe *Evening News.* An ardent Democrat, Editor Ellis supported his party locally and nationally, and became an influential figure in public affairs. He was on intimate terms with Governor Cass who saw to it that the *Sentinel* became one of the mouthpieces for Michigan Democrats. For his loyalty, Ellis was appointed postmaster at Monroe, a key post because that city

54

was an important center in the line of communication between Detroit and the East. Ellis was a member, also, of the elected Territorial Council, and it was natural that he should become a delegate to the convention where he quickly assumed a position of influence and leadership. He was a member of Crary's committee on education, and is popularly credited with having been the author of the library section of Article X.

Whether he actually wrote the section has been questioned. Talcott Wing, the historian of Monroe County, flatly states that Ellis

> was the author of the statute [*sic*] then adopted and since remaining a part of our organic law, and which has become a law in several other states, that monies paid as fines in criminal offenses and misdemeanors should be devoted to purchasing and maintaining public libraries in every town and city.

Wing also said of him:

> A very important service was rendered by him in the constitutional convention of the state of Michigan. When an enactment was under discussion for establishing libraries in all the townships of the state, without any provision either to receive books or sustain the libraries, it was Mr. Ellis who proposed and carried through the idea that all fines imposed for violation of the penal laws through the state, and all sums assessed for non-performance of military duty, should be set aside as a fund for the support of said libraries. The idea was original with him, and has frequently been mentioned to his credit.[9]

Others have been equally ready to give Ellis credit for the library clause. Silas Farmer was one of them. His father, John Farmer, was a convention delegate, and it may be assumed that Silas learned from him of Ellis' role. The same can be said of Charles Lanman, author of *The Red Book of Michigan*. In it he stated: "It was Mr. Ellis who proposed and carried through the idea that all fines imposed for the violation of the penal laws throughout the State . . . should be set aside as a fund for the support of said libraries. The idea was original with him. . . ." Lanman, or his family, undoubtedly knew Ellis personally, or at least sufficiently well to support the statement he made about him.

The Monroe *Evening News* declared editorially in 1958 that

it was Ellis' "foresight more than 100 years ago in earmarking penal fines for the support of such a library system. . . . This inspired clause in the Michigan Constitution has endured through three revisions of the state's organic law." * [10]

The public services of Crary and Ellis did not end with the 1835 convention. Crary was sent to Congress, the first duly elected member of the House of Representatives from Michigan. He served three consecutive terms from 1835 to 1840. In Congress, he continued his efforts on behalf of the school system in his state, and was responsible for adoption of the rule that federal public lands, allocated to townships, should be held in trust by the state, thus making it possible to hold them off the market until they appreciated in value. Crary later served as a delegate to the Convention of 1850 which wrote Michigan's second constitution. For a brief period, 1837–39, while still a congressman, he was a member of the University of Michigan Board of Regents. He also performed one other extremely valuable service. When the state government was organized under its first constitution, Crary persuaded Governor Stevens T. Mason to appoint his friend Pierce superintendent of public instruction. As a result of the role the latter played in that position, he became known as "the father of public education" in Michigan. Crary died in Marshall in 1854.

Ellis spent so much time in Detroit in connection with his governmental duties that he must have concluded it would be to his advantage to move there. He sold the *Sentinel* in 1836. He was elected to the state senate in 1836–37. Described as a man of culture and foresight, he was extremely liberal. In Detroit he started another newspaper, the *Constitutional Democrat,* and also a journal called the *American Vineyard.* He strongly advocated state sovereignty, opposed a central banking system, and was the first newspaper champion of labor in his section of the country. He died in Detroit on May 15, 1848.

Whether Ellis was or was not the author of the library section,

---

* It might be stated that it has endured in substance through a fourth revision. The general library clause principle was retained in the new constitution, adopted by the people of Michigan in 1963, and which became effective January 1, 1964. The provision for fines for exemption from military duty was dropped from the 1850 constitution, but the penal fines clause was retained.

his influence in the convention was great. The delegates arrived at the opening session without previous opportunities for caucuses or discussions. There were many divergent views, ideas and opinions which had to be drawn into a reasonably narrow channel of agreement if the convention was to follow a straight course. Recognizing that diffusion could be fatal, and that at least a general outline was needed, Ellis moved for the appointment of what was in effect a nineteen-member steering committee "whose duty it shall be to prepare and report to the Convention, for their consideration, the draft of a constitution." [11] Both Ellis and Crary were made members of this committee which gave them positions of power in the convention. The draft was submitted, including a proposed section on education, which stated:

> The Legislature shall have power, as soon as the circumstances of the State will permit, to provide for a system of common schools, by which one or more schools shall be kept up, at least six months in the year in each of the several townships of this state, at the public expense, and in such manner that the benefits of education may be extended as well to the rich as to the poor.[12]

It may be assumed that Ellis had a hand in that recommendation. Crary probably wrote it, but it can be taken for granted that he did so with Ellis' knowledge and support.

The report of the Committee on Education was submitted to the convention on June 2, and by that time it contained the library clause. Section 4 was thoroughly debated, and a number of amendments were offered. Had these amendments prevailed—some of them were supported by Crary—the purpose and intent of the library clause would have been much different and probably much weaker. But it was Ellis who, after listening to the arguments, moved to "strike out the whole section as amended." This motion prevailed with the result that what remained before the convention was the original section which was thereby preserved. It may have been that action, to save the original language of the section, which earned for Ellis his lasting and traditional recognition as father of Michigan's public library system.[13]

The original draft of Section 4 was only slightly modified in its final form. The first writing provided for establishment of a library in each school district. This was changed for the better to provide for at least one in each township. Also inserted was a clause which stated that "the clear proceeds" of all fines should be applied for the support of libraries. Insertion of the term "clear proceeds" protected the library fund against raids by local officials who might seek to skim expenses and costs off the top.

The origin of the library clause has not been determined. It has been said that major features of the constitution of 1835 were based upon or drawn from the laws, organic and statutory, of New York and other eastern states. These being the states from which the majority of delegates had come, it was said they were familiar with their constitutions and adapted freely from them to suit Michigan. But the Michigan education and library sections were innovations. What, then, inspired them?

In 1825 New York had on its books a law which provided for the partial support of the State Library from chancery court fees. This act provided that the assistant register of the Court of Chancery annually pay to the trustees of the State Library

> . . . the sum of three hundred dollars, to be by them expended for the gradual increase of said library; which annual sum of three hundred dollars shall be paid out of the principal, interest or profits arising from the surplus of the common fund, so called, appertaining to the court of chancery, and under the particular charge of the assistant register of said court; Provided, that if at any time the interest or profits of the said fund shall not be sufficient to discharge the contingent expenses of the court of chancery, and also the said annual sum of three hundred dollars, the court of chancery may direct that the said annual sum be so reduced that the expenses of the court shall be first paid.[14]

This was at best a vague and tenuous financial base for the support of a library system. It may be assumed that this money, if it ever was to be forthcoming, was intended for the purchase of law books or other materials primarily for the use of the court. It could have had but very small meaning to the idea of a public library. And, of course, chancery fees are a wholly different matter from penal fines. As a result, there is virtually no resemblance between the New York law and the Michigan article. The former remained on the books only at the discretion of the legislature, while the latter was imbedded in the constitution. Even in the most orderly community, the penal fines provision would have been the more lucrative. Furthermore, the Michigan article provided specifically for libraries in each township which, by implication and later interpretation meant public libraries. The best that can be said about any relationship between the New York law and Michigan's Article X, Section 4, is that Ellis or some other delegate knew of the former and used the convention as the opportunity vastly to enlarge it.

At any rate, whatever its source, whoever designed it, the fourth section of the tenth article of the Michigan Constitution of 1835, and all of its subsequent revisions, gave Michigan first rank among all states in recognizing the need for libraries as public responsibilities, and providing the means for financing them.

The convention completed its work on June 24, 1835 and adjourned "to the thunder of guns and display of fireworks." In October, the constitution was submitted to the people who adopted it with overwhelming enthusiasm. The vote was 6299 yeas and 1359 nays, a margin of about six to one. At the same October election, a slate of state officers was elected. Michigan now considered itself a state and proceeded to function under a state government. For the time being, however, it did so outside of the Union. There was still the matter of settling the boundary issue with Ohio. Eventually a compromise was worked out. On January 26, 1837, Congress approved the new constitution and Michigan became the twenty-sixth state.

Neither adoption of a constitution nor admission to the Union automatically established libraries. That could be accomplished only by statutory implementation by the legislature, and the process was a long and often frustrating one. At the outset the library was regarded as an adjunct to the common school, and library legislation was written with this in mind. The first law, passed in 1837, set up school district libraries. This was in accord with the thinking of John Pierce, who reported to the legislature relative to libraries:

> Township libraries would undoubtedly prove beneficial to the public interests, but their benefits must necessarily be confined more generally to the immediate neighborhood of their location. The central

59

district would have the advantage of all the other districts, though equally entitled to share in the privileges of the library. As the constitution leaves it discretionary with the legislature to establish one or more in each township, it is respectfully submitted whether the public interests would not be equally promoted by the establishment of one in each primary school district.[15]

The legislature responded with a law permitting districts to levy a tax not exceeding ten dollars for the purchase of books; each district complying with this provision being entitled to its proportionate share of the penal fines collected in the county. The formula for participation in this sharing was the district's percentage of the county's child population between the ages of five and seventeen years. This tax was not a popular one and was not generally levied. In 1843 it was found that the district library plan had not been a success. The 1837 law was repealed in favor of one supporting township libraries. Books were to be distributed to the districts in the township on a three-months rotation system. The town clerk was to serve as librarian, and all children between the ages of four and eighteen were to be allowed to draw books free of charge. There also was a clause in the law which permitted townships to levy a tax of not more than fifty dollars for "the purchase of books for the use of the adult residents of the township. . . ." This was the first hesitant and short step toward a free public library. The township plan continued to grow and in 1859 the superintendent of public instruction reported the existence of 487 such libraries. That the system grew to such a size cannot be attributed to the wise provisions of the authors of the Michigan Constitution. Their good intentions were flouted when, as reported in 1846, proceeds from penal fines were diverted to general purposes. As far as was known, not a single dollar had been turned over for the benefit of libraries in accord with the constitutional provision.[16]

It took strong, positive action on the part of Detroit to remedy that!

CHAPTER 4

CRIME IS MADE TO PAY

NEITHER A STATE CONSTITUTION, statutes nor good intentions were sufficient to start a public library. Another ingredient was needed—money. That was a long time coming despite the constitutional provision regarding allocation of penal fines. Very few people were thinking about a public library in 1837. The word "library" brought to mind a school facility. For about a quarter of a century after Michigan became a state, the library system was considered only a part of the school system. To understand the origins of the Detroit Public Library it is necessary, therefore, to examine the origins and evolution of the Detroit school system.

In 1837, after the public school idea had been sanctioned by the constitution and the state laws, Detroit took its first step toward compliance. In December, the Common Council re-

61

quested the city attorney to report what measures were required
to organize a local public school system under the recently passed
state laws. As a first step a school census was taken. This revealed a total of 1356 children between five and fifteen years of
age. Three school inspectors were elected, and in May, 1838 the
city was divided into seven school districts. Shortly thereafter, an
eighth district was created for the benefit of Negro children. Each
district, except the eighth which was an "at large" arrangement,
had its own directors or inspectors, levied its own taxes and had
control over its own affairs. While there was some cooperation
between the district directors, each district functioned as an independent unit. Each district built or rented a schoolhouse and
hired one or two teachers. It did, that is, if it could raise enough
money! Not until 1839, for instance, did District 2 levy a total
tax of $750, of which $500 was to build a schoolhouse.

This uncertain and far from satisfactory state of affairs continued for three or four years. Perceptive citizens and foresighted
public leaders realized that a better foundation had to be laid if
Detroit was to have an effective system of education. It had become evident that "Balkanization" of the school districts was not
workable.[1]

By 1841 it was felt that the time had come to correct the
situation. A committee was appointed by the Common Council
consisting of Mayor Zina Pitcher, and aldermen David W. Fiske
and Charles Moran. This committee reported on November 19
that there were 1850 school age children in Detroit, but that
less than half that number were enrolled in school, both public
and private. It was recommended that the Council take the
initiative and appeal to the legislature for authority to raise
money by direct city-wide taxation for the support of schools
and to create a single governing body, or board of education. A
subsequent report, with more specific proposals, was submitted
to the Council and, indirectly to the public, in January, 1842.
This called for the power to levy a one-fourth of one per cent tax
on the assessed valuation of all of Detroit's real and personal
property, and to elect a board of education consisting of two
members from each ward. The board would have responsibility
for and supervision over all public schools in the city. This plan,

particularly the tax feature, met some opposition, and petitions objecting to it were circulated and submitted to the Council. Clarence M. Burton notes that the individual heading the list of objectors signed his name by making "his (X) mark." The majority of the city officials, however, favored the idea, and endeavored to create a favorable climate of opinion by conducting public meetings at which the need and the expected benefits were explained to the people. The backing they received was sufficiently encouraging to warrant the Council going to the legislature, then in session, with an appeal for relief.

Prompt action resulted at the statehouse level. Within ten days the legislature passed, and Governor John S. Barry signed, an act creating the Detroit Board of Education and laying, as Burton stated, the foundation for all laws upon which the present school system has been constructed.[2]

This law, titled "No. 70—An Act relative to free schools in the city of Detroit," which also gave recognition to libraries, had as its salient features:

> Section 1. That the city of Detroit shall be considered as one school district, and hereafter all schools organized therein . . . shall, under the direction and regulation of the board of education, be public and free to all children residing within the limits thereof, between the ages of five and seventeen years, inclusive.

Section 2 stated that instead of school inspectors as then elected, there would henceforth be twelve, two to be elected from each ward.

Section 3 provided that every person elected school inspector who should refuse or neglect to serve, "shall forfeit to the board of education, for the use of the library, the sum of ten dollars. . . ."

Section 5 said that the school inspectors with the mayor and recorder serving in ex officio capacities "shall be a body Corporate, by the name and style of the board of education of the city of Detroit!"

> Section 9. The board of education shall have full power and authority . . . to purchase such school houses, and apply for and receive from the county treasurer or other officer, all moneys appropriated for the primary schools and district library of said city, and designate a place where the library may be kept therein.

63

From the library standpoint, Section 12 of the act was especially important, stating:

> The board of education shall establish a district library, and for the
> increase of the same, the common council are authorized annually
> to lay a tax on the real and personal property within said city, of
> a sum not exceeding two hundred dollars. . . .[3]

While the Act of 1842 was still under consideration, the school
inspectors, anxious to obtain some money for library purposes,
began to make inquiries as to why the fines collected in the courts
of Wayne County had not been turned over to the schools, as
required by Article X, Section 4 of the constitution. At the last
session of the old Board of Inspectors, on January 8, 1842,
Inspector John Farmer offered a resolution, promptly adopted,
which stated:

> That an order be drawn on the County Treasurer for the proportion
> due the township of Detroit of the moneys paid into the County
> Treasury as equivalents for exemptions from military fines, and for
> the clear proceeds of all fines for breaches of the penal laws; and in
> case the Treasurer refuses to pay, that the City Attorney, or some
> other proper person be requested to apply to the present Supreme
> Court for a mandamus to compel the Treasurer to pay the same.

No action on the part of the county treasurer was immediately
forthcoming. In June the new Board of Education began to press
the matter by appointing a committee to investigate and determine how much money the school district was entitled to. This
got minor results, and on August 7, 1842, the county handed the
board the sum of $63.14 as the city's share of fines collected in
Wayne County.

From then on, for the next eighteen years, piddling amounts
were received from time to time. No payments were made in
1843; in 1844 the proceeds from fines were $26. The city's share
fluctuated between $93 in 1846 and $856 in 1856. The average
for the 1842–60 period was $174.55. The size of this income,
derived from fines, might suggest that Wayne County in those
years was remarkably free of sin. Actually, such was not the case.
More was taken in by the justice and other courts and paid over

to the treasurer. But the money was diverted by the county to other uses. First of all, the interpretation of what was meant by "clear proceeds" was foggy. County authorities took the position that the cost of maintaining the courts should be skimmed off the top, before anything was due the library fund. This was not effectively challenged by the Board of Education for many years, although committees were appointed regularly to ascertain how much money the county treasurer was holding and how much of it he was willing to pay out. Meanwhile, library facilities were almost non-existent. They were suffering acutely from financial anemia.[4]

The Board of Education found much to complain about in the situation as it existed. Reviewing its difficulties over a period of several years, a Board library committee reported in 1860:

> A special law, passed in 1842, requires the Board of Education of the city of Detroit to establish a Detroit Library.
>
> As a fund for such libraries, the constitution has dedicated all fines for the breach of the penal laws of the State, and the Legislature has, by statute, superadded the clear proceeds of all bonds and recognizances in criminal cases. In addition to this, it is provided that certain portions of the school taxes may be set apart for the same purpose.
>
> Heretofore, in this county, the moneys accruing from these sources have been almost entirely devoted to other purposes, by the officers collecting the same. A few justices of peace, scattered through the county, have from time to time paid into the County Treasury small sums collected as fines, making an annual aggregate of from $250 to $500. The pittance which the distribution of this amount has afforded to the city has been so small as merely to enable the Board of Education to purchase a few dictionaries and maps, and such text books as were indispensible to daily recitations in the schools.[5]

Referring to the meaning of "clear proceeds," the Board itself in 1860 complained that:

> hitherto the construction put upon this provision of the Constitution by the Board of Auditors, was such as practically to absorb very nearly the entire amount of such receipts, so that no fund up to this time has ever existed which could be made available for the organization of a Public Library for the use of the schools.[6]

The lack of such a library, as well as the need for one, was brought to public attention in 1855 by John F. Nichols, principal of the high school. It was his observations which may have spurred the Board into action which, a few years later, produced results. Said Nichols:

> A library, also, of well selected books and treatises on the various sciences, and in the departments of history and philosophy, together with standard works of literature, should soon be commenced and secured for the use and benefit of the youth and the population of our city at large. The libraries of the Young Men's Society of Detroit, and of the Mechanics' Association, have accomplished great good; but they do not by any means meet the wants and exigencies of a large and populous city, especially, if as we trust, the day is approaching, when much greater attention will be given and zeal displayed for the general cultivation and diffusion of useful knowledge.[7]

From the wording of this statement, it is clear that Nichols had in mind the general idea of a real public library. At any rate, mounting impatience on the part of school officials, typified by expressions of this kind, soon resulted in positive action on the part of the Board to assert its rights and force compliance with both the spirit and letter of the law.

On April 21, 1859, another of its perennial committees was appointed to investigate the penal fine situation. This one was unusual in that it accomplished something. The chairman was Henry E. Baker, inspector from the Sixth Ward, who was also editor of the *Tribune*. Serving with him were Edmund Hall, Fourth Ward, and H. M. Cheever, Fifth Ward. Hall and Cheever were two of Detroit's leading attorneys. Baker, obviously, was the kind of man who knew how to get the facts when he went after them. When he submitted his report the Board of Education and the public knew, for the first time, exactly how much library money the schools had been deprived of. It was revealed that during the period of July 1, 1854 to January 1, 1859, more than $15,000 had been received by Wayne County from the various local courts, all of it rightfully belonging to the Board of Education and bearing the lawful stamp of library money. The entire amount, said Baker's report, "had accrued, but been diverted to other funds." Of the total collected, the report further showed, over $12,000 consisted of fines collected in the Police Court. Obviously, Detroit was not as lily-white as earlier infinitesimal returns suggested. The city had its wicked moments, but as far as the library was concerned, crime did not pay. Said Baker:

> Out of these fines, the salary of the Police Justice, the rent of the Police court-room, the fees of officers, and other incidental expenses, amounting to a yearly aggregate of over $2,000, had been paid. Beyond all these expenses, there had accumulated during the first three years a large surplus.

Up to 1859, the report continued, the county had also collected forfeited bonds and recognizances of more than $2000. Various amounts paid over by Recorder's Court, the Circuit Court, the sheriff, and certain justices of the peace, all contributed to making up "a total sum, as estimated by the committee, of $6,691.84, which, by any reasonable construction of the law, belonged to the Library Fund." This amount of nearly $7000 was figured on the charitable ground that "clear proceeds" meant what remained after expenses of operating the courts. But the committee was in no mood to be charitable.

"Under the construction adopted by the committee, and by the counsel whom they consulted, the sum due to that fund exceeded $15,000." [8]

That was substantial money by any rule of measure—a treasure worth digging for. Baker and his colleagues presented formal applications to the county treasurer and the Board of County Auditors for that portion of the $15,000 which, on the basis of Detroit's school population, belonged to the city. Actually, the committee had no real expectations of getting their share of such a substantial amount. The county, having already spent most of it, had no such quantity of cash laid away. The committee's strategy was that, by presenting a legally-supported claim for the full amount, the county might be bluffed into paying over the lesser amount—the $6,691.84. But the treasurer and auditors did not bluff easily. They politely declined to pay anything. The reason was an uncertainty on their part of their true obligation. There was neither precedent nor authority from the Board of Supervisors relieving them of the responsibility for making a decision about disbursement of public monies, especially those for which they might be held personally liable. They were not, however, unreasonable men. They were astute enough politicians to want to be on the side of the angels in a controversy which threatened, through the use of Baker's editorial pen, to become a public issue. Said the school report:

> The County Auditors, while declining to grant any portion of the funds claimed, expressed their warm approval of the aims and objects to which the fund was devoted, and their willingness to have the claim adjusted amicably, according to the true interpretation of the law.[9]

This struck the board as a reasonable solution. The matter was turned over to D. Bethune Duffield, Samuel T. Douglass and Edmund Hall, all board members, and among the city's most learned and successful lawyers. They decided to carry the matter to the Supreme Court, and Douglass and Hall, representing the plaintiffs, petitioned the Supreme Court at its May, 1860, term for a writ of mandamus to compel the county treasurer to pay into the library fund the amount of $2200. This, of course, was not all the money the board claimed. It represented the proceeds of three recently forfeited recognizances in criminal cases in the Detroit courts. Brownstown Township joined in the case as a plaintiff also, with a claim against the Police Justice of Detroit to force him to pay over a $100 fine he had collected. This was for the purpose of establishing the claim of all units of government within the county. As it was pointed out at the time, these cases were selected because they developed all the points of law and interpretation necessary to settle the entire issue in a single action.[10]

The Supreme Court acted promptly, and a decision was written by Justice James V. Campbell, recognized as one of the finest legal minds that Michigan ever produced. It is significant that Justice Campbell in later years became closely identified with the Detroit Public Library as a member of its first Board of Library Commissioners. His opinion in the penal fines case was concurred in by the other members of the court and represented a complete victory for the Board of Education on every point in contention.

As far as the disposition of fines was concerned, said Campbell, the language of the constitution "is too plain to be open to construction. No deduction for expenses or otherwise can lawfully be made from such fines. The whole amount collected belongs to the Library Fund, and no portion can be applied elsewhere."

As to other funds, such as recognizances, earmarked for the libraries by statute, a failure on the part of the legislature to specifically deduct costs must be interpreted to mean that the legislature intended the whole amount to be paid over to the county treasurer.

> Without questioning the right of the legislature to make such deductions as they deem expedient, except from fines, it is very clear that until they see fit to make such deductions—inasmuch as no money can be drawn from the treasury without some legal authority—the fund must remain inviolate.

Campbell concluded with these words:

> It is unnecessary to consider the collateral questions argued. We are of opinion that the Treasurer is bound to include in his apportionment, and to pay over to the several local officers, all moneys which are paid into his office on account of fines, penalties, forfeitures, and recognizances.

The immediate result of the decision was to compel the county treasurer to distribute to the Wayne County townships and cities, for library purposes, the sum of $2200 mentioned in the petition. Further, it recognized the obligation of the treasurer to pay over all library earmarked funds accumulated since 1854. These, as Baker's committee had determined in 1859, amounted to $17,000. Inasmuch as this sum was, by law, to be prorated among the various school districts on the basis of school population, Detroit's share was estimated at approximately $10,000. It was confidently anticipated that the Board of Auditors would take immediate steps to draw the proper warrants on the treasury "to restore to the proper Educational Boards of the towns and city, the funds of which they have been despoiled."

While the Detroit Board of Education was celebrating its victory, it did not forget that in providing it with a library fund, the constitution and statutes imposed upon it an obligation "to establish a library, and that the money derived from the above

69

sources shall be applied to no other purpose." It was its duty, the Board admitted, "to decide upon the plan, management, and conservation" of a library.

Somewhat to its dismay, the school Board discovered that a favorable legal decision was not necessarily the same as cash in hand. The Library Fund having been spent for other purposes, the county treasurer was unable to produce $17,000 or anything approaching that amount. The deficit in the Library Fund would have to be made up out of future tax levies. Meanwhile, plans to open a library would have to mark time. Actually, the Board of Education wanted neither a pound of flesh nor the last drop of blood from the public veins. The Board was more interested in having established its right to Library Fund money, and in having set up protections against future misuse. An arrangement was worked out with the Board of Auditors—a settlement, really— by which the Library Fund claim was adjusted at $10,000 as of January 1, 1861. Payment on that amount was not to be pressed for until after collection of the 1861 county taxes. In return for those concessions on the part of the Board of Education, the auditors agreed to include the claim in their estimates of the amount recommended to the Board of Supervisors to be raised by taxation. That was done, but at the time the supervisors were ready to consider the matter, the Civil War erupted in all its fury. Engrossed with other matters growing out of the war, the library item was overlooked, and the claim went unpaid into 1862.[11]

In 1862 the auditors recommended to the supervisors that the $10,000 be paid in four equal annual installments. That arrangement was acceptable, and $2500, representing the first installment, was spread on the rolls. It was stated:

> This fund is by law distributable in the same manner as the common school fund; that is, in proportion to the number of children between four and eighteen years, in the various towns and city. By this division, Detroit, containing not far from six-tenths of the children of the county, will receive as her portion, near $6,000 of the whole, or about $1,500 each year, during the four years.

In addition, current collections were to be added to the fund as the money was received. Thus, in 1861, the Library Fund was

70

credited with $601.98 from fines collected that year. In 1862 the amount received was $331.65. These amounts were smaller than anticipated because no money was paid in by the Police Court Justice in 1861 and 1862. In 1863, however, the Police Court, where most of the criminal cases were heard, began to make regular returns. As a result, the Library Fund, after purchasing some encyclopedias in 1862, carried a balance of $368.14 into 1863. On March 9 of that year, the first installment of the arrearage debt was paid—$1,512.63, and on the eleventh, the board's share of the fines and penalties collected in 1862 was paid. Thus total receipts for the year, plus the balance carried forward, were $3,555.43, the first really important money the board had ever had for library purposes. In 1864 the installment plus the regular receipts amounted to $4,210.28. With the 1863 year-end balance on hand, the library fund swelled to $7,437.08, as of April 9.

Looking at its bank book, the board decided it had enough to start putting together a book collection. Soon thereafter, Henry Chaney was dispatched to the East with approximately $6000 to purchase books for the Capitol Library.[12]

The suit of 1860 was not the last time the Board of Education was forced to go into the courts to obtain the penal fines money to which it was entitled. The Detroit Police Court did a land office business in collecting fines from vagrants, drunks and disorderly persons involved in several categories of petty crime. Both by ordinance and charter, the Police Justice was required to hold early sessions court in the central police station and dispose of the cases of those who had been locked up overnight. Disposition of these cases often resulted in fines of $200 or more a week. The aggregate to which the Board laid claim was estimated at $15,000. Yet, because this court was established by city ordinance, the justices argued that the state laws did not apply to them, and the fines, if they were turned over at all, went to the city and not the county treasurer. The former maintained that these funds could be used for general city purposes, and did not belong to the library fund. One newspaper, the Detroit *Post,* flatly stated that the greater portion of these fines "had been embezzled" by the Police Justice.[13]

71

In 1866 T. H. Hartwell, president of the Board of Education, made a formal demand upon the Common Council for the central station fines, but the Council took no action.[14] As a result, the board, acting through the county treasurer, brought suit against the city to recover the money to which it felt entitled. First heard in Circuit Court, the judgment favored the city, and an appeal was taken to the State Supreme Court. On October 20, 1868, Justice Cooley handed down the court's opinion in which the lower court was reversed. Cooley held that the city ordinance was merely a re-enactment of the substance of state law regarding vagrancy and disorderly conduct. Said Cooley:

> No argument can be needed to demonstrate that the penal provi-
> sions of a law of the State are not superseded by an unnecessary
> municipal ordinance to the same effect, or that the penalty when
> recovered in such a case, is to be regarded as recovered under the
> state law, instead of under the ordinance. . . .
> This case, therefore, only requires us to determine whether that is
> the penal law in the sense of the Constitution, which punishes by fine
> and imprisonment, in the city of Detroit, actions which are breaches
> of the law wherever committed, but which elsewhere are differently
> provided for and guarded against. Upon this point we have no doubt.[15]

The result of this second victory was the payment in April, 1869, of more than $10,000 of central police station fines. Whereas in 1868, the Library Fund had received $2,615.16 from penal fines, it positively wallowed in riches in 1869 when receipts from the county treasurer amounted to $12,962.72.[16]

The collection of penal fines money and determination of the Library Fund's right to them continued to be a troublesome issue. Regularly, over the years, those responsible for the conduct of the Library's affairs felt obliged to examine carefully the disposition of the fines. The entire situation was complicated in 1892 when the legislature passed a law extending the jurisdiction of the Police Court. Under this law, minor offenses which previously had been defined in broad categories under state statutes, were broken down into specific offenses under city ordinances. For example, the state laws provided penalties for disorderly conduct. The city ordinances enlarged on that classification by making the use of obscene language in public a matter of disorderly conduct.

72

In giving the Police Court jurisdiction over these and several other ordinance cases, the 1892 law permitted the city to retain the costs.

This provision escaped the attention of the clerk of the Police Court for awhile, and he continued to pay over to the county treasurer the proceeds of all fines and costs as in the past. In 1895 the city brought suit against the county treasurer to recover these costs. This action alarmed the Library Commission which by that time had superseded the Library Committee of the Board of Education.

"If an important portion of the revenue is thus diverted it is likely to seriously hamper the Library in its operation and may cripple it in the immediate future," Commissioner Magnus Butzel told the Commission.[17]

How serious the matter was becoming was revealed in a report made in 1897 which disclosed that for the year ending May 1, 1897, the Library Fund received from the county only $1,524.15 against $6,087.42 in the preceding twelve months. Indeed, an average of $7,414.50 had been paid over the past thirty-four years. Robert T. Gray, attorney for the Library Commission, was asked to look into the matter and his report was far from encouraging. He stated:

> We are unable to find anything which your Board can remedy in any way, or anything that should be called to public attention in any manner. We are inclined to the opinion that it is something that you must accept.

The result was a sharp drop in library income from penal fines. This became further complicated by a practice on the part of the authorities to bring more cases into court under city ordinances than under state statutes. This, in turn, resulted in the judges assessing heavier costs and lighter fines. The purpose was to make the courts more nearly self-sustaining. Suspended sentences, with costs added, were frequently imposed. Thus, it was noted that in one year costs amounted to $9545, while fines imposed were only $4416.[18]

This sharp decline in library revenue, while the city treasurer's accounts were being fattened by court costs, caused the Library

Commission further acute distress in 1905. In that year, another survey was made of the situation with results about the same as in 1897. Able attorneys were employed by the Commission, but they were unable to offer the kind of solution the Commission hoped for—and needed. Their conclusion was tersely summarized in the following language:

> The amount of the fine in each instance being in the discretion of the Police Judge, this Commission cannot complain about the amount of the fine.
> This Commission has no rights until the fine is imposed and collected.
> Where a judge imposes no fine or a grossly inadequate one, the only relief this Commission has is to call the judge's attention to the matter.
> Costs are no part of the fund to be turned over to this Commission.[19]

Despite such setbacks, income from penal fines later increased as the city grew and the courts became busier. Library revenue from penal fines was displaced as the sole source of income as new revenues were developed. Yet the "wages of sin," which first provided the Public Library with its financial foundation, continued to be, as it still remains, an important item in the Library's support. The continued income and the uses to which it has been put, reflects the far-sighted wisdom of Edward D. Ellis, Isaac A. Crary and their fellow delegates to the Constitutional Convention of 1835.

CHAPTER 5

GROWING PAINS

OPENING of the Capitol Library for public use in 1865 was not accompanied by a rush of patronage. Despite the fact that this new service was available, the people of Detroit were slow at first to take advantage of it. The opening was well publicized in the newspapers which followed up that event with generous amounts of space, telling the citizens of the book collection at their disposal and urging them to make use of it. Despite this, potential readers did not beat a path to the library rooms, much to the dismay of the Library Committee.

> Not withstanding, the committee sought to give abundant public notice that the Library was entirely free and open to all classes of citizens, the number who have availed themselves of its benefits have been comparatively small for a city so large,

75

the Library Committee mournfully reported at the end of the year. Only 475 persons withdrew books, and only 4700 volumes circulated between May 2 and the year's end.

> Although this number is daily increasing, the committee takes the opportunity again to say, that all citizens are invited to resort to the Library, and to select from its ample store, books for their instruction and gratification.[1]

By the end of 1866, traffic was heavier, although still not up to what Library officials would have liked it to be. In that year, books were drawn by 1184 patrons. Circulation was estimated at 15,000 volumes of which 3000 were consulted in the Library. Stated the 1866 annual report:

> This exhibits a steady growth in the appreciation of the benefits of the library, but it seems, nevertheless, that a great majority of our citizens still seem unaware of, or are disinclined to avail themselves of the privileges which the library gratuitously offers them. An extended impression prevails that this is a library for the pupils of the public schools, an error which would soon be cured by a cursory inspection of its shelves.[2]

Gradually, however, the public began to learn about the Library and to make use of it. New books were purchased or acquired by donation, so that by the end of 1867 the collection consisted of more than 10,000 volumes. In order to have the broadest possible appeal and develop the fullest reader potential, Henry Chaney and the committee exercised a high degree of selectivity in its book purchases. For example, in 1866, a start was made on a German collection. It was pointed out that Detroit had a substantial German population and that group was "generally educated, and in many cases a literary people." The private subscription libraries apparently did not cater to the Germans, and the latter had no place to turn for books in their own language except the Public Library. It was largely at their request that "a supply of books in a language so famed in literature as the German" was obtained. The Library already had recognized the needs of the city's old French element, still strong at that time, and had a good selection of French books.[3] But from 1866 on, the German collection was gradually enlarged by regular annual

76

purchases from dealers in Leipzig, as well as in the United States. Because the German population was so large and had become so influential in Detroit, both culturally and politically, at least one of its representatives was usually found on the Board of Education and on the Library's governing body up to the outbreak of World War I.

Perhaps one reason the Library was not better patronized at first can be explained by the hours it was open. Because Chaney was principal of the high school as well as librarian, he could only serve the reading public at times which did not interfere with his other duties, and at hours which would not disturb the school's routine. For the time being, the Library was open from 9 A.M. to 2 P.M. for reference only. Books could be withdrawn from 2 P.M. to 4 P.M. only. Obviously, those hours did not encourage use by men, particularly those who were employed. Efforts were made to provide better service in 1866, when employment of an assistant to Chaney, at a $310 annual salary, was approved. As this assistant also was a teacher, the hours could not easily be extended. The best the aide could do was lighten Chaney's burden and, perhaps, endeavor to abate one prime nuisance which the *Free Press* complained of—"the practice of 'dog-earing,' or turning down the leaves of a book. . . . Those in charge of the library desire to be understood that such practices must be discontinued or delinquents will be deprived of its privileges." [4]

In time, as facilities improved, the hours were extended. The Detroit *Advertiser and Tribune* of May 11, 1868, carried the announcement that the Library would be open for the delivery of books from 4 to 8 P.M. daily. This was encouraging progress, reflected in the year-end report which stated with gratification that 2466 persons were entitled to draw books, and the circulation for the year exceeded 35,000 volumes. [5]

As the popularity of the Library increased, and even before the public had fully accepted it, expressions of civic pride in the institution were heard. The newspapers particularly, trying to stimulate interest and wider use, devoted much space in their columns to the Library.

"Earnestly do we commend this institution," declared the *Detroit Post*. Among Detroit's institutions, "none reflects more credit on our city," the *Free Press* echoed. The Library Committee, voicing its own pride, proclaimed that "our library is fast becoming the pride and boast of the city." [6] The *Advertiser and Tribune* ran a series of about a dozen articles describing the Library and its collection in considerable detail. This interest and pride, so frequently expressed, had the desired effect of sending more and more people up to the old Capitol school to make use of the books available to them there. By 1870 the Library officials were no longer concerned because patronage was not up to expectations. With what for the moment was adequate income from penal fines, spent mostly to enlarge the book collection, the Library Committee report was able to state: "Of the free public libraries of the country, the Detroit Library ranks fourth in the number of its volumes, and second in the amount of its income." It was surpassed in these areas only by the Boston Public Library, the Cincinnati Public Library and the New Bedford Public Library.[7] The position thus attained in the short space of five years was, indeed, something to boast of.

The Capitol Library had been open for only three days when the *Advertiser and Tribune* arrived at the conclusion that the present quarters would "soon become too confined." It did not take long for that prediction to come true. As more and more patrons were attracted to the Library, and found satisfaction in the books they withdrew—a wide range of choices which ran the gamut of Jean Baptiste Duhalde's *History of China* to Lord Tennyson's newly published *Enoch Arden*—the ground floor quarters became badly over-crowded. The Board of Education was presented with the necessity of doing something about it. Prompt action, said the *Detroit Post,* was needed.

> We can see little use in purchasing additional books if accommodation cannot be found for one-half those already procured. Besides, it renders the duties of the librarian too arduous, in addition to the waste of time and injury to the books, to search among huge, promiscuous heaps for the one required.[8]

The *Post* proposed that a partition be removed, and a room occupied by the primary school be added to the Library. The Library Committee was fully aware of the situation, but for the moment it continued the policy of building up the collection. It foresaw the time when a separate building would be required, but it preferred to give the acquisition of books priority in its budget. As for expansion within the Capitol, the committee members were members of the school Board before they were library custodians, and their first concern was with classroom facilities. They felt that the primary room was needed for pupils more than it was needed for books. The *Free Press* pointed out a temporary solution to the dilemma:

> Some ready intellect discovered that by the introduction of al-coves or extra shelving, occupying the more central portions of the library room, much more book-room might be secured. By the adoption of this plan which has been put in operation, and is being carried out, the long-needed and much desired end is being reached, and the good that the Free Public Library was intended to do is in a measure being realized.[9]

But new shelving installed in 1868 afforded only a measure of relief. By the end of the next year, the Library Committee observed that the congestion had been alleviated "only in a slight degree," and the "rose-colored cloud has a lining of unpleasant hue." Fear was expressed that unless more adequate facilities were soon provided, the legislature might act with "inimical legislation, based upon the failure of the Board to make of the library that great public institution for which its generous income calls." [10]

To head off anything so drastic, the Board of Education authorized construction of an addition to the old Capitol. On October 24, 1870, it was decided to add two rooms to the rear of the high school, each room to be sufficiently large to accommodate sixty-five scholars. Work was to be pushed forward without delay. The result was a two-story brick addition in the rear with the entrance on the Grand River Avenue end of the original building. Dimensions of the new part were 40 feet wide by 70 feet long. The first floor had a 16-foot ceiling, while the second floor room was 12 feet high. It was described as being set upon a solid foundation, with special attention given to making the rooms dry. Under the structure was a basement, sufficient for storage purposes.

The original plans called for using the new quarters, upstairs and down, for classrooms, and giving the Library added space in the old building. But as construction progressed, Inspector Charles Backus, a member of the Library Committee, offered a resolution "that the room on the first floor of the new addition to the Capitol building be devoted to the uses of the Public Library." [11] The resolution was adopted, apparently without any serious opposition. If there were objections, they undoubtedly faded away when it was agreed that the Library would pay the Board of Education an annual rental of $500. The result, as the late John C. Lodge (who attended the high school) recalled, was that

> the lower floor of the building was devoted to the older elementary pupils, and the upper, or second floor, housed the high school. The Detroit Public Library occupied the first floor of a little two-story building at the rear of the lot, and the second floor of that building was used as a classroom for the high school seniors.[12]

The addition was sufficiently near completion by December 17, 1870 to warrant preparation for removal of the Library. This involved closing the Library while workmen still were plastering, installing shelves and adding final touches to the addition. The new shelving was constructed in such a manner as to make alcoves. As the *Free Press* observed on January 29, 1871, "the shelves are made in separate portions or departments, of box form, which with the books in each is easily and readily portable." About mid-February, the books themselves were transferred, and on March 20, the *Advertiser and Tribune* reported that the Library was reopened in its new quarters. The paper found these to be "infinitely superior to any which the Library has ever enjoyed heretofore, and the circulation of its books will be largely increased. Inasmuch, too, as there is now sufficient space, the Library can be increased as rapidly as the Board of Education shall deem best."

The Library Committee was pleased by what had been accomplished. It rejoiced in "an exhibit so gratifying," and proudly called attention to the fact that

> the Library is by far the largest in size and circulation in this State. . . . It now enjoys ample shelving room, tasteful surroundings, and

the long needed opportunities for convenient classification and easy management. It has thus been freed from the more serious of the embarrassments that throughout its earlier history so greatly lessened its usefulness and so constantly annoyed those charged with its care.

Almost as important as more room, was the opportunity given the Library staff, upon removal from the old quarters, to change from the ledger to the card system of keeping account of books loaned.[13]

It had been a dream of those most interested in the affairs of the Library that someday there would be a separate building devoted exclusively to the Public Library. As early as 1869 the Library Committee's annual report stated that the erection of a separate building was desirable, and the hope was expressed that public-minded citizens would contribute to such a project. Even when facilities were being expanded within the Capitol and by its 1871 addition, it was tacitly understood that something still more suitable would eventually have to be provided. As early as December 13, 1868, the Detroit *Free Press* made a suggestion along lines others must also have considered. Detroit was then in the process of building a new city hall on the west side of Woodward Avenue between Michigan and Fort. It was to replace an older municipal building, standing since 1835 on the east side of Woodward at approximately where the Soldiers' and Sailors' Monument later was erected. While the new city hall would not be completed until June 20, 1871, Detroiters already were debating the use to which its predecessor would be put when it was vacated by the mayor, alderman and other civic dignitaries. To use it as a public library appeared to be a sound and sensible thing to do. The *Free Press* proposal, whether original with that paper or not, was indorsed by other newspapers, organizations and individuals. The Detroit *Daily Union* thought the old city hall "could not be appropriated to a better purpose." [14] The Library Committee adopted the idea and in 1870 recommended to the Board of Education "that a prompt and earnest effort be made to obtain from the City Government the gift to the Public Library of the old City Hall edifice." Its interior could be remodeled, the committee suggested, "so as to furnish a superb Library apartment." [15]

The proposition, laid before the Common Council in mid-1870, was received with signs of official enthusiasm. Alderman Bagg announced that "his heart went out to the proposal." [16] Meanwhile, Charles K. Backus and Dr. David O. Farrand, of the Library Committee, were not putting all of their hopes in one basket. Consideration was given to alternatives which included St. Andrew's Hall, which the canny Scots members were willing to rent for library purposes. However, St. Andrew's Society found another tenant, and Backus and others looked at quarters in the new Seitz Building on the south side of Congress Street, just west of Griswold.[17] Interest in this location quickly faded when the Capitol addition became available. The old city hall idea did not wane, however, even when the new quarters in the high school were occupied in 1871. Backus continued to push for acquisition of the old city hall, supported by Inspectors William D. Wilkins, William Y. Rumney and D. Bethune Duffield. A new appeal was made to the Council on the basis that the city had a moral obligation to donate the building which the Library was prepared to remodel and equip at its own expense. The Council again was receptive, and shortly after the city vacated the old building on July 18, 1871, the Council leased the old city hall to the Board of Education for fifty years with the proviso that it be refitted and made suitable for library purposes within eighteen months. A clause permitted complete demolition and replacement with a new building if that should be more satisfactory.

Thus, at about the same time the Library was comfortably settling itself in the high school annex, arrangements were being made to take over the old city hall. But unexpected obstacles arose. Detroit had plans to honor its Civil War soldiers and sailors; funds for a monument had been raised by public subscription and a design had been approved. The most suitable place for such a monument would be opposite the new city hall, and it would be too bad, the citizens felt, if it should be overshadowed or crowded out by an old city hall converted into a library. The Library Committee, itself, was having second thoughts. The remodeling would be more costly than was first estimated. The Board of Education members, being elected officials, were not inclined to cross popular public desire and spoil the site of the

82

Soldiers' and Sailors' Monument. It was decided to go slowly. The Council extended the remodeling period by a year, but this was merely a formality. The idea of using the old city hall was soon abandoned, and another site was sought.[18]

Fortunately one was available. It was a triangular piece of land, almost identical in size and shape as that upon which the old Capitol had been erected. Located east of Woodward, it fronted on State Street (soon to be known as Gratiot Avenue), and lay between Farmer and Farrar streets. The latter would in time be renamed Library Street. The apex of this triangular plot touched Grand River Avenue east. As the eastside balance to the Capitol Park, it was the symmetrical remnant of Judge Woodward's plan, formed by the conflux of streets radiating from circles and plazas. This east side lot was known as East Park, Central Park, but more commonly as Centre Park. Adjoining the park, on the northwest corner of State (Gratiot) and Farmer, stood the stately First Presbyterian Church, on the site now occupied by the J. L. Hudson Company department store. In a short time, another neighbor would be the Young Men's Christian Association. A few stores, but mostly middle class residences lined Farmer and Farrar streets. Except on Sunday mornings when the carriages of some of Detroit's foremost families rolled up in front of the church, and except for the occasional rattle of a passing horse-drawn Gratiot Avenue streetcar, Centre Park was a quiet, peaceful oasis, rather removed from the bustle and noise of the city.

Like its west-side counterpart, Capitol Park, Centre Park had originally been set aside for public purposes. Where Capitol Park had been selected as the location for the statehouse, Centre Park was chosen as the place for the county jail. With proceeds from the sale of the Ten Thousand Acre Tract, a jail was built in 1819. It was a small building, 88 by 44 feet, topped by a cupola, and surrounded by a high picket fence. From all accounts, it was infrequently used and for months at a time it housed no inmates. Mostly, its prisoners were drunken Indians, debtors or others incarcerated for civil rather than criminal offenses. Ironically, its most notable guest was Detroit's earliest proponent of a library, Father Gabriel Richard. Arrested September 21, 1824 on a body execution growing out of an unsatisfied judgment in a libel case, the priest was confined for a month before bond could be arranged for him.[19]

A few years later, September 24, 1830, the jail yard was the scene of the hanging of Stephen G. Simmons, convicted of the murder of his wife. The gallows was erected on the grounds facing Gratiot Avenue, a grandstand was set up for spectators who flocked in from miles around, and every neighboring window and rooftop was crowded by a throng of people in holiday mood who turned out for the gruesome spectacle of a public execution. While Simmons had been given a fair trial, and there was no doubt about his guilt, a public revulsion developed after the hanging. The result was that the death penalty was outlawed in Michigan, and Simmons was the last man to be executed by the State of Michigan.[20]

Apparently the jail was not the most secure lockup. In 1834 all of the prisoners broke out. Concern about its security in a residential neighborhood led the courts to decree in 1847 that the jail was a public nuisance, and as city property, the county had no right to its use. A new jail site at Beaubien and Clinton was acquired, and the old building on Gratiot was torn down in 1848. Thereafter it was used only for park purposes.

This was the ground which the Library Committee selected when it was decided that the old city hall site was not suited for library purposes. Early in March, 1872, the Board of Education began negotiating with the Common Council for the use of Centre Park. A petition signed by Robert W. King, chairman of the committee, was submitted to the Council, in which it was proposed to exchange the lease of the city hall location for a lease of "said triangular lot," or Centre Park.[21] The proposal was well received by the Council, and the trade was strongly urged by Mayor Hugh Moffat. Owners of property adjoining the park would be benefited, he pointed out, and the portion of the park not built upon, if "ornamented and well kept, should be free to the enjoyment of all," and as "a thing of beauty be a joy forever." The city government and the Board of Education, as "active and effective allies . . . therefore ought to work in union for the common weal by providing for the present wants and future prosperity of this growing city. . . ."[22]

The *Advertiser and Tribune,* echoing Mayor Moffat's senti-ments, said Centre Park was the most beautiful site the city afforded. "It is spacious, retired and attractive; while as a public park it is not large enough to answer its legitimate end." [23]

The outcome was that on May 21, 1872, the Common Council voted to vacate the park, and on August 19, executed a fifty-year lease to the Board of Education. A resolution, adopted November 18, 1872 by the Board of Education provided:

> 1st. That the Library Committee be and they are hereby directed to enter upon and take possession of Centre Park, so called, for the purpose of commencing the construction of a Public Library building.
> 2d. That they be empowered to adopt all necessary measures, and to incur all necessary expenses, preparatory to adopting a plan for the building of the same, reporting their action to the Board.
> 3d. That the said committee adopt the proper measures for opening subscription books for the purpose of soliciting subscriptions for the construction of said building.
> 4th. That said committee ascertain what legislation may be neces-sary to promote the general interests of said Public Library, and make a report thereon.[24]

Before this program could be put into effect, the power of the Common Council to dedicate a public park for library purposes was challenged. Some of the property owners on Farmer and Farrar streets feared that values of their homes and lots might deteriorate if a public building was erected, and a nuisance, similar to that caused years before by the presence of the jail, might be repeated. One of the homeowners, Alida Riggs,* sought to enjoin the Council from leasing the park to the Board of Education, claiming that she bought the property in the belief that the adjoining space would always be reserved as a park. The case moved quickly to the Supreme Court where it was decided on May 7, 1873. Once again Justice Campbell came to the rescue of the Library, his opinion supporting completely and in every detail the transfer and lease of Centre Park. Recalling the Act of 1807 by which the Governor and Judges, with congressional

---

* There was a Riggs family living at 87 Farmer Street in 1872, although no Alida Riggs was listed at the address at that time. However two persons, S. M. Riggs and Fanny E. Riggs, residing there, were identified in the city directory as teachers. This suggests that the suit was arranged as a friendly test case.

approval, reserved open spaces for public use, Justice Campbell pointed out that Section 7 of the Act specifically stated:

> The internal space of ground in the middle of every section result-ing from the radial layout of streets shall be reserved for public wells and pumps, for markets, for public schools, for houses for the recep-tion of engines or other articles for the extinction of fires, and the preservation of the property of the inhabitants, for houses for the meeting of religious, moral, literary or political societies, or other useful associations, and, generally, for such purposes of utility or ornament as the City Council of Detroit may at any time by law provide. . . .

Campbell held that a public library met the broad qualifica-tions of the Act. He stated:

> The purpose for which the land is to be used is directly within the original statute of dedication. The library is a public one, main-tained and regulated by a public corporation for city purposes, and the use . . . is much more general than the former one could have been. . . .[25]

So Centre Park became, lawfully, the site for Detroit's first building devoted exclusively to housing a public library. That was more than ninety years ago. The character of the area has changed considerably in that time. Farrar Street has become Library Street. The residences which lined it and Farmer gradually gave way to stores and other commercial buildings. The First Presbyterian Church moved into a new home farther uptown, and the old edifice was torn down. Upon its site grew Detroit's largest department store, the J. L. Hudson Company. Across the street stands another emporium, the Crowley, Milner & Company. But amid the bustle of downtown business and commerce there has stood through the years, like an oasis of culture, a public library building.

From the time the Board of Education created a standing committee on the Library in 1860, until 1873 when the legal complications surrounding the Centre Park site were cleared up, a total of twenty-one different men served as members of the committee. In the brief space of thirteen years, these men not only established the Detroit Public Library but they also built a financial foundation for it, acquired an admirable nucleus for a book collection, obtained quarters, and took steps for necessary expansion. They were, in every meaning of the expression, the Library's founding fathers. The ultimate growth and development into one of the foremost institutions of its kind, could not have been accomplished without them, nor without their full understanding of the aims and purposes toward which they and the community were striving as well as the problems with which they were confronted.

To achieve what they did in so short a space of time required high moral and intellectual character. Each of those twenty-one men was an elected member of the Board of Education. Accordingly, each was and of necessity had to be to some extent a politician. It would have been easy for them to place political interests ahead of the Library interests and by so doing make the Library a pawn in municipal or community politics. It would have been easy and understandable for them to have made the Library a minor adjunct to the public schools. That never happened. It may be assumed that members of the Library Committee gave priority to school affairs, but the impression is inescapable that a majority of them, at least, derived their greatest satisfaction from their participation in Library affairs.

Thus, at the outset, a pattern of conduct was established which could be observed in several areas, i.e., the operation of the Public Library never became as deeply involved in local politics, at least not the corrupt type of politics that was accepted if not condoned in other areas of government; the precedent of naming persons of high standing in the community to administer Library affairs was firmly established.

Of those serving on the committee whose occupations can be ascertained, seven were lawyers; six can be classed as businessmen, a category which includes manufacturers, merchants and a banker; three were physicians, one an educator and one a journalist. Some members, while eminent in their respective fields, also had political interests and either had or eventually would occupy other public positions. Several of them may be regarded as representative of the highest economic and professional class in the community. But regardless of social status, or the high plateaus of vocational success to which they attained, each possessed an elevated sense of civic responsibility, exemplified in many fields of public enterprise.

D. Bethune Duffield, son of the Reverend George Duffield, pastor of the First Presbyterian Church, was thirty-nine years old when he became a committee member in 1860. He was recognized as one of the leaders of the Detroit bar. Before his death in 1891, he would also be city attorney and United States commissioner. Edmund Hall, with whom he served on the first permanent Library Committee, was also a leading attorney. During the Civil War, he headed the local chapter of the Sanitary Commission and was active in most spheres of soldier and home front relief.

William Warner (1862) was a Vermont native, born in 1812. Before going to Detroit in 1854, he was for several years treasurer of the University of Vermont. He became a successful Detroit manufacturer, but he always retained a strong interest in education. His daughter, Harriet Warner Bishop was for many years on the faculty of Central High School and still is remembered as one of Detroit's most beloved teachers. Sidney D. Miller (1864, 1865, 1869) was a Harvard graduate who became one of Detroit's most successful railroad and bank attorneys. Allied by marriage with the family of C. C. Trowbridge, he was "numbered among the distinguished and honored members of the bar" and a "prominent and influential citizen." He served a term as president of the Young Men's Society.

Colonel William D. Wilkins (1866, 1871, 1873) had an outstanding record in both the Mexican and Civil wars. Robert W. King, a native of Pittsburgh and a graduate of Washington and Jefferson College, became a successful Detroit merchant. His business, carried on in the name of his son L. B. King, is still well known in Detroit. Robert King was for many years a trustee of Harper Hospital.

Dr. David O. Farrand (1867, 1870) was a member of a Detroit family prominent in many fields. As a Civil War surgeon, Dr. Farrand was the first medical director of Harper Hospital. The hospital's school of nursing was named in his honor. Dr. Herman Kiefer (1865) was another of Detroit's medical giants. A native of Germany, and Heidelberg educated, he became a leader of

Detroit's German colony. In later years he served as a regent of the University of Michigan and was on the Detroit Library Commission. Another medical man, Dr. James A. Brown, was on the Library Committee in 1868 and 1869.

Charles K. Backus * (1868, 1869, 1870, 1871) was as much responsible as any single person for the expansion of quarters in the Capitol Library, and for the acquisition of the Centre Park site. A member of the Princeton class of 1861, Backus became a journalist. After serving as night editor of the *Advertiser and Tribune,* he became editor of the *Tribune* in 1871. He was still in his mid-twenties when he first became a member of the Board of Education and the Library Committee. Others who were prominent on the Committee were W. B. Smith (1862), one of the founders of the Detroit Young Men's Christian Association; A. Stutee (1867), an attorney and school teacher, and G. M. Rich (1866), banker, who is entitled to a footnote of fame as the landlord of U. S. Grant when the latter was stationed in Detroit as a junior officer.

The real guiding spirit behind the Library in its early days was grave, dignified and scholarly Librarian Henry Chaney, of whose breadth of vision it was said:

> He thought of the Detroit Public Library as a sound, democratic, and vigorous organization; one dedicated to providing the best means of information for the people of Detroit. . . . He was a man peculiarly fitted for the position he occupied. His undoubted sincerity, broad scholarship, sound judgment and strong leadership were vital to the establishment and growth of those two early cultural institutions—the High School and the Detroit Public Library.

As one of Detroit's cultural pioneers, Chaney deserves more from the public memory than he has been accorded. One of Detroit's elementary schools bears his name; one of the city's newest branch libraries was named for him. Beyond that, he is

---

* Charles K. Backus was born at Peekskill, New York, September 8, 1843. In addition to his newspaper career, he was engaged in the lumbering and real estate business. He also served as State Commissioner of Immigration in 1881–82. He was a member of the Board of Education from 1868 to 1874. He married Evelyn Standish, and his descendants have been prominent in Detroit's business and social life. Backus died at Sconset, Massachusetts, July 22, 1894.

little known, while others whose efforts and contributions in no way measure up to his, are remembered and honored by posterity.

Henry Chaney—or Cheney as the name originally was spelled —was born October 14, 1808, at Orange, Massachusetts. He was the son of Luther and Sabra Allen Chaney, and he spent his boyhood in typical New England village surroundings. His father, the blacksmith in Orange, also conducted an inn and was justice of the peace. The family, while of modest circumstances, was one of substance and local importance. When Henry was still a child, the Chaneys moved to Vermont and settled on a farm near Burlington. This was fortunate, because it gave Henry educational advantages which otherwise he might not have had. When he was old enough, he entered the University of Vermont where he received a sound education. Upon graduating he taught school, and in 1831 at the age of twenty-eight, he became principal of the academy at Fredonia, New York, remaining there about seven years. At the end of that period, he returned to Burlington as professor of natural philosophy and chemistry at the University. Among his students at Vermont was William P. Wells, one of the first members of the Detroit Library Committee. While at Fredonia he taught Henry N. Walker, later a prominent Detroit civic leader, and Samuel T. Douglass who, as attorney for the Board of Education, won the lawsuit which established the Library's right to penal fines.[26]

In 1854 Chaney resigned from the Vermont faculty in order to join a brother-in-law in the manufacturing business at Ogdensburg, New York. The enterprise, from Chaney's standpoint, was not a great success. In 1858 Detroit was looking for someone to organize and head its high school. William Warner, who had been associated with Chaney at the University of Vermont, remembered his former colleague and persuaded him to move to Detroit and accept the post. Always addressed as Professor Chaney, he filled the position creditably and gained the respect of pupils and school officials alike. When the Library was organized, it was really a branch or adjunct of the school system and it was natural that he should have been asked to take charge of it.

From a small beginning, the Library grew within a very few years into an important institution. What started out as a part-time job, soon became demanding of all the hours Chaney could devote to it. When the addition was added to the Capitol School in 1871, and with prospects of another move into a separate library building, either in the old city hall or in Centre Park, it was decided that a full-time librarian was needed. The job was given to Chaney, who resigned the principalship of the high school. His duties as full-time librarian dated from March, 1871.[27]

That was the beginning of a new and distinguished phase of Chaney's career. As the Library grew in size and extent of service under his direction, his burden was lightened by the beginning of a staff. He had some assistance from teachers in the original high school library rooms; in the 1871 addition he was given two aides. T. C. Prosser is mentioned as the "first assistant," although he apparently was on a part-time basis. Miss Julia Pattison, the daughter of George W. Pattison, proprietor of a bookstore on Griswold Street, just north of Jefferson Avenue, was employed full-time. Later Miss Pattison's sister, Adda, also became a permanent member of the staff.[28]

That his work was highly appreciated was testified to year after year by the Library Committee in its annual reports. In 1866, mention was made of "his peculiar fitness," his "broad and liberal culture" and "his entire and zealous devotion to his work." [29] In 1867, the *Free Press* said "he has faithfully devoted all his leisure hours for years in doing whatever lay in his power to make it [the Library] an attractive place to the general reader, as well as one of special interest to the man of letters." [30] Said one Detroiter who knew him both as a schoolman and librarian:

> Mr. Chaney was a very quiet man. He was short and thick set, but dignified, extremely so. He was even and composed, a remarkably well-balanced man. He never did anything to provoke criticism and he offended no one. He never stormed . . . Mr. Chaney was tactful.[31]

Henry Chaney was twice married. After the death in 1845 of his first wife Elizabeth Albertina Caryl, of Barnard, Vermont, he married her sister, Isabella Juliette, who lived until 1875. He was the father of seven children, four of whom survived infancy. One son, Henry Allen, became a successful Detroit attorney. The

91

youngest son, Luther Edward, studied medicine, and for years was a prominent practitioner and professor of laryngology at the old Michigan College of Medicine and Surgery. After the death of his second wife, Chaney made his home with his son, Dr. Luther, at 121 George Street (now Vernor Highway west). It was there that he died February 22, 1885.

During the Civil War, Chaney, a staunch anti-slavery man, published his only known work, a collection of patriotic poems. This appeared in pamphlet form in 1863 under the pseudonym "Vindex" and was titled *Rattlesnakes and Copperheads; or Rhymes for the Times*. It was no great literary effort; in fact he borrowed freely from other writers, giving acknowledgement, as he stated in his foreword, "when anything suited to my purpose recurred to my recollection." Perhaps he felt that he should have donned a uniform and gone off to battle, although he was fifty-five years old at the time. At least there is a certain wistfulness in one poem, "An Apology," in which he said:

> Then let me write while others fight,
> At Freedom's trumpet call,
> A cause so noble, just and right,
> Demands Purse, Strength, Life, All.

CHAPTER 6

THE CENTRE PARK LIBRARY

WITH THE REMOVAL of legal obstacles to the occupancy of Centre Park, the pressures built up to get on with the building of a new library. Immediately after Judge Campbell handed down his decision in the Riggs case, the *Advertiser and Tribune* called for action. The paper stated in an editorial:

> This decision removes the only strong objection to at once entering upon the erection of a Public Library building. . . . The library has now been for over four years in quarters far too limited for its proper administration and for the public convenience. For more than three years only dribbling purchases of new books have been possible. With the increase of its circulation, its embarrassments grow in still greater ratio, and its managers and its patrons alike suffer. . . .[1]

That statement undoubtedly was a fair reflection of public feeling. Detroit was experiencing great changes, and the people were in a progressive mood. Population had increased from 45,619 in 1860 to 79,577 in 1870, and before the 1870–80 decade was out, there would be well over 100,000 people in the

93

city. Since the Civil War, Detroit's business complexion had begun to change. An economy based largely upon mercantile enterprise was being replaced by more emphasis upon manufacturing. The stove industry came into prominence. Railroad equipment was of major importance, causing many foundries and machine shops to spring up. Drugs and chemicals and the manufacture of shoes became major industries. Detroiters developed and exploited the northern forests and a lumber aristocracy came into being.

There was a new bustle and stir in Detroit; a new spirit of civic pride arose. To provide for industrial expansion, new banks and insurance companies were founded. Free mail delivery was inaugurated. To meet new social obligations, such hospitals as Harper, Woman's and Providence were established. The new city hall, a magnificent structure for its time, was a visible expression of Detroit's pride in itself. Schools too were being built in increasing numbers as residential areas shifted from downtown out Woodward, Jefferson, Gratiot, Grand River and Michigan. The time was ripe for almost any kind of public improvement. Contemplating a Public Library which was far from adequate, Detroiters complained about the lack of facilities until something had to be done. The truth is that as the construction of new public buildings, offices, stores and palatial residences changed the face of the city, Detroiters were frankly ashamed of their Library.

"Detroit, which, being an old city, contains in its population far above the average of well educated people, cannot, unfortunately boast of its library," complained one newspaper. It was not something to show with pride to visitors. The quarters were described as "contracted and unpleasant," and it was "unattractive both in its exterior and interior."

This article continued, referring to the old Capitol,

> The building is most unfortunately situated on account of dust. The streets running on three sides of it and in such close proximity causes the dust to accumulate on the books in great quantities. It is impossible for a person to take down from the shelves books that are in constant use without soiling the clothing.

94

Worst of all was the lack of a reading room—"the most useful adjunct to every library." [2]

Obviously, the time and the public temper were right for doing something constructive about a new library.

Professor Chaney and the Library Committee were as aware of the deficiencies as any citizen or editorial writer, and were quietly proceeding to do what they could to remedy the situation, within the means at hand.

Not waiting for the final adjudication of the Centre Park issue, the Library Committee, then consisting of William Jennison, Robert W. King and William Rumney, accompanied by Chaney and Charles K. Backus, president of the Board of Education, went to Cincinnati on December 21, 1872, to inspect that city's new library, then in the course of erection. This was the first of a series of trips to look at "the best library buildings in the country." In Cincinnati, the committee had the opportunity, not only to see the best and most modern ideas in library housing taking form, but also to confer extensively with William F. Poole, the Cincinnati librarian, who was then considered one of the two or three acknowledged experts in his field.[3] The visit was brief, but they returned to Detroit with some fresh ideas and, perhaps more important, a set of plans of the Cincinnati library.

In February, 1873, Jennison and Backus embarked on a more protracted trip which took them to several eastern cities which had up-to-date library facilities. The places visited included Washington, where they inspected both the Library of Congress and the Smithsonian Institution; Philadelphia, New York and Brooklyn, Boston, Cambridge, Springfield and Roxbury, Massachusetts. In Boston, they had the guidance of Justin Winsor, that city's librarian, who ranked with Poole as one of the country's leading library authorities.

Returning from the East, the Committee made a report which amounted to a blueprint for Detroit. They observed that only two of the libraries they visited—the Library of Congress and the Cincinnati library—were of fireproof construction, a point to which they gave principal consideration. A modern library, they affirmed, should be capable of expansion. It should be of brick construction; heating should be by steam with direct and indirect radiation, and there should be adequate skylights.

> As many of the best libraries of the country, especially Gore Hall at Harvard, and the Astor Library of New York, have lost manuscripts and books by dampness, double walls with passages between are highly recommended.

Justin Winsor had decided ideas about the arrangement and placement of books, ideas which were novel and advanced. Winsor took the group to Roxbury and showed them that town's new library which embodied most of the features which he advocated. The visitors were impressed by what they saw and what Winsor told them. As a result they recommended that with some modifications, the Roxbury plan should be adopted by Detroit.

The committee report said of the Roxbury plan:

> It embodies the views of Mr. Winsor, of the Boston Public Library and is the result of his best judgment and experience. (A plan of this edifice, as well as that of the Cincinnati library, has been deposited with the Superintendent, where they can be seen by all interested.) [4]

The report then became more or less specific about what Detroit should have. The building should have ground dimensions of at least 100 by 50 feet, with enough room in the park for future additions. The interior partition walls should be solid brick with iron rafters. The building should be divided in the center so as to provide a large hall, 50 feet square. As the library proper, this room should have alcoves and a gallery, lined with shelving. The other half of the building should consist of three stories, containing administrative offices, a cataloging room, a reception room, space for the circulating department, a reading room containing periodicals as well as books in current demand and a lecture room or auditorium for meetings of the Historical Society and similar groups. The basement should include storage space, heating facilities and a receiving room with a hoist or dumbwaiter to lift books to the upper floors.

The report concluded:

Originally, your committee was inclined to favor water closets in the cellar for the public convenience, but their investigations at the East has convinced them it would be inexpedient.[5]

With or without public restrooms, it was recommended, and the recommendation was generally followed, that the prototypes of the new Detroit Public Library should be the libraries of Cincinnati and Roxbury.

Now the question of money with which to build a new library became a matter of paramount concern to the board. The idea, cherished for some time, that public subscription was the answer had to be abandoned. The reason for this change of attitude never was fully explained, but it can be presumed that the Library Committee realized that the task of obtaining the amount needed in a relatively short space of time was a hopeless one. The money received from penal fines, while sufficient to cover general operations including book purchases, was not large enough to support a major capital improvement. Moreover, the penal receipts fluctuated from year to year to such an extent that it was not safe to base long-range commitments upon them.[6] This meant that some other kind of financing was necessary, and the Board was so informed on March 6, 1873. It had been estimated that the type of building contemplated would cost in the neighborhood of $150,000. Losing no time, the Board appealed immediately to the legislature, then in session, for permission to raise that amount, either by a tax levy or a bond issue. The Detroit Board of Education already had a bill before the legislature, asking for a higher per capita tax limit for general school purposes, and the library request was attached to it.

The entire bill passed the legislature on March 27, 1873. The Board was given authority to include in its estimates a sum not to exceed $150,000, for the purpose of defraying the cost of erecting and furnishing a library building. It was required that a statement be furnished by the Board of the portions of the whole amount which would be required in each of three years. The act further provided that the estimates, either for the whole or for any part, were subject to approval of "the citizens committee or by such board as shall be vested with the power of finally approving the general estimates of the city." This committee or board was

97

given the power to reduce the amount requested for any one year, or reduce the total amount, or the period of time within which the amount was to be raised, or to reject it altogether.[7]

Prior to 1873, appropriations or estimates were subject to approval of a citizens' meeting. This was based on the New England town meeting concept, and every freeholder was entitled to attend, to express his views, and to vote for or against whatever appropriation would affect local taxes. As the city grew, the citizens' meetings became too large to be practical. The meetings often became unruly, frequently degenerating into near-riots. In 1873, at the same session of the legislature which passed the Library building bill, a Board of Estimates was substituted for the citizens' meeting. The Board of Estimates was first composed of five members elected at large, to serve two years, and two members from each ward, one to serve for one year, and the other for two years. Elections were to be held annually in April. After the first election, one member from each ward was elected every year, and five were elected at large every other year. Thus the Board's membership was staggered. Several city officials, including the controller and president of the Common Council, served as ex officio members of the board. Under the 1873 act, the Common Council was required to submit all estimates to the Board which had authority to reduce but not to increase them. Thus, the function of the Board of Estimates was to act as a brake upon any Council tendency toward extravagance. The Board of Estimates, in various forms, continued to be an integral part of Detroit's municipal government until it was finally abolished by adoption of the city charter of 1918.[8]

Acting as sponsor for the Library Committee, the Board of Education presented estimates for the new library fund to the Board of Estimates at that body's first meeting which was held in mid-April, 1873. The request was for $125,000, to be raised from the sale of bonds over a three-year period. The first year, 1873, a total of $25,000 was asked for, and $50,000 in each of 1874 and 1875.[9] Even before the estimates were presented, however, opposition developed. The 1873 general and school tax levy was unusually heavy. The *Free Press,* immediately after the legislature acted in March, pointed to the fact that the Riggs case had not been decided, and that it would be foolish to appropriate any building money until that issue was resolved. The paper said:

> Undoubtedly, a new library building is a very desirable thing; but without knowing where to put it, it would be injudicious to raise money for it when so much will be needed for objects which are indispensable.[10]

In April, the paper repeated its opposition to the appropriation, even though the question of the site had been settled, a fact of which the *Free Press* seemed unaware. In an editorial blistering the Board of Education for requesting too much money, it was stated that "it is not likely that the Board of Estimates will grant any appropriation solely that it may remain for a year or less in the hands of the Treasurer of the Board of Education." [11]

Taking the cue from such expressions, and taking itself seriously as the watchdog of the public purse, the Board of Estimates rejected the plea for the Library building fund. The matter was thus thrown over to 1874, when the request was renewed, this time with better results. On April 6 of the latter year, an initial appropriation of $50,000 through the sale of bonds was asked, with another $50,000 in 1875, and the final installment of $25,000 in 1876. The estimators gave their approval to this financing plan, but the Common Council, in whose hands remained the responsibility for levying the money, did not look favorably upon a bond issue and preferred, instead, to spread the first $50,000 and the subsequent amounts on the general tax levy.[12]

The Library Committee proceeded at once to make preparations for using the funds which would soon be in their hands. On May 11, 1874, a report was submitted to the Board of Education with specific recommendations as to construction, arrangement and furnishing of the proposed new library. On June 1, it was proposed that architects be invited to submit plans on a competitive basis, with payment of $600 to be awarded the architect whose plan should be accepted, and the sums of $250 and $150 be given for the next two most acceptable plans. Advertisements were placed in the local newspapers, announcing the competition, and calling for "detailed plans to be submitted." [13]

Only three sets of plans were received in August, and the decision as to which plan was best set off a bitter argument which split the Committee. Inspector Romeyn, the chairman, and Inspector A. G. Lindsay favored the work of W. G. Lloyd, but Inspector J. J. Martin filed a minority report, recommending adoption of the plans of the firm of Brush and Smith. The other competitor, R. T. Brooks, was never considered for anything except third place. The argument went to the full Board of Education to be resolved on August 25, and there politics entered the picture. Romeyn was denied permission to permit Lloyd to read a written criticism of the work of Brush and Smith. Finally Romeyn was allowed to read it instead. That having been done, Romeyn moved that the contract be awarded Lloyd. Martin moved to substitute the plan of Brush and Smith, and the debate began to rage.

After much shouting back and forth, it was decided that none of the three sets of plans submitted were perfect, and whichever one was accepted would have to be modified by incorporation of the best features of the other two. This had the appearance of a reasonable compromise, with each of the competitors receiving something. On that basis, Inspector Lillibridge moved that first place and the $600 prize be awarded Brush and Smith, with the $250 second prize going to Lloyd. R. T. Brooks continued to hold down third place and was given the $150 consolation prize.

The adoption of the minority report apparently outraged Romeyn and Lindsay, and they resigned in a huff. That left no committee to carry on the work of building the new library. That problem was resolved by the Board's decision that the job was too big for three men anyway and the Library Committee was replaced by a select committee of five members. This committee functioned until 1875 when, with construction actually begun, it was discharged and Library affairs returned to a regular Library committee.[14]

Once the architect's plan was accepted, the drawings were put on display, first in the city hall, then in the windows of the Roehm & Wright (predecessor to Wright, Kay) jewelry store at the corner of Woodward and Campus Martius for the edification and delight of the public. Preliminary work was assigned to the Board of Public Works, under general supervision of J. B.

Cousins, messenger for the Board of Education. (The duties of "messenger" were comparable to those of business manager.) [15] While actual construction did not begin immediately, the *Free Press* on December 11, 1874, reported that "the foundation stones for the new public library have been hauled to the site of the contemplated building." A few weeks later, in January, the detailed drawings and specifications were completed by the architects, and contractors were invited to bid. The bids submitted ranged in amount from $159,000 to $190,000, and in February the construction contract was awarded to David Knapp, the low bidder.

Knapp's $159,000 bid, while low, was substantially in excess of the original estimates of $125,000 for which appropriations had been authorized, and above the $150,000 which the legislature had set as the top figure. There was a good deal of complaining about this, particularly on the part of the Common Council, and an injunction was threatened. Some of the councilmen, jealous perhaps of the increasing independence of the school Board in financial matters, charged the Board with arrogance and extravagance. In order to avoid further controversy and the possibility of delay through litigation, the original specifications were revised, through arbitration, and the contract was scaled down so as to come within the limits of the $125,000 appropriation. This involved considerable modification of both the interior and exterior of the building. The original plans called for an elaborate ornamental front elevation, with a tower and broad, sweeping stone front steps. These were eliminated; the front facade became plain; the tower was cut out and a wooden porch and steps were substituted for stone. Outwardly, the revisions gave the front of the building a rather plain, chopped-off appearance which it never lost. Inside, some of the galleries and rooms intended for special use were abandoned. George W. Balch, president of the Board, thought the changes gave the library a "shorn and uncouth frontal aspect." [16]

Evidently the Common Council thought so too. From complaining about excessive cost, that body now felt the city was getting less than it had bargained for. A special Council committee was appointed, and held a meeting on April 4 to investigate, and "to show that the Board acted in bad faith in letting

the contract by furnishing specifications for an incomplete building so as to bring the contract price within the limit of the
$125,000 allowed them by the Board of Estimates." Witnesses
called included David Knapp, his son and partner Julius A. and
Samuel E. Pittman, secretary of the Board of Education.

David Knapp proved to be a very uncooperative witness. He
refused to produce a copy of the contract, and said he could not
recall off-hand all the changes which had been made in the
original specifications. His attorney, James W. Romeyn, then
denied the Council's right "to examine into a contract between
the Board of Education and Mr. Knapp." This statement "created
quite a sensation among the members of the committee." Pittman
was then called, and submitted a prepared statement which read:

> With all respect to this committee I have the honor to state that
> the Supreme Court of Michigan has decided that the Board of Edu-
> cation is a body not subordinate to but independent of the Common
> Council and therefore the Council has no right to review our pro-
> ceedings or the method in which we keep our records. Should the
> Board of Education, whose officer I am, instruct me to testify in
> regard to these matters, I will cheerfully do so. Until so instructed
> I must, with all respect, decline to answer your questions.

Julius Knapp was slightly more helpful. He stated that the
difference between the original and revised bids was caused by
omission of the tower, the galleries, marble tiling, front stone steps
and circular stairs leading to the galleries. He added that, from a
functional standpoint, "the Library would be just as complete as
originally planned."

The Council came off second best in this investigation, salvag-
ing what face it could by declaring that even though the school
Board was an independent agency, "it was very bad policy on its
part to create even a show of antagonism between itself and the
disbursing power of the city." Another alderman loftily declared
that "the Board had procured the passage of obnoxious laws by
the Legislature by lobbying, and he was glad that its attitude had
now come to be understood by the people." [17]

Such attacks served only to strengthen, in the long run, the
independent position of the Board of Education and, through it,
the position of the Library. A more immediate effect was to spur

the Board and the Library Committee to push ahead with the new building before more obstructions could be raised by the politically-minded city hall. The work, uninterrupted by such diversions, progressed on schedule, the excavation work beginning March 29, 1875.[18] By mid-May the first footing stone was set, and in less than two weeks the foundation, a model of substantial masonry, was near enough completion to allow for the ceremonial cornerstone laying. This took place on May 29, and was the occasion for a general civic celebration.

The *Free Press* of that morning reported the arrival of a number of persons "from the interior of the state," who had come to take part in the events of the day. A parade was formed, composed of the high school cadets, fraternal groups including the Detroit Commandery No. 1, Knights Templar and other Masonic bodies, officers of the Army and Navy, city officials including the mayor, the Common Council, the Board of Estimates and, of course, the Board of Education. The procession formed at the Soldiers' and Sailors' Monument, and at the sound of a signal gun fired in Centre Park, marched briskly to the new Library site to the music of the Light Guard and Bishop's Opera House bands. The cornerstone was laid according to ancient Masonic usage. Several dignitaries made speeches, reviewing the history of the Library, and predicting a great future for it in its new quarters. After a long draught of oratory, the high school chorus, Professor Sylvester Jackson directing, sang a dedicatory hymn composed for the occasion by D. Bethune Duffield. Along with his legal accomplishments, Duffield had enjoyed considerable local renown for his poetical talents. Regardless of the literary quality of his efforts, Duffield's verse struck a happy dedicatory note, as the chorus warbled:

> Not for church, or sect, or guild,
> Do we this proud temple build;
> Her open gates and spacious hall
> Stand free, forever free, to all.

The grand chaplain of the Grand Lodge of Michigan, a Mr. Goodman, pronounced the benediction, whereupon the high school artillery cadets let loose with a thirteen-gun salute which momentarily may have made the residents of Farmer Street wish that Mrs. Riggs had won her lawsuit. Everyone else, though, went away happy; the city had taken on a holiday appearance.[19]

Anything following the rites of May 29 must have appeared somewhat anticlimactic. The contractor and his workmen, however, did not relax. On June 6, the *Free Press* reported that the foundation was above ground and the construction of the walls would begin the next day. A series of bulletins followed, giving an almost day by day account of progress. On June 10, "the new Public Library has reached the second story." A week later, "building is progressing rapidly," and on July 9, the *Free Press* said the walls would "shortly loom above the trees." By November 13, the iron frame for the roof was in place, and on December 21, "the glass roof . . . is in position, temporary windows have been put in, and the work of finishing the interior of the building is underway." The latter work took longer than it did to raise the outer shell of the building. All through 1876, there was continuous activity inside, as the fittings and furnishings were installed. Gradually, however, each task was finished. On December 17, 1876, the newspapers carried a notice, signed by Chaney, to the effect that after December 22 no books would be loaned from the Capitol Library. "The Library will be opened again after due notice at the new Library Building in Centre Park on Gratiot Avenue."

There was one more important announcement yet to be made, and that, coming soon after the beginning of 1877, declared that all was at last in readiness, and the grand new Detroit Public Library would be opened and dedicated on January 22.

The dedication ceremonies while intended to be impressive, were somewhat less spectacular than when the cornerstone was laid to the accompaniment of brass bands, marching columns and the roar of artillery. The season of the year and a heavy snow fall ruled out the feasibility of a procession, although the contractors were made happy by the snow. It provided a test of strength for the glass roof which, to everybody's satisfaction, held up without a creak or groan. The festivities were to begin at 8 P.M. Invitations had been sent to about four hundred of the city's select, and seats for that number were provided in the main hall facing a speaker's platform which had been erected against the west wall. In addition, a blanket invitation had also been extended to the general public to inspect the building between the hours of 7 and 10 P.M. An estimated five thousand citizens came out on the cold January night to examine this newest municipal ornament. That the people were curious and pleased at having a new Library goes without saying. The turnout was proof of that. There also may have been a corollary to civic pride, expressed by one relieved citizen who now had something to show and boast about to out-of-town visitors besides the new city hall. The latter was losing its novelty as an attraction.[20]

The program for the evening was a full one. The invocation was given by the Reverend Dr. J. P. Scott, minister of the United Presbyterian Church. Mayor Alexander Lewis introduced School Inspector John T. Liggett who read an "exhaustive and interesting report" in which he talked about the history of the Public Library, described in detail the new building in which his audience was sitting and standing, and thanked everybody who had a hand in bringing it into being. The speech was long enough, and it may be assumed that the hall was hot enough, to make the crowd restless. The attendance, far greater than was anticipated or provided for, milled around, causing a distraction. One newspaper complained that

> No attempt was made to restrain the small army of youths and misses who played hide and go seek, indulged in silly noisy conversation and in a dozen other ways filled the large apartment with so many different noises that all persons except those who occupied the platform were entirely unable to catch one word of Mr. Liggett's report.

Another speaker, the Reverend Dr. Arthur T. Pierson, minister of the Fort Street Presbyterian Church, wrily observed that he felt comfortable on the platform "because if he did not make a good speech, a majority of his audience, hearing no part of it, would not know whether he had or not." [21]

Others who spoke were Freeman Norvell, president of the Board of Education, James W. Romeyn, Sylvester Larned, C. I.

Walker, D. Bethune Duffield, William P. Wells and Levi Bishop, all men of substance and associated in one way or another with the Library, the school Board, or other cultural interests. As a climax, grand or otherwise, Eben N. Willcox, an attorney of high standing, read a poem liberally sprinkled with classical literary allusions, which he had written especially for the occasion.

Despite an attendance far larger than anticipated or comfortably accommodated, the occasion was a success. But in a more real sense, the true dedication took place the following morning, Tuesday, January 23, 1877, when the Library opened for business. On that day the first arrival found 33,604 volumes neatly arranged on the shelves, with Henry Chaney and his staff—Miss Adda D. Pattison, Miss Ida Norton, Mrs. Sarah E. Doll, Miss M. E. Ladue and Miss R. Teichner, not to mention Edward Beaubien, the janitor—waiting at their stations to serve the reading tastes and requirements of the people of Detroit.[22]

CHAPTER 7

A GLIMPSE OF THE STARS

FOR MORE THAN HALF A CENTURY the old Main Library in Centre Park served Detroit and was a familiar and beloved landmark of the downtown district. For almost a quarter of a century it was the city's only public library facility—and for at least two generations of Detroiters it was a magic place in which they could lose themselves in the wonderful world of books. It was a schoolhouse for those beyond school, a meeting place of minds and ideas, a center of culture. For the young and eager, its open door beckoned an invitation to visit strange and romantic lands, to find adventure and to live intimately with the heroes of childhood, from Siegfried and Robin Hood, to Elsie Dinsmore and the star-touched gamins of Horatio Alger.

The Centre Library was no thing of beauty, regardless of what enthusiastic and prideful citizens may have thought or felt on its dedication day. Architecturally it was an ugly building, even by the standards of the eighties and nineties when "court house" design was at the height of its popularity. The economy measures, necessary to bring construction costs into line with available

107

funds, caused it always to have an unfinished appearance, particularly its front elevation, as though a giant knife had cut away a slice, leaving an unadorned facade. Years later, about the time it was ready to be abandoned, an observer found it no more than an interesting relic of a bygone day, achieving then what it never had before, "a glamour for the lover of the picturesque."

> Red brick! Not a fine glazed brick, but very positive red brick, trying to preserve an air of studious aloofness by its tiny parks, and attaining a quaint, old fashioned pretentiousness in its steep, circular steps and heavily ornate doors!
> And as the doors close on the modernity of our street, the dusky interior might be the haunt of old world scholars of a long past century. The cathedral-like columns, carrying the eyes up, tier upon tier of turreted iron balconies, dim, remote, suggesting so many books a lifetime could not read, until the dusk darkened dome, hinting at greens and reds and wine in its colored glass, shuts out the sky—how it all catches and quickens the imagination!
> Old, cramped and rickety if you will, but charming; dignified by the years and the knowledge that within its walls is held the heritage of the ages.[1]

Dim and dark it may have become with the years, but through those murky skylights more than one eager young mind caught a glimpse of the stars. No matter what effect the Centre Park building had upon the beholder's eye, the great city of Detroit would have been much less than it is without it.

However, in 1877 people saw not what it would become as tastes changed, but beheld it as something fine and new and splendid. The building, which stood back about 60 feet from Gratiot Avenue, had a front ground dimension of 64 feet on that street, and ran back 84 feet. The front elevation to the top of the main cornice was 61 feet. Including the basement, which was partially above the ground level, it had four stories. The exterior was largely unadorned, a single bas-relief head of William Shakespeare over the front entrance being its only decoration. In 1965, one could still find similar design in a few of the city's oldest remaining school buildings.

Even at the time the Library was built, it was described as "substantial, not very elaborate, and just the least bit graceful."

108

As good an over-all contemporary description as can be found was furnished by the *Free Press*.

> Beginning inspection of the interior with the basement, one sees a large room with cement floor, which is used for a storage room; a small room to the left, which is intended for packing, repairing and binding purposes, and a similar room to the right which contains the heating apparatus. There is also plainly visible all the strength of construction which characterizes the building throughout. . . .
>
> Ascending the stairway, the visitor enters the library department, which presents a handsome appearance. In the southwest corner is located the librarian's office, while in the opposite corner is a semiprivate department intended for the benefit of persons wishing to study. Across the north side of the room is the distributing counter, while six large tables placed in the center of the room furnish facilities for the hasty, temporary visitor.
>
> Ten large cast iron columns of handsome design rise from the floor to the roof, which is built of iron and stained glass half an inch thick. The columns are twelve feet away from the walls and are the inside supporters of the single gallery which extends around the building. The gallery is built of light and ornamental castings, and contains twelve recesses fitted with shelving and calculated to hold 34,000 volumes. The plans provide for three additional galleries, calculated to accommodate the same number of volumes each. As necessity requires these galleries will be placed in position. The glass roof is gaudily colored and rests upon the walls and the columns. . . . The cast iron work in the building is painted lavender, light brown, bronzed and gilded, while the names Homer, Virgil, Dante, Goethe, Milton, Shakespeare, Plato, Cicero, Guizot, Bacon, Humboldt and Franklin appear in letters of gold upon blue ribbons, in the arches which spring from the columns. The building is lighted with eight double-jet gas brackets, sixteen brackets of three jets each and thirty-two single gas jets, the fixtures being of bronze and handsome design. [In 1887 electric lights were installed in the main reading room, the current being supplied by the Edison Illuminating Company which later became the Detroit Edison Company.] [2] The furniture is all of black walnut and ash, substantial and elegant, and among other articles is a large eight-day clock, donated by Messrs. Roehm & Wright.* [3]

The main floor and the single gallery contained twenty-seven alcoves with 4400 lineal feet of shelving. There also were six cases

---

* It might be suspected that the gift of the clock was one of desperation. For several years, a recurrent item of expense had been for repair of the Library clock by Roehm & Wright. It could never be made to work well, and in despair, the jewelers donated one that would.

and desks for large books and periodicals and one glass case for rare books. That amount of space was inadequate, however, and thousands of books were stored wherever room could be found for them. Before 1877 was at its end, the Library Committee was calling for construction of a new gallery and the addition of 3000 feet more of shelf space.[4]

Every effort was made to make the grounds as attractive as possible. Circular walks, leading to the main entrance were built, the lawn was cultivated and carefully tended. Shade trees lined the streets bordering the building until late in the nineteenth century when they began to die and were removed. Park benches were installed, and until the adjoining streets were paved a regular item in the Library budget was for sprinkling the streets to eliminate the dust nuisance as much as possible. The Library Committee and later the Commission sought to preserve the park-like surroundings. They were sometimes frustrated, however, as on the occasion when the outraged librarian complained that the J. L. Hudson Company, constructing an addition to its store, was using the rear, or north end of the Library lot, to store building material and dump debris. A sharp protest remedied that situation.[5]

Once the 1877 building was occupied it quickly ceased to be the Centre Library and the remembrance of Centre Park soon faded. To Detroiters it was simply "the Library" or when given its full dignity in official references, it was the Detroit Public Library. Being the only such facility which the city possessed for several years, it did not become known as the Main or Central Library until after the branches had been opened.

Public buildings have a way of being outgrown almost as soon as they are built and the Library was no exception. This was noted at the dedication ceremonies when several speakers expressed hope that eventually it would be enlarged so as to meet the original plans. "Your committee," it was noted in the annual report for 1877, "express the hope that authority will be obtained from the next Legislature to enable this to be done and that such addition will be constructed at an early date." [6] The committee also hoped that a proper front could be added to give the building a finished look. That was a wish shared by other committeemen

110

and commissioners as long as the Library was used. As late as 1891, such plans were being wistfully discussed.[7]

For the moment, however, there were more urgently needed improvements. Early in 1878, contracts were awarded for the second gallery; the third was put in during 1882, and the fourth was installed in 1887. This, it was pointed out, completed the interior of the building "according to plans of the designer," and added 1500 shelves to the capacity. The interior, from main floor to roof, now had the appearance of a spider web of iron balconies and alcoves, a dizzying prospect for the seeker of books in the upper regions. The librarian was aware of the inconvenience resulting from vertical storage, and told the Commission it would be necessary to rearrange the books.

"The aim," he said, "will be to keep the books most in demand nearest the surface of the earth, to save the arduous labor of climbing stairs." [8]

At the time the third gallery was put in, a part of the basement was built into a vault, dry and safe, for the storage of "such manuscript and other historical material as may be given or entrusted to our care." [9]

Additional galleries, regardless of how high heavenward they soared, were not enough, and from time to time extensive interior remodeling became necessary, as well as the building of additions. All of this was accomplished over a period of twenty years without seeking extra financial assistance or appropriations from the taxpayers. As a simple expedient a portion of the regular Library Fund was set aside and earmarked for a building fund.

The first major addition was started in 1884, when it was noted that it had been decided to extend the main building by adding a two-story 50-by-60 foot addition to the rear. The work progressed slowly.

The firm of Mason & Rice was retained as architects, but to the chagrin of the Library officials, George Mason departed on a protracted European trip, and the job was not completed until 1886. The addition was opened on March 1, "affording a spacious reading room and other much needed accommodations." These other accommodations consisted of several smaller business and reference rooms, as well as a greatly enlarged basement.

These facilities sufficed only temporarily. Six years after the addition had been finished, Magnus Butzel, president of the Commission, declared that "in the near future means must be found for enlarging the Library building to be what such building should be." [10] While no grand scale program was possible, extended remodeling of the second floor of the annex was undertaken in 1893. Partitions were knocked down, a stairway was built leading from the main building, and shelves for 20,000 books were installed. When rearranged, expanded reading room facilities "where students may work to the best advantage" were available.[11]

But even this improvement did not suffice because the Library collection and the number of people using it were growing larger month by month. As a result, the north and west walls of the annex were knocked out in 1895, and a 40-by-30 foot addition was built. This provided space for a children's reading room with its own entrance at the north end, allowed expansion of the periodical reading room, and permitted doubling the space previously allotted to the reference room.[12] With this improvement, just about all of the Centre Park site was covered, except for the 60 feet in front on Gratiot Avenue. That meant that future additions would have to be vertical instead of horizontal. Accordingly, in 1900 when more room was sought, it was proposed to add another story to the main building. That idea, however, was dropped in favor of the more practical one of putting up an entirely new building—an undertaking which had to wait for two more decades.[13]

Despite cramped quarters, Library officials never were satisfied unless more people were visiting and making use of the building. After the annex had been remodeled in 1893, the president of the Commission called attention of his colleagues "to the attractive character of the new reference reading room and suggested that some steps be taken to bring it more to the public notice." City officials and prominent citizens were invited to inspect the new room and 750 special invitations were mailed asking the recipients to drop in anytime. No mention was made of how many accepted the bid.[14] On another occasion, the librarian deplored "the very small attendance of lady readers." Eventually that was taken care of when, in 1899, a space was railed off and reserved for women. This ladies' nook, as it was called, was furnished with rugs and rockers and provided with all the comforts of home.[15]

The need for enlarged quarters was clearly shown by the growth of the book collection and the use of the Library by the public. At the end of 1865, the year the Library opened, it had 8864 volumes. Ten years later, that number had grown to 24,903, explaining why an addition had to be put on the rear of the Capitol and why a new and separate building had become a necessity. Thus, by the end of 1877, with the collection housed in the Centre Park building, there were 37,703 volumes on the shelves. Thereafter, the number of books increased steadily until on December 31, 1886, the inventory showed 70,550 volumes.

But even more important, from a librarian's standpoint, was the use to which these books were put. Prior to 1880, no exact statistics were available. Only estimates were made, and these were probably not entirely accurate. Yet they are valuable as an indication of the trend of Library use. In 1865, 4700 books were withdrawn or used in the Library. The following year, the first in which the Library resources were available for a full twelve months, combined use totaled 15,000 volumes and in the next year, 1867, that number doubled. Thereafter, the rate-of-use increase slowed somewhat.

Not until 1872 was there a substantial spurt. In that year, 9200 volumes were used in the Library, 98,000 were withdrawn for home reading, making a total of 107,200. Thereafter, the use of the Library showed a steady, healthy increase. In 1880, the first year in which accurate statistics were compiled, there were 40,496 books in the Library. These were used as follows: Library reading, 12,000; home reading, 113,585. That made a total of 125,585, or a ratio of use to volumes of better than three to one. For 1886, figures reveal total use of 167,285. Only once in the entire 1865–86 period was there a decrease from the previous year in the number of books circulated. That occurred in 1882 when the combined Library-home reading total dropped to 113,042 volumes from 128,932 in 1881. In 1883, the call for books was back up to 128,274.[16] The 1882 drop was explained by the librarian in the annual report for that year.

As in most other libraries throughout the country, there has been with us a falling off in the circulation of the books. But this might only be expected from the continuance of the causes which have been commonly, and no doubt correctly assigned, viz: the general revival of business and the prosperity of the country, with the consequent increased employment of all classes of people, permitting less leisure for reading. Also, in our own case, there can be little doubt that the establishment of the Periodical Reading Department has had a like influence on the circulation—large numbers of readers, who formerly drew out books for home use, satisfy themselves instead with the periodical literature on our tables. This is easily understood. Most readers prefer the newspaper and magazine to other reading matter; and the necessity for keeping informed on the current topics of the day is too generally admitted to be questioned.[17]

The 1882 slowdown demonstrated a phenomenon with which librarians have become familiar, namely, the use of public libraries increases when employment declines. Hard times have always made the Library a haven for the jobless.

The drop-off in use in 1882 was temporary, and the use curve swung back upward and continued to rise until in 1898 the total use for the first time topped the million mark. That year's figures showed home circulation of 461,848; recorded book use at the Library, 501,742; and use of unbound periodicals, 180,617, for a grand total of 1,144,207.[18]

In order to encourage patronage and make use of the Library easier and more efficient, it was necessary to devise a better method of classification or arrangement of books, as well as a catalog. Originally there appears to have been only a crude attempt at classification; volumes were grouped according to broad general categories such as (1) general literature, (2) reference works, (3) general history, (4) American history, (5) biography, (6) poetry and drama, and (7) science and art.[19] This arrangement was not workable even when the Library's collection numbered only a few thousand volumes because it was difficult for the librarian or attendant to locate any particular book called for. A catalog of sorts was compiled in 1865 when the Library opened. This was an alphabetical listing by authors' names, and comprised little more than an inventory. A second catalog was made in 1868, and was similar to that of 1865. This was revised or supplemented in 1871. In 1877 a third catalog, the books listed according to subject, was put together. Neither type of catalog was satisfactory, but in time something better evolved, both with respect to classification and cataloging.

In 1880 the Library was closed from July 15 to November 1 to permit a complete classification and rearrangement of books, and to make a card catalog of the collection. It was expected also, that the new arrangement would enable a new catalog to be made when finances permitted, the old one "being quite imperfect and only of partial use." The arrangement adopted—or rather continued in a somewhat improved form—was generally known as the "fixed location" system, the books being grouped under general categories, and each was numbered. This proved awkward because, as it was discovered,

> It is found in practice that a more or less frequent transfer of books from one location to another is important. But now this involves the renumbering of the books so changed, which is laborious and expensive and throws our catalogue into utter confusion. All this trouble is avoided by the relative numbering.

The Library Commission was asked to approve a shift to the "relative" system.[20]

An improvement or refinement had been developed in 1876 by Melvil Dewey, and in time the Dewey Decimal System was universally adopted. Dewey was one of the first of what might be called the professional librarians. Born in 1851, he attended Amherst College and served as its acting librarian. He moved to Boston where he founded and edited *The Library Journal* and was a founder of the American Library Association. In 1883 he established the country's first library school at Columbia College. Later, Dewey become director of the New York State Library. He continued to be a dominant figure in the library profession until his death in 1931.

Detroit Library officials were aware of the advantages of the Dewey system, and the 1880 reclassification was a step in that direction, carried farther in 1886. In the fall of that year, it was suggested that a member of the Detroit staff be sent to Buffalo where a new library was being built, "to examine the practical details of the shelf arrangement . . . with a view to advising upon the proposed change in the system of this library." [21] The person selected was Sarah A. Cochrane who had become a member of the Detroit staff in December, 1883. She was allowed the princely sum of $19.10 for expenses. Apparently that did not permit her to remain long enough, because at the end of the year it was suggested that John C. Gager, of the Buffalo library, be brought to Detroit as a consultant at $30 a week, plus travel expense. Whether he actually went to Detroit or not is unclear; there is no record of any fees having been paid him.[22] At any rate, the system was put into effect, and in the 1886 annual report the librarian pointed out that "the work of renumbering is now going forward without interfering at all with the circulation and use of the books. When this work is done, it is done for all time, and no future addition of galleries and alcoves will make it necessary to change any of the numbers." [23]

Reclassification, as was indicated, enabled the Library to update its catalog. The librarian had been directed to look into the matter of a card catalog in February. Apparently his report was satisfactory, because on June 25 the Commission gave one of their fellow members, Herbert Bowen, "special authority" to look after the completion of the catalog.[24] Soon after the beginning of 1886 the work under Bowen's general supervision was progressing satisfactorily. Along with the general catalog, separate catalogs were being made for individual classifications. Thus, on January 25, 1886, a Professor Theodore Zeck was hired at $2.50 per day to catalog the German book collection, a task which he completed by December 2, when it was printed and on sale at 25 cents a copy. Prior to 1889 a French catalog also had been printed.[25]

The story of the cataloging work, the magnitude of the task and the problems involved were described in the annual report for 1886, and is worth quoting at some length.

> Early in the fall of 1885, the work of preparing a new catalogue was begun in earnest. Those without knowledge on the subject can form no conception of the time and labor involved in preparing a new catalogue of a library of 70,000 volumes. Every book has to be not only examined but carefully examined and its subject, and perhaps numerous subjects, minutely noted and in this connection there are often very puzzling questions which require studious con-

sideration. The preparation of a catalogue is, therefore, a work of time and arduous labor. Ten or twelve persons have been employed in the several departments of the work almost constantly throughout the year.

The English prose fiction and juvenile portion, covering some 12,000 volumes, was finished in March. On account of the popular demand for this class of books, this catalogue was separately issued and sold for the convenience of the public, though designed ultimately to be incorporated as a part of the general catalogue. The German portion, covering some 4,000 books, was similarly issued in December. The manuscript for the remaining portion of the catalogue is in a forward state and I feel confident that the whole will be out before the end of the year 1887.

The catalogue is to be what is known as a dictionary catalogue, that is, the authors, titles, and subjects are arranged in alphabetical order. It is to be less full than some of the more elaborate and expensive library catalogues which give tables of contents and analytical notes, but sufficiently so for all purposes of ordinary users of our library.

For complete information of the library the reader will be referred to the card catalogue, the preparation of which has gone forward simultaneously with the preparation of the manuscript for the printed catalogue. This is to be as full as it can possibly be made. There are cross references in all conceivable directions and all known subjects are covered, the effort being to meet every possible inquiry. The card catalogue of the fiction and German departments is arranged for use and upwards of 40,000 cards have been written for the other departments of the library, though this is only a small proportion of the whole.[26]

The general catalog was not completed until 1889. When published in that year, it consisted of 1113 pages and was offered for sale at $2.50 a copy. It was not, as may be imagined, a best seller. Most purchases were made by schools, scholars and other libraries. Yet, it was highly regarded by the library profession. The librarian of London's Bishopgate Public Library, Mr. Charles W. F. Goss, told United States Commissioner of Education Harris that he "considered the catalog of the Detroit Public Library the best example on cataloging according to the decimal classification." For those kind words, the Library commissioners voted to send Mr. Goss a set of the catalogs with their compliments.[27]

Supervision of the card catalog compilation was assigned to Mary E. Ladue, who became a member of the staff in 1877. Late in 1885, she was given an expense account of $4.60 to go to

117

Ann Arbor "for inspection of card catalogue." The general catalog work was assigned to Sarah Cochrane, who made cataloging her life work. Until 1891, she was a library assistant. In that year, she was promoted to assistant librarian, and in 1900 her name appeared on the staff roster as superintendent of the catalog department. She retired, after twenty-three years of service, in 1906.

In 1942, the Detroit Public Library was designated a depository for the catalog of the Library of Congress—"one of the finest bibliographic tools in the country, long sought for the city." At the same time, through joint efforts of the Library and the University of Michigan, there were compiled two composite catalogs representing book holdings of the six largest reference libraries in Michigan. These included, besides the University and the Detroit Library, the collections of Michigan State University, the Michigan State Library, the University of Detroit and Wayne State University. Another important catalog in the Library was the British Museum's author catalog of books printed through the year 1899.[28]

A notable advance in book classification was pioneered in Detroit. Known as the Reader-Interest Classification, it was first proposed in 1936 by Ralph A. Ulveling, then associate librarian. In a communication of September 24, Ulveling invited staff members to a conference on the subject of "looking toward the development of better and more helpful ways of serving the patrons of circulating library units." He said:

> For some time, I have wondered whether our popular book lending service as organized on traditional lines is pointed directly enough toward our service objectives; that is, whether the organization of our circulating units is adapted to the function we are trying to fulfill. Though circulating and reference units may be part of the same large institution the primary functions of each are different. A reference department is organized to provide a factual service from ready reference to a research level. Quite obviously in such a department it is necessary to have the book collection follow a more or less rigid classification based on subject content.
>
> A circulating department, however, is less concerned with definite subjects. In fact the reading inclinations of this department's patrons are governed by moods. Should not the scheme of classification used in these libraries attempt to parallel this natural inclination of the

persons using such a book collection? In other words, classify not by subject but by patrons' reading inclinations.[29]

This plan did not meet with the approval of the librarian, Adam Strohm, and the idea hung in abeyance for six years, or until Ulveling had become the librarian. The proposal was considered too radical by most professional librarians; only a few could at first see its possibilities. Ulveling described what he had in mind to John Chancellor of the American Library Association. Chancellor saw its advantages and discussed it with a few progressive-minded people. One of these was Lyman Bryson of Columbia University, one of the country's foremost authorities in the field of adult education. Referring to Ulveling's proposed innovation, Bryson told Chancellor: "Under a very innocent cover he seems to be handing out dynamite." [30]

When he was at last able to do so about 1942, Ulveling's plan was tried out on a limited basis in the browsing room of the Main Library. Then, when the Thomas Edison branch was opened in 1948, it became the first complete library with the Reader-Interest Classification. Soon it was installed in other branches. As Ulveling pointed out, this classification was designed for the branches, and except for the browsing room it has no place in the Main Library where the standard decimal system continues to be used.

The Reader-Interest Classification was described by Ruth Rutzen, director of Home Reading Services from 1945 to 1963 to whom was entrusted the task of putting the new system into operation. She said:

> This is a book arrangement planned to fit the needs and uses of the greatest number of people. It recognizes the variety of reasons prompting people to come to the Library. It is not a classification in the fields of knowledge but a shelving arrangement based on broad areas of interest which relate themselves to the everyday needs of people. These broad areas have been designated as interest categories. They are subdivided by a varying number of sub-headings, depending on the type of category and the size of the collection. Some categories are browsing sections for the general reader; others are subject to groupings aimed at a particular use by the reader. It does not interfere with the well-defined specific need or requests which have to be met through the use of the catalog and its subject headings, or special indexes. One of the advantages over a strict

119

classification based on content is that it is flexible and adaptable to different and changing conditions.

We use the term category to indicate the large fields of interest such as current affairs, personal living, people and places, background reading, hobbies, etc. The term "sub-heading" is used for a breakdown of the books within a category, such as house plans, entertaining, home management, under the category Your Home. Under the category Your Family are marriage, child care, health, aging.[31]

The professional library world withheld judgment on this experiment until its worth was proved by Detroit, whereupon it was widely and enthusiastically adopted, both nationally and internationally. A well-known Indian librarian, S. Das Gupta, of the Delhi University Library, after a survey of American libraries, observed that "the Detroit scheme of classification is a fine example of what the right kind of technique in its right place can achieve to liven up a mass of books in such a way that the arrangement itself communes with life." [32]

CHAPTER 8

The Library Commission is Created

SOON AFTER THE LIBRARY moved into its new building in Centre Park, an important step forward was taken in the administration of its affairs. This came about through the creation of the Library Commission and the removal of the Library from the direct control of the Board of Education and its Committee on the Library.

This transfer of authority which occurred in 1881 was a long time coming. In its annual report for 1870, the Library Committee strongly recommended this change. At that time, it was negotiating for the lease of the old city hall, and looking forward to the Library occupying its own building in the near future. The committee, headed by Charles K. Backus, clearly saw that a growing Library could not indefinitely remain a minor appendage of the school board. The inspectors who comprised the board had enough to do in supervising an expanding public school system without having to devote part of their attention to Library matters. The report stated:

> Your committee further recommend that the Board of Education propose to the Common Council, that if the City Hall shall be given

121

to the Library, the Board and Council shall unite in requesting from the Legislature at its present session such a change in our laws, as shall remove the Library from the care of the Board and shall place it under the absolute control of a Commission of our leading citizens. This must come eventually, for the Library is rapidly becoming too important to be much longer managed as a mere tender to the business more properly coming before this Board. The proposition now to make such a change would probably give our application for the City Hall strength before the Council, and your Committee here therefore recommend that it be made. One, two or three years would probably elapse before the City Hall could be prepared for its new use; meanwhile, the Library would thrive and gain in popular appreciation in its pleasant rooms at the Capitol, and when the change was finally made, it would be merely a step higher, an important event in a career of steadily increasing prosperity and usefulness.[1]

The report was signed by all three members of the committee —Backus, Dr. Farrand and J. W. Bartlett—but the language was Backus' as was, in all likelihood the idea. The proposal was received attentively, and Backus, with a newspaper voice to amplify his own, was sufficiently strong to get action, both by the Board, the Council and the legislature. The proposition was presented to the legislature and on March 31, 1871, that body passed an act which, as permissive legislation, authorized the Board of Education to appoint a Board of Library Commissioners and transfer to it the Library, its fund, and the responsibility for its operation. It specified that the Commission must be made up of six members to serve staggered terms of from one to six years each. After the first year, the Board of Education would elect one new member annually for a six-year term. That the bond between the new Commission and its parent Board of Education might not be wholly severed, the president of the school Board was designated as a member ex officio of the Commission.[2]

It was ten years before the Board of Education took advantage of this legislation and voluntarily divested itself of its control of the Library. Henry M. Utley, who became librarian about the time the change occurred, and who was familiar with school board politics, explained the delay by stating that the Board of Education was in no haste to deprive itself of the responsibility involved in the management of the Library.

That is true, but there was another reason for the Board's slow

122

motion. Backus' original idea was for a separate commission when the Library got out from under the Board of Education's roof and into a home of its own. Backus, as well as nearly everyone else, expected in 1871 that the old city hall would be taken over in a matter of months, thus providing a favorable time for a clean break. But the old city hall idea was dropped. The Library remained in the Capitol or its annex until 1877. There was, then, for a period of seven or eight years no enlargement of the Board of Education's responsibility, and therefore no urgency about setting up the Commission. It was not until the new Library in Centre Park was built and occupied that the occasion for a separation presented itself.

It might have been delayed longer except for the fact that the Board of Education fell into public disrepute about the time the new Library was built. The Board was not, as a body, corrupt, but there was some corruption on the part of individual members. At this time the Board consisted of twenty-six inspectors, two being elected from each of the city's thirteen wards. Silas Farmer refers to "a variety of evils" under this arrangement:

> As the city grew, the people moved their homes from the lower and central portion of the city, but, though their homes were removed, the representation of the wards on the Board continued, and in 1881 wards with less than two hundred children had an equal voice in school matters with those that had six thousand children.[3]

Thus, it can be understood that the temptation to play politics on the part of the inspectors from the downtown wards was strong. An increased rate of school construction provided opportunity for log-rolling and graft—or so it was hinted. There were ugly rumors, also, about crooked contracts for textbooks. Inspector John Henry Carstens, at one meeting referred to "expensive buildings which were put up and had to be repaired the next year." It had been charged," he declared, "that one member of the board had received $1,300 for his influence in behalf of certain textbooks."[4] While Dr. Carstens actually was belittling these rumors and charges, his recognition of them is indicative of the way in which many citizens regarded the Board. It was the feeling which prompted the Common Council, far from lily-white itself, to look

123

with suspicion upon the juggling of estimates by the school Board when the Centre building contracts were let.

Public opinion began to recognize that it was time to make some major changes in the Board of Education, an idea which found little favor in the eyes of many of the politicians on the school Board. But whatever opprobrium tainted the school Board, it had not rubbed off on the Library. The public feeling was that the Library would be better off detached from the control of rascals on the Board of Education. "The proposition for a Library Commission originated with the Board and the people were in favor of it," Inspector Philip Mothersill acknowledged.[5] By 1880 the public clamor for reform had reached the ears of the legislature. In an effort to stave off disaster to themselves, the inspectors finally relinquished Library control on December 27, 1880. Hastening this action was the fact that penal fines revenue had declined to a point where the Board of Education feared the Library would become a burden to the school system.

Hardly had the Library been given its freedom than the legislative bludgeon fell on the Board of Education. On March 11, 1881, an act was adopted which provided for its complete reorganization. The old ward system of electing members was abolished. Its place was taken by a new Board, twelve in number, to be elected from the city at large. (This arrangement continued until 1899, when Detroit went back to the ward system which remained in effect until adoption of the present city charter in 1918.)

Before its demise, the old school Board took the matter of library control into its own hands and as one of its final acts set up the Library Commission. This was done, in part, to offset the results of the 1880 school Board election in which, for the first time, Democrats had won a majority of the inspectorships. The outgoing Board, showed judgment by naming a bipartisan Commission which, in the words of Utley, was "carefully and wisely chosen; every one of them was above partisan considerations." [6] Such maturity of action did not come about easily, however.

The resolution to establish the Library Commission was first offered at the meeting of the Board on December 14, 1880. Two weeks later it was brought up for final action in what was one of the liveliest sessions that body ever held. Before a vote was taken on creating the Commission, Inspector C. A. Kent nominated Justice James V. Campbell for membership. That set off a bitter wrangle, one faction wanting to be sure who the members would be before they would approve of having a Commission at all. The matter was thrown into the committee of the whole. Kent stuck to his guns, declaring "that the Board had done so many foolish things, and was liable to do many more. He . . . wanted to know the character of the men they proposed to elect before they decided upon the question of having a commission or not."

Inspector Mothersill "arose to remark that the Board was still on trial before the public. Every newspaper in the city had been hounding the Board and the people were talking about it. He wanted it, therefore, to take such action as would reflect credit upon it." Inspector Carstens objected to the fact that too many lawyers had been suggested for commissionerships. He saw no need for a Commission, anyway, preferring a governing body, if there had to be one, chosen directly by the people.

These statements represented the various points of view which were at issue, and "after considerable wrangling" it was agreed to take up the nominations. Those nominated were Campbell, George V. N. Lothrop, Alfred Chesebrough, Theodore Romeyn, John J. Bagley, William D. Wilkins, August Rohns, Herman Kiefer, Alexander Lewis and William C. Maybury. Those agreed upon and their terms were Campbell, six years; Lothrop, five years; Chesebrough, four years; Wilkins, three years; Kiefer, two years; and Lewis, one year.*

---

* James Valentine Campbell (1823–90) was one of Michigan's foremost legal lights, ranking with such men as Thomas M. Cooley as an early interpreter of the state's basic and organic law. A native of Buffalo, New York, he was educated in the east and began practice in Detroit in 1844. In 1858 he became justice of the Michigan Supreme Court, a position he retained until his death. He was also professor of law at the University of Michigan and was the first to receive the honorary degree of Doctor of Laws from that institution. He wrote extensively on law, politics and history.

George Van Ness Lothrop (1817–97) was the recipient of many honors during a long public career. He was attorney general of Michigan, recorder of the city of Detroit, and minister to Russia. His legal practice was largely devoted to railroad work.

Alexander Lewis (1822–1908) was a banker, merchant and manufacturer. He was a member of the police commission from 1865 to 1875, and in the latter year was elected mayor of Detroit, serving one term (1876–77).

Having settled the Commission membership, Inspector Mothersill then moved the adoption of the resolution to create the Commission. This was the signal for several members to walk out of the room in an effort to prevent a quorum being present when the matter was referred by the committee of the whole back to the Board for final confirmation of its action. Fifteen members remained, and the final vote on the committee action was thirteen to two, sufficient to carry the measure.[7]

The *Free Press,* a Democratic paper which opposed the Commission idea, commented the next day on what had happened and censored the members who walked out.

> They resorted to means that were illegitimate and disgraceful. . . . They not only injured themselves in the estimation of the community, but they injured the cause they sought to serve. Nothing could possibly tend more directly to the creation or strengthening of public sentiment in favor of a measure than the resort by its opponents to such disreputable proceedings. . . .

At the same time, the *Free Press* had only the highest praise for the men selected to serve on the Commission. The Library, it agreed, "will be in thoroughly competent hands." [8]

On January 11, 1881, the new Board of Education, which was to be replaced by the at-large board on July 1, took office. One of its first acts was to instruct the Library Commission "to enter upon its duties on the 27th inst." [9] The old Library committee was requested to confer with the Commission. Its report of January 28, raised new complications. It recommended that the status of the Commission be only that of a permanent committee of the Board, the Board retaining control of the Library funds "as a check and balance on the unlimited authority" of the Commission. This proposal was promptly challenged. Inspector George R. Angell said the report surprised him. He declared:

> I supposed that the law transferred the entire duties of the Board to the Commission. . . . It seems to me, that if that is not the law, before we proceed to dispose of the report, we ought to take legal advice in regard to the matter.[10]

The upshot was that the report was tabled, and on January 30, 1881, the Commission held its first meeting.[11] The six appointed commissioners were joined by the ex officio member, Michael Firnane, president of the Board. On February 15, the Board took the committee's report from the table, and adopted a substitute resolution "that the secretary be and is hereby instructed to turn over the Library and its funds to the credit of the Library Commission, to be expended as their judgment may elect." [12] The Commission, meanwhile, had organized itself, electing Justice Campbell president; Chesebrough, secretary; while Alfred Ives, treasurer of the Board of Education was appointed ex officio treasurer of the Commission. The office of vice president was not added until 1884.

Soon after its establishment, the Commission adopted a set of rules for its own governing. Originally, there were two permanent or standing committees, the Finance Committee and the Committee on Purchase of Books. In 1886 a third was added, the Committee on Internal Management. The name of the latter was changed in 1892 to Committee on Administration. On occasion, temporary committees have been named for specific purposes, but the three principal standing committees have been found adequate to handle the Library's routine affairs for more than eighty years.

The Commission came into being as a nonpartisan, nonpolitical body, a character which it has maintained down to the present time, to the envy of other library systems. In 1890 Frederick M. Crunder, the St. Louis librarian, commented on the condition of the Detroit Public Library as being "free from political influences," and "congratulating you on your stable and comfortable status." [13]

Only once was that status seriously threatened. When the Democratic dominated Board took control in 1881, an attempt was made to rescind the action of the previous Board in 1880. But according to Utley, "the best legal authority held that the Board, having acted within the discretion given it by the law, and having appointed commissioners, had thereby exhausted its power in the premises and the appointments made were therefore valid." [14]

Having been duly constituted and having assumed its responsibilities and prerogatives, the Library Commission quickly discov-

127

ered that it had an institution to run, but very few dollars with which to lubricate its gears. The Library Fund which the Board of Education turned over on February 23, 1881, amounted to $3,190.17. This was the total capital on which the Commission was expected to operate until June, when the county treasurer ordinarily made the annual penal fines payment. It was obvious to the Commission that its first and most pressing concern was obtaining more money. This was recognized by a review of the Library situation as the Commission found it upon taking charge. Commission President Campbell's initial assessment of the Library's management was that it had been well conducted and no radical changes in operation were required. This later proved to have been an error in judgment.

"The system was very good and very well administered under the regulations matured by the former committees," Justice Campbell reported. Then, he added a very large "but." He said of the Commission:

> At the time of their appointment, it was evident that without some further means than we were then likely to be secured by existing methods of supply, the Library would before long become helpless. The receipts from fines and penalties under the criminal laws of the state had fallen off to an alarming extent.[15]

That was an accurate observation. After the Library's right to the "clear proceeds" from the penal fines had been established, revenues from that source increased substantially for a while. However, before many years passed, the fluctuations from year to year became marked. The high point was reached in 1869 and 1870 when income from this source was $12,962 and $12,200 respectively. In 1871 income from fines dropped to $5839. By 1879 it was down to $2908, and in 1880 only $3405 was forthcoming in penal fines. The year 1881 showed slight improvement, amounting to $5826.

Said Campbell, speaking of this revenue decrease:

> It is difficult to know why this was so, and our experience has not yet done much to enlighten us. We cannot flatter ourselves that crime has so far diminished as to show in our large population today a less amount of violation of law than when the city had less than half the same number of people.[16]

It was evident that the kind of library Detroit needed could not be supported by such uncertain and totally inadequate revenues. The first matter of business for the Commission then was to seek a new source of income. Campbell and his fellow commissioners wasted no time. Less than a month after they had taken office, they appealed to the legislature for relief. The justice of their cause, combined with their influence in local and state affairs, gained them sympathetic consideration. On March 11, 1881, legislation was obtained which provided that the Common Council and Board of Estimates should annually place in the city tax levy one-fifth of a mill on each dollar of assessed valuation. This tax was exclusively for public library purposes. The bill was enacted early enough in the year to allow the tax to be levied in 1881, and the receipts for that year amounted to $15,170.24. Thus, for the first time in its history, the Library was placed upon a secure financial footing which established for all time its right to direct public tax support.[17]

Year after year, almost without exception, the millage tax increased. The increases were not spectacular, but they were steady, reflecting the growth of the city. Within five years after the tax was initiated, it passed the $20,000 mark (1885), and by 1891 it had risen to $30,059. Added to the $12,953.59 from penal fines that year, plus a small amount from penalties for overdue books, the Library had a total income of slightly more than $43,000. In 1900 total income was close to the $50,000 mark, of which $46,295.80 was from direct taxation. The penal fines revenue that year was down to $3084, the drop being accounted for by the diversion of Police and Recorder's courts fines which, as has been noted, was to some extent corrected in following years as the result of legal action taken by the Commission. The significant thing is that beginning in 1881, the penal fines, which up to that year had been almost exclusively the Library's sole source of income, assumed less importance in the complete fiscal picture.

The transfer of the Library from the jurisdiction of the Board of Education to a separate commission marked the beginning of a new era for the institution. It had, for the first time, a new and adequate building. It was given a stronger financial base, and it was under the direction of a group of civic-minded men who took their duties as commissioners with the utmost seriousness. In the fulfillment of these duties they were aided by the librarian upon whom rested the chief responsibility for the actual operation of the Library. The man upon whom they first relied, and who filled the position ably for a period of five years was Henry Gillman. The events leading up to the appointment of Gillman as librarian requires some historical digression at this point.

Henry Chaney, who had borne the burden since the Library was founded in 1865, enjoyed the new building for only about a year after it was opened. On April 12, 1878, he retired. That date, said the Board's Library Committee, marked the "expiration of his official term." [18] He was seventy years old, and supposedly in ill health. That may have been true—but he lived seven years after he left the Library! There remains a lurking question of whether his departure may not have been politically precipitated. Certainly his successor, the Reverend Manasseh Hickey, was appointed solely on political grounds, for while that gentleman's character and reputation as a clergyman may have been estimable, one looks in vain for the slightest degree of qualification as a librarian.

No one would deny that Manasseh Hickey was a good and well-intentioned man. He also was a colorful figure, tall and commanding in appearance, good natured and possessing a wide acquaintance in Detroit. Hickey was born at Arcadia, New York, September 7, 1820, and moved to Michigan as a youth, living on a farm in Oakland County. He graduated from Albion College and became a Methodist minister. Most of his ecclesiastical career was spent as a circuit rider, particularly among the Indians of Michigan. He became recognized as an authority on the Chippewa, and learned to speak their language fluently. Several times he was selected to represent the government in negotiations with the Indians, or to serve as official interpreter. As a settled pastor, he was said to have been very effective in Sunday school work, because he could hold a group of children enthralled with stories about the Indians, and with songs and prayers in the Chippewa tongue.

After several years among the Indians, he occupied pulpits in Port Huron, Washtenaw County and Detroit. In 1872 he was presiding elder at Flint. There he suffered a mishap, being thrown from a carriage and incapacitated to an extent which ended his career as a clergyman.* [19] His friends sought some means by which he could be supported, and the Board of Education was persuaded to give him the Library post. The appointment was recognized for what it was—purely political—and met sharp public opposition.

On April 19, 1878, the *Post & Tribune* caustically remarked that Hickey "who recently dropped into the soft position of public librarian, to the surprise of nearly everybody including himself, has assumed the duties of his new office."

Robert E. Roberts, C. A. Kent and Alfred Chesebrough, three members of the Library Committee, sought to stave off Hickey's appointment by suggesting that Chaney be retained at a reduced salary, and that an assistant be appointed to help lighten his burden. Kent particularly opposed Hickey on the grounds of his lack of qualification.

"Of Mr. Hickey," reported the *Post & Tribune,* Kent

> could say nothing derogatory, but he had not heard his friends claim for him any special qualifications for the place. He is upwards of 60 years old and therefore past the time when he can fit himself for the place. He was educated at Albion, and has been a tolerably successful preacher for several years, until he was compelled to abandon that profession on account of an injury to his head, and for some time past he has been seeking a public office with considerable persistency. He had not heard that Mr. Hickey had a taste for literature, or that he was familiar with it.[20]

The following day, the *Post & Tribune* referred to Hickey as "a chronic office seeker and the Democratic party in this city have long been bothered with him. They have given him this office to rid themselves of his importunities." The *Post & Tribune* then continued editorially with a perceptive comment: "The appointment is chiefly significant because it betrays the drifting of the Board of Education more and more into the whirlpool of politics." [21]

Only the *Free Press,* the city's Democratic paper, had a kind

---

* The Reverend Manasseh Hickey died in Detroit January 2, 1903. He was the father of Dr. Preston M. Hickey, of Detroit, who was a pioneer in the field of X-ray, and who climaxed a distinguished medical career as professor of radiology at the University of Michigan Medical School.

131

word for Hickey, and even that was cautiously qualified. The *Free Press* saw the appointment as a "well deserved compliment" to Hickey, and "if he lacks somewhat of the technical experience which is desirable, he has the energy, zeal and thorough practicality which will enable him to acquire the needed experience in a very short time." [22]

The Hickey appointment was one of the brazenly political maneuvers which helped bring about the reform in 1881 of the Board of Education, and which resulted in the removal of the Library from its direct control. Unfortunately, Hickey did not possess the capacity to acquire the experience needed. Within a very short time the Library's internal affairs were in a chaotic condition. When the Commission took over in 1881, it was found that "the Library was reported to be in bad condition from lack of proper system in its arrangement and conduct and proper care of the books." [23] It would have been necessary for the Commission to make a change, but it was saved the trouble. Even the Board of Education, smarting from criticism and seeking desperately to regain public confidence, recognized its mistake. Almost exactly two years after Hickey's appointment, he was ousted from the job, and in April, 1880, even before the establishment of the Library Commission, he was replaced by Henry Gillman, a man who possessed most of the qualifications which his immediate predecessor so sadly lacked.

One of the first things Gillman did was to restore a semblance of order. With the approval of the Library Committee he closed the Library on July 15, 1880, not only for the purpose of cataloging the collection, but also to recondition the books so they could be circulated. They were in a sad state of neglect.

> Many of the books had been wantonly abused; others were really filthy and appeared to be more like pest repositories than healthy volumes. Many others had been interlined with coarse, and in several instances, indecent remarks. It became necessary at once to undertake the task of cleaning and purifying these volumes, before anything else could be done. This occupied nearly one month using the entire staff of the Library. A new set of rules was printed and inserted in each volume, specifying the several fines which would be enforced for each and every injury which the books might sustain when in the possession of the reader; a rigid scrutiny to be

exercised by the assistants upon delivery and return of the book, in order to ascertain its condition.[24]

That the manner in which Gillman took hold was most satisfactory, first to the Library Committee and subsequently to the Commission, is revealed in that body's first annual report which stated its approval of the way he was managing things. He was earning his salary of $1500, but to increase efficiency and release him from some of the details of administration which had proved so onerous to Chaney, the new Commission, in 1881, hired Lucian B. Gilmore as chief assistant librarian. He was selected because of "his considerable knowledge of books as well as his business experience." [25]

Gillman filled the position of chief librarian until 1885 when he resigned to accept appointment as United States consul in Jerusalem. Although his tenure in Detroit was relatively short, he proved himself an able and conscientious man whose attainments were notable. He can be included in that galaxy of intellects who contributed so much to the prestige of their city, but who, unfortunately, are too little remembered.

Henry Gillman was born in Kinsale, Ireland, in 1833. He had Irish and English ancestry, and his immediate forebears, if not of the aristocracy, were at least quality folk with backgrounds of public and military service. Gillman was well educated, and in 1850 he emigrated to the United States with his parents, settling in Detroit. He was soon employed by the United States Great Lakes Geodetic Survey, the beginning of a career devoted to what would then be known as the field of natural science. He traveled extensively through the northern United States wilderness with topographic and hydrographic expeditions. His reports attracted wide public attention, so much so that he was invited to contribute to scientific publications. The result was that he soon gained a considerable literary reputation.

Although he remained in government service—he was assistant superintendent of lighthouse construction on the upper Great Lakes from 1870 to 1876—his interest turned more and more to science, particularly the fields of archeology and osteology. The *Dictionary of American Biography* cites as his most important contribution to science the discovery of certain peculiarities in the bones of the mound-building Indians. He is said to have been one of the first to recognize the importance of Isle Royale as a fertile field for archeological research.

After leaving the Library he continued to combine official diplomatic duties in the Holy Land with archeological and botanical investigations, some of which attracted international attention. He returned to Detroit in 1891 where he continued to make his home until his death, which was virtually unnoted by local newspapers, on July 30, 1915.

Gillman was succeeded as librarian by Henry Munson Utley whose appointment dated from August 1, 1885. Under his long, active administration of twenty-eight years, the Detroit Public Library experienced a period of vigorous growth and expansion, and it was under Utley's leadership that the Library's true character was shaped. Utley came into the Library service through political channels, but the politicking was that of the Board of Education, not of the Commission. A former newspaperman, Utley became secretary of the Board of Education in 1881 at the time of its reorganization. He was a Republican, and in 1885, when the Democrats won a majority of the seats, he became what the Detroit *Post* described as a victim of "the ravages of politics." However, his services to the school board had marked him as a man of ability. The Library Commission knew a good thing if the Board of Education didn't, and felt that Utley's talents should not be lost. "Mr. Utley," said the *Post,* "is the man they have been looking for to succeed Mr. Gillman." [26] It proved to be a wise and happy selection.

Within a year after Utley's appointment, two key aides were added to the staff. These were Norman C. Perkins, who was made second assistant librarian, ranking just below Lucian B. Gilmore,*

---

* Although Lucian B. Gilmore was a member of the Detroit Library staff for about thirty-one years, not much is known about him. Born in 1840, he went to Detroit from his native Providence, Rhode Island, at the age of twenty-one. There is no account of his career prior to 1881 when he was appointed to the staff. In 1883 he was made second assistant librarian at a salary of $900, and by 1886 he was first assistant, a post he held until Adam Strohm joined the Library in 1911. Gilmore retired at about the time Strohm became Librarian in 1912, and he died at his home, 197 Peterboro, June 17, 1913.

and George W. Osborn, who was named assistant in charge of the reading room. Both appointments dated from March 4, 1886. Perkins' salary was $1000; Osborn's $600.

Following the six original members of the Library Commission, an even dozen additional men were appointed prior to 1900. Of the 1881 Board, Judge Campbell served the better part of two terms, resigning in 1889. Dr. Kiefer resigned in 1883, but the Library did not lose his services entirely. He went abroad, carrying with him the Commission's authority to act as its agent to purchase books in Germany. Lothrop resigned in 1885 and William D. Wilkins died in 1882, serving less than a year. The replacements, as well as those receiving new appointments, were men who in every instance measured up to the highest standards of integrity and devotion to the Library's interests. The list, starting with Levi L. Barbour,* who replaced Wilkins, further consisted of Magnus Butzel, Herbert Bowen, Joseph A. Marsh (who resigned in 1886 after less than a year on the Commission), George S. Hosmer, Richard Storrs Willis, Henry A. Harmon, Edwin F. Conely, Dr. C. Henri Leonard, John S. Gray, Dr. John

---

Norman Perkins was born at Pomfret, Vermont, April 17, 1832. An 1857 graduate of Yale, he went to Chicago where he practiced law until 1881. He then went to Detroit to be an editorial writer for the Post & Tribune. Five years later he was appointed second assistant librarian, a post he filled until his death, March 20, 1895. After his death, the Library Commission decided not to appoint a successor to him.

* Levi Lewis Barbour (1840–1925) held many public positions including that of regent of the University of Michigan. He is said to have conceived the idea of the city's acquiring Belle Isle for a public park.

Herbert Bowen (1847–1921) was a man of many interests. An attorney who specialized in real estate law, he was also an avid numismatist, and acquired an outstanding collection of bank notes which he donated to the Detroit Public Library. He was one of the founders of the Detroit Scientific Association.

George Stedman Hosmer (1855–1921) was elected judge of the Wayne County Circuit Court in 1888 and served continuously in that post until his death.

Edwin Forrest Conely (1847–1902) was a law partner of Mayor William C. Maybury. He held the post of police commissioner, water commissioner, and was minority leader in the Michigan House of Representatives. He was also on the faculty of the University of Michigan law school.

John Simpson Gray (1841–1906) and Paul Robert Gray (1867–1929) comprised one of the two father-son combinations on the Library Commission. The elder Gray, an industrialist and banker, was the first president and one of the original stockholders of the Ford Motor Company. His son Paul, a manufacturer, also was an original Ford stockholder.

E. Clark and Maynard D. Follin. These men offered a fair cross section of high standing in the community. They represented the medical and legal professions, business and industry, and several had displayed their interest in public education by having served as members of the Board of Education. There also were eighteen ex officio members of the Commission between 1881 and 1900. These were the presidents of the Board of Education. Among them were Harmon and Clark, both of whom were elected commissioners after their school board terms expired.

The provision of the law which required staggered terms proved to be a wise one, giving the Commission a continuity which always assured a majority of experienced members. Politics played almost no part, either in the selection of the commissioners, or in their conduct of Library affairs once they had been appointed. There was one notable exception which occurred in 1901 when Eugene A. Bresler was made a member of the Commission.

Bresler was a personable young man, the heir to a considerable fortune amassed by his father who had mining and commercial interests in Venezuela. He managed to dissipate most of the estate, and in the process gained the reputation of being a good fellow. For some reason, probably a yearning for public office, he "collected" members of the Board of Education, attending its meetings regularly, and turning his office over to some of his school Board cronies who used it as an unofficial meeting place. He was nominated for a seat on the Library Commission late in December, 1901, to fill a vacancy about to result from the retirement of Dr. Leonard. Bresler previously had been a candidate for secretary of the Board of Education, but withdrew his name in favor of another candidate. His nomination for the Library Commission apparently was his reward.[27]

The school Board was divided, about half the members favoring Herbert L. Baker in preference to Bresler. Baker was described as a "lawyer, scholar and gentleman of affairs." He also had the support of the newspapers which unanimously opposed Bresler.

"Those who know the Library Commission thoroughly say he is not the man for the place," declared the *News,* with reference

136

to Bresler. "His backing comes largely from inspectors who don't stand very high in the community," said *Today,* while the *Free Press* warned: "Under no circumstances . . . should the place be given to a political wire puller." [28] The *News* commented further:

> Ordinarily, the Board is unanimous in selecting some gentleman of cultivated tastes who has read and traveled and who has enough business ability to be of use to the Commission. . . . The present library commissioners are put out over the likelihood of Bresler's election, and their friends make no bones of saying that such an event will be a great disappointment to them.

In an effort to block a quorum, several of Baker's supporters walked out of the school Board meeting when the vote was taken. The result was that Bresler was elected by eight votes to seven. Despite this outcome, the corporation counsel ruled the election legal and Bresler, accompanied by his lawyer, appeared at the Commission meeting on January 16, 1902, and demanded to be seated. The Commission at first was inclined to ostracize him, but finally he was accepted.[29]

The *Tribune* found the whole affair shocking, and was caustic in its editorial comment which appeared January 17, 1902.

> If Mr. Bresler cares to claim a seat in an honorable and honorary body like the library commission on such credentials as require the opinion from the corporation counsel to uphold their legality, there is nothing to say except that his willingness to do so is conclusive and indisputable evidence of his unfitness for the place. If we are to have bitter and unseemly scrambles for library commissionships, if politics are to be projected into deliberations which should concern themselves solely with the culture and ability and character of the candidates and to effect selections for offices which above all others should seek the man, then it is time to inquire what strange influences have resulted in this loss of dignity. There is only one explanation which suggests itself to the unprejudiced mind. The probability that large sums of money are to be expended by the commission in the near future suggests the conclusion at which the general public will arrive.

It must be said to his credit that Bresler took his duties seriously; his political interests were put in the background, and his performance as a commissioner was acceptable if not distinguished. At the expiration of his single term on December 31, 1907, he did not seek nor was he mentioned for reappointment. Bresler's appointment was the only one since the Commission was established in which the election of a commissioner became a public issue.

CHAPTER 9

SOMETHING FOR EVERYBODY

POLICY MAKING was—and is—one of the principal functions of
the Commission, and in this field nothing has been more important than those decisions which have shaped the character of
the Library. Among other policy decisions the Commission had
to make was what kind of a library Detroit should have. Obviously, this course was not charted all at once; it was a matter of
evolution, emerging, changing, developing, year by year. Different
commissioners had their own ideas on the subject. When they
were men of strong mind and will they endeavored to shape the
form and destiny of the Library according to their individual concepts of what a library should be. An example of that occurred in
1904 when Commissioner James E. Scripps * raised a question

---

* James E. Scripps (1835–1906) founded the Detroit *News* in 1873. Born
in London, England, he came to the United States in 1844. After growing
up in Rushville, Illinois, he worked for newspapers in Chicago until 1859
when he became associated with the Detroit *Advertiser*. Scripps' influence
in Detroit and Michigan affairs was great and his interests were broad. In
addition to his membership on the Library Commission, he was a trustee

which related to the nature of the Library. The publisher of the Detroit *News,* Scripps qualified on every count as a man of strong ideas and convictions. Eminently successful, he could both shape and interpret public opinion. No one could deny that he had the best interests of the community at heart—or at least what he believed to be its best interests. At the same time, it cannot be denied that his strong personality occasionally made him appear autocratic.

At the Commission meeting on October 6, 1904, Scripps, who that year was vice president of the Board, submitted a communication in which he offered some thoughts in regard to the Library management. He was prompted to do this, he said, as a result of five years service as a commissioner, during which time there had grown in his mind "the feeling that we are not working altogether with the carefully considered system which should prevail."

To be worthy of the name, Scripps said, a library must be more than just a collection of books; it must be a collection with a purpose and a system. He doubted that the Detroit Library was meeting that standard. There was, he felt, too much catering to popular tastes and desires in the selection of books, and not enough fulfillment of the Commission's obligation to give the public more in the way of intellectual nourishment. He would draw a broader distinction between the reference and circulation functions, even to the point of recommending that they be housed in separate buildings. (At that time the Commission was considering a new main Library building.) But in any case, "the highest consideration ought to be given to the Reference Department."

What Scripps obviously had in mind was something that would make the Detroit Library pre-eminent in some particular field, making it, in effect, primarily a specialized, as opposed to a general, library. This suggested radical change in policy and a marked departure from what the Library had always been, since its inception forty years before. Detroit, he insisted, could and should be notable among the libraries of the world. But, he

of Harper Hospital and one of the founders of the Art Museum. He was elected for one term to the state senate in 1903.

added, the mere possession of 200,000 volumes would not make it so.

> "What is it notable for?" the student will ask. We can at present only reply, "Nothing in particular!" I would very much urge that we adopt some specialty or specialties in which we may stand out conspicuous. There are genealogy and western biography and antiquities which afford two excellent fields for distinction. Some department ought to be agreed upon and then a system devised for its fullest development.[1]

The Commission permitted this communication to lie on the table for a month, and the reply, when it came, was from Utley. In his answer, he took sharp issue with Scripps, both on the question of what the Library was and what it should be. He agreed that new book acquisitions should be carefully made, and he even conceded that special categories could be built up, but only with funds remaining after new and current books had been purchased. Whatever specialty was decided on, he pointed out, should not be that for which some other library had already gained recognition. He said:

> This idea of a specialty is endorsed by the Vice President, but his suggestion of genealogy, western history, biography and antiquities as such specialty appears to me not to have been well chosen. The Newberry Library of Chicago has since its establishment made a specialty of genealogy and having many years the start and unlimited resources furnished by an endowment of several millions, it would be idle for such a library as this to undertake to gain a reputation in competition with it. The same is true in the field of western history. The Wisconsin Historical Society has been engaged in collecting for fifty years. Its secretary is given carte blanche and travels over the country picking up what he can find. . . . In the field of antiquities and antiquarian research no library in this country can compete with the Astor and Lenox of New York. . . .
>
> It seems to me that exception can properly be taken to the expression in the document regarding this library: "What is it notable for? the student will ask; we can at present only reply, Nothing in particular." If asked the question, What is the Detroit Public Library notable for? I should not reply "Nothing in particular." It is notable throughout this country among people who know anything of the subject as one of the very foremost of good, all-around working libraries, as being abreast with the times in all plans for rendering the best and most acceptable service to the public, as being the first

141

to establish working relations with the public schools, about which inquiries have come to us from abroad, and upon which the heads of the educational departments of both England and the United States have made reports. It is notable as issuing the best printed catalog of any library in the world, copies of which have been sold to all sections of this country and to Great Britain, Austria, Australia and Cuba. It is notable for having one of the best reference departments in the country, used by vastly more people than any similar department in a city of equal size. It is notable for having on its shelves rare and valuable books not commonly found in other public libraries, including the most complete set of the periodicals indexed by Poole.[2]

This was sound rebuttal, and the commissioners must have been impressed by it, because no radical change in policy resulted. In time, the Detroit Public Library would be able to point to special collections which would give it wide renown. But it did not abandon its character of general service. Rather, both under Utley and his successors, it strengthened its position of appeal to the widest possible field of public interest.

In 1905, his last year on the Board, Scripps was elected president. He took the occasion of assuming the chair for the first time, to reiterate some of what he had said earlier:

> In his view, the reference library should be entirely separated from the circulating library. The main central library should be for reference use alone, and the popular circulation of books should be confined to the branches.[3]

The desire to provide maximum service sometimes forced the Commission into making painful policy decisions. While these may seem trivial when viewed in retrospect from the safe distance of 80 years, they were soul-wracking experiences at the time the commissioners were confronted with them. There was, as an example, the delicate issue of whether to keep the Library open on Sunday. Would such a decision, the commissioners had to ask themselves, be accepted by the majority of the people, or would they be condemned as irreverent violators of the Sabbath? Obviously, it was an issue which would, in the end, be settled from the city's pulpits.

Late in 1885, a cautious trial balloon was sent aloft by the Commission. It was in the nature of a recommendation from the librarian that the reading rooms be opened for a few hours on Sunday afternoon and evening. The Commission took the proposal under consideration and waited for the reaction. It came swiftly. Two preachers in particular unloosed their eloquence, and taking opposing stands, pretty well summed up the issue. They were the Rev. Dr. E. L. Rexford, of the Universalist Church of Our Father, who took the affirmative in the debate. The opposing thunderbolts were hurled by the Rev. William Dawe, pastor of the Palmer Methodist-Episcopal Church. Dr. Rexford led off on January 17, 1886, by pointing out that the Library was an educational institution and, if it "is a good thing, then it is better when it is more wisely used." The pious rich man, Dr. Rexford continued, spent Sunday in a leisurely manner, attending church if so inclined and after dinner had at his disposal his private library. Although he probably fell asleep over his book, no one thought the less of him. Said Dr. Rexford:

> Now the poor laboring man—a young man. I hope the doors of the library will be open to the honest laboring man who only wishes to enrich his mind. . . . When a man goes into a library he naturally removes his hat. All is hushed. There are the collected thoughts of men long dead, but who still live through the ages. Give the young men who walk the streets the privilege of walking into a great aggregation of books. . . . All things are sacred that are made so by use. I believe we can make a better use of the library than keeping it closed on the Sabbath.[4]

Mr. Dawe, in his rebuttal, warned that the tendency to open public institutions on Sunday was demoralizing and endangering the nation. The pretension that secularization of the day was in the interest of the working class was wholly false. He warned:

> The overproduction as a result of Sabbath's toil throws confusion into the world's market; throws thousands of men out of employment for weeks through the year. This is God's answer to the nation for the violation of this day. . . . There is no individual who has the use of the Library but what their wants could be met without the Sabbath day.
> I therefore charge upon our commissioners in this action the solemn responsibility of setting forces in motion which endangers civil advancement. I charge them with the responsibility of making it more difficult for the religious instruction of our young people. I charge upon them serious injury to this rudder of the ship of state.

143

I can scarcely hope that the gentlemen of this Commission will heed my voice in this matter, but its echo will be heard in the coming years, if our children, for the want of a Sabbath, shall have forgotten to worship God. . . .[5]

A good deal was heard on other Sundays and from other pulpits, including the dire warning that "Sunday books and Sunday beer" would become synonymous. Open one institution, and others will be opened. The Sunday sale of liquor would be condoned and Belle Isle would soon be turned into a Sunday beer garden. "Don't let down the barriers," Mr. Dawe implored.[6]

By the end of February, the Commissioners had heard enough to enable them to make up their minds as to what course to follow. On February 29, 1886, the doors were first opened to Sunday users of the reading rooms. No celestial thunderbolts crashed through the skylights as approximately one hundred persons made use of the service. Said the *Free Press:*

> Fully three-fourths of the men and boys present belong to the laboring classes whose limited means do not admit of their having all the reading matter desired at their own homes. They were all neatly dressed and well ordered, and both by their behavior and interest they took in reading, demonstrated the possession of liberal intelligence and of a most laudable ambition to improve their minds.[7]

The circulation department remained closed, but within a few weeks there was a movement to permit Sunday withdrawal of books. This won little support, and the Commission voted it down.[8] Reviewing the Sunday open reading room policy after it had been in effect for five years, Utley reported "the plan is now generally commended by clergymen and religious people." The cost of keeping the library open, with two attendants on duty, averaged $9.18 per Sunday, or less than $500 per year. In 1887 the average Sunday attendance was 100; by 1891 it had increased to 146.[9]

Most of the Commission's decisions having to do with the day-to-day operation of the Library were of a more routine variety. For example, it is difficult to believe that a debate of any magnitude developed in 1877 when it was found necessary to equip the Library with spittoons, which were purchased at the

144

store of R. W. King at a cost of $12.75. They served their purpose until 1909 when an advanced social note was struck by the janitor's recommendation that "the 28 cuspidors in use for the last 30 years be replaced with something more modern and presentable." The Commission learned that vessels of brass or graniteware could be obtained for one dollar each, and ordered that they be bought forthwith. The Library grounds offered tempting sites for the display and sale of seasonal merchandise, and purveyors of Christmas trees regularly asked, and sometimes were granted, permission to offer their wares along the sidewalks bordering the building. But the Commission balked when someone petitioned to have a dray stand in front of the Library.

Quite a stir ensued when Commissioner Leonard, in 1900, proposed that a special committee be appointed to consider "providing a badge for the members of the Library Commission, each member to pay for his own badge." Commissioner Scripps snorted that badges would be "cheap and snobbish" and demanded to know what good use they would be. "I want mine to swell around in," Commissioner Follin frankly admitted. On another occasion, however, tribute came more easily to a distinguished citizen when the Commission caused a notice to be inserted in the newspapers stating: "The Public Library will be closed next Monday in honor of G. Washington, deceased."

Technological progress was recognized in 1887 when the librarian was authorized to purchase "one of the Hammond typewriters, the price thereof including the necessary wheels shall not exceed $100." One was bought from the firm of W. A. Thorpe & Co., but the price was $104. Some few years later, there was grave discussion about "procuring an Edison Oscillative Mimeograph at a cost not exceeding $50." Obviously, the Commission accepted the dawn of the mechanical age.[10]

Of more serious concern was the matter of recurring thefts and vandalism. On June 4, 1887, someone broke in during the night and stole the book register, dating stamps, book cards and other items, along with about $10 from the cash drawer. The *Advertiser and Tribune* attributed this burglary to revenge on the part of a disgruntled patron

145

who has been obliged to wait an hour for a book that he ought to have been able to get in three minutes, and who took this step to abolish the unsystematic system which has so long disgraced the administration of the Public Library.

Other similar invasions caused the Commission to authorize the employment of a special policeman, but that did not halt the depredations. On December 4, 1894, the Library safe was cracked, and between $60 and $65 in cash and stamps were stolen. The police department was called on for extra protection and a man was assigned day and night. In spite of this precaution, a thief pried open a window and made off with a number of rare books from one of the glass display cases. The mutilation of books and periodicals, then as now, was a constant nuisance, and in 1897 a citizen named G. Bertram Davis claimed a reward of five dollars "for the detection of one N. J. Bradner in the act of mutilating a copy of the *Scientific American*." It was necessary to issue constant reminders that those violating the care of books were subject "to penalties imposed by the state laws passed for the protection of public libraries." In 1890 the librarian was granted authority to employ a detective "to suppress the larceny of coats, etc., which has become so great a nuisance."

Equally bothersome was the necessity to track down borrowers of books who failed to return them. If the borrower could not be located, the person who signed his application for a card, his surety, was looked to. Often the surety was as hard to find as the borrower. On one occasion, a surety claimed his signature was forged. That contention failed to impress library officials and "the matter was ordered to be tested in court, if necessary." E. C. Hall was employed in 1892 to recover over-due books. Said a library report:

> These books are not sent for until they are a month or six weeks overdue and in many cases it is necessary to hunt up sureties as well as the principals to get the books or to pay for them. During the year, 438 books were assigned to Mr. Hall for collection and of these all were collected and returned to the Library by him, but eleven, which are lost beyond hope of recovery by reasons of death, removal from the city or worthlessness of both principal and surety.[11]

Contamination of books was another problem in the days before vaccines and inoculations, when diphtheria was endemic in Detroit and smallpox a frequent visitor to the city. What to do with the books which were in the possession of stricken people puzzled the Commission. The health officer was requested to examine books suspected of contamination for "dangerous germs." That functionary reported, after five books held by persons exposed to diphtheria had been turned over to him that "examinations and animal inoculations of cultures . . . failed to reveal the presence of any disease producing germs." In 1903, in the course of a serious smallpox epidemic, the Commission adopted a rule which decreed that

> if the health officer shall place a contagious disease notice upon any house in which there is at the time a library book, the person who drew such book shall at once notify the Library of the fact, and shall retain the book and cause it to be disinfected with the other household effects . . . however, books in smallpox infected houses shall be destroyed.

The seriousness of the 1903 epidemic was indicated in that year's annual report when circulation of children's books dropped off 17,753 volumes compared to 1902. "This is believed," the report stated, "to be almost wholly due to the epidemic of smallpox and other contagious diseases which prevailed during the winter of 1902–3." [12]

The ever-present danger of fire gave everyone connected with the Library chronic sleeplessness. Fortunately the Library itself escaped direct disaster of that kind, but it did not come off completely unsinged. On the night of January 27, 1893, the alarm bell sounded. The high school which had housed Detroit's first public library was totally destroyed. In the fire 1425 volumes loaned by the Library to the school were lost. Because the fire was such a disaster for the Board of Education, and because the expense of fitting up a temporary high school was so great, the Commission generously waived all claim for the books lost.

On three occasions books were burned up in bindery fires. On October 5, 1896, the Librarian reported that fire in a downtown bindery caused destruction of 345 volumes, including a dozen or

147

so volumes of early Detroit newspapers which it was "extremely difficult, if not impossible, to replace." A year earlier, all but seventy-five copies of the German catalog were lost in the explosion of the Detroit *Journal* building, one of the city's worst disasters which cost many lives. Part of the building was occupied by Hiller's bindery. It was necessary to order the entire edition reprinted. A third bindery fire resulted in damage to Library books to the extent of $336. Fortunately they were insured. A serious fire in a building on Farmer Street in 1897 caused Commissioner Butzel to call the Commission's attention to the danger to which the Library was exposed "by the high buildings on the west and east sides." The Board adopted his recommendation that added protection be supplied by putting fireproof shutters over the windows.[13]

Discipline, then as now, was another problem facing the Library staff. As early as 1884, when the term juvenile delinquency was waiting to be coined, the librarian complained that

> large numbers of boys, "street Arabs" or gamins, visit the Library in the evening from about seven to nine o'clock. The difficulty in dealing with them in maintaining order is very great. Yet the importance of encouraging their attendance under proper direction, pointing out to them the books to read, and otherwise instructing them, is not lost sight of while preventing their disturbing the more orderly readers.

The great number of children using the Library brought complaints that they disturbed the adult readers. While admitting the problem, Utley felt it necessary to explain that the children's rights "are the same as adults, and we cannot lose sight of the fact that it was largely on their account that the Library was established." Later, some inspired genius devised the plan of persuading the more boisterous boys to act as monitors in the children's reading room, a plan which worked very satisfactorily. Yet, no one has ever been able completely to suppress the animal spirits of youth, and the problem was universal. In 1901, the head of the library in Madison, Wisconsin, addressed a plaintive letter to Utley: "I inquire what you do concerning the unruly boys in the Library, and what devices you use for their subjection or control?" Utley's reply, if he made one, is not on record. About the same time, D. J. Healy,* a prominent Detroit merchant, wrote complaining that while his son Daniel was visiting the Library, his bicycle was stolen. Whether there was any connection or not, Daniel J. Healy, Jr. in time became a probate judge, in charge of the juvenile division.

Loafers, the nondescript characters who seek refuge from the cold in public buildings, soon discovered the Library was a haven of refuge on harsh winter days. With a magazine or newspaper propped up in front of them, they could snooze away the hours in an unwashed and sometimes boozy aura which was heightened by steam heat. This prompted more than one protest from outraged citizens. One complaint signed by Louis K. Gibbs, was as eloquent as any.

> I wish to protest against the intolerable conditions now prevailing in the reading room of the Public Library in regard to the loafers who are making it their headquarters and themselves nuisances by talking and sleeping. No self-respecting person can associate with the ill-kept and vile smelling clan. . . .

The librarian's reply was sympathetic. "Within another week," he assured Gibbs, "arrangements will be completed whereby the flavory newspaper readers will be removed downstairs to a special room. . . ."[14]

There were others besides noisy youngsters and ill-flavored vagrants who went to the Library. The building was a crossroads for humanity, the meeting place for men, women and children from every walk of life. Newspaper writers, looking for human interest stories, found the Library to be a lush pasture.

"In what are the people at present interested?" an attendant was asked.

"In genealogy," was her prompt reply. "Just now [this was in 1895]

> there is an awakened interest in that subject. We have a complete set of those books, and ladies come here and spend hours at a time tracing their family connections. There is no special class of readers

---

* Daniel Joseph Healy (1862–1933), founder of the department store and specialty shops which bear his name, was elected a member of the Library Commission in 1930.

149

here. Our patrons generally are people with cultivated tastes, and students, but we have excellent facilities for supplying information to those engaged in all pursuits.

Librarians had to be deft and nimble-witted to interpret the demands made upon them. A reporter was told:

> The titles of books are ridiculously transposed sometimes by those who call for them. People come here and ask for the "Sacred Letter", by Hawthorne, "Cluster on the Hearth", by Charles Reade, and "Aristocrat of the Breakfast Table", by Holmes.[15]

But their requests, no matter how farfetched they might sound, were gladly complied with, and the reading rooms were filled with contented people, lost to all other concerns in the world of books.

> There were commonplace people and scholarly people. Some read novels, and others burrowed into books of reference. Many showed that they wished themselves elsewhere, for they fidgeted as they read, but the greater number turned the pages gently and smilingly. True and knowing readers were they.

Sometimes the reporters became as gushingly sentimental as the characters in the more saccharine novel. Said one such writer:

> It may be the green things and the spring time flowers do grow for them, but the sun shines as well for the old man with the kindly eyes or the old lady with the sweet face who sits by the west window of the Library on this May afternoon reading for the tenth time, possibly, some old story that in the days long gone lightened a childish heart or made a darkening day seem brighter.
>
> One will see all sorts and conditions of men in the reading room of a library, from the gushing young girl hardly out of frocks, who eagerly pores over the pages of a fashion magazine, to the old scholar of a theological trend, who turns and re-turns the leaves of some such a volume as "Young's Night Thoughts", or, possibly, even "Colenso on the Pentateuch."

The reporter observed with interest two giggling girls who almost collapsed with hilarity under the reproving eye of the "advanced woman with the side curls," trying to concentrate on the other side of the table.[16]

"To spend day after day in Detroit's public library would be to find oneself in a wide field of character study," remarked a reporter for the *News-Tribune* in 1898. He was particularly taken by an elderly man, whom he described as

> a thinker, a philosopher. . . . It is restful to watch him. His face is so strong and his features so expressive of a steady, never flinching purpose, that of assimilating and equalizing in his own mind, the realities of life.

By contrast there were "the flippant characters," the boys "snuggling together to take a peep in the books they have drawn." There were the men

> whose appearance indicate nearly all sorts of occupations from the classical professor to the most commonplace mechanic. Books of travel, of adventure, of historical interest, and now and again of fiction are pored over by these frequenters of the Library. Beside the delicate face of the student is seen that of the man whose bronzed features and rough hands tell of manual labor, each supplied with the books he desires with which to feed his hungry mind.

Nor was Cupid barred from those hallowed halls.

> Girls move to and fro with arms laden with tales of love, giggling and exchanging views on the latest summer novel. . . . There are worse places to meet one's sweetheart than the bookroom of a library. Particularly if one is given to poetry and romance.[17]

Clearly the old Centre building had something for everyone. From these descriptions, the Library appears to have been an almost idyllic place, with the public, the Commission and the staff enjoying a feeling of quiet well-being. Crises had arisen, been overcome and forgotten. The Library was quietly busy. Calm and complacency prevailed. Then, suddenly, this euphoria was shattered, and for a few days, at least, it appeared more than possible that the Library would collapse in a financial ruin. What ruffled the even waters was the failure of the City Savings Bank, the depository for Library Commission funds. For the moment, the Library faced the bleak prospect of being almost totally without money.

On February 10, 1902, state bank examiners finished an inspection of the books, and announced the institution was unable to meet its obligations and would not be permitted to reopen.

Most people thought the City Savings Bank was a sound establishment, and the examiners' report came as a distinct shock to the community. Hundreds of small depositors, as well as large business enterprises, found themselves in a desperate situation. It looked as if the life savings of many people would be wiped out. The Board of Education and the Library Commission were in the same boat. The bank had been designated the depository by the school Board, and, according to established practice, the bank's cashier, Homer McGraw, served as ex officio treasurer for the Board of Education and for the Library Commission. When the doors failed to open, Utley announced in a shocked voice that "every dollar of the Library's funds was in the City Savings Bank." [18] The fund amounted to $38,757.04. Other cash resources—all the money left at the Commission's disposal—counted up to only $2,222.78.

The real wrecking bar was the bank's vice president and director, Frank C. Andrews. Frank C. Pingree was the president, but it was generally acknowledged that he was little more than a figurehead. Andrews ran things, and the *Detroit News* recognized him as the "real executive head." He was a young man in a hurry. He hurried so fast to get to the top that he tripped over his own feet, not to mention his scruples, if he had any. He had come to Detroit from his Macomb County farm home when he was 19, and quickly made a reputation as a shrewd real estate operator. By the time he was 29, he was reputed to be a millionaire. His interests included streetcar franchises and local politics. He fostered the so-called ripper bill by which municipal boards were abolished in favor of one-man commissions, a move which opened the door wide to shady politics. His reward came when he was made police commissioner. A stock market gamble, which he financed by embezzling from the bank, led to his downfall. To many Detroiters who watched his mercurial success, he was a popular, admired figure. But the sounder business element was wary of him. John S. Gray, a Commission member, was in California when he heard the news of the bank's failure. He wrote Utley:

> What a frightful plunger our man Andrews has proved to be. It is some time since I became afraid of him and sold my City Savings

152

stock for just what he cared to pay, but I never dreamed of the extent of his operations and now I am thankful not to have had a dollar's interest in the bank. My poor fellow directors [Library Commissioners] must be in a terrible plight and my sympathy goes out for them.[19]

It was small comfort to the Library that Andrews was arrested, tried and sentenced to prison for fifteen years (he served thirteen months), or that Homer McGraw was thrown into bankruptcy along with other bank officers and directors. What immediately concerned the Commission was how the Library could be saved from catastrophe. The first reaction of some Commission members was panic. "At first," said Utley, "it looked as though the temporary closing of the institution and discharge of all employes was inevitable." [20] It was the Common Council that saved the day. It authorized the Library to borrow sufficient operating funds from other banks, to be repaid out of anticipated tax collections. The council also appropriated $9500 which had been earmarked for the purchase of a site for a branch library. It was agreed that the funds thus acquired should be held by the city treasurer who would release them on proper warrant in sums approximating each month's requirements.

The result was that the Library was able to weather the storm, although some belt-tightening became necessary. "The purchase of new books was practically suspended," said Utley.[21] The Union Trust Company was named receiver for the bank. In 1904 it paid an initial dividend to depositors. That of the Library amounted to $12,402.15. From then until 1911, further distributions were made until, in the end, the Library recovered $26,263.12, or about 70 per cent of its total claim.

CHAPTER 10

BRANCHING OUT

DETROIT experienced a rapid growth, almost tripling in population between 1880 and 1900. During approximately the same period, the area of the city nearly doubled, due to annexations. When the central Library was built in 1877, there were fifteen square miles within the city's boundaries. By 1900, the area was slightly more than twenty-eight square miles. The new areas added were largely residential, accommodating the greater number of people who were establishing homes in Detroit.

This expansion meant that an increasingly large proportion of the public lived farther than ever before from the Library. Whereas in 1880, Centre Park was either within walking distance or a short streetcar ride for most patrons, the situation in the 1890's was considerably different. By that time, it took more than an easy stroll to reach Centre Park. It was beyond walking distance for most people. Public transportation also became a problem. From the outlying districts it became necessary to transfer from one line to another, often at added expense and inconvenience. The Library Commission was aware of this situa-

154

tion, and realized that a library facility located in the heart of the downtown business district could not adequately service the outlying areas. The chief sufferers were children and those adults, employed and living far from downtown, for whom limited time virtually ruled out a visit to the Library.

It was this realization which finally persuaded the Commission that continued enlargement of the Library building was not the answer. As the city grew outward, library facilities also had to move outward. If the people could not easily reach the books they wanted, it became the Library's duty to take the books to them. It was out of this necessity and obligation that the Detroit Public Library's system of branches emerged.

In 1893 Magnus Butzel was president of the Library Commission.* Born in Bavaria, he went to Detroit where he established a wholesale clothing business in which he was highly successful. He was elected to the school board in 1881, and in 1883 he was made a member of the Library Commission to fill a vacancy created by the resignation of Dr. Kiefer. At a meeting of the Commission on July 6, 1893, Butzel announced that a joint convention of the International Library Congress and the American Library Association would be held in Chicago July 12–22. He urged his fellow commissioners to attend, and he and Utley went to the meeting. Chicago had a branch system in operation at that time and Butzel took advantage of the opportunity to study it first hand. He was impressed by what Chicago was doing and went home convinced that Detroit should move along similar lines.[1] He stated in his report for 1893:

> During my visit to Chicago last summer, I was favorably impressed with . . . the system of branch libraries, or delivery stations, in use in that city. I have no hesitancy in commending the system as there managed.

Chicago, he continued, had thirty-six branches, although the term "branch" as he employed it was not what modern library users understand it to be. Actually, the Chicago branches were more properly delivery stations at convenient locations in outly-

---

* Magnus Butzel was born January 14, 1830, and died in Detroit January 17, 1900.

ing neighborhoods where books drawn out of the central library could be ordered, picked up and returned. That was what Butzel had in mind for Detroit, as other statements in his report indicate.

> The plan was explained to me by Mr. F. H. Hild, the courteous librarian. Select in a convenient location some candy, book or drugstore, the proprietor of which in view of drawing customers to his shop and the small compensation, would gladly furnish bonds and act as sub-librarian.

The applicant for a book, visiting one of these stations, would fill out a call slip which was sent to the main library where the order was filled, and the book sent to the station where the patron picked it up and to which he returned it. "This simple and inexpensive system brings the advantages of the Public Library close to the door of every citizen. I earnestly advocate the establishment of such branches in this city where needed," he concluded.[2]

Utley was quite familiar with the delivery station system, but he was less enthusiastic about its possibilities than Butzel. As a matter of fact, Utley had made a survey of delivery stations in half a dozen cities as early as 1891. These included Chicago, Boston (which also had a couple of regular branches), Milwaukee, Newark and Minneapolis. Perhaps it was the replies he received in answer to his questionnaire which disillusioned him and made him cautious about recommending a similar system for Detroit. The *News-Tribune,* probably in follow-up to Butzel's report, asked Utley's opinion. He replied that he believed it would only be a matter of time before "sub-distributing" stations would have to be established in Detroit, although he did not look for such a development in the very near future. His coolness toward the project stemmed from the fear that it would tend to lower the standard of reading matter. Said the *News-Tribune:*

> He thought that the central library would be flooded with applications from the sub-stations for the poorer class of novels. He said that the person who got the most good from the Library was the person who came in contact with all its departments—reading room, reference room, etc.—and also with the attendants. If a person calls for a certain book at the Library now and cannot obtain it, the attendant will suggest another book. . . .

Mr. Utley did not offer any of these ideas as arguments against the establishment of sub-stations, but only to put people on their guard against expecting too much from them. He feels that a library serves the best ends when it is educative, not when it is merely a distributor of volumes called for.[3]

For the time being, then, the matter was dropped. But not for long. Others appreciated the problem as much as the Commission. In 1896 Hazen S. Pingree, one of Detroit's most progressive mayors, mentioned the branch library need in his annual message. He advocated two real branches—one on the east side and one on the west side of the city. The Commission, in its report for 1896, took notice of Pingree's recommendation and attempted to analyze the situation.

Branch libraries are unquestionably desirable, and when the time comes that the city authorities feel that the cost of establishing and maintaining them can be well afforded, the Commission will be sure to exercise its best judgment in selecting books therefor and in equipping such branches on a scale suitable for their economical management. At the same time, it must be confessed that there is considerable expense involved. If any are established, manifestly two will not be sufficient. . . . No branch could be placed in either the east or the west end which would so well accommodate the residents of those extreme portions of the city as does the central library. The only solution . . . would be the establishment of two branches on or near main thoroughfares in the east end, a like number in the west end, and also one some distance out Woodward Avenue. This makes five branches which would appear to be necessary, if any are to be provided, since it would be hardly fair to favor the residents of one extremity of the city to the exclusion of all others. Such branches would be very useful and would, without doubt, be highly appreciated and well patronized.[4]

Sometime later, shortly after the first branches had been opened, the Commission ordered a survey to be taken to determine whether patrons of the Centre Library paid carfare for the sole purpose of going to the Library, or whether other errands took them downtown. The results showed that only 10 per cent of the patrons paid carfare expressly to visit the building.[5] This confirmed what should have been fairly obvious. The only question at the moment was whether the emphasis should be on true branches or on delivery stations.

157

Despite all the talk about delivery stations little was done to establish them. In 1898 employees of the Detroit post office tried to organize a library for their own use. Although they asked the Public Library to make it a delivery station, no action resulted. Then, in 1899, the Library adopted a plan for supplying books to the city's fire houses. This plan worked satisfactorily for several years, eliciting from Captain Roderick Morrison, of the Fire Boat *Detroiter,* the acknowledgment that "your kindness will long be remembered by this company." In 1899 Commissioner Maynard D. Follin included in his report the observation that delivery stations were "most useful adjuncts of a library." He pointed out that Detroit was the only major city that did not have any, a condition he regarded as regrettable because "the expense of maintaining them is very slight, and the number of books thus circulated is enormous." His suggestion that something be done was referred to the book committee where it languished.[6]

The Library got its first branch in 1897, when the Detroit Water Commission set aside a building in Water Works Park to be used for library purposes.* This structure was made possible by a bequest of Chauncey Hurlbut. Hurlbut, who died in 1885, had for many years been a member of the Water Board, and its president for twelve years. His estate was left to the Water Board to beautify the pumping station grounds—the result being Water Works Park—and to establish a library intended primarily to house his own collection of engineering and scientific books. Under arrangement with the Library Commission, the latter agreed to "recognize the Hurlbut Library as a branch of the Public Library and supply through it such books as may be asked for there."

This accommodation did not work out well at all. The Water Board employees who served as librarians were not skilled in that profession, and much public criticism was heard. Disgruntled patrons failed to note the distinction in jurisdiction and, thinking

---

* The Hurlbut library building was constructed originally as a storage tank. Library Commission President Richard Storrs Willis, in his annual report for 1899, states that the building was erected expressly for library purposes by the Board of Water Commissioners. Apparently he was in error.

that all libraries were part of the Public Library, blamed the Commission for the Hurlbut deficiencies. Actually, the Water Works station, servicing an area limited by its waterfront boundary, was not well situated to attract many patrons and in 1899, the Library Commission complained that "no work was being done at the Water Works branch, except the regular drawing of salaries."

In 1905 the Water Board decided to stick to the business of pumping water and turned the operation of the branch over to the Library Commission which proceeded to staff it with its own people and stock it with its own books. From that time on, it was a "full" branch.[7] It continued as such, except when it was temporarily closed during the depression, until it was abandoned during World War II when Water Works Park was closed to the public as a security measure.

In 1901 a small branch was set up temporarily during the summer season on Belle Isle, the quarters being provided in one of the Parks Departments' administrative buildings.

Unlike most other large cities whose branch systems had their beginnings with delivery stations, Detroit moved directly into true branches without going through the intermediate step.

The Detroit Public Library's original branches were in the city's high schools, beginning with the establishment of the first one in old Central High School, now the Old Main of Wayne State University. After the destruction by fire of the Capitol High School in 1893, temporary quarters were taken in the Biddle House, a hotel, on Jefferson Avenue, just east of Woodward. A new site was selected for a permanent school on Cass, between Warren, Hancock and Second. This was completed and occupied in 1896. Meanwhile, the Board of Education was going ahead with plans for two more high schools, one on the east side at Grand Boulevard at Mack, and another on the west side at Scotten near Porter. These became known as Eastern and Western high schools. While completing the former, classes were held in the Harris School at Pulford and Ellery avenues.

These schools, strategically located, suggested the possibility of branches to the Library Commission. In 1899 the book committee approached the Board of Education and asked that a

159

room in Central High be set aside for a public library branch. The Board was receptive, and the committee reported in October that a room probably could be made available at an early date. It would be necessary, the Commission was told, "to put in a small stock of books, as well as to appoint some one from our Library as superintendent." [8]

Either late in 1899 or early 1900, members of the Commission visited the school and selected Room 18 as the most suitable for their purposes. This room was in the basement, which in reality was at ground level, fronting on Warren Avenue. Some remodeling was necessary, and a window was made into a door, providing public entrance from Warren without entering any other part of the building. This work, together with the necessary shelving and furniture, cost $250. The room was rent free, and janitor service, light and heat were provided without cost to the Library by the Board of Education.[9] Upon recommendation of Utley, Miss Mary Myler,* a veteran of the Library staff, was named the first branch librarian at a salary of $60 a month. The Central High School installation was officially designated Branch No. 1.[10]

The formal opening was held on Monday evening, April 2, 1900, with suitable refreshments and floral displays, for which Utley was authorized to spend not more than $50. The entire branch operation at that particular time was made possible by a special $10,000 appropriation made in 1899 by the Common Council and the Board of Estimates to compensate the Library Commission for loss of Police Court fines. Said the Commission:

> Being thus assured of adequate financial support, the Board has been planning measures for bringing the Library much closer to the people than ever before. . . . Branch libraries are considered essential.[11]

Within two weeks, on April 16, 1900, Branch No. 2 in the Harris School was opened. In charge was Adolph Gronkowski who joined the system as a page in 1894 and was made a regular assistant the following year. The Harris School was used as

---

* Mary Jane Myler (1867–1952) became a member of the Library staff in 1889 and retired in 1919.

temporary quarters for Eastern High School until that building was completed and occupied in 1901. But the branch library did not move, remaining in the Harris School until March 1, 1903, when a more suitable location was obtained by renting a store building at 887 Gratiot near the corner of McDougall. Opening of Branch No. 3, which had to await completion of the new Western High School, was on October 25, 1900. It was under the supervision of Miss Bessie Brow, a member of the staff since 1894.

"Branch One has the most attractive room," stated the 1902 annual report.

> It has been made still more attractive by the pictures which friends have placed on its walls. McClure, Phillips & Co., of New York, have loaned the branch for exhibition the original drawings illustrating 'Emma Lou', by C. L. Hinton; 'Madness of Philip', by F. Y. Cory; 'Indian Boyhood', by Blumenschein; also a page of manuscript of 'The Hound of the Baskervilles', with portraits of Dr. Doyle and Dr. Bell, the prototype of Sherlock Holmes. These illustrations have been a source of continued interest and pleasure to those who visit the branch.[12]

Branch No. 2 was a makeshift affair, and the Commission was never entirely happy with it. It was described as the least attractive. The room, in the basement, was small and dingy. "The books of this branch are on the same shelves with the school library . . . and the reference use of the books is indiscriminate." This arrangement placed public patrons, as distinct from school children, at a disadvantage. Branch No. 1 had a complement of 1733 books soon after it opened, while Branches 2 and 3 had about 2200 each. While these may have been comparatively small collections, they were well read. In 1903 Utley reported that

> we are beginning to see the effect of the establishment of branches upon the circulation of the main library. It seems certain that the people who patronize the branches are not wholly new patrons— although a very large proportion of them undoubtedly are—but that many who have previously drawn books from the main library are now going to the branches. This is indicated by the decrease of the home circulation from the main library. This decrease is the most marked in the children's department, where the circulation has run down from 84,633 in 1900 to 66,584 in 1903. The fact appears to be that the children who live remote from the main library have

161

transferred their patronage to the branches nearer their homes. It is a matter for congratulation, and not regret, that this is so. Certainly, it is well that children should be able to get books near their homes instead of going for them long distances to the center of the city.[13]

The commissioners could not see the branches as centers for the dissemination of frivolous reading matter. While plans were being formulated for the Central High School branch, Commissioner Scripps suggested that "the books for the branch should be only standard works of permanent value, since those of ephemeral interest can always be obtained at the Central Library." His feeling on the matter was heartily indorsed by his fellow members.

In anticipation of the establishment of branches, the Commission set up a new branch department on October 19, 1899, and shortly thereafter Jessie C. Chase * was appointed superintendent of branches, a position she held for twenty-one years. She had been a member of the Library staff since 1892 when she was appointed temporary assistant.

The number of books each branch shelved was not a good criterion of the reading matter available. Books could be ordered from the Main Library, and were delivered promptly by an efficient express service. Users' cards were issued only at the Main Library, but applications for them could be made at any of the branches. A record of card holders in its general area was kept at each branch for convenience in sending out delinquent or other notices. It was not long before each branch had its own card catalog of books assigned to it, all of which were duplicates of volumes at the Main Library. Branch No. 1 was open from 10 A.M. until 6 P.M. daily; the others were open from 10 A.M. to 9 or 10 P.M.

The branch libraries proved to be so popular with the public that before long petitions were being received by the Commission from residents in various sections of Detroit, asking that branches be opened in their neighborhoods. Members of the Commission

---

* Jessie Clara Chase was born in Cleveland, January 15, 1857. A graduate of Wells College, she became a permanent member of the Library staff in 1893. In 1920 she stepped down as chief of branches and served as a reader's aide until her retirement August 1, 1938. She died November 18, 1952, but not until after a branch, named in her honor was dedicated July 24, 1952, at 17731 West Seven Mile Road.

were eager to meet these community requests, although a lack of funds prevented as rapid a branch expansion program as they wished for. Utley was anxious to set up a branch in the Grand River-Warren Avenue area, and in his 1902 report he stated that one should be opened, finances permitting,

> in the vicinity of the junction of the Fourteenth Avenue and Cross-town lines. The Hancock School is located in this neighborhood, but if suitable quarters are not available in that building, doubtless some place could be found at a small rental which would answer the purpose. This section of the city appears to be best entitled to immediate attention in considering the placing of new branches.[14]

The commissioners would have liked to build branches, and at their January 3, 1903, meeting they voted to acquire five sites, subject to certain provisions. The site first mentioned was one at the southeast corner of East Grand Boulevard and Champlain (now East Lafayette Street). The provisos were that it could be obtained for $10,000 and that "the Board of Estimates approves the issue of bonds for the purpose." Another $10,000 site was at Gratiot and Pulford; a third at the northwest corner of Woodward and Bethune had been offered by Bothrop & Duffield Land Co., Ltd., for $13,500 which was considered a reasonable price. Selection of sites for western and northwestern branches was deferred. Although none of these sites was actually acquired, the discussion reveals the desire of the Commission to establish a pattern of branches dotting the city.[15] So much attention was being given the subject by the Commission at this time that it was proposed to set up a standing committee on branches. After deliberation, however, it was decided to leave responsibility for branches in the hands of the Committee on Administration.[16]

The branch program, in its first years, did not grow as rapidly as the Commission wanted it to, and other means of getting books to the public were tried. One such plan, discussed even before the first high school branches were opened, was a home delivery service by messenger. The Commission was attracted to this idea in 1897 when it was learned that a similar plan was being carried on by the Mercantile Library of New York. Patrons of that library purchased special stamps, costing 10 cents each which, attached to a request for a book, resulted in the book being delivered by messenger at the patron's door. A request for further information brought a reply from the Mercantile librarian which stated that the service cost considerably more than was received. While it probably increased the use of the library to some people, W. T. Peoples, the Mercantile librarian, said he was "not prepared to recommend the system to a free public library." On the basis of that report, the Commission decided not to inaugurate such a plan at that time.[17]

The matter was allowed to rest until 1899 when Commissioner Maynard D. Follin revived it, and on June 4, the system was begun. According to the president's report for that year:

> A book ordered by telephone or otherwise is sent immediately by messenger. A contract with a messenger service company provides that a boy shall be sent on call. He collects a fee of 10 cents and will at the same time return a book to the Library without charge. Thus for the cost of carfare one may have a Library book delivered at his door and another returned to the Library, with no exertion or loss of time to himself. This service does not appear to be very widely appreciated as yet, but it doubtless will be later on.[18]

That was an expectation that did not materialize, despite efforts to make the service more effective.

In 1901 Charles D. Bennett, of Automobile Service Company, offered to take over the delivery system on a contract basis, and on terms which would have added a touch of elegance and grandeur. He offered "to equip . . . ten stylish automobiles, supplying the same with uniformed attendants, properly wrap, address and handle the books at the Library and deliver the same in any part of the city at 3 cents per copy on a basis of 500,000 a year. . . ." Although this was the first official recognition that the Library had entered the automobile age, Bennett's proposal was too grandiose. The demand for the service never even remotely approached the 500,000 book figure. In fact, the delivery service came to an end in 1901, after the Commission sadly reported that while the service had been thoroughly advertised,

> experience has shown that there is practically no demand for such service. Books are still sent out by messenger when so ordered, but the fact that the fees collected during the past year amounted to $1.20 indicates that there is no general call for book delivery.[19]

The failure of such schemes helped convince the Commission that its best hope of reaching more readers was through branches. The high school libraries were proving their worth, but while the members of the Commission congratulated themselves on the system's success, they also were confronted by new problems. First of these was the need of the schools for the space occupied by the public libraries for classroom purposes; the second was that growing public use made the school library rooms too crowded. The result was that between 1903 and 1910, the Commission, still lacking sufficient funds with which to construct buildings, opened five branches in rented stores. The first of these was a location on Gratiot near McDougall to house Branch No. 2. When the new Eastern High School was completed, Branch No. 2 did not follow it into the new building but remained behind at its original site in the Harris School which proved totally inadequate. On March 5, 1903, Commissioner George Osius,* president of the Detroit Ammonia Works and a leader in Detroit's east side German community, recommended the removal of Branch No. 2 to the Gratiot Avenue store. The building, he said, was new and in fairly satisfactory condition. Moreover, he added, "the rent is $20 per month, which is very reasonable." [20]

When it became evident that vacant stores could be used as branches, the Commission was deluged with offers by property owners anxious to obtain tenants. Knowing of the commissioners' desire for a location on Grand River, an offer was made in 1903 to sell two lots to the Library at Sixteenth and Warren. Without money to build, however, the proposition was turned down. This was followed by an offer of a land owner to erect a suitable building at the southeast corner of Grand River and Hancock, to be leased upon terms to be negotiated. Nothing came of that proposal either. Instead, in December 1903, Utley reported he had found a store suitable for a branch on Grand River between Twelfth and Thirteenth, near Calumet, and in the neighborhood of the

---

* George Osius (1859–1941) was born at Bercastel, Germany, and came to the United States in 1878. For several years he was in the book and publishing business at Ann Arbor before going to Detroit in 1887. He took an active part in civic affairs, being a director of the Detroit Community Fund and a trustee of the Detroit Symphony Society. He made his home in Grosse Pointe Shores, of which he was mayor from 1911 to 1928.

165

Dickinson School. "The neighborhood is a good one," Utley said, "and quite thickly populated. The rental is $14 per month and the owner promises to put the place in good condition." About the same time, a building formerly occupied by a drugstore on Field at Agnes was also rented. It was described as "pleasant and convenient." In March, 1904, both of these buildings were opened as branches, that on Field being designated Branch No. 4, and the one on Grand River as No. 5.[21]

Also in December, 1903, the Committee on Administration reported that it had been investigating the possibility of moving Branch No. 1 from Central High to a new location on Woodward north of the railroad viaduct. "No suitable vacant store or building has been found, but we have received the following proposition. . . ."

The proposition referred to was an offer made by George A. Ducharme to build and lease to the Library a store 20 by 100 feet "on a rental basis of 6 per cent per annum exclusive of taxes and insurance, the land to be taken at a valuation of $200 per foot." This came out to between $40 and $45 per month. It was an excellent location, in the block between Grand Boulevard and Milwaukee, and was served by the Woodward streetcars. It was close to a growing residential area, and was within walking distance of several elementary schools. In the same block was the Northend Post Office and a bank. In the block south, Hook's notions store eventually became Demery's department store. The offer was too good to turn down, and in March, 1905, Mary Myler packed her books and moved out of Central High School and into her new library home.[22]

In 1907, Branch No. 3 had to give up its space in Western High School. A new store location was found for it on Dix near Clark. That was in February, and in September Branch No. 8 was opened in a store adjoining a butcher shop on West End Avenue, just off Jefferson. Designed to serve the Delray district, it was moved around the corner to 2327 West Jefferson in 1910 when the butcher shop flies got to be more than the library users and staff could tolerate. In October, 1908, Branch No. 6 was established in a store on the south side of Michigan near Thirty-first Street. With the Hurlbut branch under Library jurisdiction by this time, the first phase of the real branch system was completed and in full operation.[23]

While they were the best the Library had to offer at the time, and while their usefulness cannot be denied, the store branches still left much to be desired. Rented quarters in buildings originally intended for commercial purposes were not ideally suited for the storage of books or to accommodate large numbers of people. One of the best things that could be said about them was that they permitted a low-cost test of public acceptance in a given area before making a large investment for a permanent branch building. Beyond that, the good they accomplished was equally attributable to branches in general. Not all of the troubles encountered could be blamed entirely on the fact that stores were used. Nature played its dirty tricks, as the Commission noted on April 18, 1907.

> The year opened rather disastrously, with Branch 1 for the victim. The violent wind storm of January, blew in the transoms, carried enough icy breath to kill the plants so carefully tended by Miss Myler, and which so added to the attractiveness of the room. A few days later, this Branch was deluged by water from the flat above which left ruined books, discolored walls and a librarian with lacerated feelings.[24]

The stores, plagued by acts of God and unpredicted disaster, had inherent drawbacks as library rooms. They were badly lighted, ill-ventilated, incapable of expansion. The Gratiot branch was described as "a sorry commentary on the sense of justice of a municipality which not only permits but compels its citizens to endure such discomforts and unwholesome conditions." The Dix Avenue branch was said to be a "ramshackle old wooden building." While it was better than the Gratiot branch, it still came "perilously near being a joke." The Commission marvelled that so much business was carried on with conditions in the stores as bad as they were.[25]

The hope had prevailed for some time that not only would a new main library be built, but that the Commission would be able to construct its own branches. Contemplating either or both developments, a question arose in the mind of Scripps as to the Commission's legal power to purchase and hold land for such purposes. At the Board meeting on January 17, 1901, he submitted a note in which he suggested

> a careful examination of the legal question of the powers of the Library Board in view of the contemplated purchase of real estate and erection of a new building; also the employment of some suitable person to prepare a bill and attend to getting it through the legislature.

No action was taken until late in the year when there was fresh discussion about purchasing a site to replace Branch 2 in the Harris School. The matter was referred to the corporation counsel who reported that funds originally intended for enlargement of the Centre Library, but since set aside as a new building fund, could not be used to purchase a site for a branch.

Several months later, in the light of subsequent legislation, Corporation Counsel Timothy E. Tarsney revised his original opinion and stated that the Commission could use the money for any purpose.[26] However, his first ruling awakened the Commission to the need for legislation along the lines of Scripps's thinking. An act, therefore, was obtained which incorporated the Library Commission and gave it the right to hold and maintain property in its own name, and to condemn property for its uses. This was further supplemented in 1905 by legislative action which provided that all annual estimates, in detail, had to be submitted to and approved by the Board of Estimates and the Common Council. The latter then was required to appropriate as part of the general tax, the amounts approved. These funds, plus other revenues including penal fines, could not be less than an amount equal to one-fifth mill on the city's assessed valuation. This meant that the Library was no longer limited to living within the strict confines of five mills.[27]

Armed with these powers, and confronted with the urgent necessity for improving conditions at Branch No. 4 on Field Avenue, the Commission was in position in 1905 to take action. It was done without resorting to a special or increased appropriation, because of a dividend which was paid by the receiver of the defunct City Savings Bank. With that windfall, a lot was purchased at 285 Field, directly across the street from the rented store building. With additional money on hand, most of it from the City Savings Bank, the first specially built and wholly owned branch was officially opened on the evening of November 22, 1906, with "a large attendance and interesting addresses." Osius, president of the Board in 1906, reported that the people of the neighborhood were highly pleased with the building, and he expressed hope "that the example of a branch library in its own building will quickly spread to other sections of the city." To make the occasion more festive, Commissioner Philip Breitmeyer of the Department of Parks and Boulevards sent over a drayload of flowers and plants from his Belle Isle conservatory and Osius presented a bust of Shakespeare. The entire cost, including site and furnishings was $13,242.51. It was described as handsomely, but not extravagantly furnished.

> The Library occupies the whole of the main floor except the private office of the librarian. There is a corridor from the main entrance to the delivery desk. A turnstile entrance upon the right opens into the children's department and upon the left into the adult department. The book shelves are along the walls, the windows extending from the top of the cases to the ceiling. . . . In the basement is a pleasant lecture room, with a seating capacity for 250. This has an outside entrance independent of the Library.[28]

The building was constructed of brick and stone. The masonry and stone contractor was E. S. Piggins, who within a few years would become a member of the Commission.*

The second Commission-owned branch was acquired partly by gift. In 1905, just as he was about to retire as president of the Commission, James E. Scripps donated fifteen lots on Grand River between Trumbull and Commonwealth to the City of Detroit. He specified that the land was to be a park, and that a parcel of 4000 feet was to be reserved for a library building. Scripps died May 29, 1906, leaving a bequest of $50,000 for beautifying the city. Meanwhile, a part of the Grand River property had been selected by the Commission as a branch site, and a deed to the ground was given to the Library by the city.

---

* The building, enlarged in 1913, is still in use. Street numbering changes now locate it at 1117 Field.

In 1907 the Common Council, at the Commission's request, appropriated $14,000 to construct a branch building.

The money, however, was not used for that purpose. The residence of George G. Booth, Scripps's son-in-law, adjoined the donated property. He gave that fine manor-house type structure to be used as the branch, and as a trustee of the estate pledged the $50,000 for upkeep of what became known as Scripps Park which included the Library grounds. The $14,000 was then applied to remodeling the Booth premises which, it was stated, were suitable, both externally and internally, for Library purposes. An extension was added, providing not only a book and delivery room, but also a children's room and a reference room. The second floor was converted into a large auditorium and several small club rooms. The actual remodeling began in the summer of 1908. It was soon found that the costs would be $18,000 instead of $14,000, but the city appropriated the extra amount. All was finished by July 1, 1909, when the Scripps Park branch was formally opened and the store branch at 800 Grand River was abandoned.[29]

To complement the work of the branches in carrying library service directly to the people, a unique and highly successful plan of opening deposit stations in factories and neighborhood settlement houses was inaugurated late in 1905. This plan continued to operate for about twenty-five years. The factory station, or extension service as it came to be called, had its genesis one Sunday afternoon in November, 1905, when Utley addressed a church men's club on the functions and services of the Library. In a general discussion which followed, a Burroughs Adding Machine Company draftsman suggested a closer relationship between the Library and the artisan and skilled worker class. Utley immediately became interested in this idea. After the meeting he discussed it further with the Burroughs man who invited Utley to visit the plant. A few days later he talked to the plant superintendent who expressed a willingness to cooperate in the plan to supply books to the factory. The books were to be placed under the supervision of an officer of the Burroughs' Relief Society in space provided by the company. Each employee desiring a card was issued one, the company acting as his guarantor or surety.

170

This arrangement was approved by the Commission and promptly put into effect. About two hundred books, half of them fiction, were delivered to the factory, and about sixty employees applied for cards.

The initial experiment proved so immediately satisfactory that Utley canvassed other major plants, all of which displayed interest in sharing in the plan. By the end of 1906 other participating firms included the Hamilton Carhart and W. M. Finck companies, overall manufacturers, the Independence Cigar Company, Chicago Pneumatic Tool Company, Cadillac Motor Car Company and Packard Motor Car Company.[30]

It was the Library's policy to select factories "which employ a superior class of skilled labor," and where the employment turnover rate was comparatively low. Declared Utley:

> One establishment found that its employees were so transient and so little inclined to take advantage of the opportunities offered by the Library that after a trial of several months they abandoned the plan.

The overall and cigar factories, predominately employing women, were particularly busy stations. "The working girls read by far more than working men." The Library also could state with satisfaction that in 1907 not a single book circulated through the stations had been "marred or lost."

> Choosing a factory which has a class of employees of fair intelligence and education, there is no difficulty in interesting them in books and giving them all the mental uplift and widened horizon which books must mean to such persons," one report stated. "We know of cases in which factory employees have been able through the opportunities which the Library opened to them to fit themselves for higher grades in their employment or for other work better paid and more desirable.[31]

During 1906 similar stations were set up in the city's various settlement houses. Catering to a foreign-born element, circulation through the settlement houses was largely of foreign language books, particularly Polish and Italian. All of the Library's Yiddish collection was sent to the Jewish Institute on High Street (now East Vernor Highway).

The servicing of these "traveling libraries" required careful

171

supervision with the result that an Extension Department—really a division of the Circulation Department—was created under the direction of Miss Aniela Poray in 1907. This was separate from the Branch Department. Miss Poray's report for 1914, when there were twenty-seven stations in operation, throws light on the operations and problems. That report said, in part:

> Ferry [Seed Company] is like Acme [Paint Company] in the separation of its office and factory forces. The factory is composed largely of young foreign girls who have so far sensed no need of books, either for recreation or information. In order to awaken their interest, the Library has taken the initiative and gone to them. This class of readers needs the Library as a civic and social haven and it is most difficult to reach them. Here as at Acme there is no common meeting place, and owing to the strict rules of the firm, no one is allowed to address the girls while at work.
>
> Franklin St. Settlement decrease (465) is due to two causes—the frequent change of resident workers . . . ; the second—the continuous shifting of the population. Formerly we dealt with 'poor white'—French, German, Irish, not illiterate. The last two years we are facing the population of the Balkan provinces, some of them coming from countries where illiteracy is as high as 80 or 90 per cent. Before they can make use of a library, they must be taught to read some language. . . .
>
> Anyone who has watched men and women hurrying to their homes at the closing time will realize that those people with few exceptions live far from their place of employment. Many of them in the outlying districts are far from any library agencies. Even if the Library were within a few blocks of the factory, comparatively few workingmen or women would patronize it. They go to work early in the morning before any library agency is open, at night they hurry away to their homes, and at noon have no time to change to street dress in order to go to the Library. The location of the Library within one mile of the factory is of little value to the working people.[32]

From this it will be seen that one important value of the factory station was its ability to interest the foreign-born industrial working class in the Library, and to make its facilities available to them. The stations were performing a unique social function in an industrial community.

Other cities had attempted similar endeavors, but they lacked Detroit's success. One reason was that elsewhere the management of the station was assigned to a plant foreman or other employee. In Detroit, on the other hand, the Library maintained control of the station, and a trained staff member was assigned to duty at specified hours—often at lunch time.

From time to time the service was expanded to hospitals, and during World War I to military establishments in the area. A station was opened in 1918 in the Ford Motor Company's Highland Park plant, despite the fact that it was not in the city of Detroit. Said Librarian Adam Strohm in 1914:

> In addition to Library service, we also maintain in two factories, fortnightly illustrated lectures. . . . There is no doubt that it generates a cordial feeling between the Library and the mechanics. . . . If conducted sensibly and conservatively, I believe the station system is justifiable and well worthwhile. The drawback is of course a diffusion of one's resources and energy, and personally, I favor having these stations in those parts of the city where educational facilities or other means of public recreation are of inferior grade or non-existent. Its necessarily sentimental character has a great attraction to some workers, but at best the station is a little superficial and preparatory in nature.[33]

In 1914 the Extension Department was renamed Stations Department. Then in 1920 the Branch and Stations departments were merged into a single unit known as the Extension Department.

In 1931, the factory stations were closed as a retrenchment measure. They never re-opened, but while they existed they served their purpose, sometimes, as in the case of the store branches, doing the pioneering work in advance of the permanent branches. By 1909, the branch circulation of 364,048 books exceeded that of the central Library with 363,248. At the end of that year, the Detroit Public Library was operating, in addition to its downtown main center, five store branches, three permanent branches, one delivery station and eleven factory and settlement house extension stations. Traveling libraries, primarily for the use of children, serviced the city's playgrounds under a policy begun in 1905.[34]

Thus, by 1910, the branch system was firmly established in Detroit. Although it still was inadequate to the needs of a growing, dynamic community, within the year there would be new developments which would mark the beginning of an era of extraordinary Library advance.

CHAPTER 11

"BLOOD MONEY"

FROM ABOUT 1890 to about 1910, the Detroit Public Library system failed to keep pace with the city's growth and expansion. There were several reasons for this: they can be found in a fairly low order of politics, lack of financial support and public apathy —or at least apathy on the part of that segment of the public which should have but did not assume responsibility for leadership and financial assistance. The fault was not in the Commission. It did what it could within the means allotted; it provided a sound administration, and it resorted to many innovations which, while constructive and useful, sometimes fell short of the mark. The truth was that Detroit had become a big city.

The Library, with certain notable exceptions, remained a small-town institution, basically not much different in 1910 than it had been in 1880. From the beginning it had been the hope of the Commission that one or more wealthy Detroiters, whose number was increasing, would step forward and provide the means for a new main building and sufficient branches to serve the city's neighborhoods. With the single exception of the Scripps gift, it

174

was a vain hope. Detroiters found other ways to dispose of their fortunes in the public interest, or else they kept their pocketbooks tightly shut. Beyond the donation of a few books, some of them valuable to be sure, affluent citizens ignored the needs of the Library.

It was not until 1910 that assistance from a private source proved to be the salvation of the Library and gave it modern status. Even then, there was a span of nearly ten years between offer and acceptance. During that decade Detroit may have established some sort of record for resistance to philanthropy.

When help came, it was not from anyone whose interests were closely entwined with those of the city. It came, rather, from a Scots immigrant, who amassed one of the nation's greatest fortunes in the railroad and steel industries, and having done so, used his money to express his social philosophy. He was Andrew Carnegie, steelmaster.

Andrew Carnegie was born in Dumferline, Scotland, on November 25, 1835. His father was a weaver, and the family was a humble one. The industrial revolution was changing the old order so fast that many of the workers could not keep up with it, the result being that many families, the Carnegies among them, found themselves in dire straits. Economic distress led to the formation of radical movements, and Dumferline, hard hit by the shift from cottage weaving to steam powered mills, was a center for some of these movements. Carnegie's father and his uncles were leaders, and frequently found themselves in trouble. Out of this background emerged Andrew Carnegie's social conscience.

With nothing but a bleak future ahead of them in Scotland, the Carnegies packed up in 1848 and moved to the United States, settling at Allegheny, Pennsylvania. There young Andrew worked as a bobbin boy in a cotton mill. Although he was exposed to very little formal education, fondness for literature was bred into him by his father, and he was an avid reader and lover of books. Ambition spurred him on, and when he was a little older he found employment with the Pennsylvania Railroad as a clerk and telegraph operator. His natural ability would not be denied; before long he was the right-hand man to T. A. Scott, head of the railroad. He was as frugal in these early years as any Scot is expected to be. He made sound investments, and, foreseeing the future of the steel industry as the United States grew after the Civil War, he bought into steel mills which he consolidated into the Homestead works. By 1888 he qualified as a real tycoon, the kind the cartoonists delighted in depicting: paunchy, top-hatted and frock-coated, with the dollar sign inscribed on his vest and his heel on the neck of prostrate Labor.

Carnegie was depicted in this fashion as the result of the bloody Homestead riots of 1892. While he had expressed views sympathetic to labor, when a strike occurred at his mills his managers brought in strikebreakers. A small-scale war erupted in which several men on both sides were shot down. Carnegie was in Europe at the time, and it has never been clearly established how much of the responsibility was his. Certainly he deplored what happened, and there have been those who claimed that had Carnegie been on the scene, strikebreakers would not have been recruited and the worst trouble would have been averted. Nevertheless, the odium stuck to the steel king. The gunfire at Homestead was to reverberate years later in Detroit, and for a while it looked as though the Detroit Public Library might be another casualty of the Homestead riots.[1]

In 1901 Carnegie sold his steel holdings to a combine organized by J. P. Morgan. Out of it grew the United States Steel Corporation. Carnegie retired from active business with a Morgan & Company check for $300,000,000. Many years before that, however, Carnegie had embarked on a course of distributing his wealth through a series of philanthropical enterprises. These were based upon his philosophy that great wealth is given to an individual only to hold in trust for humanity. Carnegie once stated:

> To one to whom surplus comes, there come also the questions: What is my duty? What is the best use that can be made of it? The conclusion forced upon me, and which I retain, is this: That surplus wealth is a sacred trust, to be administered during life by its possessor for the best good of his fellow men.[2]

A corollary to this social expression was Carnegie's principle that philanthropy should not be charity but an investment in human resources. Money should only be given in such a way as to

176

enable those seeking their betterment to take advantage of the opportunities provided. He said:

> What we must seek, then, for surplus wealth, if we are to work genuine good, are uses which give nothing for nothing, which require cooperation, self-help, and which by no possibility can tend to sap the spirit of manly independence which is the only sure foundation upon which the steady improvement of our race can be built.[3]

Educational assistance seemed to Carnegie to fit this formula satisfactorily, and of all means of education none appeared to him more beneficial than libraries. As a result, establishment of new libraries and aid to existing ones became major objects of his generosity. The first one to which he contributed in 1886 was in his home town of Allegheny. Eventually, he contributed to 3000 of them all over the world, his total gifts for this purpose amounting to almost $60,000,000. He explained:

> We were soon led to see in the free library an institution which fulfilled these conditions [as expressed above], and which must work only for good and never for evil. . . . A free library occupies the first place, provided the community will accept and maintain it as a public institution, as much a part of the city property as its public schools, and, indeed, an adjunct to these.[4]

That latter statement came very close to being a rephrasing of the principles upon which the Detroit Public Library was founded. But it also reveals Carnegie's idea that means of self-help were not restricted to the individual; they applied equally to the community. Thus, the Carnegie gifts for public libraries had strings attached. He would not provide anything for the purchase of sites. These had to be supplied by the city, which also had to pledge that once the library was built, it would be maintained at public expense. There was no element of perpetual endowment in the Carnegie gifts.

Up to 1901, Carnegie had given more than $27,000,000 for libraries, and why Detroit had not asked to be placed on his list before that time is a mystery. In the early part of January, 1901, the Commission was principally concerned with how it could get sufficient tax or bond money to build a new main Library. Dr. C.

177

Henri Leonard,* who became president of the Commission in 1901, indicated that he and his colleagues were aware of the Carnegie possibilities, but no overtures were made to the steel king.

"I had the matter in mind," said Leonard, "and had consulted with several parties concerning it; but nothing definite had been done." [5] That statement was made at the end of the year, and may have been something of a second thought on the part of Dr. Leonard. Later, too, it was claimed that Mayor William C. Maybury had formulated a plan to get Carnegie assistance, and that Leonard preferred, for political reasons, to remain in the background and permit Maybury to reap the credit and glory. The *Free Press* concluded that it was better that Leonard and the Commission should take the initiative, however, because "the mayor has a way of entering upon great undertakings with a rush and exhausting his enthusiasm in the preliminaries." [6]

It remained for some outsider, whose identity will probably never be known, to break the ice and make the first approach to Carnegie on Detroit's behalf. That was indicated by the Detroit *Journal* on February 8, in a short paragraph signed by the paper's Washington correspondent, Otto Carmichael. It stated:

> A Washington gentleman, who recently had a conversation with Andrew Carnegie about library affairs, told the *Journal* that he felt certain that Mr. Carnegie would be glad to give a library building to Detroit, if the city cared to assume the necessary obligations.[7]

That was all, but it was enough to set events in motion, and from the minute Carmichael's rather obscure and veiled dispatch appeared in print, Carnegie and the Detroit Library became a joint municipal issue. Reporters called upon Dr. Leonard immediately to get his reaction.

---

* Dr. C. Henri Leonard (1850–1925) was a man of many interests and his life was colorful. Born in Akron, Ohio, he attended Hiram, Genesee and Union colleges. During the post-Civil War reconstruction period he was a newspaper correspondent in the South where, as a Yankee, he had many adventures, some of them harrowing, according to his own account. He studied medicine in Cleveland and Wooster, Ohio, and had graduate work at the College of Physicians and Surgeons, New York. He began practice in Detroit in 1874. The author of several medical books, he was a long-time member of the faculty of the Detroit College of Medicine.

If Mr. Carnegie wants to perpetuate his memory here by giving a library to Detroit, I do not know of anyone who would be more willing to accept it than I would. It would certainly be a fine thing for us; we'd get a beautiful building, and all we would have to do would be to keep it up.

Don't think that I'd be in favor of asking Mr. Carnegie to do it on the strength of this report. But if that statement could be run down to hard fact, then I certainly would be in favor of trying to get a definite proposition.[8]

In the margin of his scrapbook, alongside a clipping from the *Journal* containing this interview, Leonard wrote: "First crystallization of the Carnegie movement." [9]

Leonard then recalled that he consulted various people and he found everyone favorably inclined toward accepting a gift from Carnegie. Oddly enough, however, there was still no direct approach or effort on the part of anyone on the Commission or attached to the city government to learn what Carnegie himself thought of this. From the facts that are available, the next steps were of a somewhat devious nature, giving the strong impression that the Commission, for unclear reasons, was definitely avoiding any application, preliminary or otherwise.

Thus matters stood until about March 1, when Willard G. Sperry, president of Olivet College stopped in Detroit, en route to New York, to talk to Carnegie about assistance for his institution. While in the city, he spent a few hours with George W. Radford, a prominent corporation lawyer and alumnus of Olivet.* Radford was on close personal terms with members of the Library Commission, and was familiar with its problems and hopes. Radford suggested to Sperry that when he had concluded his own business with Carnegie he sound out the latter to see how he felt about doing something for Detroit. On his return, Sperry reported that Carnegie had expressed a willingness to talk to Radford personally on the subject. Radford so informed Commissioner John S. Gray and Leonard. They, in turn, called in Dr. John E. Clark,

---

* George W. Radford, a native of Baldwinsville, N. Y., was born in 1853, and was a member of the Olivet class of 1874 and the University of Michigan Law School class of 1875. It was said that "his clientage represents large moneyed interests." He died at Detroit in 1917.

179

another commissioner, and the proposition was discussed by them. All this, for some unknown reason, was done outside of the Commission, and apparently without the immediate knowledge of the other commissioners.

Leonard then goes on to state that while the matter was "carefully canvassed," there "was much doubt as to its successful issue." [10]

Why the secrecy? Why should there be any doubt about Carnegie listening to Radford's request on behalf of Detroit, particularly when he had given assurance that he would welcome a visit from Radford? Why was the Commission not made privy to what was going on? There are no satisfactory answers to these questions. The *Free Press* later commended the Commission for its secrecy, declaring that overtures to Carnegie "seemed too much like a begging expedition to set out with such a blare of trumpets and to rejoice over the chickens even before the fresh eggs had been provided for." [11] Nevertheless, for the moment, the air of conspiracy was maintained, and Radford was sent off on his mission on March 12, his expenses being privately paid by Leonard, Gray and Clark. If ever there was a secret emissary, it was George Radford on that occasion. [12] The other commissioners, Follin, Scripps and Osius, and the ex officio member of the Commission, Edward P. Marschner, president of the school Board, must have known what was going on, but there is no record to prove it.

Radford arrived in New York late on the 13th, bearing a letter of introduction to Carnegie, signed by Leonard, Gray and Clark. It said:

> Mr. George Radford of Detroit, the bearer of this, represents citizens of Detroit in the interest of the Public Library. Anything he may present to you in connection therewith will also meet with the hearty approval of our Board of Library Commissioners. [13]

Rushing to the Carnegie residence on 51st Street, Radford found everything in a state of confusion. Boxes and trunks were piled on the sidewalk and in the foyer, waiting a drayman to haul them to the pier from which Carnegie was sailing that same evening for a holiday at Skibo Castle, his estate in Scotland. At first Radford could not get past the front door. Carnegie was too busy to see him, he was told, and further, no more gifts would be made by Carnegie until his return in October. Radford, however, was not to be denied. He literally pushed his way into the great man's presence where he found Carnegie's manner not reassuring. He reiterated his intention to do nothing more before October. Radford pointed out the dangers in such a delay. The legislature, then in session, met only biennially and would adjourn in June, he said. If enabling legislation should be necessary, it should be framed at once, otherwise nothing could be accomplished for two years.

"Did it ever occur to you, Mr. Carnegie," Radford said, "that the mines of the state of Michigan are the foundation of your splendid fortune?" [14]

That pleased Carnegie, Radford recalled. The interview lasted less than twenty minutes, but when it ended Radford had the satisfaction of seeing the memo he had presented go into the case of papers which were being taken to Scotland.

The next day Radford notified Leonard that he had talked to Carnegie, and that he had been referred to the latter's secretary, James Bertram, with whom he had an interview scheduled for March 15. Radford reported the impressions he had gained from his brief talk with Carnegie as follows:

"He is opposed to large central buildings and sites. Is in favor of one central commodious building and branches." [15]

He added a note of caution, urging secrecy while negotiations were underway. On the 16th, following his talk with Bertram, Radford again telegraphed Leonard, asking him to "arrange meeting C. [Clark] and G. [Gray] tomorrow sure." [16]

A meeting of the full Commission, or so it would appear, greeted Radford upon his return. He was confident of success, stating that all that was necessary to meet Carnegie's conditions was to have the Library Commission given official corporate standing. A bill seeking financial assistance was already before the legislature, and the required amendments were written and rushed to Lansing where they were tossed into the legislative hopper by Representative William A. Hurst in the House and

James O. Murfin in the Senate. The bill was passed on March 27, and given immediate effect.

Anticipating its passage, Radford had already started for New York, and on the 28th, notified by telegram of the legislature's action, he called upon Bertram with a formal request for a grant, to be forwarded to Carnegie. Accompanied by a covering letter affirming Radford's authority to act on the Commission's behalf, the application, signed by Radford, read:

It is my pleasant privilege, as a citizen of Detroit, and representing the Detroit Library Commission, to ask you to add the metropolis of Michigan to the list of cities already favored with your generous gifts for library buildings.

Detroit is in pressing need of a new central library building, and of at least five branch buildings. The system of branch libraries has been for some time in use here, in connection with the public school buildings, but the demands made thereon have rapidly grown beyond the ability of the Commission to meet them, with present facilities.

At least $1,000,000.00 is now needed for buildings, and $1,500,000.00 is not too much, when the rapid growth of Detroit is considered.

By a recent Act of our State Legislature, The Detroit Library Commission has been created a body corporate, with full power to take and hold by purchase, condemnation, gift, devise or otherwise, all such property as may be necessary for library purposes, to contract for and supervise the construction of library buildings, and also to contract for maintenance thereof.

The Act also provides for a special yearly city library tax. The tax, together with certain fines of the criminal courts, will furnish, by the time the buildings can be erected, sufficient revenue to adequately maintain the entire system of libraries. But in addition to this the Act authorizes the issuance of city bonds, to an amount sufficient to furnish sites for buildings, books and maintenance.

The Detroit Library Commission, you will therefore see, is fully authorized by law to meet all the conditions you imposed in connection with your magnificent gift to Greater New York, i.e., the Commission can furnish the necessary sites, and can agree in satisfactory form to provide for maintenance of the buildings as built.

The question herewith submitted to you is, will you extend aid by generously furnishing the funds for the buildings?

It will be my pleasure to furnish you with such detailed information as you may desire.

This letter is accompanied by the written certificate of approval of the Commission, which is composed of representative professional and business men.

Your reply may be made to me, or to the Commission direct, as

182

you may choose. Trusting that such reply will be favorable, and that again you will aid in extending to the masses the blessing of good books.[17]

On April 1 Radford followed up with another letter, a supplement to that of March 28, containing some statistical information on Detroit's population, present and projected, library finances and similar pertinent data. Then, both Radford and the Commission settled back with what patience they could muster to await the verdict. Transatlantic mail service was slower in 1901, and it was not until July 1 that the postman delivered a plain square envelope, bearing the postmark "Clashmore Station, Bonar Bridge." Tearing it open, Radford found a short but much-to-the-point note, dated June 20, 1901. It stated:

> Yours of March 28 comes before me this morning. If the City of Detroit will furnish proper sites for libraries and agree to spend $75,000 a year in their maintenance, I shall be very glad to provide $750,000 as needed for the buildings. About one-half—not more, I think not so much—of this sum should be expended on the Central library and the remainder on branch libraries. The site for the Central library, however, should be amply sufficient to provide for probable additions in the future, judging from Detroit's horoscope.

It was signed: "Andrew Carnegie." [18]

A week after receipt of the Carnegie offer, the Commission, at a special meeting, took first official notice of Andrew Carnegie and his good works. Up to July 9, 1901, there is not a single mention in the Commission's records of Carnegie or of any negotiations with him. But now the bird was in the hand; the eggs could be counted. Say the proceedings for July 9:

> The President stated the object of the meeting to be the consideration of the offer of Mr. Andrew Carnegie to give $750,000 for public libraries in the city. He then called upon Mr. Radford to make a statement concerning the negotiations with Mr. Carnegie.

Radford reviewed the matter, and presented copies of all the correspondence along with his own recommendation. "Permit me," he said, "to earnestly urge your honorable body to take every necessary step, under the law, to bring to the people of our

183

City, the earliest possible enjoyment of Mr. Carnegie's preferred magnificent gift." Commissioner Gray then introduced a resolution of thanks, and Commissioner Scripps, ever the practical man, followed up with another asking the Common Council to submit to the electors at the next general election, the questions of issuing bonds in the amount of $500,000 "for purposes of complying with conditions imposed by Mr. Carnegie, and to ask the Board of Estimates for authorization and approval of such bond issue." [19]

The newspapers, of course, had the full story in their editions of July 1 and July 2. On July 1, too, the Detroit *Journal* launched an editorial attack on the whole idea, leaving the impression that instead of giving money for library purposes, Carnegie was uncorking a vial of plague germs and scattering them over the city. Radford, declared the *Journal*, had no official standing, he did not speak for the people of Detroit, and in asking outside aid, the city was demeaning itself. Blared the *Journal:*

> The city should not take a dollar. Detroit is neither a mendicant nor a pauper. It does not need Mr. Carnegie's wealth. It did not help to earn it, and it should decline it with the suggestion, made with all courtesy, that the amount be distributed among workmen who made Mr. Carnegie's fortune possible [It added that Detroit needed a library] but there are enough Detroit millionaires to provide one.[20]

The Detroit *Free Press,* more favorably inclined, answered the *Journal* by asking if so many Detroit millionaires were able and willing to provide a library, why hadn't they stepped up and done so.[21] Dr. Leonard declared he had solicited some of Detroit's millionaires, including the *Journal*'s publisher without any success. Other papers were cautious, particularly when organized labor, remembering the Homestead riots, and regarding Carnegie money as tainted with the blood and sweat of the workingman, expressed strong opposition to the whole idea. Many of the municipal politicians followed the labor line. "It strikes me," said Common Council President Jacob J. Haarer, "it would have been better for Carnegie to give some of his money to those workingmen in the steel mills." Councilman Louis E. Tossy announced he would "hotly oppose the acceptance of Carnegie's 'blood money'." C. H. Johnson, secretary of the streetcar union, declared he personally was in favor of accepting the gift, "but the workingmen of this city are not going to do anything of the kind. They will oppose it bitterly." Several prominent Detroiters including business leaders and clergymen expressed themselves as favoring acceptance, but their voices were more or less drowned out by the political screeching.

"We've got the ministers with us," observed Commissioner Clark, somewhat wistfully, "but the fellows we need are the aldermen." [22]

The shrillness of its opposition seemed to make the *Journal* slightly ashamed of itself, and its editors decided that if the Carnegie offer was thumbed down, an alternative should be found. Why not a home delivery service to take the place of branches?

> The cost of a delivery service, such as will deliver the entire library circulation of the city of Detroit, each and every book at a different house, may be estimated in the light of facts . . . to be in the neighborhood of $10,000 a year,

the *Journal* editor pontificated. That would be much more economical than a collection of branches costing a minimum of $50,000 each. The paper was sure of its facts because it had checked delivery costs with the head of the J. L. Hudson Company delivery service. The store had 26 horses and wagons which were maintained and operated at $10,000 a year. With only 14 wagons out, the store had, in one day made 14,000 deliveries. With proper routing, the Library could do as well, and with 13 wagons, making 120 stops per day each, more than 1500 deliveries could be made. That, it was pointed out, would involve only half of the Hudson layout. Recalling the almost total lack of public interest in a messenger service, tried out a couple of years earlier, the commissioners never gave the paper's proposal a moment's serious thought. Neither did the public.[23]

The Commission's only interest at the moment was in meeting as quickly as possible all of the requirements and conditions which would bring the Carnegie cash into Detroit. But instead of money, all they got was opposition and one frustrating delay after another. About the same time that the 1901 bill aiding the Library was passed, the so-called ripper bill was engineered through the legislature by Frank Andrews who, in the moments when he was not politicking, was rapidly leading the City Savings Bank down the road to ruin. One provision of the ripper bill eliminated the 1901 general city election, postponing it until 1902. The Commission opposed passage of the bill and Dr. Leonard later explained that one reason for pressing so hard for adoption of the Library bill was to assure getting a bond authorization on the ballot in 1901. But with the election canceled out, that had to wait until 1902.

One indignant citizen wrote Carnegie:

> The people of Detroit are prevented from the immediate enjoyment of the fine library which you have offered them by the atrocious political scheming of a few legislators who have taken home rule from Detroit. . . . It is shameful to say that Detroit is under the control of Rippers. . . .[24]

As 1901 drew toward a close without any action, Carnegie became a little impatient. He had anticipated a quick response by the Common Council in accepting his offer, and when none was forthcoming by the end of November, he wanted to know why. Radford sped off to New York to tell him exactly what the situation was. Carnegie assumed that the bond vote, whenever it would be held, would be favorable, so he told the Commission that as soon as the Council had adopted a resolution of acceptance, he would advance money for one or two branches, regardless of whether or not the bond money was immediately available.[25]

But the Council, still under pressure from the opposition, would not act on the resolution, or consider bonds without approval by the Board of Estimates. Those gentlemen, too, were subject to such opposition pressure as was applied by the Detroit Trades Council which, in a resolution, pointed out that while

> the shooting of innocent men and the making of widows and orphans at Homestead is still fresh in our memories . . . we request the mayor and other officials interested to assert their manhood and independence by refusing to accept of Andrew Carnegie his offer of unjust gains.

The demagogs were having a field day. Alderman Tossy shouted that Carnegie's money "is soiled with the blood of workingmen."

186

Accepting the gift, added Tossy, wrapping himself in the flag, would be un-American.

Nevertheless, the Commission kept pressing for action, and succeeded in getting a proposition to issue $500,000 of library bonds on the November 4, 1902, ballot. The voters obviously weren't too impressed by the hysterics of Tossy, the labor leaders and the Detroit *Journal,* and voted 7574 to 4730 in favor of the proposal. Now the Commission, having what it regarded as a public mandate, felt more secure and took immediate steps to have the Board of Estimates authorize issuance of the bonds. The Board stalled until December 23, when it reluctantly agreed to the sale, not of a $500,000 issue, but of one for only $150,000. The Commission refused to compromise, with the result that no library bonds were authorized that year. The *Free Press* thought the Board of Estimates had "exceeded its moral powers" when it refused to carry out the expressed will of the people.[27]

Despite the setback, the Commission tried again in 1903, persuading the Council once more to submit to the electorate a proposal to authorize a bond issue, which was rejected at the April 6 election. Major opposition, the commissioners agreed, stemmed from unwillingness to have $75,000 a year pledged for maintenance, and from newspaper feeling that a new central library building should have precedence over branches. Carnegie, then, was sounded out on the possibility of waiving two of his conditions. If he would agree to waive the maintenance require-ment, and allow the city to use his gift without reference to branches, the major difficulties would be eliminated. The reply to this proposal, written by Bertram to Commissioner Sidney T. Miller, was short and to the point. "Mr. Carnegie's letter of offer dated 20th June 1901, is to be read literally," said Bertram. Perhaps because of the failure to obtain the waiver, perhaps for other reasons, the voters this time rejected the bond proposal.[28]

The Commission's next step was to have the city transfer title to the Centre Park property to the Board of Education from whom the Library held it on lease. This, it was believed, would clarify matters, and Carnegie was asked to advance half the pledged money to build a new central library, letting the branches come later.

187

Again Carnegie was adamant. He pointed out that his offer was made, not to the Public Library Commission, but to the city of Detroit. Until the Common Council, as the city's official body, formally accepted his offer with a resolution which contained a maintenance pledge, not a single penny of his money would be released.

"Our Council as a body, can hardly be said to be amenable to an ordinary course of reason," Sidney Miller dolefully reported to Carnegie.[29]

In 1904 the Common Council refused to adopt the necessary resolution of acceptance and some Commission members began to regard the Carnegie offer as a dead issue. This attitude of defeat prevailed in spite of a marked softening of hostility toward the gift, especially on the part of labor. In a letter from Samuel Gompers, president of the American Federation of Labor, the labor leader recommended that Carnegie money be accepted. Gompers wrote in part:

> Inasmuch as Mr. Carnegie seems bent on making grants for libraries in several cities and towns in America, and as there is perhaps no means by which he can be persuaded to devote his wealth to a purpose fraught with better, more important, as well as far-reaching results in the interest of the people, I do not see why we should interfere with carrying out his purpose. After all is said and done, he might put his money to a much worse use.[30]

When all seemed lost as far as the Library was concerned, the canny brotherhood of the Detroit St. Andrew's Society suggested they would be happy to have their fellow Scot build them a new hall and auditorium. Mr. Carnegie was not receptive to the idea.[31]

Nothing more was done about the Carnegie offer during 1905 and 1906, but early in 1907, the issue was revived, partly through the efforts of interested citizens, including the Detroit Board of Commerce. For the third time, the Common Council agreed to put the matter on the ballot, this time in the form of two propositions. One applied to a bond issue authorization, the other to whether or not the Carnegie offer should be accepted by the city of Detroit. At the election on April 1, the bond issue carried by a comfortable margin; the acceptance proposal was defeated by the narrow edge of seventy-seven votes out of a total of nearly 15,000 cast. The defeat may have been the result of bitter-end opposition from the *Journal* which claimed "Detroit has got along without a Carnegie library all these years." But even the *Journal* tirade contained an admission that in the long run the Library cause would triumph.

> But no matter what the verdict of the people may be, no matter how decided they are in their refusal to provide a site at a cost of a quarter of a million and a maintenance fund of $75,000 a year for a mausoleum for the Steel King, Carnegie's admirers will admit no defeat, and the proposition may be expected to be up again at intervals as long as Carnegie lives.

Trying to be satisfied with half a loaf, the Commission, pointing to the favorable bond vote, asked that bonds be issued to allow the Library to proceed with a building program on its own account. That produced a new barrier in the form of an opinion of the corporation counsel to the effect that no Library bonds could be authorized because the city's legal bonding limit had been reached. The Commission raced to Lansing, seeking legislative relief by extending the debt limit for library purposes, but the measure found little support and languished in a Senate committee.[32]

Again nothing was done until 1909, when a determined coalition of the Library Commission and the Board of Commerce decided again to ask—this time to demand—bond approval. It was pointed out that there was always searoom when other city departments wanted a bond issue; the limit only seemed to be reached when the Library asked for something. Early in 1910, a letter was written to Mayor Philip Breitmeyer, asking his support. Breitmeyer was interested, and at his insistence, the corporation counsel wrote a new opinion, reaffirming the Library's power to issue bonds within the debt limit, and pointing out that such power had been conferred by the legislature in 1901, subject to popular approval which twice had been given. It was not necessary, then, to resubmit the proposal to the voters. It only remained for the Common Council to determine whether there was room within the bonding limit. If there was, the bonds could be authorized.

189

The Commission moved immediately with a request to the Council for approval of a $750,000 issue. The Ways and Means Committee, reflecting a changed attitude, was sympathetic. It reported to the Council that the debt limit would not permit so large a bond issue, but that actually there was no need for one. The 1901 Carnegie offer of $750,000 was still in effect. A resolution accepting it and pledging the maintenance fund would close the deal. That would provide an adequate amount of money for building. All that remained to be done was to raise a nominal sum to acquire sites.[33]

Thus, all was done in one swoop on March 22, 1910. The Council vote was 28 to 6 in favor of the resolution. The next day, March 23, Charles Sawyer, secretary to the Board of Commerce, sent off a jubilant telegram to Bertram: "City Council voted last night overwhelmingly in favor of library gift. Actual appropriation for site must pass Council and Board of Estimates to be completed before May 1." [34]

Bertram replied to the formal notification on April 2:

> When we hear that you have sites purchased and paid for, and as they are purchased and paid for, and we see plans which can be approved for a building to be erected complete, ready for occupancy and for the purpose intended within the $375,000 promised, and the same amount for branch libraries, arrangements will be made for payments as work progresses.[35]

There was no stemming the tide now. On April 14, Bertram was informed that the Council had given its sanction to the expenditure of $240,000 for acquisition of a main site and branch sites. It was agreed that bonds would be sold as the property was acquired, and to take care of immediate needs, the first Detroit Public Library bonds, in the amount of $25,000 were issued on July 1, 1910.[36]

The partnership between the Library and Andrew Carnegie had been cemented almost nine years to the day after the philanthropist had made his original offer to Detroit.

CHAPTER 12

BRANCHES, BRANCHES EVERYWHERE

ANDREW CARNEGIE waved his golden wand and branch libraries sprang up all around Detroit soon after 1910. Or at least so it must have seemed to the Library's supporters who had endured a decade of major frustration in getting the Carnegie program launched. It is true that there continued to be frustrations after the program moved into gear, but by comparison they were minor ones, offset by visible, tangible results.

Once the Carnegie offer was officially accepted, and with prospects of it being supplemented by bond money, the Commission moved ahead to obtain sites. At its meeting on May 4, 1910, "the immediate procurement of three sites for branch libraries was considered, and it was agreed that steps in this direction be taken as soon as practicable." It was determined that the most

191

pressing needs were for replacement of Branch 1, in the store at Woodward and Grand Boulevard; for Branch 3, which, having been dispossessed from its original quarters in Western High School, was now housed in a store on Dix near Clark, and for a new branch to serve the West Warren and West Grand Boulevard area. A lot for Branch 3 was found near the store library. It was on the Boulevard at Dix, and was purchased June 8 from Mrs. Sarah E. Lovett for $10,500. A second site on West Warren Avenue at the Boulevard, part of the old Bela Hubbard estate, was obtained for $5430. The idea of moving Branch 1 a couple of blocks north to Bethune was abandoned. Instead, it was decided to go farther out in the heart of the new north end residential district. Land with a frontage of 243 feet, extending the full block between Alger and King avenues, was acquired. Thus the second Carnegie condition was fulfilled. The land was available, local architects were selected—one for each branch—and everything was in readiness to begin construction.[1] Ground was broken for the two buildings on West Grand Boulevard in the spring of 1911, and before the year was over, both were near final stages of completion. The Woodward Avenue branch was contracted for in 1911, but the work did not begin until the spring of 1912. In 1912 the Commission decided to discard its old system of designating branches by number.

Such fine new buildings as were taking shape on architects' drawing boards, the commissioners felt, merited something of greater dignity than a number, and it was resolved to honor the services of outstanding Commission members and librarians by naming branches for them. Thus, Branch No. 1 became officially known as the Henry M. Utley branch; No. 3 (Dix Avenue) became Herbert Bowen branch; No. 4 (Field Avenue), John S. Gray; No. 5 (Scripps Park), James E. Scripps; No. 7, always known as the Hurlbut branch, kept that designation; and No. 10, which in 1912 had not yet been built, was to be named for Magnus Butzel. It would be on East Grand Boulevard at Harper Avenue. For the time being, names were not yet selected for branches, existing and planned for, on Gratiot at Pulford (No. 2); on Martin Avenue (No. 6) and No. 9 (Warren at West Grand Boulevard). However, these soon were named respectively: George S. Hosmer, Edwin F. Conely, and George V. N. Lothrop.[2]

Meanwhile, the Commission discovered that its financial problems had not been solved. The issuance of the first $25,000 of Library bonds—a token amount, really—was challenged, and there was serious doubt, in view of the debt limit situation, that the balance of the approved issue, $215,000 would soon be available. Lack of that money, intended for a new central site and additional branch sites, made it impossible to take advantage of waiting Carnegie funds as rapidly as desired. The Board of Education at this time also was interested in issuing bonds, and the city fathers feared that the schools and the Library, between them, would absorb the city's borrowing cushion. Mayor Breitmeyer voiced the fear that the Library bond issue might be illegal, and this statement effectively killed the market for the sale of the $215,000 issue. The question was taken to court, and a Circuit Court judge ruled that the issue was illegal because it exceeded the debt limitation. The voters were then asked to increase the bond limitation, but in November, 1910, the proposal failed to get the necessary two-thirds majority.

However, the Circuit Court ruling had been carried on appeal to the Michigan Supreme Court which in 1911 held that the right of the city to issue Library bonds to an amount in excess of the limit applying to general purpose bonds was not restricted by the municipal limitation. Library bonds, said the court, fall into the same category as school bonds. The Library, it was held, was a part of the educational system. Inasmuch as the schools' right to borrow had been exempted by the legislature from the restrictions placed on the municipal government, the Library enjoyed the same right. This was an important decision, because it strengthened the Library's position as an agency independent of local governmental control. At the same time, and as a more practical matter, it opened the way to the financing which the Library was then seeking in order to carry out its program of expansion.[3]

Much of the legal work which produced this opinion, as well as the legal preparation in connection with the Carnegie grant, was done by Divie B. Duffield.* He possessed a fine legal mind and was an authority on municipal finance.

---

* Divie Bethune Duffield was a member of a family which was long influential in Detroit civic affairs. He was born March 3, 1870, the son of

After the initial arrangements for the grant had been completed, almost all dealings involving Carnegie money were with the philanthropist's confidential secretary, James Bertram. No man ever had a more faithful or devoted servant than Carnegie had in Bertram. The latter was also a Scot. Born in 1872, Bertram attended a business college in his native Edinburgh, and worked for a short time as a railroad company clerk in South Africa. In 1897, while visiting Scotland, Carnegie hired the young man as a secretary and took him back to the United States with him. After Carnegie's retirement from active business, the details of administering the grants and charities were assigned to Bertram, and the recipients of Carnegie's generosity found his secretary to be a stiff-necked, dour man. An agreement to him was an agreement to be carried out to the letter. He kept a careful eye on every penny of Carnegie's money and woe to the beneficiary who deviated by so much as a superfluous nail from the original specifications of a library building. Every blueprint drawn by the locally-hired architect received Bertram's careful scrutiny —and frequently his caustic criticism. Bertram continued, long after Carnegie's death, to administer the estate as secretary of the Carnegie Corporation of New York. He died in 1934.

"The librarian whose privilege it was to carry on negotiations with James Bertram, Secretary of the Corporation," said one Library official,

> received thereby a bit of free education in the economic handling of a trust fund for public good. The plans mutually agreed upon

General Henry M. Duffield, and the grandson of the Reverend George Duffield, for many years minister of the First Presbyterian Church. Educated at Phillips-Exeter, Harvard and Detroit College of Law, Duffield became a civic leader at an age when most young men are still struggling to establish themselves. He was, in large measure, responsible for the success of the municipal reform movement in Detroit, and was a member of the city charter commission in 1917. He served with distinction as corporation counsel and was twice an unsuccessful candidate for mayor. He was a member of the crew of the U.S.S. *Yosemite* in the Spanish-American War and was credited with planting the American flag at Guantanamo. An enthusiastic oarsman, he represented the United States in the Olympic Games, winning the singles championship. Duffield was the nephew and namesake of D. Bethune Duffield (1821–91) who in 1863, as a member of the Board of Education's Library Committee, contributed to the establishment of the Detroit Public Library (see p. 29). Divie Duffield did not marry. He died July 15, 1935.

must be adhered to and the full amount pledged was available only when the building was properly finished and ready for service. Such exacting accounting is not always demanded in expenditure of public appropriation; the experience was a salutary one to librarians and communities alike.

The Carnegie Corporation had certain fixed business principles which one learned to respect; certain experiences and soberly conceived ideas about library buildings which one did well to digest. Waste space and vague speculations were frowned upon, while essentials and practical arrangements were stressed. In this era of Carnegie munificence it was well that governing boards and librarians were put on the defensive by the firm grip of Mr. Bertram, whose terse directions quickly checked overeager enthusiasm and hazy programs.

Good taste of design was welcomed, but ornamentation and artistic extravagances were frowned upon. These libraries were not to be show places, but useful work shops. It were better that all comers were confronted with a house of simple dignity and correspondingly simple hospitality within.[4]

At the time the Detroit branches were being planned, Carnegie (or Bertram) decided that $40,000 was enough to spend for each. The Detroit Commission felt that eight branches would be necessary, but Carnegie questioned their judgment. With four city-built branches, plus a central Library, Detroit would have a total of thirteen buildings which, said Bertram, "seems an exceedingly liberal allowance for your population." He asked for more data on population, present and estimated, and at the same time cautioned "before you enter into any contracts or make yourselves liable for expenditure, submit plans of the buildings for approval, with a note of the cost complete, ready for occupancy, and for the purpose intended, of each building." [5] Bertram did not rely entirely upon his own ideas and knowledge about library construction, although the latter was extensive. In order to get the best advice possible, he conferred closely on Detroit's plans with W. H. Brett, the Cleveland librarian. In selecting branch sites, the Commission adopted a policy of locating them near schools which were generally centrally located in various neighborhoods and therefore easily accessible. It was estimated by the Commission that it cost a minimum of $7000 to equip each branch with books. That money, of course, did not come out of the Carnegie fund.

From Carnegie's standpoint, the financial settlements were handled as follows:

> When the plans of a building have been approved and its cost determined, the total amount of this cost is deposited with the treasurer of the Carnegie Corporation subject to the order of the Detroit Library Commission. Drafts upon the treasurer to the amount of about $10,000 each are made from time to time upon the requisition of the architect, certifying that the sum asked for is required to meet obligations incurred for labor and material in the construction of a certain building. The check for the total sum drawn is made payable to a designated local bank. Checks are drawn upon this local depository on architect's estimates, from time to time, on behalf of individual contractors. Thus the details of the business locally are handled by the Library Commission.[6]

However, the Commission quickly learned that Bertram was watching matters very closely and had a good deal to say about how things were being handled. He was particularly unhappy about the Detroit architects.

"This branch library matter is getting rather tangled up," he told Brett on one occasion. "The trouble is they have an architect without experience in this branch of his profession." He wondered why Detroit didn't use the experience which had been gained by Cleveland, Cincinnati, Philadelphia and other cities.[7] When the first blueprints were sent to him by Utley, he replied tartly:

> With your plans you show a basement, but not how same is used. As a rule, the lecture room is put there; in fact, we make it a rule that if there is a lecture room it should be put in the basement. You have it in the most advantageous position for library work, on the first floor.
> I see no stack room in the building at all. Where do you propose to put your books?

Such critical comment flowed from Bertram's pen until Detroit had spent its last Carnegie dollar. It may have been a good thing in the long run; at least it gave the Commission, the librarian, the architects and the contractors the realization that every nail pounded, every brick laid and every penny spent were under close scrutiny. The pressure began to tell on Utley and his health

196

began to crack. To relieve him, Adam Strohm was appointed assistant librarian in 1912 and shortly thereafter acting librarian until Utley's actual retirement on November 1.[8]

Not all of the problems of getting the branch program underway originated in Bertram's office. Complaints began to filter in about the location of the Bowen branch at West Grand Boulevard and Dix. Nearby were some railroad yards from which cattle were unloaded and driven through the streets to the stockyards west of the library location. Dust from plodding hooves and damage to the grounds and landscaping looked like a major nuisance in the making. Strohm protested the condition to the Department of Public Works and drew a reply from the DPW commissioner who bore the appropriate name of William T. Dust. He informed Strohm:

> You are in error that herds of cattle are permitted to be driven down the Boulevard. . . . The animals are driven along Dix Avenue from the stockyards to 24th street and then north on 24th street to Buchanan. Occasionally one of the cattle or sheep will stray off Dix and go on the Boulevard into flower beds and shrubbery, and so long as the city authorities permit the driving of cattle and other animals on the streets of Detroit an occasional occurrence of this kind will happen.[9]

Despite such contretemps, building progressed, and new sites were purchased. On December 21, 1912, the Lothrop branch was opened for public use, followed on December 28, by the Bowen branch. Each had been completed on schedule, safely within the $40,000 allotment. The Utley branch, one of the first three Carnegie projects, took longer to complete. Cost of constructing the building was found, as the work progressed, to exceed the first estimates, and twice the Commission had to go back to Bertram and ask for additional allowances. Altogether, Carnegie gave about $55,000 for the Utley branch which cost a total of nearly $60,000 before its completion and formal opening May 20, 1913. The last of the Carnegie branch fund was used up during the 1916–17 fiscal year, but not before the last two branches—the Divie B. Duffield (West Grand Boulevard at Dunedin) and the Bernard Ginsburg (Brewster Street between St. Antoine and Hastings)—had been opened.

There was still about $33,000 unspent of the $375,000 Carnegie had pledged for branches. In 1916, the Commission was looking for a site on Mack Avenue and finally acquired one in 1919 at the corner of Montclair upon which a branch ultimately was built in 1921. Named the Charles I. Walker branch, the cost estimates for this building ran to about $58,000. The Commission asked the Carnegie Corporation for a supplemental grant of $15,000 which was refused. As a result, Strohm informed the Commission that "the cost of erecting new branch libraries must be wholly shouldered by the city hereafter." [10]

That unused balance of $33,000 long troubled the Commission, and in 1937 Strohm inquired of the Carnegie Corporation if it might not still be available.

Robert M. Lester, who had by then succeeded Bertram, replied that there was no commitment as far as the Corporation was concerned. He wrote:

> The Andrew Carnegie personal commitment in general to Detroit was assumed by the Corporation only building by building, nothing being written on the Corporation books except in relation to a specified building. Consequently, when the books were cleared, nothing was written off as to Detroit, the $33,000 balance from the Andrew Carnegie *personal* and general promise, never having been actually assumed by the Corporation.[11]

Detroit's branch program did not come to an end when the Carnegie spigot was turned off. It was in reality only the beginning. Development of the automobile industry in the first two decades of the twentieth century and the impetus provided by World War I caused Detroit to undergo a new era of expansion. It increased in area as peripheral communities such as Delray, Fairview and Redford were annexed. Population grew at an astonishing rate, with the result that before long Detroit was the nation's fourth largest city and the core of a large metropolitan area. This meant not only a continued need for new branches, but also a degree of fluidity in the branch system. Neighborhood change, from residential to industrial, resulted in the closing and re-location of branches. The Ginsburg branch, for example, lost patronage to such an extent that its building was abandoned in 1927, and its operation was conducted in a rented store building.

Widening of Gratiot Avenue in 1938 caused the loss of the Osius building which later was replaced by the Mark Twain branch to serve the same area. Changing nature of the neighborhood ultimately led first to a different use of the Scripps branch, and then to its being closed completely. It was no longer needed for library purposes. On the other hand, when the village of Redford was annexed in 1926, the building intended as its town hall, was taken over by the Detroit system as a branch library.

Traffic was another phenomenon of the automobile age which affected the branches; in some places it cut attendance. This was duly noted in the 1922–23 annual report, in which it was stated:

> The Duffield branch on West Grand Boulevard, for instance, situated where traffic east and west makes crossing the street a perilous undertaking for an adult, is forbidden to children by parents who are afraid to have their children run the risk. A policeman is stationed at 12th street and one at 14th street for part time, but one in front of the branch between the hours of three and seven is a necessity, if we are going to serve the children south of the branch. The use of the Utley branch, (north Woodward), is now restricted to the children east of Woodward for the same traffic reason.[12]

The fall-off in business at the Utley branch, a fairly commodious building, was in time compensated for by using a portion of its facilities as the headquarters of the Extension Department.

All in all, however, the branch program continued to be a dynamic one. In 1920, by which time the Carnegie phase had ended, there were fifteen branches in library-owned buildings. By 1930 that number had increased to eighteen. In addition to the regular branches, there were what might be termed special branches, intended to serve a special or limited need. For example, a branch was opened in the old Art Museum at East Jefferson and Hastings in 1916, and was operated by the Public Library even after the museum's removal to its new quarters at Woodward and East Kirby. In 1947 its book collection and administration were turned over to the Arts Commission. From 1918 to 1924 a business and commercial branch was located in the office of the Board of Commerce. In 1924 this was removed to the Downtown Library and became a part of the Business and Commerce Division.

199

Later branch construction was handicapped by rising costs of land and construction. Mr. Carnegie's $40,000 branches, with sites which could be purchased at from $5000 to $10,000, quickly became a thing of the past. The Parkman branch, built in 1930, cost $152,000. To obtain sites in 1942 it became necessary to resort to condemnation proceedings, and the site of the next to the last most recently opened branch, the Henry Chaney at Grand River and Mansfield (1955), brought an award of $52,800.[13]

Cost, however, while of vital importance, was never the measure of branch value. Neither, for that matter, was the size of its circulation. Andrew Carnegie regarded branch libraries as community centers. So did the Detroit Library Commission. The branches always served as something other than places where books could be read or drawn. Lectures were a popular attraction and, as the Librarian reported in 1909, "never fail to draw large audiences." During that year, topics included "Pompeii, Past and Present," "Venice," "Labrador," "Dante," "Beyond the Rockies," "Joan of Arc," "Origin of the Moon," "A Trip through Scotland," "The Weather Bureau and Its Work" and "Manual and Industrial Training." The lecturers, as a rule, were local clergymen or prominent people who gave their time without charge. Often the lectures were illustrated by lantern or stereopticon slides. The advent of the motion picture spoiled the popularity of lectures in the branches—an experience which was shared by many churches and other organizations. The still lantern slide could not compete with the undulations of a Theda Bara or the simpering of a Gish. In time, of course, the Library met the challenge with its own motion picture program.

The branches were very close to the communities of the city which they served, and in some respects assumed the characteristics of social agencies. It was stated in the 1925 annual report:

> From crowded homes of poverty and noisy streets, the residents do turn to the library. It is good to think that one place, comfortable, spacious, beautiful in a quiet way, and fairly clean, is accessible to young and old.[14]

Shifting population of an industrial center brought to the branches the "apartment house child." "Sometimes," the 1925 report said, "this pathetic travesty on real childhood seems a greater problem than the huddling of the masses." [15]

But if the branch was the haven of the slum child, it was also "an institution for what may be popularly expressed as the average man." It was a place where Boy and Girl Scout troops could meet; where classes could be taught in handicrafts and folk dancing; where neighborhood associations could gather.

> As specific instances of what is being done, may be mentioned the occasional neighborhood nights, when the library holds 'open house'; the exhibit of treasures brought from native countries; the colored women's club and large debating clubs for boys and girls at the Bernard Ginsburg branch; talks on current topics in Polish at the Edwin Conely branch; and a class in English for foreign women and a married peoples' club at the Magnus Butzel branch.
>
> The keynote of the branch library community activities is service. Whatever tends to develop community spirit and react for the good of the community deserves and receives support. When a lovely woman confides over the desk, "I am so lonely it doesn't seem as though I could stand it. We're strangers in town and don't know a soul," the answer comes, "Why don't you join our neighborhood club?" When a disconsolate youth bursts forth, "I sure would like a good time with a girl I've been introduced to," the reply is, "Wouldn't you like to join the social dancing club?" [16]

The staff of the branch libraries often were among the first to sense changes going on in their areas. An article in *Library Service,* a small bulletin covering Library affairs, published by the Detroit Public Library from 1917 to 1939, said:

> How many of even the old residents of Detroit know that there is a well developed, congested foreign district so near the well-to-do North Woodward section that about 75 per cent of the children who use the Utley Branch Library come from homes where the parents are foreign-born and often do not speak English? This district lies east of Oakland and north of the Boulevard and comprises the little known street names of Cameron, Delmar, Goodwin and Cardoni.
>
> A large proportion of these families are Russian Jews, and the children, with the thirst for knowledge characteristic of the race, are indefatigable patrons of the library. Many of them take home 'easy books' for the use of their parents who are learning English. Recently in response to a request, the branch has added a small collection of books in Yiddish, which also the children take home to their parents.
>
> This is why the children's room of the Utley Branch is crowded

201

every afternoon with eager little black-eyed boys and girls, with un-
accustomed names, who give the branch quite a different atmosphere
from that of even three or four years ago.[17]

This statement is significant in light of the fact that the Utley
branch had been opened in an upper-middle class district only
seven years before. So rapidly, then, had Detroit become the
melting pot!

Branch libraries were looked upon as such good neighbors
that when a new one was established, it was the occasion for a
community celebration. When the Chandler Park branch was
opened in 1957, a luncheon was given by the Library Commission and the Outer Harper Business Men's Association as joint
hosts, and the festivities were attended by the mayor, members of
the Common Council, and representatives of schools, churches
and service clubs in the Chandler Park Area.[18]

Regardless of the importance of the branches in the field of
community relations, books were always the first consideration,
and the Detroit system endeavored to give its patrons not only a
wide selection, but reading material to suit their tastes. Prior to
the time in 1928 when Ralph A. Ulveling joined the Detroit
system as head of the Extension Division, only books approved for
use in the Main Library could be purchased for branches. In order
to improve the branch service, Ulveling instituted a dual system
whereby separate book lists for the Main Library and the branches
were prepared. The branches could make selections from either
list. Said Ulveling:

> Any objective analysis leads inescapably to the conclusion that
> books for branch libraries must be deemed appropriate, not accord-
> ing to the competence of the author and the contribution they make
> to general knowledge, but rather they must be judged by the stimula-
> tion and enlightenment they bring to readers.[19]

How well this type of service was extended to the public can
be seen by a glance at the available facilities at the end of the
1930–31 fiscal year. Besides the Main Library, there were twenty-
four regular branches, two specialized branches, thirty-two deposit
stations in establishments so varied that they had included at one
time or another everything from fire stations to a pickle factory,
and 119 school deposit stations serviced by the Public Library.

202

Thus the city was well blanketed. After 1931 changes in library coverage occurred due to many factors including the depression, but expedient measures were taken so that, in the over-all picture, there was an extension rather than a curtailment of service.

One important innovation was the motorized library, known as the Bookmobile, which enabled the Library to reach out to areas which were not so well served by branches as might be desired. The Bookmobile was a large rig well supplied with books which could be driven to any neighborhood or location desired, placing at the disposal of children and adults a necessarily limited, but at the same time varied range of reading choices. The Bookmobile became, in fact, a branch library on wheels. The purchase of such a specially designed vehicle was first discussed by the Commission in 1939, and on July 11 of that year the committee on administration was authorized to advertise for bids. A Chevrolet cab and chassis were purchased, and the body was built by the Fruehauf Trailer Company. On February 5, 1940, it was put into operation.

"Such a service," it was stated, "although it is not an adequate substitute for a fully-developed system of branch libraries, will be an important auxiliary to them at this time." [20]

The Bookmobile operated out of the Utley branch where it was parked or garaged. By 1955, the original Bookmobile had been replaced by a new van and in the 1955 fiscal year, a second van was added. Ulveling explained:

> Such a unit, properly staffed with professional people, is a flexible and relatively inexpensive medium for maintaining a directed service for adults and children in all areas where branches are unjustified. As a supplement to the branch system it is rapidly assuming the importance of a requirement.[21]

Even with such useful devices, the Library's attention never was diverted from its important and desired goal of branches within the reach of every potential patron. Over the years it indulged in that favorite sport of municipal officials and planners, formulating long-range programs—five- or ten-year plans—some of which, happily, materialized in whole, or at least enough in part to make the ultimate goal seem attainable. In 1930, a ten-year plan was

laid out which called for expenditure of $3,386,000. This in-
cluded the remodeling and enlargement of some branches, the
replacement of two existing buildings and the construction of six
new ones. While part of this program was successfully carried out,
the Library director reported at the end of seven years that "we
are numerically short of book centers as in operation five years
ago." At that time the Commission was content with a five-year
capital investments program which called for an all-purpose expenditure of $1,070,000. In 1942–43, with new sites acquired,
further expansion was anticipated which, when realized, offered
assurance "that the branch library system will be reasonably adequate for the area encompassed by the present city boundaries." [22]

Again, in 1944–45, in cooperation with the City Plan Commission, a new long-range plan was developed "to redistribute and
enlarge" facilities. This called for thirty branches, but it involved
the relocation of twelve, and the retention of only eleven at their
existing sites. Sites for four of the contemplated new structures
already had been acquired. Two years later, the range of vision
was extended, and the Library Commission and City Plan Commission were discussing "in detail the proposed plan for branch
library development in the next fifty years." [23] There was nothing
impractical or visionary in these studies. The Commission, on the
contrary, was showing a commendable determination to plan
intelligently for future conditions which, experience had proved,
changed rapidly in a large and dynamic community.

Meanwhile, real progress was being made. The 1949–50 annual report said that "not since 1920–21 has the long-quiescent
program of branch library development moved forward as in the
past year." Two new buildings were completed; a third was near-
ing completion; contracts had been awarded for two other
branches and funds were appropriated for a new site and for
rental of quarters for still another branch.

"If we could be assured that this expansion program could be
sustained for three or four years longer, the branch library program would be completed," Henry Meyers, then president of the
Commission could report. In 1955, it was stated that with the
completion of work in progress, "the goal of twenty-nine branches
will be realized" and "three library agencies [including two Book-

mobiles] have been placed so they will bring library service within one mile of the homes of most Detroiters." Two years later, the Commission could proudly report to the Common Council that the branch situation is "in excellent condition." [24] Much credit for the remarkable progress made in the 1950's went to Albert E. Cobo who was Detroit's mayor from 1950 until his death in 1957. Cobo had great plans for the revitalization of Detroit; he was a builder at heart, and his accomplishments were solid. He was mourned on the occasion of his sudden death by a resolution of the Library Commission which pointed out that "no less than ten branches of our Library were dedicated during his mayoralty." [25]

Quantity was not the only concern of Library officials when its branch system was being developed. Quality of service was equally important and in striving for it some progressive innovations were employed. One of these was the adoption of a plan of regional branches, first tried out in Chicago. The regional branch was a much more self-contained library unit than the neighborhood branch, and was felt to be effective in large, sprawling cities. The expansion of Detroit taxed the supply of reading matter which, at best, was constantly strained. Withdrawal of books from the main storage to supply outlying branches from seven to ten miles from the Main Library, had a tendency to deplete the available supply of books and to withdraw from circulation books transported for hours each day. Such a method, Strohm told the Commission, reduced the time a book could be used, and increased the overhead involved in the distribution of the book.

> The solution for this phase of the problem is regional libraries of sufficient size to be very largely self-dependent, so serving a larger area and obviating the necessity of a too great extension of the smaller branch system.

The first regional branch, the John Monteith, was opened at Kercheval and Eastlawn on May 1, 1926. After that time, two others were established. They were the Mark Twain and Francis Parkman branches.

In calling attention to the Monteith as a regional branch, Strohm had this to say:

205

The erection of this regional branch library marks a change of policy in the extension of the library service. These new branch libraries will be in the nature of a town library or, in other words, a self-contained, self-dependent library unit with larger resources and larger service area than the branch libraries so far erected.

Where the ordinary branch was intended to serve an area with about a mile radius, the regional would have a service area of five miles or more. It would be stocked with from 25,000 to 30,000 books in the reading rooms, and more in the reserve stacks.[26]

Later evaluation of the regional branch program created doubts as to its real effectiveness, and the plan was not expanded beyond the three libraries which actually became no more than large neighborhood branches.

In the latter stages of the branch building program there was a spectacular change in which the Detroit system pioneered. This consisted of the abandonment of the traditional architectural style —the court house square type of solidity—and the substitution of a completely modern and highly functional kind of building.

Because several branch buildings of the former sort had to be closed on account of changing neighborhood conditions, and because their design and construction made them essentially expensive to duplicate, something new was resorted to. It was Ulveling's suggestion made to the Commission in 1947, that new branches should be simply designed. These could be equipped with all necessary facilities for a comprehensive library service at much less cost than "the previous monumental type of building." They would have the further advantage, in case they had to be abandoned, of being easily converted to commercial use. The new structures might be expected to have an aesthetic influence on their communities.

Said Ulveling:

> The proposed building will be of a commercial type . . . distinguished from ordinary store buildings by the dignified treatment of their facades. Such buildings, it is estimated, may be erected and equipped for about thirty per cent of the funds required under the older plan.

The monumental type building at that time cost about $300,000 to $350,000 to build.[27]

The first such building was the Benjamin Franklin branch on East McNichols Road near Gratiot. It was opened January 24, 1950. Large window space took the place of solid masonry walls. Well-lighted and well-ventilated rooms, attractively and colorfully furnished, set off by agreeably landscaped grounds made the functional branch an instant success. The Benjamin Franklin branch was quickly followed by nine more.

> The most readily noticeable exterior features of each of the new buildings are the entrances at sidewalk level and the generous glass areas in the front. The big expanse of glass enables those who pass to see the colorful and inviting interior, the books, and the people reading. The long rows of tables and chairs formerly seen in libraries have been replaced by inviting lounges equipped with comfortable chairs, sofas, and end tables. In step with modern building developments, the buildings are air-conditioned and provided with the most efficient lighting equipment.

Not only were the people in the neighborhoods delighted with these new branches, but librarians all over the world looked with envy at what Detroit was doing and began to emulate it in their own communities. Librarians, library trustees and architects from nearly every part of the country as well as from Europe, South America and India, came to Detroit to marvel, and return home with a valuable new idea.

> The fact that two of these modern functional type buildings can be erected for the cost of one of the earlier type library has not only speeded the development locally, but has influenced modern library planning in the United States and abroad,

crowed Detroit.[28]

CHAPTER 13

THE NEW MAIN LIBRARY

IN 1877 the Library Committee of the Board of Education
derived deep satisfaction from their successful efforts to give
Detroit a main library. Their pride in the building as a showpiece
adorning Centre Park was understandable. But their pride was
not shared by their successors, the members of the Board of
Library Commissioners when that body took over direction of
Library affairs in 1881. To their eyes, the Centre Park building
was too small for the book collection it was called upon to house;
it was dirty and dingy; they regarded it as an architectural
monstrosity, badly located in unattractive surroundings. Additions and interior remodeling offered only temporary alleviation.
The commissioners hoped for something better, and at least five
times between 1886 and 1901 there was serious discussion about

the need for a new main library building and some planning about how to get one.

Judge James V. Campbell, the Commission's first president, led off in 1886 with the observation that "it is evidently but a question of time how soon the building will become too small, with all possible economy, to contain the yearly additions of books and library material." At the end of that year there were 70,550 volumes stacked away in the old structure which was beginning to groan under their weight. The collection had about doubled since the opening in 1877. One can imagine, then, that succeeding commissioners could find no flaw in Campbell's prediction, because by the end of 1901—an elapsed time of only fifteen years —the Library had close to 175,000 books.

"As the Library grows and its use increases from year to year, the ill-adaption of the building to library purposes becomes more and more apparent," it was stated in 1890. "There is ample room for the erection of a building in front of the present one, and it cannot be utilized a day too soon." Yet, the old structure continued to be used to the growing dissatisfaction and distress of all concerned. It was indicted in 1898 because "it has neither shape nor comeliness, neither eloquence nor dignity . . . While we are proud of our Library, we are not proud of our building." Plans were being made, even then, for the civic observance of Detroit's bicentennial in 1901. The Commission had always cherished the hope, as did its predecessor, the Library committee, that wealthy Detroiters would come forward with gifts or endowments that would provide facilities at no cost to the taxpayers. The two hundredth anniversary of the city's founding suggested itself as a fitting occasion for some sort of outside help. The Commission issued an official hint that it hoped the bicentennial plans would involve putting up a building of permanent character, centrally located, which would be adapted later to Library use when the festivities were ended.

If all the conversation about a new building could have been preserved and stacked on shelves, the Centre Park Library would have bulged even more than it did. But along with the discussion, there was grim determination to do something, a determination which grew stronger year by year.

209

"The agitation for a new Library building has begun not a moment too soon," it was announced in 1900, along with a statement of the urgent need to get busy on necessary legislation, selection of a site, and all the other preliminaries. These, it was forecast, would require at least five years of work.

Impatient at the delay and the endless flow of words, Commissioner Scripps in 1901 called for a special meeting of the Board to consider either enlargement of the Centre building, or the construction of a new one on another site. The meeting was held on January 10, and at its conclusion a statement was issued to the effect that it was "the sense of the Board that there should be a new building." Despite all that had been said before about a new main Library, that January 10, 1901, meeting really was the beginning of a determined campaign to obtain the desired facilities. It might be added that while it was a long campaign, it was successful in the end.

Two things made the January 10 discussion different from those which had preceded it. One was the decision to drop plans to remodel the Centre building and to concentrate instead upon construction of a new Library. The other was the realization that to accomplish the set goal, public support was essential. As a first step in obtaining that support, a meeting was held with the mayor, the corporation counsel, and the president of the Merchants' & Manufacturers' Exchange. They were asked their views about attempting to obtain necessary legislation to make possible "the erection of a new library building on a new site." The meeting was held in the Russell House on January 14. It was described as entirely informal, but it produced the desired results. The city officials were interested; the members of the Merchants' & Manufacturers' Exchange—the forerunner of the Board of Commerce—pledged their support. It was unanimously agreed to start at once to secure legislation which would enable the Commission to purchase a site and erect a building with funds provided by the issuance of thirty-year bonds, with a 2.5 per cent tax levy for a sinking fund. The enthusiasm whipped up at the Russell House conference was sustained during the days immediately following by the favorable reaction and comment of the newspapers.[1]

In the first days of 1901, the Commission probably was more

concerned with a new main library than with branches. As things turned out, the legislation and financing plans actually encompassed the entire system. The legislature passed the required bill, allowing issuance of bonds to the amount of $1,000,000 of which it was intended that $250,000 would be used to purchase a site and $750,000 would go into construction of a Main Library. The bill also permitted the Commission to acquire and hold property in its own right. It will be recalled that because of the ripper bill, passed by the legislature at the same session, it was impossible to submit to the people in 1901 the question of authorizing issuance of the bonds to raise money as it was needed. Then, on June 20, 1901, Andrew Carnegie's offer of $750,000—$375,000 for branches, $375,000 for a main building—was received, and the entire picture changed. Branches, as well as the main building became an issue and, in fact, assumed precedence simply because sites and supplemental construction money appeared to be more readily available for them. However, because of opposition to the Carnegie donation from certain elements of the community, Detroit delayed formal acceptance of his offer until 1910.

During the nine-year hiatus, the Commission never entirely lost hope that the program of expanding the Library system could be undertaken. The prospects grew very dim at times, but hope of ultimate success continued to mark the Commission's planning.

"It is inevitable," declared Dr. John E. Clark in 1903, "that before long, either by gift or by taxation, a library building worthy of this city will be erected." It was Dr. Clark's idea that a new structure would be on a grand enough scale to include an art gallery and museum. The same year, the commissioners placed themselves again on record that "it is the firm belief of the members of this Commission that the city needs a new central library building without delay." [2] Another year went by without action, and the Commission once more played the familiar theme, pointing out that conditions

make it more certain that the day is not far off when the people of the city will see that the good name and standing of Detroit as an intelligent, enterprising and prosperous municipality, inevitably require the raising of funds sufficient to put the Library on a footing to compare creditably with similar institutions in neighboring cities.

211

To meet the needs of a growing town the commissioners conceded that sewers, paved streets and a good water supply were of prime importance. "But," they added, "it is also important that the city shall be made attractive and desirable as a place of residence by attention to the intellectual and esthetic side of life." [3] Four years later, there was more of the same, this time in the form of an address by Commissioner Sidney T. Miller* to the Board of Education in which there was a tinge of exasperation:

> We brag of Detroit as the city beautiful, yet, our main library building is a joke. . . . Our people have not shown a disposition to take Mr. Carnegie's offer to give us libraries, but this does not absolve you gentlemen from your duty to help the Commission to get better quarters. The duty lies partly at your door, as in Michigan the library is part of the educational system. . . . It is my recommendation that the city take immediate steps for the building of a new main library building on a new site. The present location is not good for library purposes; it is dirty and thus hard on the books, it is noisy, and thus hard on the nerves of the library force and students using this building; it is dark, and thus bad for the eyes; the building is unventilated, and thus bad for the health; it is a bad place for fire, as any of the fire department or insurance experts will tell you.[4]

Early discussion about a new library was coupled with speculation and argument about where it should be located. Once it was agreed that the Main Library should not be in Centre Park, various other locations came under consideration. As early as 1900, the Detroit *Journal* came out in opposition to a downtown building. "The trend of residence building is away from that part of the city," the paper said. "It must be placed where it can expand." [5] Dr. Clark suggested the lot on Grand Circus Park at Washington Boulevard and Bagley Avenue, the homestead of Governor John J. Bagley. The commissioners agreed this would be an ideal place, but no further action on the matter was taken. It was hoped apparently that the property would be donated to the Library. Ultimately it became the site of the Statler-Hilton

---

* Sidney Trowbridge Miller, Sr. (1864–1940) was one of Detroit's best known and most influential corporation lawyers. He was the son of Sidney D. Miller (1830–1904), also a well-known attorney, who was on the Board of Education and, as a member of the Committee on Library in 1865 (and again in 1869–1870), was one of the real founders of the Detroit Public Library.

Hotel. At this period, and even after the Carnegie offer was made, the Grand Circus area had strong appeal, both to some members of the Commission and to many of the citizens.[6]

The Carnegie offer in 1901 made it necessary for the Commission to get down to hard facts regarding a main location. The cost of a site took on new importance in the Board's calculations, and it was this consideration which, in the end, ruled out anything on or near Grand Circus Park. Accessibility was another factor, and a place farther out Woodward Avenue began to attract more attention. Within a couple of weeks after Andrew Carnegie's offer had been received, George Radford suggested that an ideal site would be the lot of Senator Palmer, a block bounded by Woodward, Farnsworth, Frederick and John R. This was the property which was later taken for the Detroit Institute of Arts. The Detroit *News* did not think well of this site for the Library; it was not served by good transportation and to reach it from most parts of the city required a transfer. It was only within the half-mile circle, said the *News,* that all lines were available.[7]

Not much more was heard, for the time being, about the section suggested by Radford. The Commission felt a place closer to the center of town would be better. In 1902 it adopted a resolution to the effect "that in case an uptown site is selected for a central library building, the same can be secured on Woodward Avenue, between Watson and Frederick streets, to cost not over $100,000. It is however, its opinion, that a site should be selected in the heart of the city near Circus Park where satisfactory sites have been offered, the cost not to exceed $380,000, and the latter is hereby recommended by the Library Commission." [8] Convinced that they were now on the right track, the commissioners on November 6, 1902, invited sealed bids for a lot or lots covering not less than 60,000 square feet. Bids were received and on December 23, the members of the Board announced their intention of inspecting the sites offered. One of them was on Adams Avenue at the northwest corner of Park.[9]

In their apparent attachment to the downtown section, an attachment undoubtedly influenced by James E. Scripps and the *News,* the commissioners reckoned without public opinion. The other papers favored going farther out Woodward, and in its 1902 annual report, the Commission admitted that considerable public opposition was expressed to the Grand Circus district. Nevertheless the Commission again, on January 15, 1903, went on record that "another site should be bought forthwith, such site to be, if possible, between Elizabeth street and Jefferson avenue and within the near vicinity of Woodward avenue." [10]

With rejection of the first bond issue proposition and the Common Council's refusal to accept the Carnegie offer, hopes for the building program were all but abandoned. Nothing could be done to obtain the Carnegie money because the Commission owned no site and had insufficient funds. The dream of a new Main Library, therefore, lay dormant until 1907, when a bond issue was approved by the voters. With expectations of getting money, interest in obtaining a site was renewed. By this time, official interest had shifted to Woodward Avenue in midtown, and a solution suddenly seemed to be at hand. There was a site available, ready-made for Library purposes. This was the space occupied by the old Detroit Athletic Club, a tract between Woodward and Cass, including most of the ground between Forest and Canfield. It was occupied by an old frame club house, built in 1887, fronting on Woodward, with a large playing field behind it. This property was available, and in 1907, the Library Commission took an option to buy it for $185,000. The DAC option was renewed from time to time, the last extension expiring on December 20, 1910. [11]

In 1910 the atmosphere was cleared both by approval of a bond issue and the City's formal acceptance of the Carnegie offer. As the matter of a site again became important, a new element entered the picture. While the Library was marking time, a group of public spirited citizens had acquired two blocks on Woodward between Farnsworth and Kirby avenues for the Detroit Institute of Arts. This included the Palmer property which Radford had earlier recommended for a Library site. The backers of the Art Institute had their own financial difficulties and needed to raise $96,000 to enable them to exercise their option. As a solution to their problem, they offered approximately half their site, 300 feet between Frederick Street and Kirby Avenue, to the Library for $100,000. Their thinking was that the Art Institute and the

214

Library would be placed side by side on the east side of Wood-ward. The Commission considered the offer, but decided the dimensions of the tract were inadequate. The Art Institute backers were not willing to give more space to the Library, so the Commission went ahead with its plans to buy the DAC property.[12]

Meanwhile, forward-looking citizens began to get ideas about establishing a mid-town cultural center. The Art Institute backers overcame their financial difficulties and definitely committed themselves to building. This seemed to offer a beginning for a cultural center, and efforts were made to attract the Library to the area. Mayor Philip Breitmeyer's aid was enlisted, and he called a conference in October for the purpose of persuading the Library to locate on the west side of Woodward opposite the Art Institute. The City Plan Commission stated that the DAC site would not be satisfactory because of commercial building in that area. Divie B. Duffield who attended the conference as the Commission's representative, told the mayor that the Commission felt that if it could secure a site of sufficient size opposite the proposed Art Museum within a reasonable time and "within our appropriation," it would be best to do so. He foresaw some difficulty in acquiring the property, some of which he feared would be subject to life-lease. He did not know what Carnegie's reaction would be to such an arrangement. The mayor offered his cooperation, with the result that by the end of the year, the DAC option was allowed to expire, and the Commission was committed to obtaining a site bounded by Woodward, Cass, West Kirby, and the north line of lots fronting on Putnam. This provided 529 feet frontage on Woodward. Many years later, the Putnam Avenue lots were acquired, the last parcel being obtained by condemnation in 1946. On May 3, 1911, Duffield was authorized by the Commission "to see what could be done in the way of getting options upon property in the desired locality." [13]

Having made its choice, the Commission was pleased and the public generally was satisfied. There was a little backstage maneuvering on the part of William C. Weber, a member of the Arts Commission, who for some unexplained reason tried to shift the Library to the museum site, and move the museum across the street. He asked Andrew Carnegie's help. Strohm saw something

215

sinister in the move and told Charles Moore, secretary of the Arts Commission, that he knew something "which I would not dare trust to correspondence." [14] The Library Commission had no desire to trade for any reasons and boasted that the Library "has a better site than has New York, Boston, Brooklyn, or St. Louis." [15]

There were fine homes of several prominent Detroiters on the Woodward-Putnam block and it was expected that the cost would be high. There were seven parcels at the outset which the Library wanted. These began with the lot of the Stevens family which ran straight through to Cass. With 130-feet frontage, the south of this lot was approximately in the middle of the block. The Stevens family, like some of their neighbors, had made a fortune in the lumbering business. The next parcel, 115 feet on Woodward, belonged to the McGraw estate. The Woodward-Kirby corner lot was owned by Mrs. D. B. Mitchell. A smaller lot on Kirby was the property of Mrs. Rice, a relative of Senator Palmer. The home on that lot was vacant. On the southeast corner of Cass and Kirby, with 106 feet frontage on Cass was a large lot and fine home. This was known as the Williams property, but was actually part of the McGraw estate. The next lot south on Cass was occupied by an apartment building owned by Mrs. C. D. Standish. Next to it, running south to the Stevens property was a 43-foot lot belonging to a real estate broker, Matthew Finn.[16] These were the seven parcels in which the Commission was originally interested. Duffield thought about $250,000 was a fair figure. Other properties comprising the south half of the block belonged to William V. Moore; Clarence A. Black, one of the founders of the Cadillac Motor Car Company, and a Library commissioner from 1911 to 1913; and Merton E. Farr, president of the American Ship Building Company, whose home later was utilized by the Library to house its technology collection. The last piece of property at Woodward and Putnam belonged to the heirs of Simon Murphy, a lumber tycoon. Some of the lots had more than one house on them. It was not until November 11, 1912, after part of the north half of the block had been acquired, that the Commission decided to obtain the south half as well in order to make the site measure up to the Art Institute property across Woodward and to allow room for expansion and beautification.

> What the Art Museum is doing is intended for all time to come. What this board believes should be done for the public in the way of a library should also be done for all time to come,

the Commission resolved.[17]

As soon as the Supreme Court decision upholding the legality of Library bonds was handed down in 1911, thereby assuring the Library of building and site purchase funds, the Commission moved to obtain the Woodward Avenue property. On February 21, 1912, the owners of the first seven parcels were notified that the Library intended to acquire the property and preferred to do so by purchase rather than condemnation. They asked for the lowest cash price on each parcel. The response was not wholly satisfactory, and in May a committee of the Detroit Real Estate Board was making appraisals, its services being donated. The chairman of the committee was James Holden. When some of the owners refused to sell at the appraised price, condemnation proceedings were ordered begun in June. The first parcel was acquired by purchase on June 9; the first condemnation verdict was obtained in 1913. The first ten parcels cost $414,000, and while this was double the original estimate of the amount to be spent for a site, members of the Commission thought they had obtained a bargain. By the time the rest of the block had been acquired, the Library possessed a total of fourteen parcels of which ten were purchased. The total cost amounted to $1,194,349.72.[18]

On September 13, 1912, Commissioner Ginsburg urged the necessity of considering, as soon as possible, the kind of Library that should be constructed. It was decided to see what had been done in other cities, so on September 27, Commissioners Black, Duffield and Ginsburg, along with Utley and Strohm, set off on an inspection trip which took them to Springfield, Massachusetts, New York, Brooklyn, Newark, Philadelphia, Washington, Pittsburgh and St. Louis. They were gone until October 5, and upon their return they filed a report, detailing many of the features and advantages of the central library buildings they had examined. They were particularly impressed by the brand new building in

217

St. Louis to which Andrew Carnegie had given $500,000. It was designed by a noted New York architect, Cass Gilbert. Ideas and impressions, however, were drawn from all the buildings they examined. They concluded with reference to Detroit:

> What is wanted is a plain, substantial structure of pleasing, digni-fied and impressive appearance. Detroit cannot afford to stand for anything mean or picayunish. It has a reputation as one of the fore-most cities of the land, and its library, as well as other public build-ings, should maintain its reputation. The new library of St. Louis is of about the right character and size for Detroit. While some of its ornamentation might be omitted, nevertheless we think the City of Detroit should make up its mind to furnish a considerable addition to the $375,000 offered by Mr. Carnegie.

The next step was to put these impressions into the form of architectural drawings, specifications and estimates. Frank Miles Day of Philadelphia, an architect of splendid reputation, was re-tained as consultant. After his first visit to Detroit and inspection of the site, it was urged that the proposed building should be capable of housing 750,000 volumes, be expansible, should cost about $1,000,000, with "a capacity to accommodate the people of Detroit a generation hence . . . . The building . . . . is intended to be of sufficient dimensions and general arrangement to serve for fifty years, at least." [19]

Day advised a competition in order to select an architect for the building. This was to be a two-stage affair, the first open only to Detroit architects who would then compete against national en-tries. Sixteen local architects submitted plans, among them such well-known men as Albert Kahn and George D. Mason. In the end, a three-man jury, of which Congressional Librarian Herbert Putnam of Washington was chairman, selected Cass Gilbert of New York. He was awarded the contract on December 22, 1913. Gilbert went to work immediately, his plans were approved, and on January 4, 1915, the first contract, for the excavation, was awarded to the Detroit firm of Irwin and Leighton for $63,800. A week later, January 12, the shovels, scoops and dirt wagons moved in. Behind an eight-foot high board fence, enclosing the entire building site—a fence which would be an eyesore for the next three years—the first sod was turned.[20] The excavation was dug in less than five months, and before it was finished bids had gone

218

out for the structural steel work and construction of the first floor. The contract for $65,750 went to the American Bridge Company on May 13, 1915, and by the year's end the framework was completed.[21]

If this beginning was auspicious, the luster quickly dimmed. All work was suspended at the end of the year. The Commission had run out of money, and for nearly a year-and-a-half the girders stood exposed to the elements, an unsightly monument to the frustrations which had plagued the Library planners for more than a decade. It took men of courage and determination to see the job through with all its delays and disappointments. Fortunately the Commission was composed of such men. Outstanding among them was Divie B. Duffield, who was president of the Board during these difficult times. A lawyer who maintained the high professional standards of the Duffield family, and who was well endowed with the clan's sense of civic duty, Divie Duffield was a towering oak of strength during those trying days. If ever the Detroit Public Library had a staunch friend it was he.

In the 1914–15 annual report, Duffield attempted to explain in detail what was holding things up. He reported that rising costs together with the modification of plans to improve the building had raised the price tag to $1,350,000. After paying for the main and branch sites out of the original $750,000 bond issue, only $311,000 remained, some of which had been spent on foundation and steel work. In addition, there was the $375,000 pledged by Carnegie but still not available. These amounts combined left a total of $664,000 still needed. The only way to secure it was through an additional bond sale. The voters in 1915 showed no inclination to give the Library any more money and the $750,000 bond issue was defeated.

An appeal was made to Carnegie to release his $375,000 donation, but that, too, was unavailing. Bertram was adamant. He stated his position in a letter dated July 22, 1915, worth quoting in full because it reflects not only his attitude, but also his current enchantment with simplified spelling.

> We hav your favor of June 14, regarding the new main library bilding for Detroit. We understand that the bilding, according to plans submitted, wil cost $1,350,000 complete and redy to occupy. When we ar advised that Detroit has expended $975,000 on the

219

bilding, according to these plans, and that by payment of $375,000 by this Corporation the structure wil be finisht complete and redy to occupy, arrangements wil be made for payment of our promist donation as work progresses.[22]

There was a good deal of public criticism of the Commission at this time. People began to ask why the construction of the Main Library had been started before the money to pay for it was assured. Duffield was called upon to explain. He said:

> It remains now to explain why the building is under way when there are not funds enough to erect such a building as the Commission can recommend. In the early part of this year [1915] there was an urgent demand that as much public work as possible be undertaken for the benefit of the unemployed. For this reason our specifications for excavation and foundation were hurried and the contract let. . . . The contract was let and the structural steel will all be in place by the middle of December. On the present price of structural steel—and it is still advancing—there has already been a saving of about $14,500. The contract is based on $21 a ton for steel, while the present quotation is $33 a ton.

He went on to explain that the building could be completed with the money at hand, but it would be a cheap affair, reflecting no credit upon Detroit. What was needed was popular approval of additional bond money which, he was confident, would be forthcoming when the people realized "that nothing extravagant is contemplated."

"Such," he added, "is the explanation which will be given for the cessation of all work on the building after December 15, 1915." [23]

The criticism did not immediately subside. It cropped up again in the 1916 mayoralty campaign in which Recorder's Judge William F. Connolly, opposing Oscar B. Marx, made the Library an issue. He charged Marx, who was seeking re-election, with the "slows" in pushing ahead a capital improvements program and cited the Main Library as an example of Marx's lack of leadership.

"At present," he declared, "there stands on the site of the public library only a bare skeleton of a building, all due to the wastefulness and laxity of the Marx administration." [24]

Duffield, who had been a primary candidate himself but now

supported Marx, came forward with a letter refuting Connolly's charges and defending the delay as necessary to getting the kind of building Detroit needed. This gave Connolly an opportunity to reply in which he repeated and elaborated on his original charges. He pointed out that he had presided at the 1913 condemnation proceedings which were represented as "a public necessity."

> Over three years have passed since then, and the "new" library is not under roof yet; it stands, to use the verbal flourish of my speeches, "a gaunt, naked skeleton of steel against the sky!" . . . Nobody knows when it will be finished.
> Nobody seems to care when it will be finished.

It was time, he concluded, that Detroit had a mayor who would "put his personal and official force behind these projects, inspire to action those who are lagging and faint-hearted, and shove these projects along to a seasonable conclusion." [25]

Connolly was defeated in the November 1916 election, but retained his place on the bench. A year later, he was called upon to preside, as a one-man grand jury, over an investigation of alleged graft in the city and county governments. He used that opportunity to look into some of the circumstances surrounding the new Main Library building. The inquiry, however, turned up no evidence of mismanagement on the part of the Commission, city administration or the contractors. Nevertheless, the idea had been planted that the job could be completed and money saved by substituting, for example, brick for marble and granite facing, and other details which, as frills, Detroit could well get along without. These complaints stirred Strohm to reply with indignant eloquence:

> There has been some public discussion as regards the architectural appearance of the new main building, the material to be used, and the subsequent cost involved. Would not tile, brick, concrete, do well enough? Why granite, marble, or artistic adornment of any kind? The answer in part is this—
> Mean surroundings make mean people; things of beauty cleanse our hearts. True architecture, as any other artistic expression of the human mind has a social function to perform in the liberal education of mankind. A building should be dignified and proper self-expression of its purpose and of the spirit within; the revelation of one's

221

self is largely by the "front" we make; our modes of expression, our taste revealed and good manners practised in public and private.

"Architecture is the work of nations." Public statues, public buildings of charm and beauty are public assets—not extravagances. They are a source of pride and affection to individuals, communities and nations. The Old World cathedrals in their grandeur will remain our universal treasures as the offerings of the human mind in its noblest hour. Venerated for centuries, they are majestic even in their decay. Surely the city of Detroit in its prosperity and courage is willing to have beautiful public buildings as monuments of its true progress.[26]

Whether it was due to such appeals as those of Duffield and Strohm, or whether the public's good sense prevailed, the skies cleared considerably in the fall of 1916 when the voters authorized issuance of bonds in the amount of $750,000. Prospects became even brighter when they approved an additional $250,000 in April, 1917. This changed the whole complexion of matters; the money was pledged and would be available as soon as the bonds could be sold. Pending the sale, working capital was needed, and a new appeal was sent to Bertram to release Carnegie's $375,000. Again he refused to turn over any cash until only that amount was needed to complete the building. This created something of an impasse, because the city controller refused to confirm any more Library building contracts until such time as the money to pay them was in hand. The stalemate was finally broken late in 1917 when Mayor Oscar B. Marx wrote Bertram, informing him of the situation and assuring him that Detroit was fully committed to spending all that was needed to complete the work. Upon this assurance, Bertram yielded a point and on December 18 the Commission was informed by the city controller that a check for $375,000 had been received from the Carnegie Corporation.[27]

Meanwhile, on the strength of the 1916 bond issue, Cass Gilbert urged the Commission to renew work on the building. Bids were called for, and on March 17, 1917, the general contract for completion of "a building of marble construction," was awarded the George A. Fuller Company. The contract was for $1,236,320 to which later would have to be added $225,000 for interior fittings. By this time, too, the entire cost of the building had been revised upwards to $1,446,607.19.[28] Costs continued to rise, and before the building was in use another bond issue of $750,000 was necessary. The final price tag bore the figure of $2,775,000 exclusive of the site. This was almost three times what the original estimates called for.

At the moment, however, the Commission was excited about getting started and enclosing the gaunt and ugly frame that had offended the public eye for two years. It was with satisfaction that on October 2, 1917, the commissioners instructed Strohm to make necessary arrangements for the cornerstone laying ceremony. That was duly carried out on November 1, with Commission President Ralph Phelps presiding. The list of distinguished citizens participating included Mayor Marx, Mrs. C. R. Wilson, president, Detroit Federation of Women's Clubs; Albert A. Albrecht, Clarence M. Burton, city historiographer; Samuel C. Mumford, president, Board of Education; John A. Russell, vice president, Board of Commerce, and Strohm. There was one vacant chair, that of Henry M. Utley who had died February 17.[29]

The work went on slowly, so very slowly, that sometimes it seemed the Library would never be finished. April, 1917, saw the United States enter World War I. The usual wartime shortages of manpower and material had their effect. Union labor complained that some of the contractors were not paying the prevailing wage which was required on city work and that out-of-town workers were being hired. The Commission replied that it was not subject to city ordinances, and that it would be illegal to enter into a wage agreement with the Detroit Federation of Labor, a contention that was supported by an opinion from the corporation counsel. In 1918 the Wayne County War Board requested the Commission to slow down in order to release labor for essential war industry.[30]

One problem after another arose, one decision after another had to be made. Someone suggested a pedestrian tunnel under Woodward Avenue to connect the Library and Art Institute, but the idea was dropped in the face of Strohm's objections that it would not be used and that it would require careful policing. Help of the City Plan Commission was called for to zone the area around the cultural center to prevent threatened commercial development. The Library Neighborhood Association was organized and won a battle to prevent a factory from being built at Palmer and Cass avenues.[31] Ralph Stone, an official of the Detroit Trust Company, whose home was nearby, complained about a smoke stack on the top of the building "which belches forth more black smoke than a dreadnought putting out a smoke screen. Mrs. Stone has taken down all her white curtains for protection." His complaint led to improvement in the heating system. And in 1920 when everybody was impatient at delay which followed delay, Cass Gilbert explained that a breakdown in the nation's railroad facilities, an aftermath of the war, made it impossible to receive materials on schedule. Still, there was always hope. On July 15, 1919, the contractor cheerfully predicted that the job should be completed in eight months, and in November the clerk of the works fixed the target date as April, 1920. Although both guesses were short of the mark, the Commission was sufficiently encouraged to ask for an appropriation of $30,000 from Library revenue to be used as a special book fund for the new Main. Things were far enough along, too, by November, 1920, to permit the Common Council to have a preview of the building. The city fathers expressed "interest and hearty approval," which encouraged the Commission to ask approval for the sale of more bonds, $300,000 worth.[32]

The last days of 1920 were ones of feverish activity as a multitude of last minute details were tied together. Shelving was installed and the books were shifted to their places in the stacks from the Downtown Library, which, in the future, was to be used for technical, commercial, municipal and economics collections. The movers had to work their way around under the scaffolding on which were precariously perched some of the nation's most prominent artists, putting the last touches on murals, decorated ceilings, stained glass windows and ceramic and bronze installations. Among those so engaged were Edwin Blashfield, Gari Melchers, Samuel Yellin and Frederick J. Wiley. Mary Chase Stratton, of Detroit's own Pewabic studios was supervising the work of setting tile and mosaic decorations. Altogether, contracts amounting to $125,000 had been awarded for paintings and other interior adornments.[33]

Commissioner David Heineman* and Strohm were appointed a committee to select a suitable inscription to go over the main entrance. Heineman recommended that the aphorism "Knowledge Is Power" would be appropriate, and the Commission concurred. Andrew Carnegie, who died on August 11, 1919, was commemorated as the Library's benefactor with the installation of a bronze tablet in the new building, paying tribute to the man whose generosity helped make the structure as well as several branches possible.

Finally, out of the welter of confusion, order began to emerge, and in the eyes of the commissioners the Library seemed just about complete. On March 1, 1921, Commissioners Kennedy (Johnston B.), Robertson (C. R.) and Gray (Paul R.) were named a special committee to set the date and arrange the program for the dedication and formal opening. The three men reported back that June 3 had been decided upon as dedication day and that the exercises would be held in the afternoon on the rear terrace, followed by a public reception in the evening. All branch libraries were to close at 1 P.M. to permit the staff to attend and also to serve as guides. William Howard Taft, former President of the United States and Chief Justice of the United States Supreme Court, was invited to be the principal speaker. Unfortunately a previous commitment made it impossible for him to be present. Not waiting for a formal dedication, the building was opened for limited use on March 29. When the dedication day finally arrived, it was bright, blue and balmy. A luncheon for fifty important guests was held at the Detroit Boat Club. At 3 P.M. several hundred people had assembled on the terrace and the ceremonies began. In the crowd were many librarians, library officials and others from out of town, assembled to rejoice with their Detroit confreres at the auspicious accomplishment of completing a new Main Library of such impressive proportions. The invocation was delivered by the Right Reverend Charles D. Williams, bishop of the Episcopal Diocese of Michigan. Cass Gilbert was introduced

---

* David Heineman (1865–1935) was an attorney. A member of the legislature, he later became the city's corporation counsel, and a member of the State Library Board. Among his other achievements, he was the designer of Detroit's official flag.

225

and accepted the applause and congratulations of the crowd. Divie B. Duffield, president of the Library Commission, introduced the principal speaker, Dr. Marion L. Burton, president of the University of Michigan. He was followed by Mayor James Couzens and, briefly, by Joseph S. Stringham, president of the Board of Education, and William J. Gray, a Detroit bank official. The Right Reverend Michael J. Gallagher, Roman Catholic bishop of Detroit, closed with the benediction. Later that afternoon and during the evening it was estimated that between six thousand and eight thousand persons toured the building. They were described as "appreciative." In addition, three hundred congratulatory telegrams were received from local well wishers and two hundred more came in from all parts of the country and the world.[34]

Those who visited the new Main Library on dedication day and on the days following, beheld a thing of beauty and architectural splendor. From the standpoint of library planning, there probably was nothing to compare with it in the United States. Gilbert had conceived and executed a massive building in early Italian Renaissance style, 210 feet square, with three floors and a mezzanine. It was constructed of white Vermont marble and entirely surrounded by a broad balustraded terrace of Indiana limestone and pressed brick. Approaching the front by a broad walk which divided the wide expanse of lawn, the visitor saw the facade which at the second floor level contained seven arched openings forming an open loggia. Across the front under the cornice were carved marble panels in relief of the twelve signs of the zodiac. In a belt directly beneath the second floor level were carved the names of eighteen literary immortals from the golden ages of Greece and Rome. Over the third floor windows were roundels containing the carved heads of twenty-nine great figures who gave Western civilization its literary heritage.

Entering the massive sculptured bronze front doors, the visitor found himself facing the grand staircase which divided into two stairways, to the right and left. To the right, upon entering, was the children's reading room and to the left, the newspaper and periodical reading room. Behind these large rooms were a number of smaller rooms for staff and administrative purposes. Bisecting

226

the building at ground level was a north-south driveway, behind which were the shipping room, bindery and other offices. Back of these, extending across the entire west side of the building was the galleried stack room rising the full three stories, and providing space for approximately 800,000 volumes. The mezzanine, along the north and south sides, contained the Commission board room, administrative offices, and other facilities for staff use and convenience.

Ascending the grand staircase from the first floor, one stood on the threshold of the high ceilinged and spacious delivery room which, at a later time, would be named Adam Strohm Hall. Directly off the delivery room, on the south, was the catalog room, beyond which was the reference reading room. On the north side of the delivery room were two smaller rooms. One was the comfortably furnished Book Lovers room; the other room, somewhat smaller, was equipped with writing facilities. Beyond this, and corresponding to the reference room, was the Open-Shelf room. Across the center front of the second floor was the Fine Arts room; adjoining it in the southeast corner was the Civics room, and in the northeast corner, the Music and Drama room.

The available floor space on the third floor was considerably less than on the second, due to the lofty dimension of the delivery room, the upper part and ceiling of which occupied the center of the third floor. Around this vaulted space ran a corridor. Off it, in the front, were the staff lunch room, the Map room, and a series of smaller rooms used for meeting purposes. The entire south side was devoted, in 1921, to the Technology Department, while along the north side was the Burton Historical Collection.

In time, interior rearrangements were made and some of the rooms were used for other than their original purposes. But in 1921, the impressive edifice, gleaming white in a park-like setting, with its adornments of paintings, sculptor, stained glass, bronze and mosaic, gave Detroit what was up to that time, its finest public building, and provided the nucleus for the Cultural Center.[35]

CHAPTER 14

THE CHILDREN'S HOUR

As THE PURPOSE and aim of a public library are largely educational,
it is coming to be felt in all wide-awake institutions of this character
that special efforts should be made to interest young people and to
direct their reading, as far as practicable, into proper channels.[1]

So stated Henry M. Utley in 1897 in his annual report as
librarian to the Library Commission. It was a statement which
elicited no surprise in view of the origins of the Library which he
headed. Considering the fact that the Detroit Public Library
began, like other public libraries in Michigan, as a constitutionally
ordained part of the educational system and came into existence
as a school district library, its field of service to the children of the
community was acknowledged from the beginning. That field of
service never failed to be recognized. As time went on, more

228

emphasis was placed upon it. Catering to the young readers became more and more its function.

In the early days of the Library, there was no great distinction between the services offered to adults and children. The purpose of the Library was to meet the demands of the people—and children were people. Books that would be of principal interest to young readers were made available at an early date, but they were available on the same basis and through the same facilities which were enjoyed by their elders. As a practical matter, children were handicapped in their use of the Library when it first opened in 1865 by a rule which set a minimum age of 18 years as a qualification for withdrawing books. That, however, did not preclude parents from taking out books for the pleasure and instruction of their offspring. It was some time later, at least by 1868, that this rule was modified to extend Library privileges to high school students and to "those outside of it who shall obtain written permission of the Library committee." [2] This rule remained in effect for several years, and later rules reduced to fourteen years the age at which a card could be obtained. For several years no distinction was made between juvenile books and those of a general character. This changed in time, too, and by 1880 the classification of the collection showed that about 10 per cent of the books were "juvenile—mostly fiction."

In 1881 a decline in total circulation was noted which was attributed in part to "the restriction upon the circulation of books of an objectionable nature among the juvenile readers, and the permitting them to draw but one book per week, except under the certificate of parent or guardian." [3] At that time, juvenile books withdrawn for home use totalled 13,395 or 11.4 per cent of the Library's total circulation.

The control of reading matter, mainly fiction, was of concern to the Library staff, but there was little that could be done about it as long as children had to rely upon the general reading room for their selections—a room where books of all categories were at their disposal. Moral suasion was resorted to, and in 1884, when juvenile withdrawals dropped to 7.76 per cent of the total, the Library had this to say:

The cooperation of parents and teachers in the labor of elevating the character of the reading done by the young is earnestly advocated, as of the greatest importance in this work of reform. Children and young people should be taught that, even for amusement, history, biography, art, science and travels are far beyond the romance, and that truth is not alone stranger, but more satisfying than Fiction. When once this is accomplished, they would as soon think of seeking their daily mental pabulum in the direction deplored, as of abandoning the use of solid food and adopting a dietary of sweet-meats.[4]

All this was a tacit recognition of the increasing non-adult patronage of the Library and the problems it imposed. The year 1886 showed a sharp increase in juvenile circulation. It was more than double that of 1885, rising to 14.36 per cent of the total home reading. The increase was attributed to the publication of a new catalog of fiction and juvenile books. About that time, the Library began to put more emphasis on periodicals. Only four such publications were for youngsters. They were the *Youth's Companion, Harper's Young People, St. Nicholas* and *Wide Awake.*

The increasing use of the Library by children brought complaints from adult patrons who had to share reading room facilities with them. Partly because of these complaints Utley recommended in 1894 that

a reading room for them is quite desirable and if any space can be found in the present building suitable for such a purpose, I earnestly advocate its preparation. If this want cannot be filled, it forms another strong argument in favor of enlarging the building.[5]

The situation was further complicated in 1894 when, upon the motion of Commissioner Henry A. Harmon, the age limit for card holders was reduced from fourteen to twelve years. This caused Utley to suggest converting the bindery room in the basement into a children's reading room by putting in two windows and cutting a door which would provide direct access to the street.[6] Such a makeshift arrangement, however, was obviated in 1895 when the Centre building was enlarged and quarters for the exclusive use of children became available.

The space acquired by the enlargement of the central Library permitted the opening of a room especially for young people and the establishment of a Children's Department. The new reading room, in the words of the *Free Press,* was "a large apartment in the basement on the west side of the building, with a door opening direct from Farmer Street." [7] A further account pointed out that the basement was only a couple of steps below the grade of the street. The direct access door toward the north end made it unnecessary for those entering to pass through the building proper.

> The children's room is 52 feet long by 33 feet wide, for about two-thirds of its length, and for the remainder about 25 feet wide. It is abundantly lighted, well-ventilated and is in every respect a cheerful and pleasant room. The walls have been decorated with framed portraits of famous authors. Across one end and a portion of one side is shelving of the capacity of about 6,000 books. These cover all classes of literature, but are mainly fiction. All the best periodicals are kept on file and the bound numbers are on the shelves. The children are permitted to go to the shelves, examine the books and make their own selections. Books are drawn out and returned here, and thus the main delivery room is relieved from the great crowds which in former years had become exceedingly uncomfortable, at times.[8]

The children's room was officially opened May 28, 1896, under the supervision of Mary Conover, a pioneer in children's library work. A native of Detroit, Miss Conover joined the Library staff in 1894 as a temporary assistant and within a year had a permanent appointment. She is said to have conceived of a children's department, although she herself gave credit for the idea to Mrs. John J. Bagley, widow of the former governor of Michigan. At any rate, the children's room was one of the first of its kind to be established in a major public library in the United States. Miss Conover thereafter continued in children's work at the Library until her retirement at the end of forty years of service. She helped organize a special library service for sick children, worked closely with the public schools, and founded the Detroit Story Tellers' League in 1912. She died in 1937 at the age of eighty and her memory was preserved by a stained glass window in the Francis Parkman branch.[9]

231

Part of Mary Conover's work was to help, advise and guide the reading habits of Detroit's youngsters, a duty which she performed for more than a generation. Said one descriptive account:

> Parents and teachers frequently come with their children or pupils and look over the books, with a view to making judicious selections. In this way there is more opportunity than ever before to direct the reading of young persons in channels that will be helpful and beneficial in increasing their knowledge and improving their taste.[10]

The department was a success from the outset. In seven months after the room's opening, it was estimated that 42,270 books were used. That figure is not wholly an accurate one because it fails to take into account the withdrawals by children from the adult section which continued to be open to those youngsters desiring to use it. Many did. The classification of "juvenile" books applied only to those in the Children's Department, used by those of fourteen years and younger. Books of biography, history, travel and other categories on the general reading room shelves also were used by young people to a large extent. But by the end of 1896, about 21 per cent of total Library withdrawals were through the Children's Department. So well was the room patronized that in a little over a year the Detroit *Tribune* remarked that it was becoming too small.

> It was started last May, and its little patrons have been steadily increasing in numbers ever since. There are not enough tables and chairs in the room and the Library Commission . . . authorized the purchase of four new tables and two dozen chairs.[11]

Youthful patronage became so heavy that in 1897 Commissioner Herbert Bowen felt obliged to remind the librarian to enforce the regulation "that children may be permitted to handle library books only on condition that their hands are clean." Use of the room became both easier and heavier in 1901 when, under Miss Conover's supervision, a card catalog case was installed. In 1908 a 215-page catalog was published and distributed to the teachers in the public school system and "has been in demand from various cities throughout the country. It has been warmly commended by library and educational experts." In 1903 the age

232

limit for card holders was again reduced, this time from twelve to seven years if requested or approved by the child's parent or teacher.[12]

Miss Conover and those who were assigned to assist her carried the message of what the department could do and was trying to do to public school teachers and parent groups by a series of talks, all of which helped create new interest and business. Pictures, of which Miss Conover began to accumulate a voluminous file, were loaned to teachers for classroom purposes in connection with important persons, events and occasions.[13]

Another phase of children's work was developed in 1902 at the suggestion of Commissioner Osius. He proposed that Saturday afternoon talks or story-telling hours be inaugurated and this was done with great success. It was reported:

> On the occasion of these lectures the room has been packed to its utmost capacity. Perfect quietness has prevailed and close attention to the speakers was noticed in every instance. The talks have been limited to twenty to twenty-five minutes.

While these story periods had a tendency to disrupt the routine of the children's room during the period they were held, they proved invaluable by attracting youngsters to the Library and familiarizing them with the facilities available. Usually a reading list was compiled on the subject of the talk or story and these "drew the attention of the children to good books, and resulted in an extensive use of those books." [14]

In 1905, reporting on the previous year's activity in her department, Miss Conover stressed the necessity for responsibility on the part of the staff for guiding children toward the best in literature. She stated:

> We want parents and teachers to believe that we are guardians at the gates of the book world, and will admit to the children's companionship only what is sweet and wholesome and of good report— only such books as are pleasant to an uncorrupted taste and good for intellectual and moral food.

Perhaps there was need for moral sustenance. The Henty and Oliver Optic books were in heavy demand and *Toby Tyler, or*

Ten Weeks with the Circus was a steady favorite around the turn of the century. The Horatio Alger books in which honesty, perseverance, manliness and youthful enterprise offered the sure way to adult success and fortune, were read until they were quickly worn out. Somehow their message seems to have been lost, because when a report was made on the books stolen from the Library, it was sadly remarked that "the Alger books seem to offer the greatest temptation." [15]

Once the Library was well embarked upon its branch program, the children's work began to take new direction. Youngsters were encouraged to make use of the branches nearest their homes; the same facilities which were provided at the Main Library downtown were offered at the branches. In addition, the difficulty of traveling downtown for books or for story hours became greater as the city grew, and to some extent, children were discouraged from making the effort. Then, too, in the first and second decades of the present century, new diversions such as enlarged recreational activities and the neighborhood motion picture house began to compete for the attention of the young people. The problem was one which the Children's Department quickly recognized, and to which it gave attention as the following excerpt from the annual report of 1909 reveals:

> A growing city needs, for its young men and women, counter attractions to contest the field with the cheap, and often unwholesome amusement places which flourish like toad stools downtown, and which are even now springing up in scattered clusters in home sections. It is a significant fact that money and tremendous energy expended on juvenile courts and charities are found to be necessary only in the larger cities. It may be said, almost with complete truth, that during the childhood of the youngest voter of today, a boy or girl could be safely allowed to go downtown in this city without encountering the lure of harmful amusement places. Such a possibility, most emphatically, no longer exists in Detroit where life is supposed to be worth living.[16]

The drive to locate new branches was the result of this challenge, and the needs of children were taken into account in 1910 when it was stated that the new buildings being planned included as "an important feature," separate rooms for children.[17]

Once the branches had been established and the various factors contributing to the diffusion of activities had made themselves evident, an administrative reorganization became necessary. As a result, the Commission decided in 1914 that "the chief of children's work be hereafter known as the Supervisor of Children's Work, and as such be in charge of all the library work with children in the Main Library, Branches, Stations and School Divisions." As head of the new department, the Commission imported an experienced librarian from Pittsburgh, Miss Elisabeth Knapp. A native of Stamford, Connecticut, Miss Knapp was born August 18, 1874. She graduated from Lake Erie College for Women, at Painesville, Ohio, and studied library science at Simmons College, Boston. She remained as chief of the Children's Department until her death, April 15, 1931.[18] A branch library, opened in 1950, was named for her.

The effect of this reorganization was significant. Originally the Children's Department proper was under Mary Conover who supervised the children's reading room at the Main Library. Later, she assumed responsibility for children's work in the branches. At the same time, public library work in the schools was under the supervision of a separate division. When Miss Knapp arrived on the scene, she took over-all charge of children's work. The Children's Division remained under Miss Conover; the Schools Division, heretofore a part of the Branch or Extension Department, also was transferred to the Children's Department. With the shift in emphasis on children's work from the Main Library to the branches, there was a change in Miss Conover's status. This was officially noted in 1914 when she was given charge of the newly created Intermediate Division of the Children's Department. It was explained in this way:

> The service of the Children's Department in the Main Library has been modified. It was felt that with a dozen branches and various stations attending to the wants of children in the home districts, the need of a downtown book collection for minors was a diminishing one as it had been of late years. The books now available in the children's room are especially adapted for young people from 14 to 18 years of age.[19]

The reorganization permitted a "uniformity in juvenile book selection," to which considerable care was given. "The number of separate book titles in the collection," it was pointed out, "is decreasing while the number of books on hand is increasing. Dupli-

235

cates of good books is the guiding principle." Miss Knapp reported a couple of years later:

> We are doing a large work among the children of the working men. The children of the more comfortable homes in many of our districts need the same kind of care and the advantages which the public library can give. Parents are afraid of our dirty books, contagions and sundry other more or less valid excuses, and books are *bought* for these children. The book tables of such offerings in our local book stores do not warrant the idea that most of the buying is of the best sort.[20]

Whether rich or poor, children flocked to the branches and filled the children's rooms. In 1923 the department could claim with satisfaction that during the past three years 67,842 children were given borrower's cards. Juvenile withdrawals in 1914 were 53,345 books out of the Library's total of 731,047. In 1923, 124,009 juvenile books were withdrawn out of a total for the entire Library system of 1,719,712.[21]

While the Children's Department work was going on there was another important library service for the benefit of young people which predated it and actually was serving more children. That was the service extended by the Library to the public schools. In 1874, the *Free Press,* calling attention to the Library's origin as a school district library, said that "libraries whether public or private, are a supplement or part of the educational facilities of the people." Three years later the same newspaper declared that it was the duty of the librarian to guide the reading of young persons.[22]

In 1882 the Board of Education, having surrendered direct control of the Library, resolved "That this Board, through its President, respectfully ask the Library Commission to take into consideration the advisability of compiling a catalogue for the use of public school students, or others of tender years." There is no record that the Commission took action on that request at that time, although five years later, in 1887, there is mention of co-operation with the schools to the extent that the Library had deposited two hundred volumes in the high school. At the same time, it was noted that the Main Library was receiving heavy use by students of the high school and the Detroit College (now the University of Detroit). The following year the Committee on Books reported it had conferred with the president of the Board

236

of Education and had agreed to furnish books to the high school which could be used "in connection with the studies and text books of the pupils." Under an arrangement worked out, the Board assumed responsibility for delivering books to and from the Library and for the books themselves in the event of loss or damage. The selection of books was left to the discretion of the superintendent of schools, subject to the Book Committee's approval.

"Such books," it was pointed out, "are not, however, to be used as text books, or in the place of text books in the schools, but for examination and reference in connection with the studies of pupils in the schools." [23]

The Commission stated shortly after making this agreement with the Board of Education:

> The fact is that the call for books for investigation by students was very much greater than before. . . . It is a matter for congratulation that ways and means are being devised to promote a closer intimacy between the Library and the public schools. Great expectations are based on the success of the scheme. . . .[24]

Largely through the influence of the principal of the high school, the same service was extended to the seventh and eighth grades in the grammar schools, and by the end of 1889, twenty of the elementary schools were being supplied with supplementary books. In 1890, the Commission again congratulated itself on how well the school program was working out. The book list had been considerably enlarged, and the larger proportion was sent to those schools most distant from the Main Library.[25] Said the report:

> It is found that these books are in great demand in the families of the school children, many of whom live so far from the library that it is very inconvenient for them to come to it for books. The school houses thus become practically branch libraries from which books are obtained for home reading.
> It is on the basis of the service thus rendered the people, that the maintenance of the Library by public taxation is justified.

The number of schools benefiting was steadily increased. To encourage this, a pamphlet entitled *Good Books for Young People* was published in 1891 and sold for five cents a copy. The first edition, five hundred copies, sold out immediately, and one thousand more were printed. The pamphlet stimulated interest to such an extent that in 1892 more than 12,500 books were sent to the schools; of these 4850 were fiction. Some teachers complained about the extra work in checking the reading matter in and out. The Library sought to offset that by making special lists which would appeal to the teachers, and by granting them free run of the Main Library stacks.[26]

It was not long before any school child above the third grade could claim library privileges, and by 1910 "selected books for children above the second grade are placed in 750 schoolrooms in the 83 public school buildings of the city." Prior to 1902, the distribution of books to the schools came under the Circulation Department. In the latter year, it was taken over by the Branch Department which continued to handle the work until 1914 when, as noted, there was a reorganization of the Children's Department, and the Schools Division was made part of it under Miss Jessie Tompkins. Books were ordered by the principals of the schools at the request of teachers for specific titles. The Library staff made up these orders, the books for each school going into a wooden box which was picked up by a Board of Education dray or truck and delivered to its proper destination. These boxes "traveled"; after a reasonable time in one school they were sent on to others. All of the books thus circulated were duplicates of copies in the Main Library.[27]

In some cases, the reading material drawn by the school children was more advanced and more sophisticated than the material circulated from the children's rooms in the Main Library and the branches. That was because much of it was taken home for the use of parents. Nevertheless, the childhood favorites were well read by the pupils.

"It is interesting to note that the fourth grade, which had about 20 different titles, shows a total circulation of 19,692," said the 1896 annual report.

> The most popular books, apparently, were *Brownies Around the World, Stories from Arabian Nights, Little Folks in Feathers and Fur, Robinson Crusoe, Black Beauty, Captain January, Under the Lilacs,* etc. In the fifth and sixth grades the circulation was 20,756.

238

The different titles numbered about 40. Those which had over 700 readers each were, in the order of their popularity, as follows: *Beautiful Joe, Good Old Times, Polly Oliver's Problem, Patriot Schoolmaster, Sara Crewe, Joyous Story of Toto, Donald and Dorothy, Ten Boys.* In the seventh and eighth grades the circulation was 8,932. The books are naturally of a character which requires more time for their reading. No one book was read 700 times. The one which came nearest to it was Mrs. Hamlin's *Legends of Detroit,* with 622 readers. It may be noted that there were more copies of this than any other book, which will, to some extent, account for its large use. Other books most read were Baldwin's *Siegfried,* Fiske's *War of Independence, Zigzags in Classic Lands,* Henty's *Young Carthaginians, Rudder Grange,* Cooper's *Pioneers,* etc.[28]

In later years, while tastes changed, the works of Mark Twain remained perennial favorites. But whatever the children read they read avidly. In 1897 the public schools circulated 94,473 volumes with an average daily withdrawal of 8276 books. Circulation fluctuated somewhat from year to year. Thus in 1910, 77 schools and the summer playgrounds circulated 77,896 books; in 1920, the figures showed 53 schools and 81,617 books; in 1930, 119 schools and 406,960 books; 1940, about 50 schools gave out 223,595 volumes. By 1950, the statistics were no longer comparable, although there were still 55 deposit stations in public schools and 45 collections in summer camps. In 1950 there were 97,306 juvenile card holders, and while the circulation figures cannot be exactly determined, juvenile use may be reasonably estimated at more than 1,000,000. By 1960 the number of juvenile borrowers had increased to 176,704.

There were problems connected with servicing the schools, and the Library authorities sometimes had moments of acute unhappiness. There was, for example, the librarian's melancholy report in 1896 that 10 per cent of the books loaned to the high school were never returned. A bill covering their cost which was sent to the Board of Education was ignored. This led to the suggestion by Utley that thereafter books purchased specifically for the high school should become the property of the school and the Library should be relieved of all responsibility and expense in connection with them. This produced from Principal Frederick L. Bliss of the new Central High School a somewhat apologetic reply, which also contained an appreciation of services rendered. He attributed the loss of books to the confusion involved in moving from the Biddle House to the new school building on Cass at Warren. Then he went on to say:

> I cannot say too much as to the educational value to the young people of Detroit that the books furnished us by the Public Library have been. I believe no other body of books in the world has had a larger circulation than these, and have reached so large a number of students in direct connection with school work. . . . I most earnestly hope that the Board of Library Commissioners may consider favorably the idea of continuing and extending this privilege in the future.[29]

By 1914 the public school work had become so important that the Commission seriously considered having the operation of the high and normal school libraries placed in the hands of the Library, which would have meant that librarians would have been assigned to the individual schools. Another factor which contributed to the large circulation through the schools was the heavy street traffic which prevented small children, in many cases, from going to the branches for their books. They got them, instead, in their schoolrooms.[30]

There were other services provided for children by the Library, not least of which were the Hoyt Henshaw Stevens libraries for sick or shut-in children. These were provided by Mr. and Mrs. F. W. Stevens as a memorial to their son. In January, 1906, the Stevens offered two special libraries for the benefit of sick or crippled children confined to their homes. Each collection consisted of about twenty books in a specially constructed wooden case bearing a plate with the inscription "Hoyt Henshaw Stevens Memorial Library." Mr. and Mrs. Stevens bore the total expense of procuring and cataloging the books, and furnishing the cases, and also replaced the books as they were worn out. Within a short time after their original donation three others were added to supplement the first two.* These cases were permitted to stay in the possession of the young invalid as long as they were desired. They were under the supervision of the Children's Department,

---

* These libraries for sick and shut-ins were not endowed, but were supported by private contributions.

and the only restriction was that they could not be sent to patients with contagious diseases. One case was kept permanently at Children's Hospital. The first case of books was sent out on April 11, 1906, to a Sammie Roof, a seven-year-old who had been run over by a truck. During 1906, the cases were sent to the homes of 16 youngsters, ranging in age from seven to fifteen years. One case went to Grace Hospital where it was used by two children.[31]

Always seeking ways to enlarge its corps of youthful patrons and to shape their reading habits, the Children's Department over the years extended its services in a number of ways. In 1926 a Parents' and Teachers' Room was opened in the new Main Library. It was stocked "with a representative collection of books suited to the tastes and capacities of children of elementary school age." Under the supervision of the Schools Division, this room provided guidance to adults in their selection of reading material for home and school. A collection also was added of books of a non-technical nature to assist the parent, teacher and social worker.[32] In 1944 a Youth Service Division was set up to cater to the needs of teenagers. The wide range of activities of the Children's Department was summed up in the 1944–45 annual report in the following words:

> In the Library's work with children individualized book and reading guidance is supplemented by story telling, by music appreciation and musical entertainment programs based on selected phonograph recordings, by educational films to stimulate and inform, and by a variety of special activities developed in close association with the schools, the Junior Red Cross, and other group work agencies. Through this broad range of activities library service makes an important contribution to both the mental and the emotional growth of children.[33]

While it looked after the interests of the younger children, particularly the grade school pupils, the older students were not neglected, and the Library long has worked closely with the area colleges and universities. In 1891 Commission President Hosmer called attention to the fact that the University of Michigan had organized extension courses in Detroit in history, Shakespearean literature, political economy and chemistry. The Library lent its facilities and large numbers of those attending the classes made use of Library books in their studies.[34] In 1917 a junior college was organized in Central High School, and over the years it evolved into the College of the City of Detroit and then Wayne State University. Lacking adequate collegiate library facilities of its own in its early years, the nearby Main Library served it as a virtual college library. So great was its use by students, that they became a serious problem to Library authorities, threatening to crowd out the general public. In 1926 the Commission noted that

> use of the Library by college and high school students . . . is still a problem and not satisfactorily solved. The dividing line between the proper field of the public library and of the school library exists too often in our minds only, not in those of teachers and students, and the service we are able to give both to students and the general public suffers in consequence.

Again, in 1931, the Commission further complained:

> The cooperation extended to the formal educational institutions of the city is of considerable volume. Indeed, in the case of local institutions of collegiate education, some of our departments at the Main Library function as a school and college library in a degree disproportionate to the services we are under obligation to render for the good of the general public. . . . We are not in a position to be held responsible for complete college library service. The develop-ment of the colleges of the city has been rapid without a correspond-ing development of such necessary departments as their libraries.[35]

It was not long thereafter, however, before Wayne State University was able to establish its own library, magnificently housed on the campus. Thereafter, the University and the Detroit Public Library worked in close cooperation, and to a large extent avoided duplication of books and services, preferring, rather, to comple-ment each other. A joint committee was set up by the two institu-tions for the purpose of determining which of the more expensive books and periodicals would be acquired by either one or the other, but not by both.[36]

To evaluate in precise terms the social and educational achieve-ments of the Library is not possible, although no one questions the value of the services to the community which the Children's Department performs. This was recognized in 1919 when Elisabeth Knapp explained it in eloquent terms which also serve to explain the exalted mission of the Library in reference to children's work. She said:

> There are no figures for the following: an American ideal instilled, a sluggish brain quickened, imagination stirred, artistic sense developed, civic pride taught, a lesson made vivid and hours of real enjoyment given free; there is only faith that we may have done some of these things for many children. . . .[37]

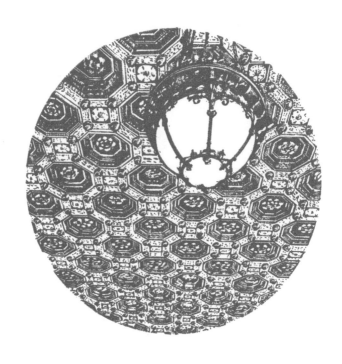

CHAPTER 15

THE PEOPLE'S LIBRARY

A PUBLIC LIBRARY, like any enduring institution, in time acquires
its own unique character. The result of such formative factors as
the personalities of those who have directed it, the peculiarities of
its community, how it is intended to serve and how well it serves,
all combine to give the library what might be called its "mission."
What has been the mission of the Detroit Public Library, and how
well it has fulfilled it, bears examination. Two questions may be
asked: What makes a library, and what should a library be?
Applying those questions as yardsticks to the Detroit Public
Library, clear-cut answers are found in a statement by Librarian
Henry M. Utley which reveals not only a sense of mission, but a
course which the Library has pursued for a century. In 1887,
when the Library was firmly established, Utley stated:

244

The Library is making substantial progress, not only in the addition of books to its already creditable collection, but in extending the circle of its influence and increasing usefulness. . . . It is the people's Library. Its literary treasures are free, to be used and enjoyed by those to whom such things must otherwise have been denied.[1]

The People's Library! That is the character which the Detroit institution early acquired and which it has consistently maintained. As distinct from a public library, the phrase expresses a mission which has not been lost in the succeeding years. Magnus Butzel explained the purposes of the Library as a municipal asset when he stated in 1892:

> The fostering, maintaining and enlarging of a public library is a steady invitation to men of culture and men of means to settle among us. . . . Even more: The addition of books, works, treating of, illustrating and furnishing new ideas in the arts, sciences, mechanical, etc., employments, of necessity must develop higher cultured and more competent helpers in our industrial enterprises . . . improves local products, enlarge their markets, and logically adds to the enlargement of factories, increase of population. . . .[2]

Time after time this basic truth was repeated. Adam Strohm saw things in much the same way Butzel did, but he went beyond the economic values. More than some of his predecessors, he recognized the educational functions of the Library and its potential for the cultivation "of good taste and clear thinking." He looked upon the Library as a people's club "to which they may resort to enjoy worthy things and noble associations and to sense with gratitude that none needs to be denied an understanding of and participation in the heritage that belongs to us all." [3]

There was always a recognition on the part of the Commission, the librarian or director and the staff, that the Library must never be permitted to become ossified, to jell into a fusty treasure house which acknowledged only the past. It had to be, in a city such as Detroit, both dynamic and progressive; one which lived in the age of today and looked toward tomorrow.

> The old order of things is past, and the Library, among other institutions, is feeling the effects of it in meeting with new patrons, new ideas, new demands, and different backgrounds.[4]

245

In 1943 the basic purpose of libraries was said to be "to assemble and preserve books and materials in organized collections, and through stimulation and guidance to promote their use. . . ." [5] Ralph Ulveling, the director, enlarged upon this broad statement of principle by stressing the importance of the words "stimulation" and "guidance." He applied them as a background for the general functions of a library which cover the categories of information, research, education, aesthetic appreciation and recreation.[6]

This sense of and acknowledgment of the necessity for being a vital force in the modern age was further stated in an essay written in 1951 by Richard Malone, chief of the Downtown Library.

> As today's public library patron utilizes the tremendous resources for education, and information that are the modern library's stock in trade, he probably little realizes how a hundred years of developing attitudes and aspirations have changed yesterday's libraries into the great public institutions they are today. The student, businessman, housewife, researcher, engineer, and historian, and a thousand others on a thousand different quests use today's library—intrinsically and traditionally still a place of books, but also a library assuming a new place in a world where communications are made with dizzying speed and ideas are multiplied and distributed by the millions.

He saw the library as "a vital agent of the general will and need for a free, democratic intelligence," an "arsenal of weapons to be used in the battle for men's minds." [7]

All of this implied the continuing need of the Detroit Public Library to serve the people under modern conditions. And as it was successful in doing so, it filled that 1887 role of the People's Library.

Regardless of what was done to keep the Library abreast of the times, its real cornerstone in 1965 as in 1865 is books. The Library was and is "intrinsically and traditionally still a place of books," or to repeat a statement already made, a place "to assemble and preserve books." The character of a library is determined to a large extent by the quantity as well as the quality of its collection. As new ideas keep coming forth as a rushing torrent, so does the literature which presents them. Failure to keep abreast, to acquire and preserve, would mean a static library. And that is something the Detroit Public Library has successfully avoided becoming.

The Library opened in 1865 with a collection of 5000 volumes, representing an outlay of $7000 made by Henry Chaney on his eastern buying junket of 1864. That number of books, or something closely approximating it, represented the Library's stock when the doors were officially opened in the old Capitol building, March 25, 1865. By the end of that year the collection had grown to 8864 volumes. The acquisitions continued thereafter at a regular although not uniform rate. When the Centre Park library opened in 1877, there were 37,703 books on its shelves. By 1881, when the Library passed to control of the Board of Library Commissioners, the public had 42,413 volumes at its disposal, and by 1886, the number had increased to 70,550. The 100,000 mark was reached in 1890, and at the end of 1909 the Commission reported that the Library possessed more than a quarter of a million volumes—a then astronomical figure. The collection's growth could be counted, of course, only in terms of net gain. While acquisitions in 1890 may have been 10,646 books, the net gain for the year was only 9657. Books lost, worn out beyond salvage or repair, or in various ways disposed of accounted for the lower net figure. The new acquisitions were distributed among eight categories, the net gain for each being as follows: fiction, 1899; biography, 1411; travel, 981; history, 934; religion and philosophy, 575; English literature, 516; natural science, 305; arts, "fine and useful," 270.[8] These figures, which were representative of other years of that general period, serve to indicate the reading preferences of the public.

In the early days of the Library, the administration of the book fund, which is to say the responsibility for the number and kind of books acquired, was left largely to the discretion of the Commission's book committee, or the subcommittee on books of the Board of Education's Library Committee. The members largely took upon themselves to determine what should be bought. The librarian's recommendations naturally were given weight, but so were the suggestions and preferences of various groups and individuals who had no official Library connection. When Commission members traveled abroad, as did Dr. Kiefer, Magnus Butzel or Edwin Conely, they often were given a sum of money, and carte blanche authority to make such purchases as they saw fit. Thus in 1890, Butzel took $500 or $600 of the Library's money on a trip to Germany and spent it in Leipzig, an important German publishing center. In the same year, Utley was requested to go east and "purchase such books as he may find which in his opinion are desirable for the Library and offered at reasonable prices, not exceeding $5,000 in amount." Nothing, it will be noted, limited Utley in the full exercise of his own judgment. Other purchases were regularly made through local channels, contracts being awarded annually to one or more bookstores or distributors on the basis of the highest discounts. For many years, John McFarlane was a consistently successful bidder, his discount as in 1886, being 31 per cent on imported books.[9]

Usually one member of the book committee took it upon himself to supervise purchases, and the other commissioners usually deferred to his judgment. Herbert Bowen, a man of scholarly inclinations, devoted much of his attention as a commissioner to purchases and acquisitions, with the result that additions to the book inventory reflected to a large degree his personal tastes. J. A. Marsh was another whose influence was strong until 1886, when he took a position with a book distributing firm, and resigned as a commissioner to avoid a conflict of interest.[10] It was not until some years later, when the increase in publishers' output, and the larger purchases made individual supervision virtually impossible, that more professional attitudes became evident, and responsibility for material acquired was turned over to staff committees and professional procedures began to be followed.

After inventorying 250,000 books in 1909, the Library had to wait nine years—until July 1, 1918—to reach the half million mark. The milestone of 1,000,000 was passed at the end of the 1940 fiscal year; another half million were added in the following thirteen years, with the collection totaling 1,573,525 volumes July 1, 1953. The Library at that time found itself embarrassed by riches, for the Main Library had run out of space, and 250,000 volumes had to be removed and stored where, the administration sadly pointed out, they accomplished very little good. By 1963, this situation had been rectified, and the system's inventory revealed 1,994,553 books possessed by the Library.* It might be pointed out that the June 30, 1955, count was 1,638,194 volumes a net gain of 33,238 in twelve months. During that period, 135,-279 new volumes were added, but 102,041 were worn out and discarded.

While the growth of the collection was impressive from a numerical standpoint, it was also impressive when compared to other cities in the same general population class. A 1904 survey of 10 cities disclosed the following: [11]

	Population	No. of Volumes
Detroit	285,704	186,449
Buffalo	352,387	208,969
Cincinnati	329,902	233,744
Cleveland	381,768	208,981
Milwaukee	285,315	145,315
Minneapolis	202,718	136,359
Newark	246,070	89,705
Pittsburgh	321,616	180,702
San Francisco	342,782	150,884
St. Louis	575,238	165,658

In 1942, however, the record was not as good. Of the public library systems of nine major United States cities, Detroit ranked lowest in the per capita number of books available. Its figure was .829, compared to 5.14 for Cincinnati, 4.88 for Boston, 4.20 for Minneapolis–St. Paul, 3.58 for Cleveland, 3.06 for Pittsburgh, 2.92 for St. Louis, 2.55 for Los Angeles and 2.23 for Milwaukee.[12]

The condition of the Library's finances naturally determined the amount which could be spent annually to build up the collection. Relatively, the Library did better in its earlier years, especially after the penal fines money began to be paid regularly and in full. At that period, of course, administrative and capital costs

---

* The June 30, 1963, book count was only part of the Library's inventory figure. In addition to the books, there were also the following: films and film strips, 2253; maps, 107,074; microfilm cards and microfilms, 20,322; pictures, 520,247; newspapers and periodicals (filed), 4350; phonograph records, 20,000; miscellaneous pamphlets, manuscripts, etc., 3,000,000 (est.).

were lower, so that the book fund represented a larger part of the Library's total income. Following the opening of the branches there was a shift in requirements, and the book fund showed a percentage decline. Thus, beginning about 1905, complaints began to be heard about the need for a larger book fund—a complaint which was fairly chronic for the next fifty years. In 1905 the pinch began to be felt when it was found that publishers had formed a combine, and prices were jacked up 20 to 25 per cent. For a time, it was cheaper to buy books in England, but British publishers soon formed a combine of their own and refused to grant library discounts. Conditions were eased somewhat in 1906 after the millage ceiling was raised, permitting slightly increased book purchases. The book fund over several years during this general period was about $20,000 annually. The book fund was not wholly devoted to the purchase of new books, however. Part of the money went for rebinding. (The Library maintained its own bindery after moving into the Centre Park building, although much of its work was done outside on contract.) In 1913, for example, about 10 per cent of the fund went for book maintenance. During that year, the book fund was virtually exhausted, and the purchase of books was practically suspended.[13]

"It may be stated as a matter of fact rather than as a matter of criticism," Strohm pointed out in 1923, "that the book fund at the disposal of the Library for a city of over a million people is at present insufficient." At that time the average cost per book was $1.39. The Commission reported at the close of the 1929–30 fiscal year:

> Our book resources are wholly inadequate. The book appropriation this year is even less than last year and all signs indicate that the book circulation for the year now progressing will top the figure established, at a ratio at least equal to any on record.[14]

In 1939–40, when the book fund appropriation was cut to $79,200, Strohm declared that the book fund should be at least 25 per cent of the total appropriation. He said:

> For the past 10 years, our book fund has fluctuated from 10 per cent in 1930 to 7 per cent in 1940. . . . If the city cannot furnish the ways and means to equip the Library with its most essential

tools, books, then a large economic unit like the state or the federal government should be approached.[15]

Time after time complaints were heard, accompanied by warnings of what could be expected if relief was not granted. Thus we hear in 1945: "Despite substantially higher unit costs for books . . . the total book fund . . . today is 14 per cent less than that of 15 years ago." In 1961, the trouble was compounded by still higher book costs and a continually increasing publishers' output. Said Ulveling in 1961, taking up Strohm's refrain:

> One quick way in which a library can become a second rate, "dated" institution is through failure to acquire an adequate supply of new publications. The older books give a library background and depth; the new publications give it timeliness, for which there is no substitute.[16]

Beginning in 1880, when the first accurate statistics were compiled and circulation amounted to 113,585 volumes, the Library's patronage steadily increased. In a period of more than eighty years, the number of withdrawals has rarely failed to show an annual gain. The year 1882 provided one such occasion, and the slight falling off followed a national trend, attributable to "the general revival of business and the prosperity of the country, with the consequent increased employment of all classes of people, permitting less leisure for reading." [17] This was a phenomenon with which librarians soon became familiar; that the state of the economy has an influence upon the nation's reading capacity. Librarians have also learned, as they did in 1884, that the weather is another factor. "As is commonly the case in other libraries," said the Detroit annual report, "with the decline of the thermometer the reading increases, and the reading is at its minimum when the thermometer reaches its maximum."

It was frequently pointed out that the withdrawals were not a true reflection of readership. Often a book would be read by more than one member of a family. Thus in the 1952–53 fiscal year, it was estimated that the 4,135,842 books circulated were read by an estimated 6,000,000 persons.[18] It is also interesting to note, as the Library did in 1898, that despite heavy withdrawals few books were lost.

251

Though almost 1,000,000 books were put into circulation by the Public Library last year, only one was lost. That was a 45-cent copy of *Three Girls in a Flat*. Two hundred twelve slips of unreturned books were put in the hands of the collector of delinquent books, and he succeeded in recovering 211.[19]

As an index of the popularity of the Library and the use made of it, the number of registered borrowers may be of more significance than the circulation. In 1865, 4700 Detroiters took out Library cards; nearly a century later, in 1961, there were 257,925 adult and 176,704 juvenile registered borrowers, a total of 434,-629. Again, the branches and school libraries were responsible for a big increase in the number of card holders, the number growing from 38,872 in 1904 to 73,028 in 1912, and 173,672 in 1921.

Impressive as the figures indicating use were, they did not always satisfy the Library. In 1924 less than 20 per cent of the city's population held cards. "We should have at least 25 per cent of our people on our books," it was pointed out.[20] In 1927, it was stated:

> The registration records disclose a list of 247,455 book borrowers in good standing which just about equals the number of registered voters who articulate their interest in our community life at elections. . . . If the foregoing number of people by exercising their franchise practically determine the political trend and communal drift of over a million of their fellow citizens, then one may be permitted to speculate how the minds of our citizens, their intelligence, their understanding of things worth while are affected by an institution where a quarter of a million people foregather to enrich their own existence, to add to their own capacity by tested information and stimulating knowledge.[21]

To process the daily withdrawal of books by a number of patrons equal to the population of a fair-sized city, to keep a running record of the inventory, and to check back into normal circulation channels the returned books, became an involved administrative problem. It was solved in 1929, and put into operation in 1930. This was a simplified method of recording loans in which a withdrawal card was filled out by the borrower instead of the attendant at the charging desk. This system marked another pioneering effort on the part of the Detroit Public Li-

252

brary, and was soon being used by other major libraries. In 1947, the book and inventory control was improved upon with a punched card system using IBM machines. The Library reported after it had been in operation about three years:

> Adapting this business practice to library procedures involved considerable effort. We are happy to report, however, that the project after several discouragements has proven successful and will be retained. . . .[22]

To keep pace with public demand and to satisfy reading tastes was no small task for the Library. Preferences changed, reflecting the interest and the mores of the times. One day's best seller was quickly read by hundreds or thousands, and then relegated to the shelves to gather dust, forgotten. A newspaper article of 1892 found such authors as Rider Haggard and Robert Louis Stevenson no longer in demand. Similarly, Kipling, "the erratic and irrepressible," was on the wane, although he had a renewal of popularity later. Most called for were J. M. Barrie, Louisa May Alcott and Hawthorne, while *Uncle Tom's Cabin* maintained a perennial popularity, and *Ben Hur* was a prime favorite. The Library stocked twenty-five copies of that book. The writer continued:

> Shakespeare is extensively called for, largely as a result of the university extension course. The works that are in steady use are those of Sir Walter Scott, Charles Dickens, William Black, George Eliot, Thackeray, George Ebers, E. A. Poe, J. Fenimore Cooper, Mrs. Craik, Jules Verne, Oliver Optic, Mrs. Burnett. . . .

Many more, some of whom like Dumas, Charlotte Bronte, W. D. Howells, Mark Twain and Washington Irving, to cite but a few listed, continued to be called for in the mid-20th century, due to the interest of students in lasting literature, and the revival of interest resulting from motion picture or television dramatization.[23]

"There are various ways in which demand for books reflects the times . . ." it was stated in the 1922–23 annual report.

> The interest in psychoanalysis, character reading and various forms of "practical psychology" makes it difficult to equalize supply and demand with books of that sort. An editorial in a newspaper sends

up the circulation of books on astronomy; the moving picture of the *Three Musketeers* booms not only the circulation of the novel, but also that of the historics of France and the life of Cardinal Mazarin. . . .

The following year, an interest in science was reported, and soon thereafter, the phenomenal wave of speculation which swept the nation as a prelude to the Great Depression, found expression in the call for books on investments and investing practice. This was accompanied by an esoteric taste, reflected in the demand for "a rather motley class of philosophy, psychology, palmistry, ethics and astrology," set off by Durant's *Story of Philosophy* and correlated reading of Plato and other philosophers, and by an interest in child psychology and child training. How much of this trend was attributable "to the presence in town of a lecturer on Yogi philosophy, or the recommendation by Henry Ford of the Ralph Waldo Trine books, is the kind of speculation that makes work with the public forever stimulating." By 1936, readers were off on a new tack, stemming in all likelihood from the social and economic changes of the New Deal. "Books bearing upon human relations and the amenities of civilization are being asked for," it was observed.

Members of the Library staff often admitted their puzzlement at the direction readers' preferences took, and they were put to great trouble as they had to trim their sails to the prevailing winds of taste. A 1919 staff memo discloses the problem of trying to be abreast, if not ahead, of popular demand. Referring specifically to fiction, the memo pointed out that

> The need extends all along the line. A request for "anything by Arnold Bennett" should be filled easily, but a few days ago, in response to the appeal, a trip to the shelves revealed the fact that not a single volume was there. . . . A similar inadequacy will be found in connection with books by Mark Twain, H. G. Wells, Locke, etc. No one would speak of Hardy or Howells as "popular" authors, and yet often there are only three or four volumes representing them on our fiction shelves. The demand for western and detective stories is constant, but often a close examination of the shelves yields but two or three. This same deficiency is found with tales of adventure.[24]

The Library found satisfaction in the fact, more than once noted, "that in our foreign neighborhoods the reading done is uniformly

254

of a higher character than that done in the American neighbor-hoods." [25]

In 1951, reviewing eighty-five years of its history, the Library printed a recapitulation of the favorite reading choices during that period. Classified in six groups, that for 1865–70 listed under Romance and Sentiment: *Under Two Flags, Little Women* and *Lorna Doone;* under Local Color and Humor: *The Innocents Abroad;* Faith and Religion: *Gates Ajar;* Self-Help: Alger's *Ragged Dick;* and Significant Books: Tyndall's *Sound.*

From that time on there appeared a whole galaxy of authors and titles, ranging from Arnold Bennett to Zane Grey and Edgar A. Guest; from Dreiser to Sinclair Lewis, from *David Harum* to *Tobacco Road* and the first Kinsey report to the oracu-lar histories by Sir Winston Churchill.[26]

Throughout much of the time that this catalog of modern literature was being compiled, Library officials, and particularly the members of the earlier Commissions, felt they had an obliga-tion to set standards of good taste and act as arbiters in determin-ing what the people should or should not read. This was well expressed in a letter which Butzel wrote to Utley in 1895:

> I am willing to go on record about the duties and privileges of a Library commissioner, that we are the sole judges what books shall and shall not be incorporated into the Library. . . . It is our duty to guard the reading masses against impure literature as far as such comes under our observation.[27]

Fiction, in the minds of the early Commissions, was an instru-ment of the devil, tending to corrupt and degrade. It pained them greatly to have to put "romantic trash" on the Library shelves; and the pain became more intense when they saw people passing by the classics and lugging fiction home by the armful. There was a constant—and losing—battle to wean readers away from light fiction and into more worthwhile channels. As chairman of the book committee in 1882, Commissioner Wilkins asked his fellow members for guidance in authorizing purchases. About 50 per cent of the book fund, he said, was expended for "fiction of the better class and carefully selected juveniles," all of which were drawn as soon as they were placed on the shelves. Should the

Library, he asked, reduce the fiction proportion, so as to "guide, direct and in a measure force or control the public taste"? [28] The Commission mulled over the idea, but gave Wilkins no help in escaping from his dilemma.

The newspapers lent their moral support to the Commission, and the *Free Press* solemnly assured its readers that it "could tell of one young woman . . . of fine education, who gratified a vitiated taste for novel reading till her reason was overthrown, and she has, in consequence, been for several years an inmate of an insane asylum." [29]

The "reading of fiction," the Commission agreed in 1883, "is a vexing problem," and there was some discussion about applying "heroic surgery" and cutting off the supply completely. That was opposed by the librarian Henry Gillman who suggested instead that

> the judicious supply of the best fiction and periodicals, in fair quantity is, it appears to me, the more salutary remedy, instead of ignoring a desire or craving common to mankind in general, and inherited from a long line of ancestry. . . . It may be added that the modern novel of the higher type is often cultivating influence in art, science, morality and religion, and that its claims for recognition in an educational direction are not to be disregarded.[30]

Nevertheless, it was an occasion for congratulation when he reported that the use of fiction in the Library had been reduced to 61 per cent from 65 per cent a year earlier. This, he proudly proclaimed, was a much better record than could be shown by most other libraries.[31]

As president of the Commission in 1905, James E. Scripps declared he would admit fiction to the Library only after it had stood the test of time and had attained the rank of literature. The argument raged on and on, with the public blithely ignoring what the Commission felt was good for it. The issue, although diminished, was still alive in the mid-1920's when Strohm, defending the high percentage of fiction dispensed through the branches, pointed out that "some of the fiction is merely sociology, economics, religion, etc., in disguise." [32]

Far outshadowing the Library's efforts to keep a few books from the public has been its valiant labors to encourage people to read more books, and to make them as available as possible. To this end all manner of devices have been employed. As early as 1896, if not before, weekly lists of new book acquisitions were furnished the newspapers, and in 1901 what was then a startling innovation was put into effect. This consisted of opening the fiction alcove to the public, a procedure which worked so well that it was enlarged upon in the years following. Placing books at the fingertips of readers, permitting them to browse, proved to be an incentive both to reading room use and home circulation. By 1912 it was the Library's policy to eliminate counters, railings, turnstiles and other obstructions and to open up the Library and the branches as much as possible. With few necessary exceptions, the stack room was the only room not available to the public. How well the people responded to this sort of privilege was made clear years later in a librarian's statement that "our open shelf room at certain hours is suggestive of the bargain counter rush." [33]

Strohm was an innovator, and in 1912 he eliminated the necessity for an adult card-holder to provide a guarantor. It was found that this was immediately reflected in an increase in the number of people applying for cards. Strohm later declared:

> Obviously, it would seem senseless to assume that everybody is a possible 'prospect' for library influence; but we are, nevertheless, under obligations to increase our points of contact so as to embrace everybody in a practical and convenient way within our sphere of influence.

The application of that influence, which proved to be considerable, was exemplified by another statement by him:

> With the risk of claiming too much, we still submit that we have democratized the institution as never before. We have endeavored to make our citizens familiar with library service rather than with library rules.[34]

But merely opening the gates and inviting the public in was not enough. They had to be persuaded to come in, and in this endeavor Strohm was equally effective. He established a public relations program which benefited the Library, and which became and has remained an important function. Even before his time, as

257

early as the turn of the century, the Library was distributing annual bulletins listing each year's important acquisitions. By 1915, bulletins and special publications listing certain categories of books, or intended to let the public know of the Library's services were being issued in considerable volume. In that year, a Division of Publications had been set up, and its output included a monthly *Bulletin on Social and Municipal Affairs;* and another on *Manual Arts;* a list of books for foreign-born who were learning English; a pamphlet on municipal government and one on automobiles. Sometimes, as in later years, some of the Library's publications were rather pretentious things. A case in point is *Michigan in Books,* a bibliography of Michigan books, and a chronology, *Detroit in Its World Setting,* published in 1953 with financial help from the McGregor Fund. On September 22, 1917, there appeared the first issue of *Library Service,* a four-page pamphlet (later increased to eight and twelve pages), containing Library and book news. *Library Service* was actually a house organ of the Detroit Public Library. It was continued until 1939, and during its life it drew the attention of professional librarians all over the world.

This type of enterprise was considerably facilitated when opening of the new Main Library in 1921 permitted installation of the Library's own modern, well-equipped printing plant. In the same year, the annual report listed for the first time a Publicity Division. The Library took to the air in 1938 with a series of radio programs, and later, through cooperation with local educational and cultural institutions, it presented a regular course of television programs over Channel 56.[35]

Developments after World War I enabled the Library further to extend its services by offering what became a comprehensive program of professional aid and guidance to readers. The growing complexity of the social and economic structure of society, in which a degree of specialization became almost necessary for everybody, opened up new opportunities for the Library to help the public read more intelligently and completely in the fields of each individual's personal needs and interest. Thus there were created in 1926 the posts of Educational Director of Reading and the Readers' Adviser. In 1938, in cooperation with the public schools, a reading clinic was established to assist adults to correct poor reading habits in order to obtain "the maximum of information and enjoyment from their reading." [36] This, as well as related effort in the adult field, developed from a growing interest in adult education, which manifested itself in 1927 with the organization in Detroit of the Adult Education Council of which the Library became an eager partner.

In some areas of this field, the Detroit Public Library did valuable pioneering work, as in the case, about 1934, of extending the reader's advisory service through its branches instead of making it the specialized function of one individual. This was described to the library profession in an article titled "Is Detroit Again Pointing the Way?" by John M. Chancellor, in the *Bulletin of the American Library Association.* According to Chancellor, the Detroit Library's existing professional staff was formed into a corps of advisers and sent on to the floors of circulation rooms in both the Main and branch buildings "to meet and assist the increased number of searchers for informal education and profitable use of leisure. . . ." Qualified assistants from the various divisions were designated for this duty, part of which was to help prepare a planned course of reading.

"Perhaps," said Chancellor, "this Library, which was one of the very first to provide its public with a specialized readers' adviser, is again pointing the way." [37]

One of the most satisfying services the Library has performed has been its programs for the benefit of the sick and afflicted. In 1889 Edward W. Kuhn, a blind Detroiter, petitioned the Library Commission to place books for the blind in the Library. Nothing was done immediately, but the request was not forgotten. Commissioner C. Henri Leonard, a physician, interested himself in the matter. With the support of the newspapers, the Commission established a collection of seventy books in Braille in 1896. Some of these were purchased, others were donated by blind persons. Kuhn contributed nine volumes, among which were a Bible, a play by Shakespeare and *Imitation of Christ.*[38] This original collection was sufficient to provide for the reading requirements of twelve individuals. More books were acquired in succeeding years, small appropriations being made, with about half of the acquisitions being donated. In 1910, the collection was lodged at the Scripps branch, but as it increased in size, it was moved to the Lothrop branch in 1919. There the books not only were circulated, but classes in reading Braille were taught. Volunteers were recruited to visit the homes and read to those unable to learn Braille. With an estimated 14 per cent of the city's blind population using the service, it was considered sufficiently important to be given division status. The cost of translating books into Braille, a fairly expensive process, was borne in part by Lions Clubs and other service groups in the Detroit area. Contributions for that purpose in the 1928–29 fiscal year totaled more than $12,000. In that year, too, the Library was servicing not only the blind of Detroit, but of the entire State of Michigan.[39] Financial support for the program was provided by the Federal government which supplied material and equipment.

By 1932, library service for the blind had become such a large-scale operation, both in and outside of Detroit, that it was thought advisable to transfer it to the Wayne County Library, which was then largely under the operation and jurisdiction of the Detroit Public Library. The transfer was made July 1, 1932, and the collection was returned to the Scripps branch where the County Library had its headquarters. When the County Library separated from the Detroit system, and eventually moved into quarters of its own in Wayne, the Blind Division went with it.[40]

The sick and infirm also were the concern of the Library and its friends. Mr. and Mrs. F. W. Stevens, who established libraries for sick children, in 1909 presented five libraries of ten books each, for the benefit of elderly women and invalids. Known as the "Mary E. Brewer Libraries for Invalids," each collection was boxed in an oak case, with an inscription plate bearing the donor's names.[41]

Hospitals, too, became in effect deposit stations. Well before the turn of the century, books were being sent to local hospitals, but not, as far as can be determined, on a regular basis. Later, through a project maintained by the American Library Association and administered locally, arrangements were made to serve hospitals. The Detroit Tuberculosis Sanitarium and the United States Marine Hospital became the principal beneficiaries. In

1945 the Commission recommended that "serious thought be given to the establishment of a specialized hospital service." This policy was adopted in the fall of 1950 when Harper Hospital came under the program. A substantial collection of books was placed in Harper. Their availability was made known to patients, and were circulated by the hospital's professional library staff. The service subsequently was extended to other area hospitals.[42]

In 1947, the Library obtained fifty-five ceiling projectors which were made available to bedridden people. This program was first advocated by the Detroit *News,* and was aided by Detroit area Lions Clubs, the Wayne County Medical Society and the Visiting Nurse Association. Through these various services, the Library was able to carry its facilities to hundreds of people who would otherwise be denied them and obliged to spend long, weary hours of unrelieved boredom.[43]

All of these things, taken together, were designed to make the Library truly a Peoples' Library, and in so doing, meet the standard outlined by the distinguished educator, William F. Ogburn, who stated, "The Library is a part of society as a whole and does not exist in any sense in a vacuum nor does it pursue its own course isolated from the happenings around it." [44]

CHAPTER 16

Thou Shalt Not Read

FRAUGHT with more significance than whether the public should
be exposed to romantic novels was the question of the degree of
latitude Library officials should exercise in circulating books
which might be considered against the public interest, obnoxious
to certain groups, particularly religious, obscene, subversive or
simply in bad taste. How far could the Library properly go in
exercising its judgment in such matters without infringing upon
the right of a free press; without assuming the role of self-
appointed guardian of public morality, without draping itself in
the censor's vestments? At the opposite pole, there was the question of resistance to the demands of various groups and organizations which demanded the removal of books because they were
objectionable or offensive to a minority element. To resolve these
matters was never easy. From time to time they became controversial issues and the decisions, whichever way they went, demanded a good measure of common sense, integrity and courage.
Unfortunately there were seldom rule-of-thumb guides; only occasionally were there judicial opinions which could be leaned on.

For the most part each determination had to be made on an individual basis.

One of the first such recorded incidents occurred in 1895 when the librarian removed from circulation a book titled *The Priest, the Woman and the Confessional,* by Charles P. T. Chiniquy. Utley felt the book was immoral, and judging from its title it must have been offensive to a substantial part of Detroit's population. Some few people, prompted either by bigotry or a sincere feeling that Utley's action was capricious and a violation of constitutional safeguards, demanded that the Commission restore the book to the shelves. The Commission, however, stiffened its backbone, and with a minimum of debate backed the librarian. The book remained out of circulation.[1]

A major issue developed in the early 1920's when the Dearborn *Independent* was dropped from the Library's periodical list. The *Independent* was Henry Ford's publishing venture, and it attracted wide and unfavorable attention for the publication of a series of anti-Jewish articles, purporting to show a world-wide Jewish conspiracy to control banking, industry and communications. The documents which were cited were proved later to be forgeries, but their circulation under the prestigious name of Ford was wide.

As protests began to be heard from the Jewish community, Strohm's first inclination was to do little about the matter. In a communication to a branch librarian he said:

> It seems to me that the policy of dropping a magazine off our list because it has an objectionable number does not seem very fair. Would suggest that any such number of irritating matter as the alleged anti-Semitic issue discussed by you be simply not made available for the public as we have occasionally done in the case of other periodicals.[2]

Other issues also were withdrawn, and William J. Cameron, the *Independent's* editor, protested. Strohm replied that the Library's action was based on "sincere and worthy objections to such publications," filed by "citizens and patrons of the Library." [3]

In 1939 Hemingway's *To Have and Have Not* was withdrawn from circulation, and in reply to protests Strohm stated:

263

In accordance with Library precedent, to preserve the complete record in case of writers of some standing, the Committee on Books recommends that a copy be retained in the Main Library for examination only under conditions satisfactory to the Library Commission.

Other books banned about the same time, or under attack, were *Grapes of Wrath, Peacock Feather, All the Young Men, Friendly Tree, Yesterday and the Day Ahead.*[4] Efforts were made before these books became controversial to establish a definite policy, and the Commission's right to do so was challenged by some. There was newspaper criticism, as early as 1922 of the number of books on the Library's restricted list. In a letter of June 28, 1922, to the editor of the Detroit *News,* Strohm explained the Library's position:

> The Library occasionally exercises caution about the display and accessibility of certain books and is thereby exercising a discretion which is strictly within its duty. The reason therefore is not based on any paternalism or tyrannical power or prudish concern about the moral welfare of the reading public. We are simply practicing a principle that has obtained and is likely to obtain in responsible library service, to wit, an endeavor to place the right book in the hands of the right person.[5]

The issue was a recurrent one with which the Library had to live, and it frequently reflected a change in public attitudes or hysteria arising out of the day's passions or prejudices. Thus, in the 1950's, the Library came under criticism from some quarters because it had on its shelves a fairly complete collection of Communist literature. Ulveling, pointing out the social importance of such material at the disposal of serious students, remarked that the chief users of what might be termed subversive matter were agents of the Federal Bureau of Investigation.

What the Library and a large segment of the community felt to be a truly dangerous threat to the Library's right to determine its own policies of book selection as well as the public's free choice of reading matter developed around 1944 and continued in the 1950 decade. This was the result of an aggressive and overzealous police censorship. This type of censorship was not peculiar to Detroit. It was national in scope, brought about in part, at least,

264

by the demands of religious and other organizations to clean up motion pictures, lurid novels and magazines. Admittedly there was much that was in bad taste; much of it was downright pornographic. The result were efforts, noticeable in many parts of the United States, to effect purity by dictum. And as in most such endeavors, one abuse led to another at the opposite extreme.

Like many states, Michigan had statutes which sought to protect the public, particularly children, from the effects of distribution of obscene and immoral material. One of these statutes stated, in part, that it would be a misdemeanor to publish or distribute material "containing obscene, immoral, lewd, or lascivious language," or to "introduce into any family, school or place of education" any book or other type of publication that should contain such objectionable material.[6] This statute was clearly intended to protect the morals of children. The trouble was that it did not define what was "obscene, immoral, lewd, or lascivious language," or who was to determine the standards to be applied in making a definition. The area of interpretation was, therefore, wide open, and organizations and individuals, often prompted by sincere intentions, set themselves up as arbiters.

Frequently politically powerful, those groups found a ready ally in the police censor. In Detroit at the time, he was Sergeant (later inspector) Herbert Case, an able officer whose probity was never seriously doubted. His judgment was questioned, however, as were his qualifications to determine what was and what was not pertinent under the terms of the anti-obscenity laws. Certainly he was diligent in the exercise of what he or his superiors construed as his duty, and he became a center of controversy among book dealers when a number of books became the objects of his scrutiny and action.

Frequently a visit from Sergeant Case and a warning to a book dealer was enough to cause a controversial book to be removed from the counters and the sale stopped. The merchants for the most part did not relish the prospect of testing Sergeant Case's judgment in court with the expense of a trial and the possible results of a conviction. It was their feeling that action should be brought against the publisher, particularly when books which the local censor proscribed, could be purchased through the mails.

To his credit, Sergeant Case also felt that way. Thus, in an effort to be diplomatic and to handle the problem with a velvet glove, an informal "gentlemen's agreement" was worked out by which a word from the censor would cause local bookstores quietly to remove from stock a book about which complaints had been made.

This comfortable agreement came to a head in 1944, partly because one bookstore decided not to play along, and partly because the Detroit Public Library refused to become a party to the gentlemen's agreement and remove a certain book from circulation.

The book in question was *Strange Fruit,* a novel by Lillian Smith. The subject involved the racial-social problem of the South, and in depicting her characters and presenting their dialog with realism, Miss Smith employed words which are sometimes seen scrawled on fences, but are not normally heard at polite tea parties. The book was banned in Boston, and certain of its passages containing the earthy words were called to Sergeant Case's attention. He later admitted that he had read only those passages and not the entire book. He followed his usual routine of calling on the bookstores and asking their voluntary withdrawal of *Strange Fruit* from sale.

But this time he ran into a snag. He asked the Library to remove the book from circulation.[7] The Library had several copies on its restricted shelf. They were not withdrawn from circulation. What was disturbing to the Library was the implication that it was subject to the censor's arbitrary edict, a proposition which could not be accepted without a complete surrender of its authority and its abdication of independent responsibility. The Library's refusal to eliminate the book completely encouraged the bookstore operated by the United Automobile Workers Union to declare that as long as the book was available at the Library, it would continue to offer it for sale.[8]

By this time the matter had been aired in the press, and Library officials felt that a firm position would have to be taken. The issue hinged upon whether *Strange Fruit* really was an obscene book, and whether the judgment of a police officer could be accepted as a final criterion. At the instigation of Ulveling the

Library Commission called a public meeting on May 23, 1944, to which representative citizens were invited to discuss the matter. The list of those responding included educators, clergy, journalists, lawyers and clubwomen. Dr. Leo M. Franklin, rabbi at Temple Beth El and president of the Commission, presided. He declared:

> I wish to make this statement at the very onset. This book which is under discussion this afternoon has never been on the open shelf of the Detroit Public Library. We have three methods of handling the circulation of books. The first covers those books that anybody with a library card or otherwise eligible to the use of books of the Library may have. The second applies to that group of books on the open shelf which may be given only to adults. And then we have a third class which we call the closed shelf group. To this classification are sent those books which we believe should not be given out to everybody who asks for them and which in any case are never given to persons under twenty years of age and then only after the most careful scrutiny of the individuals asking for such books. The particular book in question has from the beginning been put into the third grouping, i.e., the closed shelf.[9]

The point of that statement was to show that the Library was not contributing in the slightest degree to the corruption of children. The ban, then, if the censor had his way, would have been against adult, mature readers. That could be justified, if at all, only on the grounds of obscenity.

The police department censor who was present with Assistant Prosecutor Harold Helper pleaded he had only been doing his duty; that isolated words in the book had been pointed out to him; he had considered those words to be obscene, and had sought advice from the assistant prosecutor. Helper, he said, agreed that the words were obscene and violated the statute. That left the censor no alternative but to take action and he began his rounds of the bookstores.

"I then came to the Library," he stated. "If the Public Library puts that book out on loan, every dealer and every lending library also has that right."

Helper, too, admitted that his decision was based not on the book as a whole but on a few words of the text. Both his admission and the censor's served to bring the issue into focus: Can an

267

entire book be ruled obscene because it contains words which, taken out of context, are in themselves obscene? Those at the May 23 meeting proceeded to demolish any such premise as that upon which the censor stood.

Dr. Robert Foster, of the Merrill-Palmer School, said he not only had read *Strange Fruit* himself, but had given it to his wife and eighteen-year-old daughter to read, and had also recommended it to his students. He found nothing in it, he said, which could not be found in the dictionary, the Old Testament, and a number of modern books recently in the best-seller category. But what made him indignant was "whether or not a sergeant in the Police Department or the Police Commissioner himself has any business telling me what my daughter should read or what I shall read myself."

The discussion came back to the specific words which had shocked or offended the police department censor and Helper, but Dr. Franklin was able to direct the inquiry into its proper channels.

> We are dealing, I thought, with a book and not with a few words in it. I am stressing this because I am sure that *Strange Fruit*, despite an occasional ugly word or phrase is a book of social significance and value.

Others agreed. Several said they had read the book and were unaware of any obscenity. The Reverend Hugh F. Smith, a Catholic priest, was not too impressed with the book, he said, but he added that he thought it peculiar to judge an entire book by a few words. Others thought the book's social message far outweighed any other consideration, and some felt that the use of the challenged words were necessary to provide realism and factuality.

Lee A White, newspaper official, was more concerned with the censorship threat than with the book itself, although he ascribed merit to it as a literary work and hoped it would focus attention on a social situation which needed correction. But, he added:

> I should be particularly unhappy if as a result of the law or the activity of individuals, we should be deprived of an opportunity for forming an intelligent opinion. . . . I regret the limitation of circulation of books in the Library. I don't know of a library board, a

police officer, or legislator whom I would like to have choose for me the books that I would like to know. . . .

Dr. T. T. Brumbaugh, a Protestant clergyman, admitted he was aware of vulgarity, but reminded those present that vulgarity was part of the life about which the author was writing. "In that case," he stated, "with that definition which may be my own, this does not classify as obscene literature at all."

So it went, with speaker after speaker. Some felt that the language could have been toned down somewhat without losing the effect sought; others thought the so-called obscenity was an integral and honest part of the atmosphere Miss Smith sought to create. Some were more impressed than others by the book's social message. But almost without exception, those present whose voices carried weight in the community deplored the idea of censorship, and felt that a book should not be condemned by a single word or a few words taken out of context. The sole dissenter was Dr. Burt R. Shurly, member of the Board of Education, who feared the effect of putting the book in the public or school libraries.

The entire discussion was summed up by Ralph A. Ulveling who acknowledged the responsibility of the Police Department in dealing with the use or misuse of certain kinds of pictures and print. But at the same time, he said, the Library also had its responsibility. He pointed out:

> We are trying to do an honest educational job. That is our function. We know that we have a responsibility to serve all segments of society. We cannot deny one segment of society what they legitimately should have simply because another segment disapproves. Such group disapprovals may be based on economic situations, political differences, or other reasons. But if we were to honor all such protests presented, the Library could not carry out its fundamental responsibility as an educational institution serving the needs of all. Therefore, we have found it necessary to select the best materials available to all who are competent to use them. This implies at once that not everything in the Library will be approved by all Library users. In other words, prejudices, or restricted views, cannot provide a sound basis on which to build an educational service.

The meeting ended, and the Library Commission met May 24, to consider what action should be taken in regard to *Strange*

Fruit. After the members had heard from a cross-section of representative community leadership, they had no difficulty reaching the decision that the book should "be kept available on the closed shelf for restricted circulation." A directive to branch librarians and department heads warned that the book should not be issued to anyone under twenty years of age; that rental copies should be transferred to the closed shelf; that no reservations should be accepted by telephone, and that all applications for the book should be made in person.[10]

In the face of the kind of public support that the Library was able to muster, the police department censor was not eager to press the matter further. The day after the Commission's hearing, the censor quietly called the bookstores, according to the Detroit *Free Press,* and announced that the ban on *Strange Fruit* had been lifted. Within a few days thereafter the book was at the top of the best seller list.[11]

While a battle had been won, it was recognized that it still was only a battle and not the war. For that reason, the cheers were muted.

Ulveling told an American Library Association official:

> Off the record, I don't know whether ours is a final victory or not. . . . I hope the matter is settled. Had it not gone as it has up to this point, it would have presented a very serious situation for this Library; with an unfavorable decision for us, or if we had refused to fight the issue, the Police Censor, to all practical purposes, would have had a veto power over every book that we selected. As it is, I think the Police will be reluctant hereafter to move in as high-handed a way as they did, at least until after they have consulted with us.[12]

Ulveling was right when he assessed the situation with caution. Police censorship in Detroit, far from being beaten, became a more potent force than ever, and the police department censor was increasingly active. His influence became apparent beyond Detroit. In 1954, the censor and the power he exercised was the subject of an article in the Minnesota *Law Review,* the journal of the Minnesota State Bar Association. The article pointed out that publishers submitted manuscripts to the censor for his verdict before accepting them for publication. Each month the censor

would send Detroit book sellers a list of what he considered objectionable books. As a result, these would not be offered for
sale. Police officials in other cities sought copies of the censor's
monthly bulletins or lists and applied the Detroit standards in
their own towns.

> Since it is obviously impossible for a publisher to print two edi-
> tions—one for Detroit and other cities using the Detroit lists, and
> the other for the rest of the country—the Detroit censor is able to
> this extent to censor literature for the entire country,

the *Law Review* article pointed out. It continued:

> So far, the local distributors in Detroit have withheld from circu-
> lation every book banned by the censor bureau and the county prose-
> cutor. From 1950 to 1952 more than 100 titles of paper-bound books
> have been withheld in this way.[13]

Obviously, this state of affairs could not continue indefinitely
without seriously impairing the principle of freedom of the press.
The power of the censor had to be challenged and the law clari-
fied. It is only remarkable that it took as long as it did before
the rights of the public were asserted in court. That was finally
done in 1954 when a Detroit bookstore proprietor, Alfred E.
Butler, decided to test the law and the censor's powers. A copy
of a novel, *The Devil Rides Outside,* which the censor held to
be obscene was sold by Butler who was promptly arrested by
Case—by this time an inspector—and brought to trial in the
Detroit Recorder's Court on July 7, 1954.

The Public Library was not a party to this case, but it was, of
course, interested, and the first witness called by the defense was
Harriet Goode, chief of the Library's Book Selection Department. She testified as to the method of selecting books, and said
that *The Devil Rides Outside* had been acquired by the Library.
Stating that in the opinion of the selection committee the book
had literary value, it had been placed on the closed shelf, and was
available only to adult readers who specifically requested it. The
procedure thus followed was, as with *Strange Fruit,* intended to
keep the book out of the hands of children.

The trial of the People vs. Butler continued for several days

271

with the defense calling as witnesses, besides Miss Goode, a number of university professors, clergymen, and club women. Most of them testified as to the book's literary value and, in their opinion, its inoffensiveness. Nevertheless Butler was found guilty by Judge John A. Ricca and fined $100.

The case was appealed directly to the United States Supreme Court which, in the opinion written by Justice Felix Frankfurter and delivered February 25, 1957, reversed the Recorder's Court verdict. Justice Frankfurter pointed out that Butler was convicted under a law which made it an offense for him to make available to the general reading public a book which might be harmful to children.

> The State insists that, by thus quarantining the general reading public against books not too rugged for grown men and women in order to shield juvenile innocence, it is exercising its power to promote the general welfare. Surely, this is to burn the house to roast the pig.

He pointed out that, while Michigan had a statute specifically designed to protect children against obscene matter, Butler was not convicted for violating that statute. The opinion concluded:

> We have before us legislation not reasonably restricted to the evil with which it is said to deal. The incidence of this enactment is to reduce the adult population of Michigan to reading only what is fit for children. It thereby arbitrarily curtails one of those liberties of the individual, now enshrined in the Due Process Clause of the Fourteenth Amendment. . . .[14]

This decision did not settle the issue of censorship, nor did it rule against the constitutionality of Michigan's statutes against obscenity. It did not attempt to define what was or was not obscene. That question has not yet been answered by the courts to the complete satisfaction of everyone. Nevertheless, the Butler decision was a milestone in that it limited the grounds upon which the censor might proceed, and in so doing placed some needed limitations upon his wielding an arbitrary power. That was a matter of comfort and satisfaction to the book sellers and the Library alike. It also vindicated, if vindication was necessary, the Library's established procedure of not allowing a book to be banned merely because it offended someone. The Library's policy to make a book available to the general public while at the same time restricting its use by children continued in full operation. Following the decision by the Supreme Court, the Commission reiterated its policy in the following statement, a policy which has generally earned the approval of the public:

> The matter of book censorship was raised in rather acute form during the year. This came about by reason of the activities of the police and other law enforcement agencies. In the operation of a public library the problem is not quite the same as in church or other special libraries or as to book dealers. To the librarian in a public library it is a matter of book selection and manner of permitted use after being put on the shelves. Obviously, if a public library is to fully serve its purpose it must have on its shelves some books which are not appropriate for general circulation but which should be available under restrictions to adults, scholars, professional persons and the like. No substantial question was raised as to the propriety of the methods and results achieved in these particulars in the Detroit Public Library. The policies and methods so tested are being continued.[15]

CHAPTER 17

ENTER THE PROFESSIONALS

"IT MAY BE OF INTEREST to you that during the long history of
the Public Library in the City of Detroit from the year 1865 to
1951 there have been only six Librarians," Dr. Lawrence Reynolds, a Library commissioner, pointed out in 1951. His statement
was equally applicable in 1965. The cast of characters was the
same. Henry Chaney, Manasseh Hickey, Henry Gillman, Henry M.
Utley, Adam Strohm and Ralph A. Ulveling appeared in that
sequence. But in the strict sense of the word, only Strohm and
Ulveling, whose terms of office spanned a period yet unended of
fifty-three years, qualify as professional librarians. Chaney was
a schoolmaster, Hickey a retired preacher and Gillman was a
scholar and scientist. While they functioned effectively as librarians, with the possible exception of Hickey, they were not professionals because, in their days, there was no such thing. It was not
until the regime of Utley that professional standards began to be
evident in the field of library administration. His predecessors
were supervisors of the library and caretakers of the collection.
In the beginning of his term, Utley was in the same category.

274

Utley's appointment was frankly a political one, a fact which in itself placed an obstacle before any claim he may have had to being a professional librarian. A native of Ypsilanti, he was born in 1835 and was graduated from the University of Michigan with the class of 1861. He went to Detroit where he became a newspaperman, serving several years as city editor of the staunchly Republican *Post* and then with the *Post & Tribune*. He later moved over to the Detroit *Free Press* where he was an editorial writer. His newspaper affiliations led him by the usual paths into active political participation and resulted in his appointment as secretary of the Board of Education in 1881. When that Board was reorganized in 1885 and a Democratic faction won control, Utley was rewarded for faithful service by the lame-duck Republican members by being made head of the Detroit Public Library at a salary of $1800 a year.

Utley's background gave him the same qualifications most librarians had in those days. Actually, he was better qualified than most because he was well educated; he already had published two books, and would eventually co-author a third, a history of Michigan which is still consulted. A scholarly man who knew and loved books, he assumed his tasks of librarian with a determination to make the Detroit system a useful, efficient and outstanding one. He succeeded. He took an active part in civic affairs, but more important he promptly associated himself with outstanding library leaders through affiliation with the American Library Association which had been founded in 1876. Utley regularly attended its annual conventions and urged members of his staff and commission to do so when circumstances permitted. He was ALA president in 1894–95 and continued to be an active and influential member until his death at the age of eighty-two in 1917. He led the movement in 1891 to found the Michigan Library Association, and for thirteen years served as its president. Utley's efforts to keep the library in step with Detroit's growth and to raise constantly the standards of service earned him considerable distinction. At the time of his retirement in 1912, he had attained the status of a trained librarian, if not that of a professional.

His successor, Adam Julius Strohm, was a professional in every sense of the word, and on the solid foundation which Utley had

275

built, he created a truly professional staff. Strohm was born in Venersborg, Sweden, February 16, 1870, and was educated at Uppsala University. He graduated in 1888 with a degree of bachelor of arts. Four years later, he came to the United States, settling in Chicago where he lived for several years. Deciding to advance his education, he enrolled in the University of Illinois library school, at the same time working in the University library. He earned his degree of Bachelor of Library Science in 1900 and was made librarian at the Armour Institute of Technology. After a year there, he became head of the Trenton, New Jersey, public library from where he was called to Detroit in 1911 to be assistant librarian. He became librarian the following year when Utley stepped down.

Strohm was called in as assistant librarian—it was intended then that he would shortly succeed Utley—to embark the library upon the greatest expansion of its history. It was the time when the Carnegie program, just getting under way, made possible the build-up of a branch system. The new Main Library was in the near future, and a strong guiding hand was needed which Strohm provided. It was, by no means, an easy job. Strohm was a man of strong character, dedicated to the job of building up the system and providing a staff worthy of it. To this, he devoted administrative ability of high quality, but he necessarily trod on toes, and he charged head on into controversy. In the beginning, some of the staff thought him arbitrary and high-handed, and the dissidents had newspaper support. The *Free Press,* for example, charged that he ran the Library to suit his personal tastes and disregarded the public. But Strohm also had his journalistic backers, and Detroit *Saturday Night* said:

> A lady employee, whose name has been frequently mentioned as one of the martyrs, has said she could not get along with Mr. Strohm. That is altogether regrettable. In an ideal world, of course, everybody would get along in perfect harmony with everybody else; but in the kind of world we so far have, it is customary to sacrifice the man or woman in the ranks when issues of harmony and cooperation are raised rather than the officer in command who is usually not so easy to replace as the privates. . . . We feel constrained to say from our own experience, however, that under Mr. Strohm's

276

management the public library has been more serviceable to the public, has enlisted a wider public interest and has followed more enterprising methods than at any time in its history.[1]

Strohm had a well-developed feeling for public relations and good publicity timing. He was a voluminous writer—mostly about the Detroit Library and its problems and library service generally. A perfectionist, he displayed small patience for inefficiency and stupidity, and he exhibited this trait with a caustic tongue and pen. Once, when he sharply disagreed with the staff book committee's judgment on recommending an accession, he vetoed their action with this note:

> The book is not admissable. It labors. The dialogue is poor and it plagiarizes both plot and characters. . . . Whatever moron taxpayers require this sort of reading should be encouraged to go elsewhere.[2]

Within a short time, Strohm became internationally recognized as a leader in his profession. He was president of the American Library Association, the Michigan Library Association, and was often consulted about library matters concerning other cities and the nation as a whole. He retired in 1941 and died in 1951. His stature and his accomplishments were well summed up in a Michigan Library Association tribute, which stated:

> Possessed of extraordinary energy, he was the sterling leader of a devoted staff, always requiring that library service be dispensed intelligently and generously. In his own words, "We will endeavor to furnish a service in integrity; we will search for facts and tested information for those requiring it; we will offer some of the best interpretations of the findings that have guided generations past and survived for our enjoyment; we will select what may appear most worthy and helpful in the minds of today." He brought to the high responsibility of book selection an impersonal and unbiased perspective, an enjoyment of the finest in the world's literature and an urge to share the satisfaction to be gained from good reading. His watchwords were workmanship and honesty.

What he accomplished in a physical form, also was described in these words:

His was the motivating force that saw the present Main Library building to its completion, an architectural masterpiece that was the inspiration for more recent civic buildings and for Detroit's Cultural Center. The nine branch libraries of Detroit's system in 1912 were increased to twenty-two before his retirement.* [3]

In 1928 William Webb, chief of the Extension Department, resigned to become librarian at Flint, and it became necessary to replace him. Strohm turned to the American Library Association and asked it to recommend some candidates. A list of half a dozen prospects was received and each name was considered and followed with investigation of the individual's qualifications. Hazel B. Timmerman, assistant in the ALA personnel division, wrote Strohm in the highest terms about one prospect:

> Another student at Columbia, who is especially interesting is Ralph A. Ulveling, whom we are told will be in a few years one of the ablest men in the public library field. He has already had excellent experience and has the personal qualities which will make him an able executive.[4]

The position went to Ulveling who was advanced to associate librarian in 1934, and who succeeded Strohm as director in 1941. Born in Adrian, Minnesota, in 1902, Ulveling graduated from DePaul University. After serving a library apprenticeship at the Newberry Library, Chicago, and as librarian at Amarillo, Texas, he took further studies at Columbia before joining the Detroit system. Miss Timmerman's letter about him proved prophetic, and he gained national and world-wide renown as a consultant for many municipal library systems throughout the country, and as adviser to the federal government in providing library services for the armed forces and foreign countries. His range of other activities of a professional nature was also wide, including memberships on the United States National Commission for UNESCO, the board of the Great Books Foundation, and the advisory committee for Academic Freedom Study; a trusteeship of the Cran-

---

* Adam J. Strohm died October 31, 1951, in Asheville, North Carolina, where he made his home after his retirement. His widow, Cecilia B. McConnel Strohm, died at Kensington, Maryland, in 1963. Their two children, John, of Los Angeles, and Harriet (Mrs. William Carey) of Kensington, survived.

brook Institute of Science. He was president of the American Library Association, the Michigan Library Association and vice president of the American Association for Adult Education. In 1956 he was given the cherished Joseph W. Lippincott award for being "a courageous defender of free access to all shades of opinion and types of information, and an effective proponent of interracial understanding." In 1958, he was honored by the Republic of West Germany for his work in aiding that nation to develop an adult education program. Ulveling was one of three nominees for the post of Congressional librarian in 1945.

A successful library system requires a professional staff as well as professional directors, and in Detroit's case, it was a long time a-borning. Utley understood its necessity as far back as 1885 when he became the first Detroit librarian to attend an ALA convention. He returned with some definite ideas, including one that more men attendants should be employed. He reported to the Commission:

> I wish to draw the attention of the Board to the question of dispensing entirely with women assistants for climbing the gallery stairs and for evening work, and the substituting of young men. It is not exactly right to require women to come to the library for evening work, especially if their homes are a long distance away and they have no escorts. I am told that young men are more efficient and satisfactory for library work and that there is no difficulty in finding bright students who would be glad, for small compensation, to work evenings.[5]

He was not prepared to go as far as Dr. C. Henri Leonard, a Commission member, did a few years later when he advocated employing men as branch librarians because they were mentally superior to women. Declared the doctor:

> The additional four ounces of brain in the male cranium indicates their superiority for executive work. No female head connected with the library has enough executive ability to take charge of the branches. . . .[6]

Despite such misogynic and inflammatory utterances, the Library staff continued to be, as it had been almost from the beginning, made up predominately of women. In 1885, for example, exclusive of the librarian, there were nine employees, only one of whom was a man. By 1925, the ratio was even smaller with only five men listed among the 235 professional employees (as distinct from administrative, maintenance and clerical help). In more recent years there has been a greater attraction for men in library service, but they are still greatly outnumbered by the women. One drawback, if it can be called that, has been the turnover among women librarians who leave to be married. Utley complained to the Commission in 1908 that "the Matrimonial Microbe found its way into the library during the year and carried off five victims." [7] Aside from matrimonial prospects, library work, particularly in the earlier days, held a strong attraction for women because it offered both prestige and equality of opportunity which were often lacking in other fields of activity. In 1920 George N. Fuller, the secretary of the Michigan Historical Commission, looking for a job for his daughter, asked Strohm if he would recommend a library career. Strohm replied:

> I do not know of any profession where you will find so many well bred and happy ladies as in the public library. It furnishes an outlet for almost every talent and every worthy desire of rendering public service along local as well as broad national lines.[8]

Perhaps it was because the library was for so long a "woman's world" that pay scales were traditionally low. As women achieved equality in other business and professional activities, this became a serious recruiting problem for the Detroit Public Library as it was for almost all libraries. Over the years, the Commission conducted a continuing campaign for a more realistic level of compensation. In 1883 the Detroit rate for assistant librarians ranged from $400 to $550 a year, and while the salary scale gradually improved, it took a long time to become competitive—if it is that today. As recently as 1948, Dr. Harvey M. Merker, then Commission president, pointed out that

> We are failing to obtain the number of trained people necessary to operate the institution's established program. . . . The situation appears to be growing worse rather than better. Before further disintegration of the organization takes place, it is hoped that corrective action to improve the salary schedules for the professional staff may

be obtained. This is urged as an immediate need of primary importance.[9]

While this gloomy statement was partly for the benefit of the municipal budget-maker, it was true that high standards were demanded. In 1954, applicants for staff posts were required to fill out questionnaires covering schooling, experience, ability to search out knowledge, personality, health, special skills, books read and cultural interest, extracurricular activities, memberships, and experience in work with industrial and social and racial groups. This, according to Ulveling, was required as a basis for selecting new staff members because "it is deemed requisite that persons becoming employes in the Library shall be known to possess certain occupational qualifications." [10] These high standards added to the Detroit system's prestige, prompting the observation that "the Detroit Public Library has an enviable reputation in the library profession. Experience here is generally regarded as a valuable asset in any young librarian's service record." [11]

The high professional standards which helped make the Detroit system outstanding were manifested in other ways as the result of evolving activities and policies. In 1935 it was decreed that "eligibility for the higher brackets is predicated on a college degree. . . . The library exacts education and maturity as an irreducible minimum in its staff." [12] At that time the professional staff numbered 283 members, of whom 167 were college graduates and 148 had library school degrees.

> The basis on which the librarian may claim the status of professional must in a large part rest on his ability to assume responsibility and give expert advice. Such is the relationship between counsellor and client in the older professions.

He was expected, it was added, to be something more than a "mere passive attendant." [13]

That definition was elaborated upon in 1945 by Ulveling with particular reference to the Detroit system. He stated:

> Librarians must have not only a knowledge of books but a genuine interest in people and their needs. They must, therefore, have

281

understanding and sympathy, be socially-minded and enthusiastic. In addition, they need the same basic qualities that make for success in any professional field—good health, emotional maturity, a responsiveness, out-going personality, resourcefulness, capacity for leadership, and alertness to changing conditions.[14]

Detroit staff members have long displayed these qualities, including that of leadership in many activities, civic as well as professional. In the latter field, their contributions have been outstanding. In 1891, it was largely through their efforts, with the strong support of Commissioner Butzel, that the Michigan Library Association was organized. In 1936, the staff members organized their own staff association, through which was established the annual staff Memorial and Fellowship award which recognizes outstanding ability and achievement. The first award was given in 1951 to Miss Mabel West, and it has generally carried with it a paid leave of absence, granted by the Commission. In addition to the honors accorded Strohm and Ulveling, there have been many others, notably that conferred upon Charles M. Mohrhardt,* associate director, who in 1954 was cited by the senate of Berlin for appreciation of his work in helping design and organize the American Memorial Library of Berlin.[15]

Throughout its history, the Detroit Public Library has been relatively free from political influence, a fact which contributed much toward the development of a professional staff. Patronage was never a factor; on the other hand, merit has always been the basis for selection and appointment. This was acknowledged in 1905 by James E. Scripps, who pointed out: "If I mistake not ours is the only department of the municipal government strictly conducted under the so-called merit system." [16]

The merit principle was first observed in 1883 when Commission President Campbell announced that "it has been found ex-

---

* Charles M. Mohrhardt (1904–) was a native of Hubbardston, Michigan, and a graduate of Michigan State University with a degree in engineering. He took graduate work at Columbia University. He was employed at the Olds Motor Works, Lansing, until 1928 when he was appointed chief of the Technology Department, Toledo Public Library. He became chief of the Technology Department at Detroit in 1930, and was made associate director in 1941.

pedient to have examinations of candidates for positions in the Library upon such topics as will best indicate their fitness. . . ." [17] From that time on, competitive examinations were regularly held for all but top administrative jobs. On September 22, 1886, there were sixty applicants who took the test to fill a single vacancy. Helen C. Bates scored highest and received the appointment, although eleven others who did well were placed on the substitute list.

The questions of broad range asked at that examination have been preserved. Applicants were asked to list all the presidents of the United States; the names of the principal writers on American history; the chief American poets and dramatists and their works. Similar questions covered the fields of English, French, German and Italian literature, as well as the Greek and Roman classics. A general familiarity with painting and sculpture, invention, theology, travel, geology and botany was also required. Finally, applicants were asked to identify and discuss in more detail the principal figures in American and English literature and their works, and to display a familiarity with contemporary literature.

The pressures to fall into the error of favoritism were great, and it was to the credit of the Commission that they were resisted. Attempts to win patronage must have been particularly strong in 1897, prompting Richard Storrs Willis,* Commission president that year to offer "a preliminary word or two . . . for those who are unaware of certain rules obtaining in the library."

The commissioners, he explained, were sometimes asked to use their influence to secure a position for "a friend of a friend" and to have the formality of an examination waived in that "exceptional" case.

---

* One of the most interesting of the early Library Commissioners was Richard Storrs Willis. Born in Boston, February 10, 1819, he was educated at Yale, and in 1841 went to Germany to continue studies in music. Upon his return to the United States, he became editor of various musical publications, and also gained considerable recognition as a composer. His best known work was the familiar Christmas hymn, "It Came Upon a Midnight Clear" (1857). His brother was the poet, Nathaniel Parker Willis, and his father was Nathaniel Willis, founder and editor of *Youth's Companion,* of which the Detroit Public Library is the proud possessor of a complete file. Willis died in Detroit on May 7, 1900.

This is rather trying as, after a statement of the case the commissioners sometimes become interested themselves. Impracticable, however. Every applicant must rely upon personal fitness and the ability to pass the civil service examination. Personal influence is not recognized in the Library.[18]

For many years, also, the Commission had to fight to control its own selection procedure. Thus, when a general civil service system for city employees was set up in 1913, the secretary of the first Civil Service Commission, Fred W. Smith, called on the Library to submit its personnel records with the idea that it would thereafter assume jurisdiction. Divie B. Duffield replied for the Library Commission with a flat refusal, pointing out that city civil service did not cover the educational system of which the Library was a part. Smith threatened that if the Library list was not turned over to him, the payroll would not be approved. Duffield warned:

Before any such unwarranted and unjust action as proposed is taken, namely, the withholding of salaries of those who are in no wise responsible for the conduct of this Commission, it is hoped that your Commission will seek an opinion from the Corporation Counsel and so avoid a hardship upon the innocent and trouble for itself.[19]

Duffield's advice was followed, but shortly thereafter the Library Commission had to fight infringement upon its legal autonomy. In 1922 the Common Council demanded that the Library submit all of its contracts for Council approval, and again Duffield offered an opinion in which he was less rigid than in the civil service matter. He advised Strohm:

I do not believe as a matter of policy in being at all "edgy" with the people in the City Hall unless something of importance required it. I can see no particular harm in submitting our contracts to the Common Council, although it may be annoying, and if they are inclined to insist upon it we could then consider whether we wish to take a definite stand against it.[20]

It was the civil service issue, however, which most tried the Commission, and the matter came up again in 1940. Reviewing its successful personnel policies, the commissioners on that occasion pointed to the necessity for maintaining control over the selection of professional workers and for establishing and maintaining its own standards. The Commission stated that "such transfer of powers was not advisable, having regard to the best interest of the library service and thereby the public interest." [21]

As recently as 1960 the matter once more arose in a different form, when the Budget Bureau declared its intention of passing upon the need for filling vacancies on the Library staff. The Commission's reaction was placed in its minutes.

> The Director, in a rejoinder, stated that effective operation would not be possible if the Library's Administrator is unable to plan and carry out a program because of reference to an outside agency which is not fully cognizant of or competent to pass on professional matters for which its representatives are not trained.[22]

In order to make professional librarians out of those who successfully passed the application examinations, the Library found it necessary to institute intensive training programs for beginners, or apprentices as they were called. The apprentices were not actually employees of the library. They were young people who took the qualifying examinations to become apprentices, and while they were frequently employed as substitutes, they had to wait completion of their training course before becoming eligible for staff jobs. The first record of an apprentice class was in 1903 when the Library rules were amended to provide for one. In June of that year, three passed their examinations with grades ranging from 92 to 77 per cent. The system was strengthened in 1909 when provision was made for "giving instruction in library technology to the apprentice class by a member of the library staff." The twelve students in that year's class were instructed in classification and cataloging, bibliography and use of reference books, charging procedures, simple book mending and a study of general literature. Classes met each week day except Saturday from 8:30 to 9:30 A.M. The next year, they were paid fifty cents a day during the term of instruction which, in 1911 was extended from six months to a full year. A passing grade of 75 was required. Candidates were required to be at least eighteen years old and not more than forty, citizens of Detroit, and high school graduates. In 1919, Strohm was able to report that during the previous six years, ninety-five apprentices had won staff positions. He commented:

> This training of our own staff guarantees a certain stability of our personnel which is important and has also a stimulating effect on our "regulars" in making them realize the necessity of increasing their professional competency in order to keep ahead of the ambitious newcomers.[23]

To keep the "regulars" abreast of new developments in library service, a series of staff seminars was begun in 1937 "at which selected staff members would informally explain the essential features of their departmental services." [24]

A particularly important forward step was taken in 1956 when a cooperative arrangement was worked out between the library and the University of Michigan's School of Library Science. It was explained to the Commission in this manner:

> The Director discussed the shortage of librarians locally and nationally. He also told of exploratory conversations held with Dr. Rudolph Gjelsness, director of the University of Michigan Library School, regarding co-operative arrangements whereby selected college graduates having the desirable personal qualifications might obtain professional training largely in Detroit while employed at the Library on a pre-professional status.

The plan was approved by the Commission "as a means for rebuilding the depleted ranks of professionally trained librarians for the library's service." [25]

One of the big handicaps which made it difficult for Detroit in particular and libraries generally to obtain personnel of professional quality was the previously mentioned wage situation. The Commission constantly fought for a more reasonable scale. From time to time, the city granted increases, but the Commission just as often felt these to be inadequate. It referred to one such general raise in 1927 as "a waiter's tip," a poor token "of appreciation of faithful community service devoted to the promotion of education, social intelligence and an enriched citizenship." The Commission consistently sought over the years, to bring the librarians' scale into conformity with that of school teachers. Conditions did improve, even if the improvement was slow in coming and left much to be desired. In 1955, Library employees along with all city employees became entitled to longevity increases, although the Commission complained that the city's Budget Bureau set higher rates for window cleaners than for librarians with Masters' degrees. In 1961, the Commission finally was able to set up a long-range salary plan which compared favorably with salary schedules in effect in other library systems.[26] The Detroit induction rate, which was increased from a range of $4993–5329 in 1961–62, to $6069–6295 in 1964–65, was said to be the highest in the country.

Many of the modern so-called fringe benefits, intended to make employment more stable and more attractive, were in many cases hard come by, and in that respect Detroit Library staff members were no exception. The first of these advantages came in 1884 when, after the staff had petitioned the Commission for summer vacations, they were each granted a month holiday.[27] A retirement or pension system did not come as easily, despite the Commission's recognition of the need for one. A long time elapsed from the day a retirement system was first discussed until one was put into operation. From all available records, the original force behind a Library pension plan was Commissioner George Osius who in 1911, if not earlier, was advocating a pension program and working out the details. In the annual report of 1912, Commission President Ralph Phelps, Jr., recommended "for early consideration and adoption the establishment of a 'Public Library Staff Retirement Fund' similar to the Public School Teachers' Retirement Fund which is now in successful operation in this city." [28]

Opposition to any such idea immediately came from some of the journalistic guardians of the public treasury, notably the Detroit *Free Press* which claimed that municipally financed pensions could not be afforded. Meanwhile, in other cities, particularly Chicago which was the first to grant library pensions, plans were being put into effect. A bill authorizing benefits for Michigan libraries was submitted to the legislature in 1913, but with no success. Nothing more was done until 1925 when a new bill was written, and support of the Detroit Common Council was sought. Librarians, it was pointed out at that time, "constitute about the only class in Detroit for whom provision is not yet made by law for old age and long-service pensions." The bill was passed in 1927, but to have application, it required local sanction and that was not forthcoming until 1936 when a public referendum approved revision of the general city retirement plan and made it possible to include Library employees. This became effective in 1938, and was hailed by the Commission as of benefit to the Library because its "retirement provisions will strengthen the robustness of the institution and loyalty to the service." The effect became immediately noticeable with a pickup in recruiting. "Among these recruits we have a fair nucleus of young men," it was stated.[29]

The first Library employee to take advantage of the new system was Mildred Garvai who retired in 1938 after twenty-seven years of service. Her pension was $900 a year. Altogether, there were eight members of the staff in the first group to retire in 1938. Among them was Emma White. She was seventy-nine years old and had worked in the Library for forty years. She received $440 a year. At the end of 1938, the Commission observed that the pension system had permitted "several superannuated members of our Library staff . . . to retire with a sense of modest security for their old age." A good effect on morale of younger employees was noted by the Commission with "a sense of relief." [30]

In 1946 Library employees were given additional security when they were included in the general city employees benefit plan which made them eligible for hospital and surgical benefits.[31]

The retirement system created some problems for the Library administration. In 1946, it was pointed out that the institution had passed through a period of great expansion between 1910 and 1921, and numbers of people who had entered the system at that time had become eligible for retirement. As these older, experienced people left, it was difficult, the Commission noted, to find qualified candidates to replace them. This led in 1957 to adoption of a policy which permitted sixty-five-year-old employees, eligible for retirement, to remain temporarily if they so chose. This was done, as it was explained, because of the "shortage of qualified people for virtually all classifications of the Library's personnel," leaving many vacated positions unfilled for long periods of time.[32]

Despite such difficulties, however, the staff of the Detroit Public Library had evolved over a period of nearly a hundred years from a small group of clerks and attendants, whose chief qualification was an interest in books, into a corps of highly trained technicians, competent and qualified to serve a complex social, economic and industrial order not even dreamed of a century earlier.

In building a professional staff, the Detroit Public Library contributed to raising the general standards of the library profession. It served as a training school for many young librarians who left its employ to win distinction in other library posts throughout the nation and in many parts of the world. Its list of "alumni" is impressive. The names of but a few who have attained high places in librarianship would include Douglas W. Bryant, director, Harvard University Library; Benjamin A. Custer, editor, Dewey Decimal Classification, Library of Congress; Elmer M. Grieder, acting director, Stanford University Library; Joseph Groesbeck, deputy director, United Nations Library; Eugene B. Jackson, librarian, General Motors research laboratories; Irving Lieberman, director, School of Librarianship, University of Washington; M. Ruth McDonald, assistant to the director, National Library of Medicine; Ernest I. Miller, director, Cincinnati Public Library; Everett N. Peterson, head, public libraries section, UNESCO, Paris; Edward B. Stanford, director, University of Minnesota Library; Genevieve M. Casey, librarian, Michigan State Library; and Loleta D. Fyan, former Michigan State librarian.

CHAPTER 18

DETROIT'S MEMORY

WHEN SOMEONE has something he wants to get rid of and has no
place to put it, he usually offers it to a library or museum. Sometimes these donations have to be accepted for political reasons.
Sometimes they turn out to be white elephants, taking up valuable
space which could be used for more worthwhile purposes. Often
they turn out to be of great value to the recipient institution, enlarging its field of service and endowing it with greater distinction.
The Detroit Public Library has been the repository for both types
of collections, and between the extremes there has been a middle
ground where a collection has served a good purpose for a period
of time before it became a burden.

One interesting collection consisting principally of natural
history specimens occupied an important place in the Library
between 1886 and 1893. It was the property of the Detroit
Scientific Association, organized in 1874 by a group of men, some
of whom had close ties to the Library. One of them was Henry
Gillman. The original members pooled their personal collections
of fossils, stuffed birds and animals, Indian artifacts, coins and
other odds and ends later described in more dignified language as

"appertaining to Natural History, Archeology, Numismatics, Local History, etc." The combined collection was large, and what to do with it and where to display it were problems. For several years it was shunted around town, being housed in various office buildings, the Odd Fellows Hall, the YMCA, a vacant building on the Harper Hospital grounds and in rooms in the Detroit Medical College on Farmer Street. In the course of time, the Scientific Association acquired the library of the old Mechanics' Society, and when the Public Library which wanted those books finally succeeded in getting them, the Scientific Association thought it had a solution to its troubles. It would get the Library to take over the whole collection, books and specimens, and create a museum in the Centre Library for display of the latter.[1]

In 1885 the Centre building was enlarged, and the added space, it was felt, would accommodate the museum. Negotiations were conducted in the summer of 1885, and the Library Commission agreed to take custody of the specimens. They were to be housed on the second floor of the addition, and the Commission felt it was

> fortunate enough to secure the deposit of the valuable collections of the Scientific Association, the educational value of which is very highly regarded by those most experienced in public teaching. The collection is large and choice and will add very much to the attractions of the Library.

Arrangements were made with Bela Hubbard* who held a mortgage on the collection, to release it to the Library. The cost of moving was $144.12 which the Library paid.[2] Henry B. Smith, who had apparently looked after the collection in its Farmer Street quarters was employed as janitor at $45 a month, later increased by $5. In 1888, Smith who added his own coin collection to the museum, was dignified by the title of antiquarian. He threatened that year "to resign and establish himself in a cigar store, with his collection of coins and minerals as an attraction to draw trade, unless his salary of $50 a month is increased." [3]

---

* A branch library, opened February 15, 1951, at 12929 West McNichols, was named in honor of Bela Hubbard.

291

Parnassus on Main Street

The museum was opened to the public on March 1, 1886, and at first it was regarded as a great asset to the Library. School classes in botany, zoology and geology were brought by their teachers to see it, and various organizations, such as the Detroit Microscopical Society, held meetings in the museum. For a while, the University of Michigan extension service used the room for lectures. These activities served the double purpose of exposing Detroiters and their children to the regular Library facilities. The museum, the Commission reported at the end of 1886,

> has proved a great attraction and is found to be of much service in the teaching of Natural Sciences in our schools. . . . The museum is one of large pecuniary as well as educational importance, being well selected and extensive, and furnishes means of illustrating what cannot be adequately described in books, to which it is a potent auxiliary.[4]

Within three or four years, though, this enthusiasm waned. As Library patronage increased and the book collection grew, the space occupied by the museum began to be the target of acquisitive looks. Early in 1892 a committee was appointed to consider putting an annex on the Centre building for library and museum purposes, "or, if an annex is not thought legal or advisable, what other disposition should be made of the museum, to vacate the room now occupied by it, for the uses of the Library." Two months later the committee recommended "the early removal of the museum," and an architect was hired to prepare preliminary sketches for remodeling the room into a reading room. Once more facing the bleak prospect of being dispossessed, the Scientific Association looked about for a new home. It suggested a separate building at the rear of the Library, to be erected at its own expense. This idea did not prove practical, and the Commission applied new pressure to force the museum out. "It was never intended," it was stated, "that the Library Commission should be its permanent custodian. . . . We are forced to insist that this museum find other quarters."

The dilemma was resolved by the Detroit Art Museum, then in process of building a museum at East Jefferson and Hastings. Its director, A. H. Griffith, suggested a willingness to take over the natural history collection, and thought it would also be a good idea if the Library threw in for good measure the manuscripts and other materials of the old Michigan Historical Society which had been deposited in the Centre building. The Commission was willing to give up the mounted butterflies and the mastodon bones, but not the original records of early Detroit and Michigan. On March 23, 1893, the Commission announced that remodeling of the Museum room would start on April 1. That brought Griffith back with an offer to take the collection if part of it could temporarily be stored in the Library basement, while the larger items were placed in rented quarters. That had a reasonable sound, and the transfer was made to the Art Museum, the museum quarters in the Library being vacated on March 28, 1893. For the time being, the major part of the collection was stored in a vacant part of the Biddle House block. On April 1, the carpenters moved in, and before the summer was over the remodeled museum room was being used for a much-needed reference reading room.[5]

Another collection which, from time to time, must have seemed to the Commission like an albatross hung round its neck was the medical collection, inherited in 1895 from the Detroit Medical and Library Association. The latter, organized in 1876, was a forerunner of the Wayne County Medical Society. Having gathered a respectable number of books, pamphlets and periodicals, and having no place to put them, the Association offered them to the Public Library on condition that they should be "so placed that they can be freely used." The "offer," which had the considerable weight of the medical profession behind it, was one which could not have been turned down diplomatically had the Commission been so inclined. About 1700 volumes were delivered to the Library, along with a quantity of professional magazines which were sent to the bindery. More of the latter kept coming in, because the Association agreed to continue half a dozen or more subscriptions at its own expense. The collection was placed in an alcove of the reference room.[6]

Within a year, the Association was asking that "an analytical index of the medical works" be made—the cost, naturally, to be borne by the Library. This task was given to Dr. J. V. Becelaire, who was appointed medical librarian. He was the nominee of the Association. Becelaire proved to be a difficult man to have around, and before long he was acting as if the rest of the Library was subsidiary to the medical collection. He insisted that use of the medical books be restricted to practitioners and medical students, and a little later, curtains were ordered placed in the glass doors of the bookcases in order to discourage curiosity of the general public. Becelaire also began to give orders to the general staff, thereby creating a good deal of resentment. Meanwhile, his own work of cataloging was neglected. In 1897, Utley told the Commission that the indexing of periodicals was supposed to be a short job, but that Becelaire had been at it for five months.[7] The Commission was told:

> In the opinion of the librarian, Dr. B. has not devoted his time as industriously as he might to the special work for which he was employed, but has undertaken to do the work of a reference librarian, with the result that friction has arisen between him and some of the Library assistants. There are intimations among the latter that his conduct toward them has not been at all times agreeable.

The Commission instructed Utley to advise Becelaire "that his duty is not to assist patrons of the Library in reference work, but to write catalog cards, and that he should proceed with that work as expeditiously as possible. . . . also to amend his conduct." [8]

Before long the Association announced that, having run out of money, it no longer could keep up subscriptions to medical journals, and suggested that the Library continue them at its own expense. It was about this time, a most unpropitious one, that a group of dental students asked the Commission to purchase a number of books on dentistry.[9] For one reason or another, patronage in the medical department was not holding up. Representatives of various medical societies which in 1901 merged into the Wayne County Medical Society, proposed that the book collection be enlarged and brought up to date. The doctors offered to have a telephone installed at their expense so they could be reached by their offices and patients. Another group of forty-five doctors agreed to subscribe for one each of "the best class of medical periodicals" not already on the Library's list. After three months in the doctors' offices, these periodicals would be turned over to the Library. Yet in spite of these and other efforts to draw professional patronage, the Commission reported that the "chief value of the department appears to be to the students in the medical college." [10]

These conditions continued to prevail until 1910, when the Wayne County Medical Society purchased a building for its headquarters at 33 East High Street (now East Vernor Highway). The building had a library room already containing about three thousand volumes, and it was proposed that the Commission turn all of the medical books in the city Library over to the society. The Commission was only too happy to do this, and the transfer was made on August 24, with the proviso that the books would continue to be Public Library property and as such, available to the general public.

"Their removal," the Commission sighed, "gives us much needed shelf room in our badly overcrowded old building." [11]

The relief was only temporary. Within a dozen years, the Wayne County society sold its building and, like dispossessed chickens, the medical books came home to the Public Library to roost. There was some talk about a separate building to be built on the new Main Library grounds at the expense of the profession, but nothing came of that. Instead, in 1923, the books were placed in the Detroit College of Medicine quarters on Mullett Street. The collection, at this time numbering about 15,000 volumes, became known as the Medical Science Department, and was staffed by the Public Library. The department was supported largely by Library appropriations, supplemented by grants from the Wayne County Medical Society and the proceeds of two small endowments, established by the heirs of Dr. Theodore McGraw and Dr. Benjamin R. Schenck. Later these were augmented by another fund set up by the widow of Dr. Andrew P. Biddle, for many years a member of the Library Commission. The Detroit College of Medicine and Surgery, a privately owned institution, provided free space, but benefited in turn by the fact that its students were the principal users. Public use was confined mostly to the "do it yourself" clientele—"the pathetic figure who comes for home remedies; the chronic invalid who berates the medical profession and has taken diagnosis into his own hands." [12]

A survey of facilities in 1926, made by James F. Ballard, librarian of the Boston Medical Library, found the Detroit collection inadequate, so in 1926 the Commission appropriated $12,500 for the acquisition of research materials. It was an expensive and troublesome "branch," but the Library made the best of it, declaring in 1927 that "Detroit has the distinction of being the only city in the United States which has a complete medical library as a part of the Public Library." Although this was a proud boast, the air was let out of it by a survey which pointed out that no public library system had any business trying to maintain a medical library.[13]

Although the department "contains most of the important medical literature in English," more money was constantly needed.[14] An unsuccessful attempt was made in 1935 to obtain a grant from the Horace and Mary Rackham Fund. Besides suffering from chronic financial anemia, the patient had too many doctors for its own health. The combination of the Medical Society, the Medical College which in 1918 was taken over by the Detroit Board of Education and eventually became the Wayne State University College of Medicine, and the Public Library, each with its own interest and sphere of influence made for an impossible situation. It was clear to all that something had to be done.[15]

A happy solution was found. Aided by a Medical Society grant, a new survey was made in 1947–48 by Dr. Keyes D. Metcalf, director of the Harvard University Library, and Miss Janet Doe, assistant librarian, New York Academy of Medicine. Their major recommendation was for the Public Library to get out of the medical library business and turn the collection over to the sole jurisdiction of Wayne State University. "What is everybody's business may be nobody's business," was the gist of the Metcalf-Doe report. No one was more eager than the Library Commission and administration to follow the recommendation, and on January 1, 1949, an agreement was signed, giving the Medical Science Department to the Wayne State College of Medicine. The transfer included the whole collection of more than 50,000 volumes, the proceeds of the McGraw and Biddle endowments and, more important, full responsibility for the collection's custody and operation.[16]

If medicine and natural science specimens left something to be desired as institutional assets, the Library lived more comfortably with history, particularly that of the local or regional sort. From its beginning, or at least as soon as it had adequate facilities, the Library indicated an awareness of its community background and willingly assumed the role of repository for Detroit and Michigan archives and records. Within a year after the Library was created, it was given the private library of Governor Lewis Cass who, up to the time of his death in 1866, was undoubtedly Michigan's foremost public figure. As territorial governor, ambassador to France, cabinet member, United States senator and presidential nominee, Cass was on intimate terms with world and national figures and played a part in great events. He was known both as an author and historian, and his collection of books, papers and records, the first such private collection the Library acquired, was a distinct asset forming the starting place for what developed into a renowned and matchless group of materials on Detroit, Michigan and the Old Northwest.

Other distinguished persons followed the example of Cass's heirs, giving or bequeathing their books and papers to the Library. Among the early materials thus acquired were papers and books belonging to John S. Newberry and governors Robert McClelland and John J. Bagley. Individual items, many of them rare and valuable were presented by interested citizens and organizations. In 1885, a young businessman, already a local history buff, donated a book to the Library. His name was Clarence Monroe Burton. Silas Farmer, Detroit's first outstanding historian, in 1891 made a gift of 62 books and 190 pamphlets. A valuable accumulation of back numbers of early newspapers was made. Civic societies, such as the old volunteer fire companies, gave their records and portraits of their members, among whom were some of the city's most prominent men. The old Michigan Historical Society turned over to the Library for safe-keeping and eventual ownership, its maps and documents relating to Michigan as a colony, territory and state. From time to time these donations were supplemented by the purchase of material for which the Commission appropriated the necessary funds.[17]

The Commission's awareness of the important and necessary function of the library in preserving the written and printed record of Detroit's and Michigan's heritage was clearly demonstrated in 1900. Commissioner Scripps produced a copy of Farmer's *History of Detroit* and showed a chapter in which Farmer had listed all the known almanacs, directories, maps, gazeteers and similar material published in Michigan. Scripps offered a resolution directing the librarian

> to search for and purchase every volume and map mentioned . . .
> except so far as they may be already in the library and also to pre-
> pare as rapidly as possible, a supplement to Farmer's list, to em-
> brace all books and pamphlets relating to Michigan and her citizens;
> to the end that the Detroit Public Library may be most complete in
> publications relating to or published in our own city and state.[18]

As a result of this and other evidences of interest in local and regional history, the Library gradually built up a very respectable collection and had become in effect, if not by official action, the archivist for Detroit and Michigan.

One of the most important meetings the Board of Library Commissioners ever held took place on January 7, 1914. Present besides the members of the Commission was Clarence Monroe Burton, head of a Detroit abstract and title company, who over a period of thirty years had amassed a remarkable collection of material pertaining to Detroit and the Old Northwest. The purpose of his attendance was to announce his desire to donate his private library to the City of Detroit, and to place it in the custody of the Library.[19] There had, apparently, been some previous discussion of this matter between Burton and individual commissioners. More than two years before, an article had appeared in a local newspaper, reporting that Burton intended to make such an offer and stating that if his terms and conditions were not acceptable to the city, the material would be given to the University of Michigan, "which institution is very eager to get it." [20] But when the time came, the Library Commission was certainly not disposed to impose any barriers. The importance of the collection was well known and was described as being "without doubt one of the most important historical collections made by an individual scholar." [21]

The offer was officially accepted on March 16; an agreement

was signed, and what was known as the Burton Library became the property of the people of Detroit. Burton's collection was housed in his residence, a substantial Victorian-era mansion, liberally adorned with the "gingerbread" so popular in the late 1800's when it was built. It stood on two lots at 27 Brainard Street between Cass and Woodward.* The house and land were conveyed to the Commission along with the books, manuscripts and other materials with which the residence was crammed, and which overflowed into the barn or garage which was used for storage. Burton, who was building a fine new home on fashionable Boston Boulevard, reserved to his use personal effects and furnishings, as well as books of a nonhistorical nature. The deed stipulated:

> The library is to be retained as an entirety to perpetually bear the name of Burton. . . . The public shall have access to the library in general for consultation and study. No books, documents or photographs shall be loaned from the library, except under such rules as the Commission may adopt.

It was further agreed that the Library would provide suitable quarters for the collection, separate from the general Library, in fireproof rooms. Use of the collection was, at all times, to be under careful staff supervision. Finally, the Commission agreed that it would undertake to increase the collection by adding

> books on American history, genealogy, and kindred subjects, and especially by obtaining and preserving manuscript collections that relate to American and Canadian history and to the history of Detroit. We agree to expend not less than $500 each year in the purchase of books of American and Canadian history to be added to the Burton Library and to form a part of it.[22]

Burton turned over the deed on March 19, and in accepting it, the Commission announced that "this gift to the Library is by far the most noteworthy in the history of the institution." [23] An unofficial valuation of $35,000 was placed on the property and $500,000 on the library. Actual possession of the premises was

---

* Under a later street renumbering, the Burton house became 473 Brainard Street.

299

taken by the Library on July 1, 1915, and on September 21, announcement was made that it was open to the public.

> A comfortable room is available on the first floor for general reading, and a quiet study room adjacent to the stacks has been provided for special students. The administration work rooms also are on the main floor. In accordance with the suggestion of Mr. Burton, a room on the second floor has been reserved and will be equipped for a prospective historical museum.[24]

Clarence Monroe Burton was born at Whiskey Diggings, California, November 18, 1853. He was the son of Annie Monroe and Dr. Charles Seymour Burton. The father, a Battle Creek physician, had taken his wife and their first son, Charles Francis, to California during the gold rush. The infant Clarence led an adventurous life almost from the start. In 1854 Annie and her two children, returning home by sea, were marooned briefly on a deserted shore after their ship had been scuttled by pirates. Adventure colored all of Burton's life. His later life experiences in tracking down rare and elusive documents provided many exciting episodes, although they were less violent than shipwreck and piracy.

Back east, the family resettled in Hastings, Michigan, where Clarence grew up and helped work on the family farm. In 1869 he entered the University of Michigan from which he graduated with a law degree. He settled in Detroit, became a law clerk and, for the next several years lived and raised a family on the verge of what amounted to almost abject poverty. But he was studious and industrious, and eventually he began to prosper—even to the point of being able to indulge his hobby. As a student, he became interested in books, and resolved to purchase at least one a day. Before long, he developed an interest in early Detroit and began to specialize in that field. The law firm with which he was associated devoted much of its practice to real estate work, and the result was that in 1891 he organized the Burton Abstract Company. Abstract and title work only sharpened his interest in his avocation, because it gave him access to deeds and other public and private records and documents, some of which he was able to acquire and which had great historical significance. He soon became known as one of the leading collectors of materials relating to the Old Northwest. Bookstores, dealers and other collectors were on the lookout for items in which he would be interested. He was recognized as the foremost authority of his time on the history of Detroit, Michigan and the surrounding area. He was one of those individuals who became better known for his hobby than for his profession, but he pursued it wisely, and knew how to use it for the public good.

Clarence Burton was a public spirited man in other ways. He served as a school inspector, and was active up to a point in politics. He sought office on occasion, being a candidate (unsuccessful) for the University of Michigan Board of Regents, a delegate (successful) to the State Constitutional Convention in 1907; for Congress (unsuccessful) and the Detroit City Charter Commission (successful). He wrote extensively on Detroit history. He was honored in 1908 when he was appointed City Historiographer by the Common Council, a post held previously by Silas Farmer. Burton held that office, as well as the honorary title of Consulting Librarian of the Burton Historical Collection, conferred upon him by the Library Commission,[25] until his death, October 23, 1932.

Some idea of the scope of the collection and how it was put together may be obtained from a letter which Burton wrote to the Commission in 1926 in which he reported that he had obtained the letters and papers of John B. Blois who published the first gazeteer of Michigan in 1839; the papers of John Allen who founded the city of Ann Arbor, the documents of the Campau family including those dealing with the original title to Belle Isle, and the papers of the Duffield family, two of whose members were closely identified with the establishment and later fortunes of the Library. This collection, said Burton, "had been handed around from one person to another for a century (some of the papers are more than a hundred years old)" and had been "finally halted on its way to the paper mill to be destroyed." Burton said:

Mr. Sidney Trowbridge Miller has presented the original book of minutes of the first academy in Detroit, and of the forming of the Lancastrian school. Mr. Miller hesitated whether to give this manuscript to our Library or to the University, but finally gave us the preference. It will go nicely with the Sibley and Trowbridge Collection, where we very recently placed a manuscript work of Charles C. Trowbridge on Indian legends. . . . Another exceedingly interesting document has recently come to us. It is the original letter book of James Sterling, extending from 1761 to 1765. Mr. Sterling was a trader at Detroit during those years and married Angelique Cuillierier, the daughter of Jean Batiste Cuillierier (or Beaubien). It is supposed that Sterling obtained information from Angelique regarding the proposed attack of Pontiac on the settlement in 1763, and that he imparted this information to the Commandant Gladwin, and thus prevented a massacre. The letters cover the entire duration of the siege and are very full of the details of transactions in Detroit during those troubled times.[26]

Another extremely important acquisition was the papers and records of John Askin, a Detroit merchant who elected to retain his British citizenship and removed to Canada at the time of the American occupation in 1796. These were discovered in an old barn, and were hauled to the Library in a horse-drawn wagon driven by Burton himself. The Askin papers detail not only commercial information, but contain descriptive accounts of events along the United States-Canada border during the War of 1812. Under Burton's direction, early church records were copied, and the Reverend Father Christian Dennisen compiled in twenty-five volumes *The Genealogies of French Families in Detroit*. Additional material was obtained in the form of original papers and letters pertaining to the area's participation in the War of 1812, the Civil War, and the two World Wars. Said Burton's biographer:

> However, the largest section of the Manuscript Division, as now set up in the Burton Historical Collection, is that containing the papers of statesmen, businessmen, clergymen and lawyers from 1837 to present. The papers of William Woodbridge, C. C. Trowbridge, James Joy, Governor Austin Blair, Judge Solomon Sibley, General Alpheus Williams and the Reverend George Duffield, bring one to the eve of the automobile manufacturing era.[27]

It might be added that since that was written, recent accessions have extended the collection to the eve of the atomic era.

The Collection long had a very respectable group of Lincoln materials. This was augmented in 1955 when, through the generosity of a Detroit businessman, C. Allen Harlan, the outstanding collection of Lincolniana assembled by the late Reverend Edgar DeWitt Jones, was purchased for $17,000 and added, as a reserved section, to the Burton Collection.

The purpose of the collection was defined in the following terms:

> To continue the development of a good working library, especially as it is related to the Old Northwest, and with particular attention to the Revolutionary, Constitutional, and War of 1812 periods; to strengthen the section on American genealogy, including vital records of countries from which the immigrants forming the chief race elements in the United States came; to secure everything obtainable that is essential to the history of the Old Northwest, with special reference to Detroit and Michigan; to conserve early American imprints. . . .[28]

Burton cherished the hope that the collection could be expanded to include a museum, and proposed that the Library join with other organizations to acquire a building at Jefferson and Griswold for museum purposes. The Commission went so far as to agree to turn over to a museum items other than printed materials "outside the traditional functions of the Library." Burton's plan was not realized. The present Detroit Historical Museum was built after his death. A next door neighbor of the Library at Woodward and Kirby, it is part of the Cultural Center. The Museum and the Burton Collection have always maintained close working arrangements, it being tacitly and generally understood that printed matter goes to Burton; other items to the museum.[29]

Burton's contribution to the Library did not end when he gave it his own collection and the building in which it was housed. To enable it to keep up its high standing and to expand, he endowed it liberally, beginning in 1921, with a gift of money which was added to until he had given an amount in excess of $50,000. Wisely invested, the endowment increased in value until it was worth $150,000 in 1950, at which time the Commission voted to stabilize it at that figure. Income was to be spent to purchase historical data unless the principal fell below $150,000 in which event the income was to be used to restore the corpus. Despite that decision, however, the annual report of 1958–59 disclosed that the fund was valued at $325,000.[30]

Once the original gift was made, the Library assigned four of its staff members to service it. They were under the supervision of Gracie B. Krum, who joined the system in 1901 and served first as a cataloger and as a branch librarian. Her first title in the Burton Collection was that of bibliographer, but it was changed to chief in 1916. She continued as directing head of the collection until 1941 when she retired and was succeeded by Mrs. Elleine H. Stones. Mrs. Stones retired in 1957 and James M. Babcock became chief.

The Burton residence on Brainard Street was remodeled from time to time, but was quickly outgrown. As the contents increased, taking up every available foot of space, there was danger that the public and even the staff would be crowded out. In 1914, when construction of the new Main Library was begun, Miss Krum proposed that facilities be provided in the building to house the Burton Collection:

> It would have ample room. The already valuable collections of American and local history now owned by the Public Library could be brought under the same administration as those of the Burton Collection, and all would be within easy access of the U. S. documents, magazines, etc., so that the public could be much better served and at less cost to the city than by maintaining separate buildings.[31]

Cass Gilbert, the architect, was consulted, and he revised his original plans, adding the third floor to the new building which originally was intended to have but two. This was in part responsible for the cost of the building exceeding the original estimates, but it resulted in good quarters for the Burton Collection. When the new building was opened in 1921, the contents of the Brainard Street house were moved, and that building was returned to Mr. Burton.[32]

In order to share its treasures with scholars and the public generally, the Burton Historical Collection began issuing a series of publications. To do that as well as to organize its materials, the position of editor of the collection was created in 1923. After surveying the field of eminent scholars to find a man for the position, Dr. Milo M. Quaife was appointed, effective April 1, 1924.

Quaife was well known as a historian, archivist, writer and editor. He had been previously associated with the Lewis Institute of Chicago and the Wisconsin State Historical Society. An acknowledged authority on the Old Northwest, he began the publication of a series of pamphlets known as the "Burton Leaflets," which were monographs on some phase of local history based upon materials in the Burton Collection. Among one of his most ambitious and important undertakings was the editing of the John Askin Papers which the Library published. In addition, Quaife's busy pen turned out a score or more of his own books, gaining for him the reputation of one of America's foremost historians. In 1935 financial considerations forced suspension of publishing by the Burton Collection, and Quaife's status was changed from editor to secretary, a post he continued to hold until his retirement in 1947. In 1959 he was the victim of a tragic fatal automobile accident.

Together, he, Clarence Burton, Gracie Krum and others who worked with them and followed them built the Burton Historical Collection into a renowned (perhaps the most renowned) division of the Detroit Public Library. It was stated:

> To this department have come writers and scholars from every part of the country. . . . Its treasures of early maps, manuscripts, diaries, log books and early printed items are being extended annually. . . . So important has this collection become that it may confidently be said today no adequate history of this part of the Great Lakes region can be compiled from source records without consulting the Burton historical library.[33]

In support of that contention are the authors' acknowledgments in literally hundreds of books, articles and dissertations. Among a few of the nationally-known historians and writers who have used the Burton Collection are Allan Nevins, Walter Havighurst, Harriet Arnow, Harlan Hatcher, F. Clever Bald, Arthur Pound, Howard H. Peckham, Bell Irwin Wiley and Langston Hughes.

As the Library's "most distinguished assemblage of research materials," the Burton Collection has been accurately described as "Detroit's Memory."

CHAPTER 19

THE BACKBONES

PEOPLE turn to the public library for the fulfillment of two broad, general needs. They expect the library to provide means of recreation and relaxation and to satisfy an aesthetic craving; and they expect it to gratify a desire for self- or community improvement. It is difficult—impossible, in fact—to draw a sharp line between these two general needs and the techniques employed by the library to satisfy them. The effort to do so—and again general terms are employed—is demonstrated by two basic functions of the library. They are to provide books for the general reader and reference and research material for the patron in quest of specialized information or knowledge.

Each of these basic functions are stems with many offshoots or branches which, representing the organizational structure of the library, have appeared through a process of evolutionary growth. These shoots have been put forth as the requirements of the patrons have become more sophisticated, as the structure of society itself has become more complex. The structural growth of the Detroit Public Library, as it has evolved since 1865, fairly

306

reflects the social and economic character of the entire community.

A progressive public library endeavors to keep pace with social change, not only by expanding its book collection, but by expanding it selectively. Thus, as in the case of the Detroit Public Library, a collection was built up over a period of a hundred years, which became so diverse and diffuse, that to manage it efficiently, it became necessary for the Library to departmentalize.

When the Library first opened in a single room in the old Capitol organization was a simple matter. Books for circulation were on one shelf; those for reference were on another, and the patron was served by a single attendant. By the very nature of the books called for, a book of fiction or an encyclopedia or dictionary, the reader himself informally established the first two basic Library departments: Circulation and Reference. Even this rudimentary organization was not apparent until, in 1877, the Centre Park building was occupied and space was set aside for a general reading room and check-out desk with a separate reference room. This was the real beginning of departmental organization. The Circulation Department, while not entirely divorced from reference, supplied the demands of the general reader. The Reference Department generally assumed supervision over those books the use of which was restricted to the premises. In order that the patrons could make better use of a growing book collection, a third division, Cataloging, was shortly added. After a while, a Periodical Department became necessary, followed by a Children's Department.

As these departments were set up, there appears to have been no clear cut division of administrative functions. The librarian and his staff served each division at the same time. There was no specialization until a staff member was first assigned to the task of cataloging. The general arrangement prevailing elsewhere in the Library, in which each attendant wore many hats, was not conducive to providing the reader with professional guidance and advice.

The need for true departmental organization was first recognized in 1899 when Commissioner Maynard D. Follin called for reorganization of the Library into six separate departments, each

307

more or less independent of the others, and each with its own chief who would be responsible to the librarian. There was nothing functionally new in the organizational chart which Follin wanted adopted. The departments called for were (1) Cataloging; (2) Circulating; (3) Reference; (4) Branches; (5) Juvenile; (6) Periodical. By giving each a certain degree of autonomy under its own supervisory head, Utley quietly put Follin's plan into operation upon his own initiative, without formal action by the Commission.[1]

By 1910 new major community interests resulted in three more departments or divisions being added to Follin's original six. The new ones were the Extension, Registry and Bindery divisions. The latter two were, like cataloging, "behind-the-scenes" departments, having little or no direct contact with the public. In 1911 the Order Department was created. The Burton Historical Collection of 1914 functioned more or less as a separate department. The Technology Department was set up in 1917. This completed the list until after the new Main Library was occupied. The 1921 building was built to accommodate a departmental system. Rooms were specially designed for special categories and collections of reading material. The Main Library extended the opportunity not only to provide for existing departments, but to add new ones housing Music and Drama, Fine Arts, Civics, and others. The result was that by 1941 the Commission was able to boast that "today the institution has twenty-one such departments, instead of nine general divisions which sufficed thirty years ago." [2]

In 1925 the position of business manager was created. A fairly formidable list of duties was assigned to that office. The responsibilities included being assistant secretary to the Commission; custodian of all Library funds, legal documents and supplies; supervisor of bids, contracts and leases, inventories, alterations and repairs. In addition, the business manager had charge of purchasing, approval of invoices, and payrolls and general disbursements. That need was felt for such an official to take over duties formerly borne largely by the librarian, was indicative of the fact that the Library had attained status as big business.[3]

After nearly a quarter of a century, the feeling emerged that the time had come for new structural changes if the Library's high standards of service were to be maintained. Except for the Social Science Department, created to replace the Civics Division, the 1945 departmentalization was essentially the same as when the Library moved into the new Main building. In 1945 the officials had definite hopes for the enlargement of the Woodward-Kirby Library and felt it would be wise to update the organization in anticipation of physical expansion. Ulveling presented a report to the Commission which contained recommendations concerning departmentalization. He stated:

> Through the years . . . , it has become increasingly evident that two extensive fields, History and Literature, cannot be adequately developed or properly serviced as mere segments of a much broader general department. Each should be organized as a separate unit with specialized staffs, catalogs, and indexes.

At the same time, he proposed establishment of an Education, Philosophy and Religion Department, stating: "With these three changes, the departmentalization of the Main Library will be completed from a subject standpoint and there will remain only the possible creating of a Rare Book Room for future consideration." [4] (The Rare Book Room was soon forthcoming.)

Ulveling's program received Commission approval, and the reorganization was undertaken, based upon preliminary studies made in 1942 and 1943. In 1948 a report was made to the effect that

> Five years ago the latest reorganizational study was inaugurated. The year just concluded has brought to fruition the first of the changes developed from that study. Others are now being installed and will be realized before the current [1948–1949] fiscal year draws to a close. . . . The Language and Literature Department has been established as has the Rare Book Room. The History and Travel Department and Philosophy, Religion and Education are awaiting the installation of equipment.[5]

Two years later, Ulveling was able to announce that with the opening of the Philosophy, Religion and Education Department on March 6, 1950, the reorganization had been completed, "insofar as present building facilities permit," and the reference-research materials of the Library were fully organized on a subject basis. What had been accomplished and the reasons for it were explained in the following words:

1. The great undepartmentalized core of the Library's book collection, embracing History, Literature, and Philosophy, had as a single unit become so large and unwieldy that necessary specialization, both in selection of books and in rendering service to patrons, was extremely difficult.
2. Existing departments having subject materials that form a natural supplement to each other for certain types of research work were not conveniently accessible to each other.
3. For the general reader whose concern is a variety of good reading rather than intensive study of one or two circumscribed subjects, the books of interest were too widely scattered.[6]

The result was a completely new table of organization which, with some additions, was still in effect twenty years after the reorganization. The chain of command, as shown on the organizational chart, naturally starts with the Commission to whom the Library director is directly answerable and under whose supervision all administrative functions are carried out. These are listed as follows: business management, personnel, reference services, home reading services, publications and exhibits, book selection, cataloging, community and group services and building maintenance.

Under business management are shipping, purchasing, stores, the bindery and the printing unit. Building maintenance, a second category under administration, has eight divisions concerned with repair, upkeep and operation of the Library's physical properties. Of principal interest to the user of the Library are two broad and large categories, Home Reading and Reference services. Each is under an assistant director.

The Home Reading Services is the Library's largest activity. It has ten departments or divisions besides certain administrative or "housekeeping" functions. They are: (1) Branch Libraries, (2) Downtown Library, (3) Extension Service, (4) Browsing Library, (5) Children's Library, (6) Children's Service, (7) Education Film Department, (8) Schools Department, (9) Young Adult Service, (10) Loan and Registration Bureau.

The Reference Services includes thirteen departments or divisions. They are: (1) Fine Arts Department, (2) History and Travel Department, (3) Municipal Reference Library, (4) Automotive History Division, (5) Language and Literature Department, (6) Business and Commerce Department, (7) Philosophy, Religion and Education Department, (8) Gifts and Rare Books Division, (9) Burton Historical Collection, (10) Social Science Department, (11) Technology and Science Department, (12) Music and Performing Arts Department, (13) General Information Department.[7]

Here, then, is the structure of the modern Library equipped and organized to meet every foreseeable demand which the public may make upon it, and yet sufficiently flexible to allow for expansion or addition of any new services which, experience has taught, must periodically be added as new fields of inquiry and knowledge open up.

It may be noted in the table of organization that one time-honored Library department is conspicuous by its absence. That is the Periodical Department, one of the first specialized services developed in the early days of the Library.

Other than the divisions of reference and general circulation, the periodical services may be regarded as the Library's first attempt at departmentalization. Periodicals became an essential ingredient of the Library almost at the beginning and one of the most used. So great, in fact, was the reading room traffic in the old Capitol by those calling for newspapers and magazines that in 1871 it was found necessary to open a periodical reading room. Most of the material at that time was donated, either by the publishers or by private citizens who, having read the papers and journals to which they subscribed, turned them over to the Library. Upon removal to the Centre Park building, no separate facilities seem to have been provided periodical readers using the general reading room. This was changed, however, in August 1881 when a "serial room" was established as a result of enlargement of the building. At that time newspapers, which were the core of the collection, were moved from the first floor to the basement, and an attendant was placed in charge. This new facility gave the Commission the opportunity to expand the periodical service by subscribing to a select list of magazines and newspapers, both foreign and domestic. Among the titles were the

311

English *Blackwood's, Edinburgh Review, London Quarterly, Anthropological Institute Journal* and *Nineteenth Century.* The French magazine *Revue des Deux Mondes* also was added, as were two German language publications, the selection of which was left to the discretion of Dr. Herman Kiefer. The domestic list included *Fortnightly Harper's, Scribner's, Atlantic, Popular Science, Scientific American, North American Review, American Naturalist,* the *Historical Magazine* and, for the younger readers, *St. Nicholas.* Besides the local newspapers, the collection contained the New York *Herald, Times, Tribune, World,* and the Chicago *Times.* Efforts were soon made to acquire back numbers of the periodicals, and by 1886, 754 volumes had been added. There were also 340 bound volumes of newspapers, comprising almost complete sets of all papers published in Detroit.

"We own, perhaps, one of the most complete collections of magazine literature in this country," it was stated in 1892. By that year the subscription list had been enlarged, and a careful record was kept of the reader use of the various publications. The humorous magazines *Puck* and *Judge* were called for 7445 and 6947 times respectively. *Scientific American* was read by 3987 persons, *Harper's Illustrated* by 3116, closely followed by *Century, Scribner's, Cosmopolitan, Outing* and *Lippincott's. Youth's Companion* was popular with 1909 readers, and others high on the list were *North American Review, Army and Navy Journal,* and *Art Amateur.*[8]

In 1907 the amount of money allowed for purchase of periodicals was reduced, causing the periodical room attendant to complain that in one afternoon twenty-five people were turned away because their choices had been stricken from the list. They left, said the attendant, muttering "Poor poverty-stricken Detroit! It's nothing but a big country village and never will be anything else." Nevertheless periodical circulation that year, according to G. E. Miller, periodical reading room assistant, was 190,320, due, in part, to the compilation of a subject index. Because the country was experiencing hard times, every chair in the room was always occupied, the patronage consisting largely of men temporarily out of work. Crowded conditions produced other problems, and Miller—as well as the patrons—was distressed by the reading room's poor ventilation. It was impossible, Miller said, to open the windows in the winter, and the rich, ripe odors resulting from over-crowding caused women to faint, and men to depart, exclaiming, "It's too much for me!" Miller recommended the purchase of an electric fan.[9] Improvements were made, first by separating the newspapers and magazines, moving the latter into the reference room. They remained there until 1914 when a new periodical room was opened on the first floor, with a corner or alcove reserved for women.

When the new Main Library was opened in 1921, the periodical room was on the first floor, to the left of the entrance. It was well patronized, but in 1925 Strohm reported certain difficulties. He told the Commission:

> We are beginning to experience the same problem we had downtown, a considerable number of Library boarders are drifting in with newspapers of their own with no intention of using any of the Library material but quite determined to occupy a comfortable chair for hours.[10]

The reorganization of the 1940's changed everything. The periodical room was given over to the History and Travel Department, and the Periodical Department, as such, went out of existence. There was no diminution of the collection—in fact it was constantly expanded as new fields of technical or specialized interest were opened up. However, the journals were distributed among the various departments where they appropriately belonged.

Fundamentally the reorganization went deeper than merely to create a few additional departments and services. It expressed an advanced philosophy in library administration. To begin with, it defined the major functions of the Library by setting up two administrative arms—Home Reading Services and Reference Services—each with its own director who was answerable to the Library director. Employing the simplest terms, the function of each might be described as follows: Home Reading Services provided books for the general reader, principally through the branches and extension services. The Reference Services provided the specialized books for the reader plowing in a particular or specialized field of knowledge. Home Reading Services books, intended for the general reader, were described as being expendable, i.e., they are with certain exceptions books in the "popular" category. Those provided by the Reference Services, on the other hand, consist of books which specialized readers, students and researchers call for, and whose use and value are continuing. Among them are those books and materials which make up the various special collections of the Library.

In his 1943–44 annual report, Ulveling explained and defined the nature of Home Reading Services in these words:

> Its first fundamental service is as a medium for the furthering of popular education, a center to which individuals, regardless of the level of their educational background, may come for books and guidance. They come with reasonable assurance that whatever their interests may be—vocational, recreational, informational or cultural—the materials required will be available to them. The very flexibility of such an educational institution makes it a great community asset. To fulfill this obligation in the community life it is essential that there be great diversity in our book holdings covering such fields as art, music, literature, the various trades and professions, crafts of all types, history, current problems—whether political, social or economic—religion and philosophy, biography, travel books descriptive of all places throughout the world, languages and language study, as well as recreational materials designed to provide the daily relaxation which is a fundamental part of every person's daily needs. Though this service is made available primarily through the branch libraries, it is literally impossible because of the broad scope of these requirements for each branch library to be a self-sufficient unit of the service. Great central stores of the less frequently called for books are therefore maintained at the Main Library from which place they are sent to any branch library as local neighborhood needs require.
>
> This part of the institution's book collection remains relatively constant in the over-all number of volumes included. As new titles which present the latest competent opinion and discussion on topics of current interest are added, the books which have become obsolete for purposes of helping an individual with his problems of everyday living are withdrawn. Other books which continue as standard reading for generation after generation are replaced when they become unduly soiled or physically worn beyond the possibility of further useful service. Therefore, from this part of the Library's total book holdings nearly 70,000 volumes are withdrawn annually and a corresponding number are added.[11]

With this background, the mission of Home Reading Services is to work primarily through the branches to find better ways of reaching more people—adults and children—and to serve that population which comprises the core of the city. It is, in a sense, providing a tailor-made service which will satisfy the individual's taste, desires and interests. To accomplish this it is necessary first to attract people, to make them aware of what is available to them in the branch nearest them, or, as one librarian remarked, through the great reservoir of books maintained at the Main Library upon which they can draw through the branches. This involves the projection of community programs. Through them the Library staff goes to the public in various ways, talks to them, and observes what interests them. Children are reached through programs in the schools, and even through pre-school programs, in which they are told about the Library and invited to visit it. Other programs are arranged to attract adults. Lectures are given on various current topics, usually designed for the particular neighborhood served by the branch. Films are shown, discussion groups are organized, radio and television programs are employed in which books are talked about and reviewed. In one neighborhood lectures may be given on investment practices or setting up estates. Those topics might be wholly unsuitable in another neighborhood where the people would more quickly respond to problems of the aging or various phases of homemaking.

A branch survey made in 1957 had this comment on the Conely branch, one of the city's oldest ones:

> The general character of this neighborhood has changed but little through the years. It is still predominately Polish, with the older generation still speaking and reading only in the Polish language. The other foreign groups are largely Ukranian and Russian. It is a section of neat, small homes. There are few renters and few transients. Chief reading interests are in the technical field, family living and how-to-do-it books.

The Edison branch, a newer installation, was analyzed this way:

> Lower middle income group. Young couples with many small children. New homes since World War II. Interested in child care,

315

homes, auto repair, etc. About 60 per cent circulation is juvenile. Many schools, three high schools. Considerable interest in new fiction and non-fiction.

The analysis of still another branch, the Hubbard, had this to say:

> Hubbard serves an older, established upper middle class neighborhood which is made up largely of professional people, white collar workers and small business owners. The reading public, which is extensive, is literate and intellectually alert and the Library is an accepted part of the individual family cultural pattern. Reading interests are varied and diverse, but tastes tend toward the more sophisticated, with emphasis on the arts, the theater, books of social comment, history and business.

Specific programs at the Hubbard branch which attracted interest and attendance covered such topics as investment know-how and mental health.[12] Whatever subject is covered, there is sure to be a table or shelf filled with specially-selected complementary reading matter waiting to be taken home by those wishing to explore the subject further.

To assist in planning and setting up these programs and other special events is the Community and Group Services, a department created in 1956. It remains under the direct supervision of the Library director. While the Community and Group Services Department is of inestimable value to Home Reading Services, its facilities are also at the disposal of Reference Services. The three major areas of this service are adult education, television and press relations.[13]

The adult education work is almost entirely branch based. Some idea of how it touches the lives of Library patrons and prospective patrons can be gained from the programs mentioned in the 1957 branch survey, although it might be pointed out that adult education is sufficiently elastic so that it can and will offer almost any type of subject program if enough people in a neighborhood desire it. Many of these programs, while tied to a branch, are conducted for community, social or church groups. An outstandingly successful example is the Great Books Discussions. This was started in the mid-1940's in Chicago by the University of Chicago. The results encouraged the sponsors to believe it would be equally well received elsewhere. The Great Books Discussions consists of a program in which small groups of adults under expert guidance meet regularly to discuss a certain book which each member has read and in which he is presumably interested. The effectiveness of the program depends largely upon trained leaders. When the University of Chicago decided to expand the program nationally, it selected three cities—Detroit, Cleveland and Indianapolis—as testing grounds. Local leaders were chosen and trained by University of Chicago experts. These in turn trained leaders in their own communities. The Public Library was the first local sponsor, the program being inaugurated in 1946. The University of Detroit and the University of Michigan also supplied leaders and helped in the organization of groups. Since 1946 the program has been a continuing and popular one, reaching into many—sometimes unusual—community areas. For example, one group was organized among those serving sentences at the Detroit House of Correction. Library officials stated that it was one of the liveliest and most interested groups.

This type of enterprise indicates the expanded activities of the Home Reading Services. Yet, basically, except for its housekeeping departments and divisions, the Branch and Extension departments, which in the past had been combined, remain the hard core of Home Reading Services. In tracing its lineage through the Branch and Extension departments, some important personalities, beginning with Jessie C. Chase, chief of branches, stand out as the contributing factors in the growth of this phase of the Library.

Miss Chase was succeeded by William Webb, as Extension chief, in 1921. Born in 1893 and a graduate of Haverford College, Webb earned a degree in library science at the New York State Library School. He served as legislative reference assistant in the New York State Library before joining the Detroit system in 1920. He resigned in 1928 to become librarian for the Flint Public Library. He was followed by Ulveling and he, in turn, by Mohrhardt.

In 1945 when the Library reorganization took place, Ruth Rutzen, a member of the staff since 1924 and chief of circulation

317

since 1930, was made the first Home Reading Services director. A graduate of the University of Wisconsin Library School, Miss Rutzen gained a national reputation among librarians and the public for her work in Detroit and Michigan. Not only did she help carry through the reorganization by putting the Home Reading Services on a firm footing, she also set up the Reader-Interest Classification in the Detroit branches, of which, incidentally, ten were added during her reign as director. She was president of the Michigan Library Association and is credited with organizing the movement for state aid grants. She was elected president of the Public Libraries Association, and at one time was urged to accept the nomination for president of the American Library Association, but declined the honor. The Detroit Public Library's increased participation in community affairs was largely the result of her efforts. She retired from the Detroit system early in 1963.[14]

Miss Rutzen was succeeded as Home Reading Services director by Kenneth E. King, a graduate of Brown University and the Simmons College Library School. King joined the Detroit Library in 1951 and in 1956, after having had branch experience and work in the young adult program, he was made coordinator of the Community and Group Services Department.

An important accomplishment of the 1945–48 reorganization, other than to improve the Library's general administration, was to strengthen the reference-research library. Not only was this in line with accepted library practice, but it carried on a policy to which the Detroit Library adhered almost from its beginning, namely to place emphasis upon reference service. As early as 1875 this policy was expressed when the Board of Education's committee on the Library declared:

> Your committee are inclined to recommend the purchase, so far as practicable, of books of solid value and permanent usefulness— books which shall serve for reference and instruction, rather than for mere amusement and mental dissipation.[15]

From the time that the Centre building became the main library facility, the librarians and the commissioners were concerned with providing separate and adequate reference quarters. It was determined at an early date that something better was needed than making the Reference Department share the general reading room, or equipping it with a few tables and chairs in an alcove off to one side. Judge Campbell in his annual report as president of the Commission in 1883 remarked with a ring of satisfaction that "the Reference Department has been enlarged and the rooms containing works of this kind have been extended on the main floor of the Library, so as to be quite convenient." [16]

A year later, Librarian Gillman made a statement which showed what importance was placed upon reference facilities:

> The Reference Department, with its use it seems to me, may well be accepted as a criterion of the strength or weakness of the Library. It is the vertebral column, to which the entire frame is so intimately related that imperfection or inadequacy here makes itself felt throughout. A strong "back bone" is an admirable thing and generally indicative of the strength of the structure. Since the enlargement of the division devoted to works of reference, about two years ago, the additional shelving has rapidly begun to fill with some of the best books of this class and as already mentioned, recourse to it for consultation in connection with systematic study is constantly on the increase, being more appreciated as visitors are instructed in the better methods of using these aids to research and education. Of the 11,722 volumes consulted within the walls, all but a very small number were works of reference of the better description.[17]

From that statement it may be concluded that in 1884, the Library was taking on the characteristics of a research center, an assumption further borne out by the Commission's 1884 report on the subject, in which it was stated:

> The value of the Library in its higher purposes and as an educational aid is more thoroughly appreciated as its beneficiaries become better acquainted with the more advanced methods for its employment. This is perhaps more apparent in the consultation of the books within the building than in the circulation of the volumes issued for home use. During the last two years there has been a greater recourse to works of science, and art, cyclopedias, dictionaries, gazeteers, and other books of reference than ever before in the history of the Library.[18]

It will be recalled that this was the era in which the librarians and commissioners, reflecting the attitude of the clergy and other defenders of the public morals, viewed with certain apprehension the reading of fiction and endeavored, as far as they dared, to limit the amount of light literature available for public consumption. It was for that reason that everything possible was done within the resources of the Commission to improve the reference facilities, to provide better, more attractive quarters and to make the public aware of the fact that the Library had something to offer other than literature of an "ephemeral" quality.

A new reference room was opened in 1893 in the space formerly occupied by the Scientific Museum, and was decorated and equipped at a cost of $10,822. It was reported that within a few days after its opening it was being used daily by an average of two hundred to three hundred persons.[19] It was pointed out soon thereafter:

> The reference room now has twice its former capacity. This enlargement was timely, for so greatly has the popular use of this department increased that already the room is completely filled at all times. The books most likely to be wanted in reference work are placed in this room on open shelves, accessible to all. These include all bound periodicals and works which are strictly for reference in philosophy, literature, art, archaeology, genealogy, etc.[20]

In 1896, 335,000 books in the reference room were consulted, compared to 291,000 used in 1895.

At this period there had been no important efforts to departmentalize the Reference Department, and books of all subjects and categories were included in the reference room collection. Divisional separation would come later when more room was available. Accordingly, the patron studying a book on metal working would use the same table as the person engrossed in a rare work of philosophy or, perhaps, the young attorney with political ambition making notes from the latest, most authoritative book on taxation or public administration. So heavy was the traffic in the Reference Department that by 1892 the services of three full-time attendants and one page were required. Said Utley:

> Our sneering critics who say that the main business of the Library is to supply cheap novels to persons who would be better off without them, should look into the reference room sometimes. Such a

glimpse would be enlightening. They would find it crowded with people intently engaged in serious study.[21]

The Reference Department became—and still is—a sort of mirror in which are reflected the interests of the people of Detroit at any given moment. Because of the city's industrial character, men became users of the department in large numbers, a fact officially noted in 1916 when it was stated:

> Detroit is singular in one respect—men predominate as users of the reference room, at least. Boys on debating teams, young artisans, architects, designers, older business and professional men are all much in evidence. Libraries often are considered as intended mainly for women and children, but Detroit men have elected otherwise for they appear in the proportion of four to one.[22]

"As the community's interests have broadened the Library's book collections have been broadened," it was said several years later by Ulveling.

> I need only point to the recently awakened interest in Latin America, as well as in far-off parts of the world to which American military forces have gone, to provide examples of the type of subjects which in recent years have had to be developed in the Library's book collection.[23]

Not everyone who made use of the Reference Department got his information directly from the books, periodicals and pamphlets. The telephone proved to be a convenient means of communication for questions to be answered or arguments to be settled. Before long an important part of the Reference Department's work consisted of giving this kind of service, as well as that provided by personal solicitation and by mail. The Reference Department was happy to give this service which soon became a highly specialized one. In 1919 the public was being invited to telephone, and the questions asked and answered fell into every conceivable category, taxing the knowledge and ingenuity of the staff.

"How long is it necessary to cook peaches by the cold pack method?" "What are some of the good hotels in Philadelphia?" "Is it necessary to have a license to operate a stereopticon ma-

321

chine?" "How much space does a ton of anthracite coal occupy?" These were typical questions in 1919. Now, as then, major news stories produce a flood of queries for more detailed or background information. When the state marriage laws were tightened with requirement for a five-day wait after application had been made for a license, reference attendants played the part of Cupid, directing couples to the most convenient Gretna Green in neighboring states. Sporting events produce a demand for records and statistics, frequently generated by arguments which follow an afternoon or evening of imbibing strong spirits. A student needs a date or a fact to complete a term paper; a housewife with a culinary problem goes to the phone and dials the Library number. A busy executive needs a date or some other kind of information, and he needs it quickly. There is no time to hunt through the books. "Call the Library!"

It was pointed out in 1922:

> The use of the various reference and research departments may be measured by the volume of questions answered which numbered approximately 61,342. The adequate response to such inquiries required sometimes only a few minutes' attention but, in many instances, called for research and compilation of information for days and weeks, involving copying, loan of material from out of town, voluminous correspondence—all carried on by specially trained assistants. The range of topics covered was identified with the scope of the General Reference Department and its Civics division, departments of Fine Arts, Music and Drama, Technology and Industry, and the Burton Historical Collection.[24]

So important did this service become that in 1944 a special telephone desk was set up in the general reference room, with ready reference materials at hand. Trained assistants devoted their time exclusively to answering telephone questions. In 1963 the volume of incoming calls was at a rate exceeding 182,651, keeping eighteen trunk lines busy. The volume of calls often exceeded the questions asked in person at the Main Library.[25]

Prior to 1893 reference work was handled by all staff attendants. In that year, however, Lizzie Hurst was placed in charge, first as a special attendant and then as chief in 1901. She was succeeded in 1913 by Joanna Strange, and in 1914 by Jeanne

Griffin. In 1915 Helen C. Bates, who had joined the staff about 1887, became chief and continued to head the department until her death in 1937. She was followed by Mabel L. Conat. When Miss Conat was made assistant librarian in 1945, she was succeeded by Helen M. Crane, and upon her retirement, Katherine G. Harris became head of Reference Services.

Since World War II, two things have caused a great increase in public reliance upon the Library's reference services. These, according to Miss Harris, have been more used by students, resulting from the up-grading of high school courses. In Detroit, said Miss Harris, 60 per cent of the Main Library reference patrons are students. The other factor has been the necessity of the Main Library to furnish reference-research service to an enlarged metropolitan area—a necessity which has increased so phenomenally as to prove both a challenge and a problem. Wrote Miss Harris:

> In a survey of organization use of the Detroit Public Library, made during one month in the fall of 1960, it was found that the Ford Motor Company, for instance, used every one of the nine subject departments of the Main Library, not just science and technology material.[26]

Ford Motor Company, of course, has not been the only beneficiary of reference-research services. Its competitors have also used the facilities, as have smaller manufacturing firms, advertising agencies and virtually every other type of industrial and commercial enterprise within an ever-expanding area. So great have these demands become that Detroit has had to cry "Help!" and in 1959 the Commission suggested to Mayor Louis C. Miriani that state legislation be sought "to provide for reimbursing the Detroit Public Library for providing reference and research service for the Metropolitan area." [27]

This problem and some of the measures taken to solve it will be discussed further in more detail. But when the solution comes, if it ever does, it is a reasonable prediction that the agency of government providing it will seek the data and information it requires to do so in the storehouse of accumulated information that is the Reference Services of the Detroit Public Library.

CHAPTER 20

A FINGER ON THE CITY'S PULSE

IF HENRY GILLMAN could return and look at his Library as it is today, he would undoubtedly concede that its reference-research facilities provide a very strong backbone indeed. Taking into consideration the several important departments with their highly specialized collections, he would concede that the institution has become a physiological phenomenon—a body with several backbones.

His successor, Henry M. Utley, was of a mind with Gillman. In 1891 he strongly urged the Commission to concentrate upon building up a special category of interest which would make the Library distinctive. To accomplish this he recommended the use of any surplus funds to augment some special collection after "general, well-balanced" book purchases had been made. He pointed out:

> After a few years, this specialty of the Library would become its marked and distinguished feature. There is no reason why this Library should not acquire a national reputation; even a world-wide

324

reputation is possible within the lines of a special character. Such a reputation would not only redound to the credit of our city, but would bring hither from all quarters of the globe students who would find nowhere else so large and complete a collection of books upon a subject in which they were interested.

Utley made no specific recommendations as to what category of interest and knowledge this concentration should be. He mentioned navigation, marine architecture, minerals, mining or metallurgy, anything, in fact, "appropriate to our environment, or suggested by our city or state resources, industries or social life." [1] Commissioner James E. Scripps, it will be recalled, had somewhat the same idea about 1905, although he was prepared to sacrifice some of the character of a general library in favor of a high degree of specialization. Utley was unwilling to go quite that far. Nevertheless, if the shades of Utley and Scripps could join Gillman on a midnight tour of the Main Library they, as well as he, would undoubtedly find satisfaction in finding their ideas realized. For the Detroit Public Library in some of its specialized departments has achieved pre-eminence and has become the Mecca for scholars in several fields. In achieving this distinctive position, the Library has built wisely by recognizing that which is appropriate to Detroit's environment and its "resources, industries or social life."

None of the Library's specialized collections suddenly sprang into existence as full-fledged departments without prior antecedents. Each grew out of the general reference collection, and was the product of evolution—a combination of the acquisition of books and other materials on a more or less specialized subject, combined with a cumulative interest in and demand by the public for that sort of material. The Fine Arts Department provides a case in point. It became a department in 1921 when it occupied a beautifully-appointed, specially-designed room in the Main Library. But many years before, in 1891, the beginnings of the department were clearly discernible when it was reported that "alcoves containing books on architecture and fine arts are open to the public and are constantly used, frequently to over-crowding. . . . Many art school students and young architects who desire to make use of the Library are hampered by the lack of adequate conveniences." [2] Cass Gilbert sought to remedy that situation on his drawing board, and it is more than likely that interest in providing Main Library facilities was undertaken with as much or more enthusiasm and personal satisfaction going into this phase of his plans than in any other. At any rate, the department which emerged in 1921 contained a broad range of subject matter, including aesthetics, religious art, costume, history of art, architecture and landscape architecture, house plans, pottery, glass and china, coins, textiles, furniture, photography and even flower arrangement. Books, pictures and periodicals covering every phase of these subjects are available and are constantly being added. A comprehensive clipping file is maintained, and as an added public service a day by day calendar of art events in the metropolitan area is kept current.

The Music and Performing Arts Department, more than some others, was to a large extent inspired by public demand. Musicians and music lovers combined to press for a collection in their field which would satisfy their personal interests as well as a wider cultural field for the public generally. This was expressed in a letter of 1919 written by Ossip Gabrilowitsch, conductor of the Detroit Symphony Orchestra, in which he said: "A thoroughly equipped music department seems to me as essential to a public library as a department of technical books on the industrial sciences. . . ." He was supported by such leaders in the field as Francis L. York, head of the Detroit Conservatory of Music, and Charles Morse, of the Detroit Institute of Musical Art. As a result of their urgings, along with others, Strohm announced that a music room would be included in the Main Library, with attention given "to the more expensive compositions which the music student cannot afford to buy for himself." Also promised was a collection of "Victrola records," largely operatic, and consideration was given to construction of a soundproof room for their enjoyment.[3]

Soon after the new department was opened, it was pointed out that the collection had been substantially enlarged with particular emphasis on violin and organ works. It was soon discovered that there was a great demand from the churches of the city for anthems, with the result that by purchase and gift this collection also was increased and became extensively used. Some notable gifts were made, among them the private collection of William H. Murphy, president of the Detroit Symphony Society, consisting of orchestral scores which were made available, not only to local groups, but to others all over the country. Later, an outstanding collection of the works of Michigan composers was built up. Through the efforts of the Detroit Musicians' Association, the E. Azalia Hackley Collection of Negro Music was established in 1943. Named in honor of a Negro music teacher, its scope covers the entire field of Negro contribution to the performing arts, including material from other countries, traditional and folk music, rare editions of spirituals, popular music and jazz, scores, recordings and books. A third group is the Hashofar Collection of Jewish content. Through the accumulation of these and other materials, the Library was able to claim that it possessed one of "the really extensive music libraries in the country, especially in music for the violin and orchestra and in chamber music."

The drama collection was divided—literature went to Literature and Fine Arts; performing material to Music and Performing Arts. The collection covers the field of theatrical literature, including representative plays of all nations starting with the Greek and Roman classics, and also theatrical history, biography, books on stagecraft and playwriting. In addition, there are materials on such associated subjects as puppetry, radio, television and the dance, all supported by an impressive periodical list, a clipping file, playbills, and, as in the case of Fine Arts, a calendar of planned and scheduled events. The drama collection, by its ability to furnish materials, has had a strong influence upon the little theater movement in the area and to it can be attributed at least in part, the renaissance of interest in the theater generally in Detroit.

One of the earliest specialized services of the Library, one which already has been mentioned, was the Business and Commerce Department, originally housed in the offices of the Detroit Board of Commerce and later moved to the Downtown Library. This widely used asset of the Library provides specialized business information with a collection of materials which include financial and trade publications, corporate reports and directories.

327

Two departments, History and Travel, and Language and Literature, are somewhat similar in their backgrounds to Fine Arts. Each was from the Library's earliest beginnings an integral part of the over-all collection, but as the amount of material in each category increased, it became easier from both the administrative and public-use standpoints to establish them in separate categories. Each was the result of the reorganization of the 1940's, and each dates its departmental status from 1949. History and Travel, consisting of about 100,000 volumes, covers not only the specific title subjects, but also those in close interest alliance such as archaeology Indian lore, and geography. It also maintains an extensive map collection. The Language and Literature Department specializes in literary forms such as poetry, essays, criticism, the short story, the novel; translations; and folklore. Its tools consist of grammars and dictionaries in many languages, encompassing such matter as slang, dialects and idioms. It also provides material on public speaking. The foreign language collection in the Downtown Library is composed of about 50,000 volumes in twenty-nine foreign languages.

The most recent department to be established is Philosophy, Religion and Education. Covering the subjects its name indicates, as well as psychiatry, child training, family living and vocational guidance, the department in its present form dates from 1950.

Of all the Library's reference departments, none so accurately reflect the mood and character of the city as do the Sociology and Economics and the Technology and Science departments. Each came into existence to meet public requirements which were largely the result of unusual circumstances and conditions. Each continues to occupy a place of unique importance within the Library and the community.

The Sociology and Economics Department started out simply as part of the general reference collection, an assemblage of books and pamphlets dealing primarily with political science. During the later years of the 19th and early years of the 20th century, the United States experienced an awakening of social and political conscience. The people and their political leaders began to show interest in slums, working hours and conditions, child and woman labor, penology, monopoly, and a host of similar matters.

The era was marked by a strong progressive movement which in a relatively short time manifested itself in political, economic and social reforms. It produced among other things, anti-trust and pure food and drug laws, the graduated income tax, the Australian ballot, woman's suffrage, and national prohibition. At the local level, and in Detroit especially, the period produced major political reforms in the administration of the public school system and in the adoption of a new municipal charter. Public interest in the latter two movements was mirrored in the Library by the call for books and other material on the subjects. The Library's response was to create a Civics Division out of its collection on sociology and political science.

The times called for change in the local picture. Detroit was probably no worse than other major cities, but it was bad enough. Corruption had crept into the Board of Education and the City Hall. It was claimed by many, and not without reason, that the real seat of Detroit's government was in its saloons. There, certainly, the political machines were on solid foundations.

"Serving without salary, the 'honorary' school inspectors, one from each of the twenty-one wards, never failed to mix politics with education," declared William P. Lovett, a leader in the reform movement.

> As a force in politics the school board faction rivalled the Common Council. . . . Graft there was, no doubt, in plenty. . . . An event of significance in the long list of Detroit reforms was the election campaign and referendum vote of the people abolishing the old school board and, in 1917, beginning the present plan of placing public control in a board of seven members, elected at large for terms of six years each.[4]

The school Board reorganization was followed in 1918 by the adoption of a new city charter. The old Board of Aldermen, elected on a ward basis and by partisan vote was abolished. That corrupt and cumbersome system was replaced by a nine-man Common Council, elected at large by nonpartisan ballot. A strong mayor with appointive power over most city commissions also was provided for. The result of these changes was like a breath of fresh air blowing through the political jungle. They made Detroit's government relatively pure, and kept it that way.

While all of these changes were being agitated, the Civics Division was established in 1915, mainly to furnish enlightenment to the voters. Strongly behind the reform movement were such men as Divie B. Duffield and Clarence M. Burton. Even Adam Strohm, forsaking the neutral ground which librarians were traditionally expected to occupy, worked for change.[5] Stated the 1915–16 annual report:

> The Civics Division which functions as a special bureau of information on municipal and social subjects has reason to look back upon its first full year of service with considerable satisfaction and encouraging confidence in future usefulness. . . . Interest in good government and the social well-being of the community appeared to be on the increase. The local agitation and adoption of the seven member school board produced many demands for material on that subject, which was on several occasions supplied to the agitators themselves.[6]

Library Service claimed that the Civics Division was originally organized through demand of students for material on city government, taxation, prohibition. It was soon being used by women's clubs, and then by city officials. Debating kits on a dozen subjects, containing pro and con data, were prepared. Reading lists were published on school reform and charter revision. These were widely circulated in clubs, business places and churches.[7]

"We have numerous and frequent opportunities to aid in the solution of really big problems—political, industrial and social—which are today facing the city of Detroit," the Library proclaimed.[8]

In 1918 fashion raised the hemline of women's skirts to six inches below the knee, and as if that were not sufficient emancipation, women also won the right to vote in general elections in Michigan. The Library was silent on the first issue, but not on the second. Women were reminded that they "will need to read up on 'how to use the ballot.' The Public Library is ready to help in meeting this new public responsibility. Books on citizenship and voting have been duplicated." [9] The ladies could obtain them, as well as reading lists, at the Main Library and all the branches. It all added up to one thing: the Detroit Public Library was a vital and influential force in the municipal reform movement.

330

The 1917–18 war opened another field of interest, and the need for information followed. The Civics Division began to expand with material on food control, war finance, submarine warfare, rehabilitation and similar subjects. After the war social problems became of paramount interest and continued to be so.

"In the field of sociology, we find that 75,000 volumes have been withdrawn [for home use]; indicating a very fair sense of responsibility and interest among our library readers in civic and public matters," the Civics Division reported in 1928.[10]

The scope of the Division was considerably enlarged in 1937 by the acquisition of one of the Library's most important and valuable collections. This was the Henry Glover Stevens Memorial Library which had been in the possession of the Detroit Council of Social Agencies and which was donated to the Public Library.

Henry Glover Stevens, who built the collection, was a man of wealth and culture who devoted himself to charity and philanthropic enterprises. His father, William H. Stevens, amassed a comfortable fortune in the mining business. Henry Stevens was born in Detroit, January 18, 1879, was educated in the city's public schools, and was graduated from Yale. Extensive travel aroused in him an interest in art, particularly that of the Orient. He established a school of design in the old art museum, which he served as director for a short time. It was largely through his efforts that when Detroit's government was reorganized in 1918, the Arts Commission was set up as a public agency, and the new Art Institute became a public instead of a private institution. Stevens shared his enthusiasm for art with an interest in organized philanthropy and helped establish the Council of Social Agencies and the Community Fund. As a long time director of the former, he gathered a collection of books relating to the field of sociology. In doing so, he was prompted by the conviction that to meet social problems intelligently there had to be data for research.

Stevens died February 11, 1934, and three years later, the Stevens library, augmented by cash gifts from social agencies, friends and relatives was turned over to the Public Library. It was described as "a magnificent collection of books dealing with

331

the social sciences and is invaluable as a reference collection." [11]

The addition of this and other material shifted emphasis from what had been largely a concern with political science to a broader and better balanced reference service. The result was that the Civics Division, having become so large that it required more adequate space, was given a new name and a new status. Technology was moved out in 1938 and placed in a separate building, and Social Sciences took over its rooms on the third floor of the Main building. Within a year it was reported that "the Department of Social Sciences is now functioning at a good tempo in its new spacious quarters." It was able to present for public use a broad range of material on sociology, political science, economics, law, race relations, criminology, insurance, city planning, and legislation at all levels of government.

An important addition to the Social Sciences Department was made in 1952 when the Library purchased the outstanding labor collection of the John Crerar Library of Chicago. Described in a Johns Hopkins University publication *Trade Union Publications* as "one of the six most important labor collections in the country," this material was developed by merging the private collection of the noted economist Richard T. Ely and that of the Dutch scholar Carel V. Gerretson. Added to earlier materials already in the Library's possession, plus later acquisitions, all phases of labor economics were covered. As a research tool, the collection is rich in material on the history of the labor movement both in the United States and abroad, and offers scholars a fertile field for reference and investigation of modern labor economics. An unusual feature of the collection is a file of labor-management contracts which were precedent-setting or unique. This material has been drawn upon by negotiators. In one such instance, it has been claimed, the Detroit Public Library contributed to development of the contract which contained the first escalator clause. With the organized labor movement becoming such a vital force in Detroit, beginning in the early 1930s, the labor collection has become a most valuable addition to the Library's collections which uniquely reflect the city's background and image.[12]

Due to the scope of the social sciences collection, such as the addition of the labor material, the name of the department was changed in 1963 to the Sociology and Economics Department. Claiming close kinship with the Sociology and Economics Department is the Municipal Reference Library, organized April 9, 1945, to provide reference service principally to municipal officials and employees. Although it is housed in Detroit's City-County Building, its facilities are available to the general public and it is frequently used by students.[13] Need for the Municipal Reference Library became apparent after World War II when, as the Library pointed out, "governmental planning and administration had been recognized as an important study with a growing literature." [14] In addition, municipal government expanded just prior to, during, and after the war. New committees and commissions were created to handle specific matters, and often those charged with these duties had little experience with them. Information about what other cities were doing in the same fields, together with findings reported in technical publications would, it was felt, be of value. The result was the opening of the Municipal Reference Library in quarters provided in the Water Board Building. It quickly proved its usefulness. Within days after its establishment the city clerk reported to the Commission that he had been directed by the Common Council "to advise the Library Commission that the Council feels that the establishment of the Municipal Reference Library is a progressive step." [15] Official recognition was given it when the Council adopted an ordinance providing that the Municipal Library "be made official depository, for all printed or processed reports and documents currently issued by each committee of the City Council, the various departments, divisions or commissions of the City of Detroit." [16] When Detroit's present City-County Building was completed in 1955, space for the Municipal Reference Library was provided on the tenth floor, adjacent to the offices of the corporation counsel.

Probably no place in the Main Library complex is busier than the Technology and Science Department. Its traffic and use offers ample proof of the Library's sensitivity to the community's character and its needs. Technology, with its collection of about 200,-000 books and its 2000 periodicals currently received, provides the Detroit area workshop with background and up-to-date material on a wide range of technical subjects—from how to build a ship model in a bottle to the latest unclassified developments in the field of atomic energy. Through the Technology collections, the Library's gears are effectively meshed with the Detroit industrial machine.

The Technology Department was a war baby, coming into existence in 1917 at a time when Detroit for the first time was essaying the role of democracy's arsenal. The area's manufacturers had learned a good deal about the mass production of automobiles and their parts. They were not as familiar with the techniques of turning out airplane parts, Liberty engines, guns, and ammunition. They sorely needed research materials, and the Library mobilized its resources quickly to supply them.

Of course the Technology and Science Department had antecedents which could be traced back almost to the Library's beginning. A sure starting time for the beginning of the accumulation of technical reference material would be 1868, three years after the Detroit Public Library was founded. It was then that the Library was placed on the list of institutions designated by acts of Congress as depositories for public documents, and publications of the Smithsonian Institution.[17] Before long there were received the first bound volumes of records of the United States Patent Office, the beginning of a collection which now numbers about 15,000 fat tomes containing details, specifications and illustrations of every patent granted in this country. With that as a foundation, technology reference in Detroit may fairly be said to have begun. From that time on, the build-up of the collection, which prior to 1917 was divided between the general reading and reference reading rooms, gained momentum from both a quantitative and qualitative standpoint.

As Detroit became more and more industrialized, the Library kept pace with developments. The Commission declared in 1883:

> We are constantly reminded in various ways of the great increase of all kinds of industrial work in our city and its vicinity, and we have endeavored to make provision which will need constant enlargement to meet the demands of those who desire to be acquainted with the new applications of science to the different industries as they are

developed. Detroit is becoming a prosperous centre for many branches of enterprise.[18]

Efforts were made to cater to persons interested in design and illustration, but "so also have the mechanics and artificers of our city been frequent in their attendance, and have drawn largely on our departments of mechanic trades and useful arts." [19]

The collection of technical material had a strong attraction for youths and young men—those with ideas or visions. It was, in a sense, the poor man's college of engineering. Among those who visited the Library was a young train butcher and telegrapher who dropped in between runs on the Detroit-Port Huron line of the Grand Trunk to pore over books and the latest periodicals. His name was Thomas Alva Edison, and his borrower's card is still preserved among his effects. Another who visited the Detroit Public Library, examining, in all likelihood, those Patent Office records, and who by his own admission got some of his best ideas from the Library's copies of the *English Mechanics and World of Science,* a popular mechanical publication, was another young man, Henry Ford. During his early years in the city, while employed as a stationary engineer for the Edison Illuminating Company, he found the technical collection of inestimable value.

No effort was made in those early years to separate or departmentalize the technological books and periodicals, although some of the individual commissioners were thinking along such lines. George Osius suggested in 1906 that a special collection on forestry would provide "an exceptional opportunity" to be of service to the State of Michigan. Two years later, the Detroit Engineering Society deposited its books and journals in the reference room. The material was accepted on condition that it would be available to the general public.[20]

As the United States moved toward World War I, use of the technical collection increased, but the user interest was not confined to problems directly tied to manufacturing. The step-up of industry and an influx of workers brought on a housing boom, and the Library welcomed an increasing number of architects and builders, as well as the "do-it-yourself-ers" who wanted home building plans and instructions.[21] The demand for technical information of a widely diversified character became, in fact, so great that in 1917 it became necessary to group it and form the Technology Department. To head it, Strohm looked to the John Crerar Library of Chicago where he found a reference assistant, D. Ashley Hooker.* He was appointed Technology librarian, effective September 1, to head the new department which was officially established on that date.[22] New books were purchased, with the emphasis on aeronautics, iron and steel, machine shop practice and mathematics. Subscriptions were taken to new periodicals, trade catalogs were added and pamphlet and clipping collections were started. Another service, special research, was offered. This involved the gathering together of all available material on any specific subject in response to telephone or mail requests.[23]

The department was described as "an answer to a distinct and repeated demand for intensive work in engineering and allied fields." Within a year after its establishment, it was receiving praise from local industry. The Library was proud of it. The Commission reported:

> The service along more practical lines, viz., furnishing information to engineers and mechanics, more especially those identified with our local war industries, has been one of the most tangible advances in our activities. The Technology Department organized last fall [1917] appears now almost as a war measure. Its birth was certainly timely, its usefulness has been attested by representatives from some of our largest industries.[24]

"We have come into direct touch with the men who have been doing things in Detroit," was another comment.[25]

The post-World War I years found the Technology and Science Department established on a firm foundation of public acceptance

---

* Despite the importance of his position as the Library's first chief of Technology and acting librarian during Strohm's World War I leave of absence, very little biographical data is available on D. Ashley Hooker. He was a graduate of the New York State Library School, and worked in the U. S. Military Academy Library, West Point, and the Cleveland Public Library before going to Chicago's John Crerar Library. It was from the latter institution that he was called in 1917 to establish the Technology Department at Detroit. He left there April 30, 1923 and went to southern California, presumably for his health. Some time later he was a member of the staff of the public library in Birmingham, Alabama. He died December 5, 1951.

and use. Hooker found a steady stream of men—engineers, mechanics and chemists—coming to him for advice and help. He had to devote his Saturdays to personal interviews for which it became necessary to make advance appointments.[26] The Commission observing the busy aspect of the department was impressed, as its 1922–23 report showed. It stated:

> Perhaps the field where the best prospects are being developed with the richest yield is in our department of Technology. It has already received more acknowledgements from exacting experts and local research men than many of our departments older in history. . . . This fact should never be lost sight of, namely, that the prosperity of the city is based on an industrial specialty and that an outstanding amount of ingenuity, courage and trained minds are devoted to ever new processes and methods in manufacturing. New solutions are being asked for; new ventures and new leads are being followed up. While this growth is based in part on a remarkable background of experience, every step is, nevertheless, taken after thorough searching and testing in literature pertaining thereto, in laboratories, in scientific and industrial records here and abroad. The young men of our city are naturally attracted to this local adventure in manufacturing which has given to Detroit a character of its own. In their eagerness to learn and to play in with the industrial explorers and inventors today they very readily drift to our department of Science and Technology.[27]

If the "drift" continued, the Commission felt, it might soon be necessary to provide Detroit with a special science building. During the early stages of the depression when efforts were being made to curtail expenses, the technology librarian defended the work of his department by pointing out that it was regularly used by thirty-four firms, including Bohn Aluminum & Brass Corporation, Chrysler Corporation, Detroit Edison Company, Ford Motor Company, General Motors Corporation, B. F. Goodrich Rubber Company, Kelvinator Corporation, and most of the city's leading patent attorneys and advertising agencies.[28]

Since Detroit lived by the automobile, it was frankly admitted that the Technology Department put special emphasis on books dealing with that and allied industries. But the other fields of technical interest were not neglected, and the use of the department accurately reflected at all times what the men and women in the Detroit workshop were thinking about and what they were doing.

In the Centre Park building, the technology collection was quartered in the Circulation Department, an arrangement which was far from satisfactory, but for which a lack of space left no alternative. The situation was rectified in 1921 when the new Main Library was occupied and the Technology Department was given two large rooms on the third floor. This was an improvement, but not a permanent one. About the time the Henry Glover Stevens collection was added, the Social Sciences Department was moved into the Technology Department quarters and one of the residential buildings acquired through the condemnation of the Main site was remodeled, a stack room was added, and it was converted into a separate library building for Technology. That building, on Putnam at the corner of Cass, had been the residence of Merton E. Farr and the Technology Department occupied it from 1938 until 1963 when new space became available in the enlarged Main building.* At that time the old Farr house was

---

* The Farr building seems to have stirred the emotions of the Library staff. When the former residential building was being converted into a home for the Technology Department, the muse nudged Ralph A. Ulveling with the following result:

The Technology Building
Clever men,
Like Christopher Wren,
Only occur just now and then.

No one expects
In perpetuity
Architects of his ingenuity.

Yet we wish he had lived to plan complete
The Technology building, Putnam Street.
Though a sketch was made by W.P.A.
It should be done again in another way.
Farr Hall is much too tall
For the long horizontal stackroom wall.
The garage addition is decidedly bare,
Perhaps a spire would help back there.
Chimneys arise
To one's surprise
From corners and gables of every size.
The entrance door
And the lower floor
Rest at the ground as never before.

torn down, the last of the private homes which once stood on the Main Library site.

In order to support the weight of the Technology and Science collection, reinforced concrete floors and supports were added. As a result, the demolition process took about four weeks, a job which normally could have been done in a few days. One member of the Technology staff watched the wrecking crew at work with a nostalgic feeling and, observing the difficulties, remarked: "I'm glad the old building is fighting back!"

Immediately after World War I, as the citizen soldier returned and sought to pick up where he had left off, interest was high in the Technology Department in subjects related to new or expanding vocational fields. Demand for home building information exceeded supply, and continued to be a popular subject for the next twenty-five years. After World War II, home-building interest, particularly of the do-it-yourself variety, suddenly waned, a fact the Technology staff found hard to explain. It was reported in 1929:

> Always we have a preponderance of practical men from the factories and railways who are working out their problems with the aid of our books. It is interesting to note the recent changes in their interests as reflected in our inventory report. Where heretofore we have suffered a large loss among automobile and radio books, we now find this entirely transferred to the airplane books.[29]

That shift in interest can be explained by Charles A. Lindbergh's successful New York to Paris flight in 1927, arousing public enthusiasm in aeronautics. For awhile Detroit fancied it was going to become the aircraft center of the world, just as it held the center of the automotive stage. Corporations were formed, investors put their money into airplane stocks, and everyone, it seemed, rushed to the Library to learn about this new

---

But its mixed designs, on unclassical lines,
Soon may be screened by growing vines.
Till then, however, it faces the street,
A sin against architecture, still incomplete.

No, never a cleverer dipped his pen
Than clever Sir Christopher,
Christopher Wren.

339

industry. However, aircraft building found a more favorable climate elsewhere, and Detroit turned its attention in other directions.

During World War II, the cry was for material on tool making and machine tools. But after the war that demand subsided. Whereas skilled and semiskilled mechanics were frequent wartime patrons of the department, their attendance dropped off when peace was restored. A new trend was noted as automation, data processing, and the whole field of electronics came to the forefront. The call for reference material of a highly sophisticated type now came from special libraries and information departments of area industries on behalf of their highly trained technicians and scientists. Instead of the man in overalls carrying home a book on shop practice, trucks from the large plants made regular stops at the Library and took away vast quantities of the most up-to-the-minute technical data.[30]

"New areas of knowledge are constantly increasing the number of subjects for which books must be bought each year," the Library stated in 1959. "Nuclear energy, space exploration and automation are making new demands on the book budgeting just as television did ten years ago." [31]

Asked to describe the department's strength in 1964, Robert Runser, its chief, stated that it lay in the categories of metals and metal working, all phases of engineering, and mathematics. To these had been recently added nuclear physics, the result of the Library becoming a depository of the Atomic Energy Commission beginning in the early 1950's. Biology was another active field in which the Technology Department was becoming strong. Botany became still another impressive addition. The collection in this field had been built up over a period of years and its addition to Technology resulted in the Technology and Science Department. Recent years were marked by secondary and high school level interest in mathematics and biology due, said Runser, to new teaching techniques and enriched courses in those fields. Hobbies continued, as always, to bring people to the department, and noted in recent years was a shift from home basement woodworking to boat building and sailing. Another recent active area was the demand on the part of those seeking civil service positions of a technical or semi-technical nature for data to help them to meet requirements and pass examinations.[32]

There was one particular division of the Technology and Science Department which gave the Library a unique and distinctive status among the libraries of the nation. This was the Automotive History Collection which dates from 1944. Like so much other material in the Library's specialized collections, automotive history represents a process of long accumulation from small and scattered beginnings. The first book purchased in 1896 was *Notes on Motor Carriages: With Hints for Purchasers and Users,* by John Henry Knight.[33] But for many years Detroit was too concerned with experimenting with the "horseless carriage," in manufacturing and marketing it, and creating a huge industry to devote much attention to gathering and preserving the records of its accomplishments. Time passed and the pioneers of the industry died. Companies flourished briefly and then faded into oblivion. The industry which changed civilization and which had such a tremendous impact upon Detroit, gradually was concentrated in a few surviving manufacturers, mostly in the Detroit area. Historians and social scientists began to pay more attention to the early days of the industry and the personalities who created it. It became necessary to gather the archives in a central location as far as possible. Detroit was the logical place and the Detroit Public Library assumed responsibility of assembling and preserving the records.

Much of the credit for the Automotive History Collection must go to Charles M. Mohrhardt who joined the Library staff in 1930 as chief of the Technology Department. Mohrhardt's hobby was automotive industry. Before going to Detroit he was with the Toledo Public Library where he became familiar with that institution's outstanding collection on glass, one of the Ohio city's principal products. In Detroit he was surprised to find that the Library had materials on the automobile and the automotive industry, but these were not organized into a regular collection. He suggested to Strohm that such a collection be started, but he received little encouragement. Ulveling, who succeeded Strohm as librarian, saw the importance of an automobile collection to Detroit and, with Mohrhardt, who was promoted to associate

341

librarian, set out to make the automotive section one of outstanding importance.

In 1944 formal steps were taken when the then chief of Technology Ernest I. Miller and Commissioner Edwin S. George
drafted a communication to the Commission proposing "establishment and development of an automotive history collection
and setting forth that for the proper accomplishment of this undertaking it would be necessary to solicit private holdings of automotive history materials and invite endowments or special gifts." [34]
The Commission gave its approval to the plan and a special room
was set aside to house the "extensive holdings" which soon covered the mechanical, financial, social, distributive and biographical aspects of the industry.

A considerable lift was given to the project when the Friends
of the Library took it upon themselves to aid in gathering, through
leaders of the industry and other interested persons, "the complete
records essential to a proper development of the Automotive History Collection."

Through the help of the Friends and others, significant acquisitions were made. Among these were the private papers of
Charles B. King who drove the first automobile on the streets of
Detroit. King was persuaded to give his material to the Library
largely through the efforts of Mohrhardt who was personally
acquainted with the automobile pioneer. Another important collection which was acquired was that of Sir David Salomons, an
early British motor car enthusiast. The automotive section of his
library was purchased by Vincent Bendix, the American industrialist. In 1945 it was obtained by R. L. Polk & Company by
whom it was presented to the Library. Another part of the Bendix
collection was presented by the Drusilla Farwell Foundation. The
D. Cameron Peck Collection, numbering more than 60,000 items,
the Andrew Lee Dyke Collection, the Henry Cave Collection, the
Andrew F. Johnson Collection and the Leland Collection of early
records of the Lincoln Motor Car Company also became important additions to the Library's Automotive History Collection.
Another was the collection of more than 100,000 photographs
belonging to Nicholas Lazarnick of New York. Lazarnick was
the official photographer for early national automobile races and

shows. He had acquired a large number of photographs made by two Detroit photographers, F. E. Spooner and Charles S. Wells. As a result, the Lazarnick collection included much important material covering the early days of the industry in Detroit. Also of particular significance was a complete set of records of the Selden patent litigation presented by Ralph J. Burton who served as president of the Friends of the Library in 1962–63. Hal H. Smith, the Friends' president from 1942 to 1944 donated the records and exhibits assembled in the litigation involving the Ford Motor Company stockholders at the time Henry Ford assumed complete control of the company in 1919.[35]

The accumulation of these and other materials placed the Library in such a uniquely strong position in the automotive field that it was designated the major center for automobile history under the Farmington Plan. The latter is an arrangement whereby the great research libraries of the United States have been allocated special subject responsibilities to avoid duplication of effort and expense.

The Automotive History Collection has become of inestimable value to historians, technicians, commercial artists and those seeking data for the restoration of vintage cars. The collection comprises not only United States material but many European publications. Including memoirs of the early manufacturers, with their notes on their cars and companies, original sketches, tape-recorded interviews and extensive clipping files, the collection provides a comprehensive record of the men and their machines which ushered in the automobile age. So large and important did the collection become that in 1953 it was given divisional status. Now enjoying world-wide recognition, the collection has become, indeed, a bright star in the Library's crown.

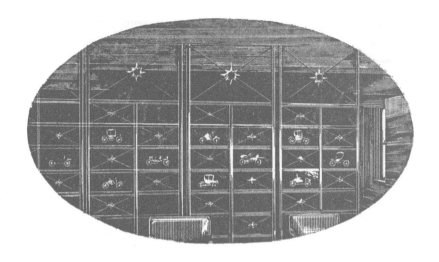

CHAPTER 21

THE LIBRARY GOES TO WAR

THE DETROIT Public Library was a "war baby," having come to life in the closing days of the Civil War. Three times thereafter it went to war, facing up to the conditions imposed by national emergencies and fulfilling important home front functions. The Spanish-American War created only a small ripple on the placid surface of the Library's life. Detroiters shared the indignation of the rest of the nation when the battleship *Maine* blew up in Havana harbor. They sang "Captain Jinks" just as lustily and waved enthusiastically as the militia and the naval reserve brigade were mobilized, but there was not much reflection of the war fever in the Library's reading rooms. In the early part of 1898 the Commission was more concerned with its own affairs than what was happening in Manila or at San Juan Hill. Officially, at least, it gave more attention to its internal structure by adopting a rule which provided that the member of the board "whose term of office is soonest to expire" would automatically become president of the Commission.[1] In 1951 this was changed and the presidency was filled by rotation.

344

By the end of 1898, however, after hostilities had ended, the Library could look back and assess events in terms of the war's effect on circulation. War excitement, it was noted, almost emptied the reading rooms and circulation of books dropped sharply. Up to May, when war was declared, home reading had increased month by month. But then, the Library reported,

> The war news apparently took precedence of everything else, and the demand for books fell off in a decrease of 21 percent, compared with the previous May, and the June circulation showed a decrease of 16 percent. . . . The reading rooms were almost deserted, and the card registry office indicated that people were giving very little attention to the attractions which the Library offers. The public mind was absorbed by passing events. The daily newspaper furnished all the reading matter for which the people cared. . . . Another noteworthy incident in the same line was the almost total cessation of book publishing. The uncertainty as to the importance and duration of the war led publishers to exercise great caution. Even books in hand were held back, for the obvious reason that during the war excitement there would be no sale for them. The market was practically dead.[2]

The Spanish-American War was of blessedly short duration. It was all over by August and normal conditions were quickly restored. The quickness with which the conflict ended prevented and made unnecessary the kind of home-front organization in which the Library could play a role. In that respect it was vastly different from the two world wars. The fight with Spain gave the United States its first territorial possessions which resulted, particularly in the Philippines, in some military pacification action and the establishment of overseas garrisons. This provided the Library with its only real wartime job which at best was a modest contribution. It consisted of the shipment of a box "containing not more than 200" books to the soldiers in the Philippines.[3]

World War I was a different matter, and the Library of that period was far different from the Library of 1898. New concepts of service and of the institution's place in the community occupied the thoughts of the administration on the eve of the holocaust which was sparked in 1914 by the bullet of an assassin in Serbia. With its field of responsibility growing, the Library was better

345

equipped to meet the demands of a society which war in Europe would disrupt. Declared Strohm in 1915:

> As an educational and social institution, the Public Library has certain definite opportunities and responsibilities in its relations to the municipality. It has invaded the recreational field, the social welfare movement, the childhood problem, the aesthetic life, the political activities, the industrial and commercial marts.[4]

All this meant organization, preparation and readiness. The United States was to a considerable extent conditioned to the war long before the country was involved as an active belligerent. That was also true, of course, of Detroit and the Public Library. The situation was summed up in 1916 by the following statement:

> The Library service registers very quickly the interests that are uppermost in the public mind. The international struggle swaying back and forth in Europe has generated a chronic craving for war literature. Numerous readers have vented their deep-rooted racial feelings in terse annotations discovered in books and journals returned to the Library. The intensity of these feelings is balanced by the not less pronounced tenderness of the human mind, its deep sympathy voiced in the growing volume and widening interest of poetry, especially the many remarkable war poems of lasting literary value. Possibly the political rapprochement and racial reconciliation at a future day will come about through the efforts of scholars and men of letters whose intellectual intercourse has been severed and who realize that the highest triumph of the human mind is the property and pride of all nations.[5]

There was a reflection in those words of the groping for spiritual values which found expression on the Library shelves in such literary works as *Mr. Britling Sees It Through* by H. G. Wells, Joyce Kilmer's *Trees,* and on the screen by D. W. Griffith's "Intolerance." Thousands "hit the sawdust trail" under the persuasion of Evangelist Billy Sunday who held a giant meeting in a huge frame tabernacle, built for his use on the DAC grounds which the Library had only lately relinquished as a new Main site. But as the German U-boat sinkings increased, and the voice of Allied propaganda grew louder, America's mood changed to

346

anger, flaming patriotism and acceptance of the inevitable. On April 6, the United States declared war on Germany. Three days before, on April 3, the Library had in effect issued its own declaration of war when the Commission authorized the librarian "to place the Library system at the service of the national Red Cross Association and the Army and Navy department for such cooperative work in registering members for the Red Cross service and giving information relative to recruiting in the Army and Navy service as may be rendered." [6] To prevent sabotage, the Hurlbut branch at Waterworks Park was ordered closed. At the request of the War Department, books on explosives were removed from the shelves, and restricted to use by authorized persons after Strohm reported: "We have several ammunition factories here, and our technology librarian advises me that books on explosives and chemical technology are in constant demand. . . ." [7]

Because the staff was made up largely of women, the Library's World War I service flag contained few stars. Strohm, however, was called upon by the War Department in November, 1917, to organize the library service at Camp Wheeler, Georgia, and later at Camp Gordon. During his absence of almost six months, D. Ashley Hooker, chief of the Technology Department performed the duties of acting librarian.[8]

The Main building and the branches became centers for community activities and information centers, providing necessary liaison between official governmental agencies and the people. This was the Library's principal war service. It was pointed out in the 1917–18 report:

> We had not only to learn how to fight but to understand what we were fighting about. This was the opportunity of the Library. The Library has unceasingly kept before its public the historical, economic and social survey of Europe and against this background we have silhouetted the corresponding conditions, responsibilities and ideals of America. . . .[9]

Red Cross instructional and sewing groups met at the branches; special book exhibits were set up, special reading lists were published. Book collections were assembled and sent to Selfridge

347

Field, the naval station at the Ford Rouge Eagle boat works, Ford Hospital, and other military stations in and around Detroit. The Detroit Library was one of thirty which was assessed $1000 by the American Library Association to help organize cantonment services. The Library cooperated with the government in its campaign against venereal disease by preparing reading lists on "sexology" for various age brackets, stressing youth groups. When a "victory garden" program was started to help relieve a food shortage, the grounds around the Centre Park building were turned over to the J. L. Hudson Company for a vegetable plot. Library employees bought more than their share of Liberty Bonds —they subscribed over $14,000 to the fourth campaign alone— and contributed generously to the Red Cross and other relief organizations. The Library even sacrificed progress in the construction of its new Main building to help conserve manpower for essential industry.[10]

When the nation was faced by a coal shortage in 1918, most business places not directly engaged in war work closed on Mondays to conserve fuel. The Library closed its buildings too for a while, but reopened them so that citizens who had idleness forced upon them would have places where they could profitably spend their time. The buildings were partially closed in late 1918 when the influenza epidemic struck. Operations for several weeks were confined to book circulation only and reference facilities were shut down—"Closed for study and research." [11] When the Library was open, which of course was most of the time, one of its busiest departments was Technology.

"The service along more practical lines," it was stated, "viz., furnishing information to engineers and mechanics, more especially those identified with our local war industries has been one of the most tangible advances in our activities." [12]

During the war as always, the Library's chief function was the circulation of books. Both the number of patrons and the number of books they drew out increased in the 1917–18 fiscal year, although there was a slight drop in readers' cards, reflecting, perhaps, the number of young men in service. The report of the Circulation Department for 1916–17 is worth examining for what it shows about war time reading. In part it says:

An analysis of the statistical report of circulation by classes shows some very interesting and significant facts. It bespeaks the trend of the times in no uncertain way. Current magazines show a falling off in use. Philosophy, religion, and sociology have made a decided gain. This is especially true of religion. . . . Useful and fine arts are also on the gain. Modern poetry has been much read and since the entrance of the United States into the war, books on the science of warfare, United States history and civil government have been in constant demand. Reading in the German language has decreased decidedly. This singularly enough, was true also of the French up to the last quarter. During the past six months, however, the reading of the French classics has received a decided impetus. Men who have enlisted or who are planning to enlist are reading in French so as to be familiar with the language when they reach the other side.

The so-called thrift, or food conservation, campaign caused a rush on the shelves containing books on household economics, cooking and gardening. Women readers devoured everything in print on the subjects of sewing and knitting. "The interest in books on auction bridge is very slight," the librarian reported, indicating that people had a serious outlook and better use for their spare time.[13]

Over on Brainard Street, the Burton Historical Collection knew a war was going on. It became, it was noted, a popular factor in the patriotic activities of the city. "With the advent of war," said Miss Krum, "came a decided 'boom' in the genealogical field, numbers of people desiring to become members of the various patriotic societies. . . ."[14]

In the fall of 1918 the Allied cause prevailed and on November 11 the armistice was declared. From that moment on, the thought uppermost in all minds was to get back to normal basis as quickly as possible. This was gradually accomplished and among its other visible signs was the resumption of progress in building the new Main Library. Strohm, who watched this conversion to peacetime status was surprised. He expected, apparently, that the emotional uplift which the war had provided would be carried over into the postwar period. When it did not materialize, he wrote:

> The predicted spiritual revival, searching of hearts, and enriched intellectual life are not particularly manifest in the statistics of books used. The economic problem of meeting the mere material need of the world is no doubt too urgent; our participation in the great war

was more of a plunge than a test of endurance, and we emerged from the fire without having suffered the sacrifice and anguish that chasten. . . .[15]

It remained for Ashley Hooker, Technology chief, to bring the war to an official end as far as the Library was concerned. Up to the time of the armistice, he observed, people came to his department with questions about aeronautics, ship building, military manuals, and the testing of materials used in war work. But after the 11th of November, 1918, the questions asked "deal with the usual occupations of peace times." The subjects, he said, which were in greatest demand were "real estate, oil and gas, salesmanship, scientific management and accounting. The increased mathematical collection is much appreciated." [16]

World War I and the period immediately following it opened up the opportunity to work with and for the large foreign-born population of Detroit in an Americanization program. The war brought an awareness to the nation as a whole that greater efforts should be made to bring the alien element, the immigrants who had flocked to our shores in the early 20th century, into the American family and to eliminate the "hyphen" which characterized nationalist groups. There was a realization born of the 1917–18 emergency that the Irish-American, the German-American, the Italian-American, the Polish-American should all become just plain Americans. This called for education, largely at the adult level, and the Library had a unique usefulness in this endeavor.

The Library cooperated with the Board of Commerce, the Board of Education and other agencies in promoting night school Americanization classes by distributing circulars at the branches and displaying posters. The county clerk's office distributed leaflets to aliens applying for their first citizenship papers describing the services of the Library.[17]

By 1918 the Library was engaged in a fairly broad citizenship program which consisted of the following activities: English classes for women at the branches; reading lists and circulation of books as aids to study of English and Americanization; cooperation with night school classes, with arrangements for teachers and their classes to visit the Library in order to become familiar with its services; preparation of special collections and reading lists on civics, citizenship, American aims and ideals, history, etc. Some of these lists were distributed in the schools for the children to take home to their parents.[18]

In a detailed report to the librarian, made about 1918, the chief of the Circulation Department discussed the Library's Americanization work and made recommendations about more that could be done. During one month, it was pointed out, circulation of foreign books was 3564 volumes, but this was not an accurate measure of the collection's use.

The foreign section at this time included extensive collections in French, German and Polish, and smaller collections in Arabic, Armenian, Bohemian, Danish, Dutch, Finnish, modern Greek, Hungarian, Italian, Lithuanian, Norwegian, Portuguese, Romanian, Russian, Serbian, Spanish, Swedish, Ukranian and Yiddish. It was suggested that printed matter, book lists and Americanization material be provided in larger quantities in the "minor languages." In 1922–23 the influx of Russian refugees "has brought to the Library a class of rather superior foreigners who are much interested in getting information about their adopted country. . . ." [19] As a result of this activity, particularly in the postwar period, the Foreign Division was reorganized in 1923 and given greater departmental status than it had previously enjoyed as a section of the Circulation Department.[20]

World War II placed greater demands upon the Library than did the 1917–18 conflict. But the Library through enlarged facilities was better able to meet its obligations to the home front in 1941. As in World War I, there had been a period of preparation and conditioning prior to the country's involvement. It might be said that when the attack was made on Pearl Harbor the Library already was mobilized and on a war footing.

The role of the public library in America in the war was well explained by the enemy. In an article published in 1941 in a Nazi magazine, prior to United States entry into the war, it was stated with reference to the American library system:

"Public libraries are a powerful weapon in the forging of public opinion. It depends to a great extent on their policy which path the American people will take in the present world conflict." [21]

While the European continent was already locked in conflict, and America was waiting to see which way the winds of chance would blow, the Library celebrated its seventy-fifth anniversary on March 25, 1940, with a civic observance which attracted hundreds of visitors. As if in preparation for the great events about to occur, there was the change in command in 1941 when Strohm retired and Ralph A. Ulveling succeeded him as director. Foreshadowing things to come, the nation's manpower was being mobilized and the armed forces were being built up. In 1940 the Commission made provision for its employees entering the service with the assurance that their jobs would be waiting for them upon their return.[22]

The blow fell on December 7, 1941, and the United States was involved in total war. Every effort, every resource, was dedicated to the preservation of the nation and its ultimate victory over the Axis allies.* Immediately the Library's program and policy was defined. It offered three areas of service:

> 1. The citizen must have easy access to accurate, reliable information on all questions which confuse him, whether those questions stem from uncertainties about the proper way to adjust his personal and family life to new regulations and changed conditions, or from the broader facts concerned with countries, peoples, resources or political and social obligations.
> 2. Every individual and every corporate structure must be aided in preparing for a larger, more useful contribution to the war effort.
> 3. The morale of the citizenry as a whole must be fortified through understanding the issues involved in this world conflict and the great objectives to be achieved by it, as well as through opportunities for wholesome relaxation and recreation so necessary for all, particularly in times of stress.

Added to this general declaration was an elaboration upon specific fields of service, such as providing the public with the multitude of wartime regulations which flowed out of Washington. This was accomplished by setting up War Information Centers at the Main and Downtown libraries. These became clearinghouses at which questions could be answered and new directives could be channeled from official agencies to the public.

The Library agreed to set up its war information center on con-

---

* With the closing of Water Works Park as a security measure, the Hurlbut branch also was closed, this time permanently. Its personnel and book collection became the nucleus of the Sherwood Forest branch.

dition that all agencies of the government involved in the war effort would cooperate. This was done with the result that the center became a very busy place indeed, and one which occupied an important place in the community. At the end of the war, those directing this service endeavored to make the home folks happy by reporting the sailing dates of troopships bringing their sons and husbands back to the United States. Few things ever attempted by the Library were more appreciated. People, not only in Detroit but in other cities, phoned for this information in such numbers that the trunk lines became overburdened. On one occasion, Mayor Jeffries, attempting to call the Library director, was unable to get through for two hours. Finally, the telephone company had to call a halt, admitting that its facilities were inadequate to carry such a load without disrupting traffic in the center of the city. Ulveling appealed to the newspapers which carried front page notices to the effect that no more information about troop sailings would be given out over the phone, although it would continue to be supplied to those applying in person.

Cooperation with the government, with the armed forces, and with industry, was often of a highly technical nature. The full resources of the Technology Department were made available and it became one of the busiest places in the Library system. Then there was the area of morale. The Library maintained its traditional functions of working closely with civic and social groups; of continuing its services to children. Beyond that, there was a new field of providing books to the armed services through such agencies as the American Red Cross and the United Service Organizations. Much of this work was conducted along the lines of a broad program adopted by the American Library Association which called attention to the need to maintain, even under the stress of war conditions, better library facilities—more books, protected budgets—and long-range postwar planning.[23]

The Detroit Public Library rose to the challenge in every instance. Within a week after the commencement of active hostilities, each member of the staff signed an affidavit of allegiance to the United States and, anticipating the greater physical and mental strain to which each would be subjected, physical examinations were given. An inventory of the Library's automotive equipment

353

was turned over to the War Department for civil defense purposes. The Map Room became, almost overnight, a headquarters for the Army Map Service and Naval Intelligence. At the end of the war this cooperation was rewarded by the Army Map Service which designated the Detroit Public Library as a depository for 50,000 maps.

One of the biggest wartime difficulties the Library faced was that of adjusting to extraordinary personnel problems. Many members—fifty-three by early 1943—had enlisted. Many others had taken leaves of absence at government request to set up and operate libraries at various military installations. The situation became sufficiently acute by 1942 to warrant steps to seek selective service deferment of essential personnel. The staff shortage forced most of the members to work six days a week and by 1945 the situation was so critical that 14 branches were closed on Wednesdays and Sundays and hours when they were open were curtailed. The situation was summed up in retrospect in 1946, when Ulveling recalled:

> [The war years] have been difficult because the book markets were inadequate and disorganized; they have been challenging because the services were continually being readapted to changing needs and conditions; they were crowded because of the multiple programs being planned for the new era we are now entering; they were strenuous because in every level of the staff normal duties of those serving the nation had to be shared by those remaining at home.[24]

In 1943, when World War II was in its more critical stage, the Library was called upon to perform a spectacular and unusual war service for the community. This opportunity grew out of the most brutal and shocking episode in Detroit's history. This was the race riot which swept the city on June 20 and 21, which resulted in millions of dollars worth of property damage, dozens of deaths, and which seriously threatened the war effort. Born of fatigue and war nerves, sparked by tension and abnormally hot weather, the rioting broke out on Belle Isle late on Sunday, June 20, and was continued the following morning throughout wide areas of downtown and the near east side. By mid-day on Monday, the situation with its killing, looting and destruction, was clearly out of hand and beyond the control of the police. Mayor

Edward J. Jeffries, Jr., appealed to Governor Harry F. Kelly who, in turn, called upon President Franklin D. Roosevelt and the War Department for help. Federal troops stationed near Detroit were ordered to the scene of the rioting and a state of semi-martial law was declared.

There was a battalion of military police, about eight hundred men, already stationed at River Rouge Park. This force, however, was not considered adequate. Racial tension also was high in other cities and there had been some sporadic outbursts of trouble elsewhere. Since it was feared that the Detroit riot might set off similar ones in other places, a show of strong force was determined upon. Another military police battalion was ordered into Detroit from Fort Custer, along with other, unassigned troops of the 6th Service Command. Altogether, the force dispatched to Detroit numbered approximately 2500 men.

The Fort Custer troops arrived by train at Dearborn between 2 and 3 P.M. on Monday. At 6 P.M., with jeeps, armored personnel carriers, a tank and other equipment, they moved into the city. They were divided into small units and assigned to patrol the troubled areas. Before nightfall they had the situation well in hand and aided by a curfew, Detroit began to quiet down. One detachment of troops, about three hundred men of the 6th Service Command, was based at the Main Library, and from Monday night until the following Thursday noon when they were withdrawn, the spacious Library lawn was converted into a military encampment. Tents were pitched, and equipment was parked along the streets. As an institution dedicated to the welfare, advancement and education of mankind, the Library provided an anomalous backdrop for this war-like display.

Following the departure of those troops, another contingent was moved in to replace them on June 24, simply as a precautionary measure. The 9th Infantry Regiment, 2nd Infantry Division "assumed control of the East District, Detroit," according to official Army records, and remained in control until relieved on June 30, 1943. "The command post of the East District was located at the Detroit Public Library." [25]

The Library itself was not content to play a passive role in the face of this emergency. Ulveling immediately summoned his staff into meeting and pointed out the Library's responsibility to the community, not only in easing the existing situation, but in help-ing to create a climate in which it could not be repeated. The first step was the fast publication and distribution of a small pamphlet entitled *The Events of the Week of June 20th.* It contained short articles by recognized authorities which exploded the myth of racial superiority, pointed out how racial strife served the pur-poses of the Axis enemies, and called for assumption of responsi-bility on the part of both whites and Negroes. At the end was ap-pended a short reading list of books amplifying the excerpts in the pamphlet.[26]

This pamphlet attracted wide attention both in Detroit and elsewhere. A labor union asked for 4500 copies to distribute to its membership; the Detroit Council of Social Agencies called for 1000 more and the President's Committee on Fair Employment Practice asked for 500. In addition, another reading list intended for children was issued and the Library set up exhibits to comple-ment the reading lists. The response to all this effort was remark-able, both from the standpoint of volume and source. Articles appeared in several publications, describing what the library had done; words of commendation poured in from civic and religious leaders. It was an example of responsibility by an institution which quickly mobilized its resources in the face of an emergency. Moreover, it was a demonstration of inspired leadership on the part of the Library. A few weeks later, in an article in the American Library Association *Bulletin,* Ulveling stated:

> The Library assumed a positive role in an issue of major impor-tance to the citizenry. I don't mean by this that the institution took sides in assessing blame—it did not—but it pointed squarely to the crux of a social issue of concern to its own constituents in contrast to a quite general library practice of either ignoring a major con-troversy of local importance or approaching it in such general terms that it fails to focus attention on the subject properly.[27]

With the end of the war in September, 1945, the Library, along with the nation, entered a new era in which soul-searching was combined with planning for the future. "The immediate and invaluable result of the current war," declared Ulveling, "is that we as a people have become conscious that the established ways of conducting our activities are in need of scrutinizing."

He called for a new assessment of library objectives, social alignments, staff resources necessary to implement community-wide programs, and "from these findings to develop at least a skeletonized library program, with special attention focused on principles." His conclusion was that a broader community program was essential, involving more staff participation, closer cooperation with civic and social agencies and, essentially, greater emphasis on the general area of adult education.[28]

As a postwar objective, Ulveling on another occasion pointed out what he considered to be the Library's function. Briefly stated, it was to enhance the dignity of the individual human being by enriching his personality through wider appreciation of music, literature and art; to encourage economic competence by improving the skills of dislocated war workers, to help foster wholesome family life, and to enlarge the individual's recognition of his obligation to society as a whole. More specifically, and with reference to the Detroit Library's postwar outlook, he cited the need to restore and catch up on the book collection and to rebuild the staff.[29]

Even while the guns were still roaring in Europe and the Orient, forward-looking postwar plans were being formulated. Speaking before the Chicago Regional Institute on Demobilization and Readjustment in 1944, Ulveling discussed some of the things that would be expected of libraries when hostilities ceased. Among these would be assistance in formulating vocational training programs for veterans and civilian war workers, helping to satisfy the broadened interest of the people whose outlook had been enlarged to global proportions as the result of the war; aiding in providing basic education for a shifting population, covering such areas as health, race relations and, in general, promoting an orderly psychological shift from a war to a peacetime outlook.[30] That the Detroit Library contributed much along these lines can be attested to by its own successful program of aid to the veteran and the war worker, and of aiding, through its various services, particularly its Technology and Social Science departments, the transition of industry and the general social organization to a new order.

There is a footnote to be added to the Library's war story.

357

After World War II the country entered the period of the "cold war," and found itself in the atomic era. This was reflected in two minor, but—from the standpoint of civilization's future—significant matters. In 1951 the librarian called to the attention of the Commission that the New York Public Library was microfilming its card catalog to insure its preservation against destruction by "fire, storm or enemy attack." Ulveling suggested it would be wiser for Detroit not to follow New York's example as a catalog would be of little value if the books were destroyed. He suggested, instead, that it would be better to microfilm the rare and unique holdings of the Library. The Commission concurred. Then in 1962, as another grim warning of the jeopardy in which mankind had placed itself, the Office of Civil Defense designated the Main Library as a "fallout" shelter! [31]

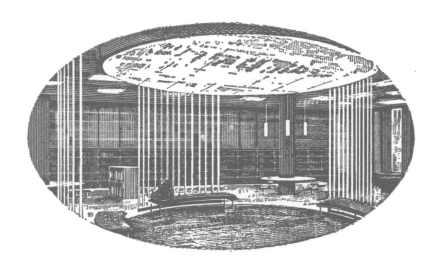

CHAPTER 22

DAYS OF DESPAIR

DURING the hundred years of its existence, in war and peace, the Detroit Public Library knew good times and bad. But it never knew a worse time than during the great depression of the 1930's, when the economy of Detroit was brought to a virtual standstill. Yet, during the most critical days of depression—a period roughly from 1931 to 1936—the Library not only survived, but reached a new height of service to the people of the city.

It is not necessary here to examine closely the causes of the depression. The Library did not contribute to them. The concern is with effect—effect on the patrons of the Library and upon the institution itself. It need only be said that America probably never has known a time like it, and Detroit, as a center of highly concentrated industry, suffered as much or worse than most other communities. Those were bleak and desolate years, years in which banks and businesses failed, homes and savings were lost, and unemployment reached the proportions of disaster. The beginning of the depression is generally fixed, for want of a more exact date, as October 24 to November 13, 1929, when the stock market

359

collapsed, wiping out investors, large and small, and creating a fiscal crisis which spread rapidly through business and industry generally.

Always sensitive to economic fluctuations, the Library quickly felt the effects of the disaster—for such it was. Automobile factories and other local industries which were highly specialized producers of luxury goods were among the first to lay off their workers. These people, with idleness forced upon them, flocked to the Main and branch libraries in unprecedented numbers. That set off a sort of chain reaction, because increased patronage ordinarily called for increased service. But the times were not normal. The same factors which caused plants to close and lay off their employees also reduced the amount of taxes they paid. The result was belt-tightening in every phase of municipal government, the Library included. The situation was viewed from the Library's standpoint in this way:

> When it was a question whether the city could maintain its destitute unemployed and when an actual admission of bankruptcy was avoided only by the issuance of scrip, the city government saw no way to avoid curtailment of Library expenditures.[1]

The challenge was great, but the Commission and the staff accepted it and made valiant efforts to meet an abnormal social need.

"The story of their Library during the depression years . . . is one of a courageous and cheerful attempt to make the best of a bad predicament," it was recorded.[2]

As indicated, the Library felt the brunt of the depression sooner than most other municipal agencies with the possible exception of the Department of Public Welfare. In a little more than six months after the stock market debacle of late 1929, the Commission issued its 1929–30 annual report in which it noted a circulation of more than 6,000,000 books. The following year it reached the 7,000,000 mark, the highest figure ever attained before or since. This was an increase of 1,775,000 volumes over 1928–29. The rise in patronage was noted in nearly every department, including the Children's. It was stated:

Just why unemployment should send children to the Library in increasing numbers is rather difficult to understand, but come they surely have; probably money is lacking for shows and other paid amusements, and when games and outdoor amusements have been exhausted, the urge to read becomes greater for the reader and even attacks the non-reader. . . . Children have trooped to the Library. . . .[3]

Sadly enough, within a year a loss of children's patronage was reported. This was due, in part, to the trend of many families, their resources exhausted, to leave Detroit and return to their homes in the country and in other cities from which they had come to take advantage of the high-wage scale in the motor plants, and the World War I industrial boom.* But there also were other, more pathetic reasons, such as a "lack of warm clothing and shoes," illness, and no money for carfare.[4] At the adult level, the Library noted, "the student group, the professional class, the 'white collar worker' and the block of business men had increased in percentage of attendance; skilled labor on an indefinite leave also reported at unwonted hours." Obviously, the depression was no respecter of persons or status. More men than women used the facilities, and a tendency toward more serious reading was noted. Not all the visitors, of course, drew books. The reference and periodical rooms where material was not circulated were crowded to capacity. In one two-week period more than 250,000 persons were counted at the central and branch buildings. Many, perhaps, came to get warm, others to escape boredom, but many more sought to use their enforced idleness to improve their capabilities. There was a great demand, it was observed, for books on bachelor cooking; for plans for building and operating roadside stands, and other forms of self-help by which men hoped to get back on their feet financially. "Vocational and 'hobby' reading took a spurt in Detroit, as in other cities," it was reported. An excellent technological department, including what is probably the best collection in the

---

* The high-wage pattern was established in 1914 when the Ford Motor Company announced a $5 per day minimum wage, attracting thousands of workers to Detroit.

361

country dealing with the automobile industry, and the Business Department in the Downtown Library helped to meet this demand. The unemployed worker, eager, at least during the first months of his idleness, to prepare for a better job or to catch up with reading he "had always meant to do when he had time," was a familiar figure. The class of visitors described by some rather unfeeling observers as "bums" did not become a serious problem in Detroit. "Bum," said Strohm, "is, in fact, a difficult word to define. If it signifies the externals of abundant leisure, ragged clothes and an appearance of under-nourishment it may be applied to those who in happier times were considered desirable patrons. . . ." [5]

The social role which the Library played in these times of stress, when many were hungry and bewildered, and ripe prospects for the evangelists of radical change, cannot be overemphasized. The Library had at its front door the familiar apple vendor—the symbol of the depression. But for each one like him, thousands were inside making constructive use of their time. There was occasional rioting by those who sought to force demands for aid on authorities unable to supply it. Their ranks might have been considerably swelled had those who found haven in the Library joined them.

> It cannot be too strongly stressed that in days of economic depression when many thousands of our citizens are without employment, when many of them are without adequate shelter and food, the Library becomes a safety valve for those who, physically hungry, are willing to compromise with conditions if only their souls and their minds need not be absolutely starved.[6]

That statement by Adam Strohm whose compassion for the distressed people was matched only by his almost superhuman efforts to make the Library of service to them, is a fair representation of his and his staff's understanding of their grave responsibility in that time of abnormality.

It took some heroic efforts on the part of the Commission and the staff to furnish the kind of service it did with the means at its disposal. During the last pre-depression good years of 1929–30, the Library budget including operation, maintenance and capital costs, was $1,627,288. This budget was prepared before the crash and accordingly it did not reflect the straitened circumstances which would soon be felt. It would be ten years before the Library would have that much money again to live on. Actually, the 1929–30 budget did not provide anything near the amount originally appropriated. By November, 1930, the bad days had come, and the Commission decided that it would not go ahead with its plans to acquire any more property. And in December, a strict economy program was adopted which included restriction of special services given private business and industry, suspension of salary increases except in the lowest brackets, and reduction of new positions to the lowest possible number.[7]

If this was austerity, it was nothing compared to what was coming. In August, 1931, tax receipts had dried up to a mere dribble, and Mayor Frank Murphy called on all city departments to cut their budgets drastically. The Commission had anticipated such an order and on January 20, 1931, cut its own budget by 12 per cent, soon to be followed by a second 12 per cent slash. For that fiscal year, the Library's budget was $1,330,436, and for 1931–32 it was reduced further to just over a million dollars. Again, these figures did not accurately reflect the money the Library had to spend. The budget merely represented a credit on the books. Revenue was insufficient to provide the budget amounts. Mayor Murphy pointed out:

> The cuts recommended in the budgets of all departments were made necessary by an extreme situation that department heads can appreciate only if they have before them the general finance picture of the government rather than the local finance problem of the department. From each department comes the protest that damage is done by retrenchment, but all must appreciate the responsibility that is ours to preserve the financial integrity of the city—its credit and capacity to borrow. It will be hard work, nevertheless it must be done, and I am sure that your Commission, which has thus far been helpful and sympathetic, will continue to be cooperative.[8]

In retrenching, Murphy suggested, wage cuts should be avoided as far as possible. Such economy would be "unwise and dangerous," he declared, because salaries of public employees were relatively low in prosperous times, and to reduce them further might lead to governmental chaos and panic and set an unnecessary example for private industry. Yet they became unavoidable.

363

Financially, the 1932–33 fiscal year marked the low point for the Library. Its budget was down to the starvation level of $748,214. On February 14, 1933, Governor Comstock declared a bank holiday, and on March 6, the newly inaugurated President Franklin D. Roosevelt ordered all banks in the United States closed. Major banks in Detroit went into receivership and never reopened. Funds were impounded, adding to general distress. Among the funds frozen were some belonging to the Library. The city had little cash with which to pay its bills; what money was available was prorated among the departments and all employees went on short rations. Even crime seemed to take a holiday, and penal fines revenues fell off. The Commission pondered the plight of its employees, noting that they were encountering growing difficulties, even in maintaining decent living quarters. Lacking cash, the City of Detroit paid its workers in scrip. While landlords and grocers accepted the scrip to the best of their ability, (it carried a small interest rate and was redeemable in payment of taxes), it was a makeshift arrangement at best, and proved to be small compensation for salary cuts which ranged from 10 to 14.5 per cent. During May and June, 1932, a $25-a-week salary base was set, and all salaries above that amount were reduced 50 per cent. Also, in 1932, the staff was reduced by fifty-three employees —about one-tenth of its regular force. There was a further cut effected by not filling vacancies caused by death or resignation.

"Such savings as these, of course, reflect nothing but a desire to economize in the easiest way," it was pointed out. "They help to make librarianship an even more poorly paid profession than it was before, but they throw no light on Library policy." [9]

It was not just the staff that bore the brunt. It was decided on July 1, 1932, to conserve manpower and other operating expense by closing the Main and Downtown libraries on Wednesdays and Sundays. In addition some departments in the Main building were shut down completely, and five branches, twenty-eight sub-branches and deposit stations in industrial plants, settlement houses and similar installations were closed, most of them never to reopen.[10]

There would have been a sixth branch marked as a casualty of hard times had it not been for direct action on the part of

364

people in the neighborhood it served. When word went out that the Outer-Gratiot branch in the northeast part of the city was to be shut down, the Outer Gratiot Branch Library Association was organized. This group approached the Commission with an offer to raise money by small service charges, card parties and other fund raising devices, and agreed to meet all overhead expense if the Commission would provide books and a limited personnel.[11]

The idea of a fee system suggested a way by which the Library generally could benefit, and a charge plan, calling for an annual registration fee of 25 cents was adopted June 7, 1932. During the first month in effect it produced $4530, but it never yielded the amount hoped for, and it was dropped with a feeling of relief on March 15, 1934.[12]

What must really have torn the heartstrings of the Library staff during the depression was the sacrifice of the book collection on the altar of economy. On November 11, 1931, the Commission temporarily suspended the purchase of books in order to meet deficiencies in anticipated revenues. After that, books became expendable. Whereas the 1931–32 book allowance was initially set at $175,000, it was soon reduced to $72,000, and the next year the allowance was a mere $39,600.[13] It was stated in a report to the Carnegie Corporation:

> The slashing of the book fund clearly strikes at the very heart of the Library. The proper returns on the city's investment in library service can be realized only if the tools and material essential to that service are reasonably available. . . . When only necessary books can be bought, and sometimes not even those ordinarily considered necessary, a librarian's philosophy and wisdom are put to the test.[14]

Despite this serious concern, there were no dollars, and new titles on the shelves as well as replacements dwindled to almost nothing. Fiction, it was decided, could be dispensed with easiest of all. A rental system for fiction was instituted, but for the most part Detroiters had to turn to commercial lending libraries for the "best sellers." In 1930–31 copies of only three hundred fiction titles were purchased, and the full effect of the depression was still to be felt. The situation was alleviated somewhat by outside help. The Louisa St. Clair Chapter of Daughters of the American

Revolution headed a book drive and collected 15,000 volumes which were turned over to the Library. Every conceivable make-shift was employed, even to having the staff repair worn or damaged books instead of sending them out to be rebound, or they might, "to the librarian's regret, be kept in circulation after they should be withdrawn." [15]

In time, however, the darkest of the depression days passed, and so gradually as to be hardly discernible, the prosperity which was "just around the corner" began to return. Government relief programs were set up and the Library benefited. Unemployed workers were taken out of the bread lines and given jobs under the Works Progress Administration and the Civil Works Administration. The Library benefited when WPA workers were assigned to clean, repair and paint Main and branch buildings which for two or three years had had little done to them in the way of maintenance. These programs continued for some time, and eventually were extended in the form of grants and aid for new buildings. In the 1935–36 fiscal year, the Federal government contributed $149,000 for Detroit Library projects. Against that amount, the Library was required to lay out only $22,300.[16]

As America's industrial giant began to flex its muscles in 1935, the Library along with other municipal agencies began to feel that better times were at hand. The 1935–36 budget was more than a million dollars, and it increased steadily thereafter until 1937–38 when it was back close to pre-depression levels. More money began to be spent on books; closed branches were re-opened and regular hours were restored. In 1935–36, too, the salary schedule of the staff was increased and vacancies began to be filled.

"From the standpoint of employment, the City has recovered," it was announced. "The day has now disappeared when large numbers of unemployed were resorting to libraries." [17]

There would continue to be abnormally high unemployment in Detroit for a few more years; the city would feel the effects of the bank closings and failures. There would be erratic bumps in the lines on the economic graph, but the worst was over. The Library, too, had survived and in doing so had helped pull the city through.

Even a depression as devastating as that of the 1930's left something good in its wake. In the Library's case, it was a splendid replacement for the old Main building in Centre Park. Built and equipped at a cost of approximately $300,000, it was a project which provided employment at a time when it was badly needed.

Before the new Main building was completed and occupied in 1921, thought was being given to what use would be made of the old central library and its site at Gratiot and Farmer. In 1917 the Commission called attention to the fact that: "It is confidently hoped that within two years administration headquarters will be located in the new building, but in the unanimous opinion of the Library Commission a library agency should still be maintained downtown, preferably in the old building, if remodeled." [18] Two years later the Commission again pointed to the need for downtown facilities for a reading room, and for "technical, commercial, municipal and economical reference purposes" and decided that the old building should be used "until some other permanent and adequate location is provided by the city." The latter statement implies that the Commission was not wedded to the idea that Centre Park had to be used, but upon later reflection that site, already city-owned and used by the Library, offered the best possibilities.[19]

Then, in 1919, what appeared to be a happy solution was offered, probably by Joseph S. Stringham, an engineer who served as a member both of the Board of Education and the Library Commission. The suggestion was made that the Board and the Commission pool their resources and put up a building for joint use for school administration offices and a branch library. The Board of Education was worse housed, if possible, than the Library had been, and the plan had appeal. By 1920 both agencies had approved the idea and the destiny of Centre Park seemed assured. At least it continued to appear assured until 1925 when financial troubles besetting both the schools and the library resulted in the plan's abandonment.[20]

Meanwhile, in 1921 the functions of the Main Library were transferred uptown to the new building. The Centre Park building became a branch, rattling around in gloomy space of which only part could be used. Designated the Downtown Annex, it

occupied parts of only two floors and its book collection was reduced to 18,000 volumes. Patronage, however, continued to hold
up remarkably well, all things considered. But it soon became
evident that any operation conducted in those obsolete quarters
was uneconomical and inefficient. Still holding to the hope of a
joint school-library structure, the Library began seeking temporary quarters elsewhere. A better building had become available.
A new police headquarters had been constructed, leaving vacant
the old headquarters built in 1884 in East Park, another small
triangular location bounded by Randolph, Bates and Farmer
streets. It had been turned over to the Water Board as the site for
a projected administration building, but those plans were still in
the indefinite future. An accommodation was worked out, and at
the end of 1923 the Commission turned the Centre Park building
over to the Board of Education and on November 15 moved into
old police headquarters. A remodeling expense of $1012 was
approved. It was fitted up to house, besides a general reading
room, the Business and Commerce Division, which was moved
from the Board of Commerce offices.[21]

The old Centre Library now was in the custody of the Board
of Education which proposed to spend $13,000 to remodel it.
The Library Commission cautioned the Board against making too
extensive interior changes, because it held old police headquarters
on a three-year lease which would expire on November 28, 1926.
At the end of the lease, the Commission said, it might have to re-
occupy the Centre building. Then the idea of a joint building was
dropped, and the Commission resolved that the "north portion of
the lot be set aside upon which to erect a downtown annex." That
statement implied that the lower or south side of Centre Park
might be used by the Board of Education for its own purposes.

In 1927 the Commission's time was running out at old police
headquarters. The Water Board was going ahead with its own
building plans and notified the Library to move out. The Library
commissioned the architectural firm of Smith, Hinchman & Grylls
to prepare plans for a new branch in Centre Park, but the
Common Council refused to include the requested $300,000 con-
struction item in the budget. The result was that the Library
again was forced to seek new quarters, and in 1928 it moved into

368

rented space in the Barlum Tower (now the Cadillac Tower). There it occupied 8000 square feet under an 18-month lease at a rental of $18,000 a year. The Commission kept pressing for new building funds, pointing out that the interest on a bond issue would be about half the rent being paid.

At the same time the Barlum Tower quarters were occupied, the first floor and basement of the Reid Building at 130 Cadillac Square were leased for a newspaper reading room and for storage.[22]

By 1929 the Board of Education's hopes of being able to put up an office building had faded. It realized that in the old Centre building it was cherishing a white elephant. A proposal was made that it either be sold or razed. The Library Commission, still hopeful of using the site, was not interested in a sale, but was heartily in favor of tearing down the structure. The Department of Public Works agreed to do the demolition work for $18,000, primarily to make work for the unemployed. There was feeling among some of the Commissioners, after the demolition was begun, that perhaps the decision to raze the building had been hasty. Commission President Clarence A. Lightner* in his annual report, declared:

> The old library building, the pride of Detroit in 1879, has, contrary to my advice and wishes, been ordered to be razed, with no definite provision for placing a suitable building thereon for a downtown library. I have apprehended that, if the little public space which was dedicated to public use only by the Governor and Judges in territorial times were cleared of the shell (which at least served as a constant reminder that the city half a century ago used its public property to better purposes than it seems to be able to do at this time), library needs would be forgotten.

He expressed fear also that the Library's right to the site might be forfeited.[23]

Such worries, however, proved to be groundless. Efforts to obtain a new building were renewed, and the "undesirability of leaving the site unused and unproductive" was discussed with school and municipal authorities.[24] The upshot was a proposal

---

* Clarence A. Lightner (1862–1938) was for many years one of Detroit's leading attorneys.

made by the Commission to the Common Council on a take-it-or-leave-it basis. The Commission, with Council approval, would undertake within a year to begin construction of a new building; if the Council refused to authorize a bond issue, the Library would surrender all claim to the site which would then revert to the Board of Education.[25] With men standing in bread lines; with the building trades clamoring for work, the Council had little choice but to go along. The architects were told to dust off their plans, and Commissioner John F. O'Hara triumphantly proclaimed that "the decision to erect at once a downtown library building on the site of the old Library is a matter of deep satisfaction. It will supply a much needed service." [26]

Things moved very rapidly. In 1931 there was no labor shortage, no scarcity of materials, and nothing to impede progress. Bids were called for on March 3, and on March 17 the contract was awarded to the firm of Bryant & Detwiler, whose low bid was for $243,895. A sign was put up stating in bold letters: "The contract for this building was let for the purpose of furnishing employment." [27] So rapidly was the work pushed that the building was completed and ready for occupancy in December. On January 4, 1932, it was opened for public use. No longer to be known as a branch or annex, it was officially designated as the Downtown Library.

"It is an Indiana limestone structure of two stories, with several mezzanines," reported the Detroit *News* on the day following the official opening. "Because of the unusual shape of the lot upon which it stands, it is triangular in form, with a broad curving face on Gratiot."

That brief description did scant justice to the attractive appearance of a graceful and well-proportioned structure. The dim recesses of the old Centre Park main building had given way to a comfortable, efficiently planned, well-lighted library. In 1958 a touch of dignity was added when the statue of Abraham Lincoln which formerly stood on the grounds of the Lincoln Motor Car Company at West Warren and Livernois was moved to the north side of the Downtown Library.

370

CHAPTER 23

PLOWING IN NEW FIELDS

WORLD WAR I and the boom in the automobile industry which followed it combined to bring about profound changes in Detroit and its environs. Population swelled and the city burst its old bonds, resulting in the annexation of communities on its perimeter. It was an era of frantic subdividing, real estate speculation and home building. The effect was felt beyond the city. Suburbs which had been quiet little rural villages turned into populous cities in their own right. Thousands of acres of Wayne County farmlands were transformed into housing developments. Suddenly Detroit awoke to the realization that it had become the core of a metropolitan area.

The Public Library was aware of what was happening and found itself confronted with the problem of how to meet conditions which this regional expansion created. How far could the Library go in extending its services? If it had to stop at the city boundaries, how was adequate library service to be furnished to the new outside communities which were springing up? The problem, while it had suddenly become acute about 1920, was not exactly new as far as the Library was concerned. For years there had been provision for issuing borrower's cards to nonresidents for an annual fee of one dollar. There had also been some consideration given to providing direct Library service throughout Wayne County. The possibility of making the Detroit system into a county library was first suggested in 1899 by Commissioner Maynard D. Follin.* As Commission secretary for that year, he included the following statement in his annual report:

> I find there exists in Cincinnati a condition of things that makes for largely increased usefulness on the part of the library; and that is that the Cincinnati library has been recently changed from a city to a county institution. This enables it to supply books in a much larger field than is possible when it is supported by the city alone. Thus instead of establishing delivery stations throughout the city, this library has them throughout the entire county. The advantages to those living outside the city are manifest; the benefit derived by the city lies in the fact that a larger fund is devoted to the maintenance of the library, making possible the purchase of numbers of books that we must now pass by at a sacrifice of the importance and efficiency of our collection. It is quite possible that it will be found desirable at some future time to make this change in our own institution. A full and free discussion of the plan at that time will no doubt bring to light many advantages over the present system.[1]

Follin's vision lighted no fires, but he was convinced that he was on the right track. Five years later, in 1904, he raised the subject again. He declared:

> I am still of the opinion that it would be an advantage to have the scope of the Circulating Department enlarged to take in the entire County of Wayne, with frequent and regular deliveries of books to each post office or other convenient point for the villages. By this means those who live near Detroit would secure a very valuable privilege at a comparatively slight expense. In case this change were made an amendment to our Act making the statutory library tax apply to the whole county would be necessary. It would enable the Library to follow up the educational work of the District School System as has been done in the Cincinnati Library for some years.[2]

---

* Maynard D. Follin (1864– ?) was one of the "political" members of the Library Commission. Born at Troy, New York, he was employed for many years in clerical positions for the City of Detroit, and in 1912 was involved in a graft exposé. In 1904 he endeavored to have Henry M. Utley removed as librarian and to be appointed to that post himself. He was the beneficiary of a substantial estate left by an aunt, but apparently he lost most of the money he inherited. His later years were obscure.

Sixteen years were to pass and the effects of a world war and its aftermath would be felt before really serious thought was given to the idea first advanced by Follin. But in time it had become evident that the needs of a mushrooming population outside of Detroit proper had to be met. Of all the suburbs, only three had their own library systems in 1920. They were Highland Park, Hamtramck and Wyandotte. The remainder of a vast area of towns, villages and farm communities was deprived of the recreational and educational advantages which a free public library system offer. It was time to do something about it. The Michigan legislature in 1917 had passed legislation which provided for the establishment of county libraries, and the Detroit Commission, meeting on October 8, 1920, informally discussed the extension of the law's privileges to Wayne County. The outcome of that meeting was a letter addressed to the Board of County Supervisors, requesting an item in the county budget "in the nature of an appropriation for its inauguration." The supervisors were receptive, agreeing "in principle to such a service." [3] A sum of $10,000 was put into the budget which became effective December 1, and it was stipulated that the Detroit Library Commission would function as the governing body of the county library system, aided by an advisory board of three members, two appointed by the supervisors, with the county superintendent of schools as the third member, ex officio. The first meeting of the Wayne County Library Board was held December 21, 1920. Bryant Walker and William Van Dyke were the appointed members and School Superintendent Eber Yost was the ex officio member. It was agreed that the $10,000 available would only finance exploratory work, and a survey was made to determine where and how the county system could best function. A formal contract was entered into with the Detroit Commission which provided office space and facilities in a corner of the shipping room in the Main Library.[4]

The survey, conducted by Lydia E. Kinsley, a member of the Detroit staff, was completed in January, 1921, and resulted in the establishment of four centers at Grosse Ile, Belleville, Flat Rock and New Boston. Before the year was ended, five more branches had been added at Cherry Hill, Ecorse, Elm, Grosse Pointe Shores and Dearborn. The collections were housed in township halls, general stores, schools, or wherever they could be accommodated.

Administrative offices were moved from the Main Library to a second-floor room at the Scripps branch. By 1933 the County Library had grown to such proportions that it took over practically the entire Scripps building which it continued to occupy until November 1959 when it moved into its own specially constructed headquarters on Van Born Road in Nankin Township.[5] At that time the Scripps branch was closed. Plans to demolish it had not been carried out up to 1965.[6]

Meanwhile, the County Library grew rapidly. Moving into new communities and areas, it operated a truck or bookmobile in those places not within easy reach of a branch. By 1963 it had twenty-five branches, many of them in permanent buildings which were a credit to the communities they served. In addition, services were extended to schools, hospitals, and penal institutions. In 1951 the County Library was referred to as "the second largest public library service in the state." In 1962 it had a book collection of 650,000 volumes, and circulated 2,761,497 books. It operated on a revenue of $713,019 that year. To show its truly metropolitan character, the Wayne County Library operated branches in West Bloomfield Township and the city of Southfield, both in Oakland County.[7]

Eventually this offspring of the Detroit Library was full-grown and ready to leave the nest. Its operations had become too large, costly and extensive for the Detroit system to handle well. As a result, the contract between the county and the Detroit Commission was canceled by mutual consent, and on December 1, 1943, the Wayne County Library became a completely independent system, continuing to operate as such ever since. Yet from the beginning, as a ward of the Commission, the County Library was a credit to its foster parent which derived considerable satisfaction from its success.[8]

Although the Detroit Library had divested itself of its responsibility for the operation of the Wayne County Library, the city institution continued to be a "good neighbor" to the metropolitan area at large. The demands made upon it by outside Detroit business and industry, particularly in the broad fields of governmental, social, economic and technical reference, became burdensome and costly, but at the same time they created for the

Detroit system the image of a metropolitan research library. It was pointed out in 1960:

> One of the great concerns of the Library Commission is the future growth and importance of the reference-research function of the Main Library. The Main Library is the only important public library research facility in the area and it would be unsound, wasteful and physically impossible to attempt to duplicate this public service elsewhere in southeastern Michigan. . . . Today, although Detroit alone supports the service, more than 50 per cent of the population and much of the industrial research is to be found outside the city limits.[9]

The Detroit Library had never taken the narrow view and had always endeavored to provide service to anyone needing it. In 1877 a policy was adopted of granting nonresidents the privilege of drawing books. That policy remained in effect, although a small registration fee has been required of out-of-towners.[10] But there were no restrictions on those visiting the Library and using its reference facilities. Sixty years ago, when the suburbs were beginning to sprout, the Library looked upon them as part of the family, and frequently extended privileges to suburban neighborhoods on the same basis as those enjoyed by city residents. The people of the suburbs, the Commission declared in 1905 "are to all intents and purposes citizens of Detroit. . . . The right to use the Library has already been extended to those living as far east as St. Jean Road. The line was drawn there for the reason that the street railway company makes it the terminus for a single fare." [11] Many years later, reference was made "to the service this metropolitan institution is giving to libraries in the state at large." [12] Use of the term "this metropolitan institution" indicates how the Library regarded itself.

World War II, with its highly specialized industrialization which continued after the war, together with higher educational standards, caused a heavily increased demand upon the Library facilities from the metropolitan area. This was anticipated in the spring of 1941 when Ulveling called a staff meeting to consider the problem. Pointing out that only the Detroit Public Library was equipped to serve the new defense industries springing up around the city's perimeter, the following action was taken:

375

With these peculiar conditions emphasizing the immediate need for the Detroit Public Library extending its service area to the entire Metropolitan district, and with such an enlarged service program in line with the best planning of political scientists, Mr. Ulveling asked all present to consider the advisability of attempting to set up a regional library for the Detroit Metropolitan area with the Detroit Public Library as the core of the organization. . . .[13]

No positive action along these lines was forthcoming at the time, and the Library had to be content to lend a helping and often overburdened hand whenever and however it could. In 1949 a meeting was held attended by the heads of nine area libraries. Out of it came a plan for a cooperative film service. It was stated:

We believe the pattern here established may be helpful in other metropolitan districts or even among a group of county libraries, and we hope, too, that this experience in united effort to work out a better and stronger library service in Greater Detroit may lead to many more joint projects.[14]

This sort of mutual accommodation was carried a step further in 1958 when the Commission gave approval to an inter-library loan service arrangement with the Oak Park Library. This service for the southern Oakland County suburb, which involved payment of a fee to Detroit, was to be given a one-year trial. It worked satisfactorily and the contract was renewed at the end of the year. Encouraged by the success of this plan, the Michigan State Library in 1961 proposed a limited experiment involving area-wide borrowers' cards between Detroit, and the Oakland County suburbs of Detroit, Berkley, Huntington Woods and Oak Park. At the end of eighteen months, Ulveling asked for an extension of the agreement in the hope that through this project data could be obtained "which will eventually lead to wider financial support for the Detroit Public Library." The participating suburbs paid the Detroit system $5792.50 during a period from January 1 to June 30, 1963. The amount was credited to the book fund, "since our costs were primarily for books." [15]

The big problem, however, continued to be the furnishing of reference service to metropolitan area industry. It was stated in 1956:

The Main Library furnishes reference and research facilities and service for the people of the metropolitan Detroit area with very little, if any compensation for the services rendered to corporations and people outside the city. In this respect, we are initiating a study and inquiry as to ways and means whereby the Detroit Public Library will provide these particular facilities and services for the metropolitan area with an equitable sharing of the expense involved by the outside-Detroit metropolitan area.[16]

In 1959 Mayor Louis C. Miriani held a conference with Library officials to discuss legislation "which will provide for reimbursing the Detroit Public Library for providing reference and research service for the metropolitan area." [17] A year later, suburban libraries agreed to support the Detroit Library's effort to obtain state funds for Main Library reference and research services. An April, 1962, survey disclosed that 31 per cent of those using the Main Library came from outside the city limits, "and the survey of use by business and industry in November 1960 showed that 22 per cent of the organizations using the Library were from outside the city limits." With this survey to support a claim for compensation, a bill was introduced in the legislature in 1963, seeking a new state-aid formula which would have given the Detroit Library approximately $500,000.[18] The bill died in committee, but a rewritten version was to be offered in 1964. Eventually, it was expected that some kind of financial support for metropolitan area service would be forthcoming. By the same token, the Library saw a new role for itself. From a school district library in 1865, it looked to a new destiny after a hundred years as a truly metropolitan institution.

The growth of the Library and the extension of its service, both quantitative and qualitative, imposed financial problems which were constantly acute. The penal fines, the Library's original financial base, continued to be a source of income, but the amount received annually became proportionately less important when compared to the whole requirement. Also, penal fines receipts fluctuated widely from year to year as they had done in the past. The annual variations made budgeting difficult. Immediately after World War I, Detroit experienced a "crime wave," which was reflected in revenues from fines of $157,325 in 1920–21.

In 1932–33 when the depression was drying up other revenue sources, the penal fines receipts were $60,278, and in 1936 when the economy had not yet fully recovered, court income was $35,151. Thereafter, variation with no predictable pattern is noticeable in the following penal fines returns: 1944–45, $143,834; 1954–55, $93,292; 1964–65 (estimate), $114,000.

The 1881 law under which the Library Commission was created provided for the Library's support with a one-fifth of a mill tax. This was the first time that the Library had the benefit of taxes directly levied by the city. The law was strengthened in 1905 by the provision that not less than one-fifth of a mill should be levied, and that the city could augment that tax by additional appropriations.* This was generally done thereafter and the Library enjoyed an annual income consisting of penal fines and a fifth-of-a-mill-plus in taxes. This income fluctuated from year to year, depending chiefly upon the mood of the Common Council and mayor, but generally it was adequate and in proportion to amounts appropriated for other departments of the city government. Thus there was reliance upon the city despite the fact that, legally, the Library was not a part of the municipal government, but a more or less autonomous institution existing under separate constitutional and statutory provisions. In order to justify its right to benefit from city taxes, the Library had to permit the Common Council to pass upon its budget. Under the 1901 law, the budget was submitted and considered as a whole package. In 1921 the legislature passed a new law, under which the Library budget had

---

* The improved financial situation was acknowledged by the librarian in the 1906 annual report (p. 13) in which he stated:
  The change in the law by which the Library was made a department of the city government on the same basis as other departments, with its financial estimates and accounts subject to the control and approval of the Common Council, has resulted in a more liberal appropriation for Library purposes. The experience of this, the first year since the law [of 1905] went into effect, furnishes the Library authorities no reason to complain. The aldermen and estimators were most cordial and sympathetic and seemed to understand and appreciate the needs of the Library and the importance of its suitable maintenance. Substantially the whole sum asked for was allowed, and this was considerably beyond the fifth-of-a-mill, to which the Library was by the old law limited.

to be itemized and was treated by the mayor and Council exactly as that of any other city department. These conditions, under which the Library lived in reasonable financial security, if not affluency, remained in effect until 1932.

In that year the Michigan constitution was amended by adoption of the so-called 15-mill limitation. A depression-born measure which reflected a taxpayer revolt against high levies against property, the amendment placed a 15-mill maximum on the amount of taxes on all property, except that in the home rule cities such as Detroit which operated under their own charters. What the amendment meant locally was that the combined tax levied against Detroit property for the support of the county government, the Board of Education and the Library could not exceed 15 mills of assessed valuation. A tax allocation board was provided for and it was its duty to determine how much of the 15 mills should go to each of the three agencies affected by the limitation. The result of this was that regardless of how generously the Common Council was disposed toward the Library, the amount that it appropriated each year for the institution's support could not exceed the Library's portion of the 15 mills as determined by the allocation board.

The effect was felt almost immediately. City tax revenues appropriated for the Library either were frozen or began to drop off. Other Michigan cities found themselves in the same unfortunate situation. It was not long after the amendment became effective that the Library Commission was describing the Library's financial situation as "precarious." To afford a measure of relief, as well as to provide better library facilities generally throughout the state, the legislature in 1937 passed Michigan's first library aid bill. This provided for an appropriation under which the State Board for Libraries, following a prescribed per capita formula, could make grants to library systems. Michigan was one of the first states to provide grants, and in doing so got in at the beginning of a national movement. Detroit's first grant, payable July 1, 1938, amounted to $122,834. Unfortunately, however, the state was experiencing its own financial troubles which for the next twenty-five years were almost annual and chronic. The treasury ran dry in 1939 after only $68,824 of the first grant was paid. The Library was unable to collect the balance of $54,000 until 1940.

Having granted initial relief, only to run out of funds, the legislature omitted a library aid appropriation from the next state budget. The Commission announced in mournful numbers:

> A great disappointment this year, in contrast to the relief afforded last year, has been the discontinuance of the State Fund for the aid of libraries. During the one year this relief fund operated—the total amount received being approximately $120,000—many needed and much appreciated services to our readers were maintained, and new ones inaugurated. The book fund, so drastically cut in the current budget, was also greatly benefited by the funds from this State Aid grant.[19]

After a lapse of two years, during which time no manna from Lansing fell on the Library, the aid program was reinstituted. For the 1941–42 fiscal year—a year in which the war placed extraordinary service demands upon the Library—the Detroit grant was $32,469. The following year it was increased to $98,498. From that time on, state grants have been a regular prop for the Library's financial structure. Unfortunately, Michigan's fiscal landscape had its peaks and valleys—with deeper and deeper valleys —in the postwar years, and the amount of money Detroit received fluctuated according to the fatness or slimness of the state purse. The grants varied from a high of $186,046 in the fiscal year ended June 30, 1945, to $80,000 in 1962. For the ten-year period of 1955–64, the average annual state grant was slightly in excess of $100,000.[20]

The Library regularly joined with other library agencies, including the State Library in an effort to persuade the state budget director and legislature to a more generous attitude, and lobbying in Lansing became a way of life for the Commission. In 1962, when a Constitutional Convention began to study revision of the 1908 Constitution, Ulveling and others from Detroit appeared before the convention's committee on education to explain the needs of the Detroit system and to add the weight of their arguments against any drastic revision of the ancient and honorable library clauses which would deprive the system of its cherished and valuable rights and prerogatives. In that effort they were largely successful, and the new Michigan Constitution which was adopted in 1963 and became effective January 1, 1964, contained essentially the same library provisions as did Michigan's original document of 1837.

Helpful as the state grants were, they were not enough to make up for the shrinkage in appropriations which were the result of the 15 mill limitation. A postwar tendency toward general reduction of property assessments in order to afford relief to home owners and business, a loss in assessments because of removal from the roles of property condemned for expressways and other public uses, and greater reliance upon nonproperty taxes, reduced the base upon which the 15 mills was calculated. The Library's tax revenues were further jeopardized by the mounting cost of operation of the county government and the school system, which led the county and the Board of Education, with their greater political influence, to seek from the tax allocation board larger shares of the 15 mills at the Library's expense. That the situation was developing serious undertones was shown by the Library's 1942–43 report in which it was stated that "an increase of not less than $50,000 per year in city appropriations for books should be sought for developing the reference facilities of the Library." Two years later, the Commission voiced concern about the 15 mill amendment "which restricts the amount of funds that can be budgeted for the Library." It was shown that the combined current operating costs of the county, the Board of Education and the Library "which must share this millage are already so close to the maximum permitted under the amendment, that a salary increase is almost impossible." [21]

The situation resulted in talk among the commissioners about the possibility of a city charter amendment. A new charter adopted in 1918 contained no mention of or provision for the Library. The amendment which the Commission had in mind would allow the city, under its home rule exemption from the 15 mill limitation, to appropriate additional funds beyond the amount allowed as the Library's share of the 15 mills to permit supplementary service or to enable the city to contract with the Library for addi-

381

tional service.* In these discussions, the Commission relied heavily for advice upon one of its members, Thomas G. Long, an attorney with broad experience in tax and constitutional matters. Long, who had been elected to the Commission by the Board of Education in 1944, acquired the standing which Divie Duffield had had before his death in 1935. He drafted a proposed amendment in 1948, and the question of having it placed on the ballot that year was discussed with a City Charter Committee, then conducting a study and review of the need for general charter revision. The Charter Committee proved to be unsympathetic to the Library's immediate need for relief and refused to sponsor an amendment. The Commission appealed that decision, with Long and Commissioner Henry Meyers as its advocates. They were not much more successful. Alarmed, the Commission decided to sponsor the amendment themselves, and persuaded the Common Council to put it on the April, 1949, ballot. Civic groups and the newspapers rallied to the Library's support with a favorable result at the polls. The city now had the power "to supplement funds obtained by the Library through its millage allocation," the Commission triumphantly proclaimed. The amendment, designated as Title 3, Chapter 1, Section 10 (as amended), added to the stated powers of the Council so as "to provide by taxation under the authority of this Charter the funds by the Council deemed requisite to be made available to said Commission. . . ." [22]

Now another stone had been placed in the Library's fiscal foundation. Besides the penal law revenue, the millage levy and state grants, there had been added shared taxes and supplementary grants by the City of Detroit. The first of these grants was

---

* Adoption in 1932 of the constitutional amendment limiting general property tax levies to 15 mills materially affected the Library's financial structure by wiping out the city's supplemental appropriation power granted by the Act of 1905. After the amendment became effective, the Common Council had the power to set the Library budget, but the total could not exceed the Library's share of its allocation under the county's 15-mill limit. Because the Library, under the amendment, was considered to be a unit of local government rather than part of the municipal government, its allocation had to be made from the county's total allocation rather than from the city's. The only way supplemental funds could be provided by the city was by appropriation based upon its own 20-mill limit. This required special authorization by charter amendment.

forthcoming in the fiscal year ended June 30, 1951, and amounted to $433,174. This was in addition to court fines of $47,041, the general property tax levy of $2,494,632 and a state grant of $128,291. With other miscellaneous non-revenue income, the Library for the 1950–51 fiscal year had a total of $3,282,589 compared to $2,882,700 for the previous fiscal year. That represented an increase of $399,889. Since the receipt of that initial city grant, the amounts have varied according to the city's ability to provide additional money. In 1956–57 the amount appropriated by the Council was $800,000; in 1960–61, with considerable unemployment in Detroit and a municipal deficit which was threatening to get out of hand, the city grant was only $365,000. In the fiscal years ending June 30, 1963 and 1964, however, the city administration recognized the further strictures of the 15 mill limitation and the grants were increased to $1,209,-796 and $1,468,570 respectively.

Mention should be made here of the members of the Commission who saw the Library through the times of stress marked by the depression, the Second World War, and the period of tribulation which followed those events. Perhaps at no time in the Library's history was it governed by a more capable and dedicated board. While politics never played an important part in the selection of the Library Commissioners by the Board of Education, that was notably apparent after World War I. During the 1930's and thereafter, the Commission was made up of such distinguished legal minds as Duffield, Long, Meyers, Oscar Hull and M. Hubert O'Brien. The tradition of having physician members was upheld in Drs. Andrew P. Biddle,* Charles S. Kennedy † (who resigned

---

* Dr. Andrew Porter Biddle (1862–1944), born in Detroit, resigned as a midshipman from the United States Naval Academy, Annapolis, because of bad eyesight. He continued his education abroad and later studied medicine at the Detroit College of Medicine. He was recognized as one of the country's foremost dermatologists. He saw service as surgeon (major) with the 31st Michigan Volunteer Infantry in the Spanish-American War. He was elected to the Board of Education in 1917 and served until 1925. He also was a member of the Michigan Board of Health, secretary of the Michigan State Medical Society and editor of its journal.

† Doctors Johnston B. Kennedy (1858–1927) and Charles S. Kennedy (1887–) were a father-son team who served as members of the Library Commission. Both were outstanding members of the medical profession, Dr. Charles being chief-of-staff of Grace Hospital.

383

in 1945 to become a member of the University of Michigan Board of Regents) and Lawrence Reynolds. Rabbi Leo M. Franklin,* of Temple Beth El, was a member from 1927 until his death in 1948. Few men in Detroit public life have ever been more respected and beloved than he. Business and civic leaders who added their talents and abilities included Edwin S. George, Daniel J. Healy, Frank H. Alfred, Edward J. Posselius, and Henry J. Brennan and Rabbi Leon Fram. Harvey M. Merker, an official of Parke, Davis & Company, joined the Commission in 1946 and, like Long, was still serving in 1964. In 1951 Mrs. Hedley V. (Florine) Richardson † became the first regular woman member of the Commission, although Mrs. Laura F. Osborn, whose principal interest lay with the Board of Education, was an ex officio member first in 1923. Mrs. Richardson became as eminent a member of the Commission as any of her male colleagues. The entire city, and particularly those people in any way interested in or affiliated with the Library, felt a deep sense of personal loss when that capable and gracious lady died June 19, 1959. The successors of those who served so ably through so many trying years, the present members, are equally respected, and their presence on the Commission gives assurance that the high standards of the past are being well upheld.

---

* Leo Morris Franklin (1870–1948) was born at Cambridge City, Indiana, and studied at the University of Cincinnati and Hebrew Union College. He was rabbi at Temple Beth El, Detroit, from 1899 to 1941.

† A native Detroiter, Florine Whittaker (Mrs. Hedley V.) Richardson (1878–1959) was the daughter of Herschel Whittaker, state official and early conservationist. Her civic interests were many and varied. Besides her membership on the Library Commission, she was a founder and president of the Women's City Club, a member of the Fine Arts Society, the Women's History Club, Friends of the Detroit Public Library, a trustee of the Detroit Historical Society, and was active in the organization of the United Foundation.

CHAPTER 24

FRIENDS AND TREASURES

ON THE EVENING of September 24, 1942, a group of thirty-eight Detroit area citizens met in the Main Library and organized the Friends of the Detroit Public Library, Inc. Those who were present had been invited to attend by a more or less spontaneously formed, unofficial committee, whose members had previously discussed the plan at a luncheon. It had been decided on that occasion, and in subsequent conversations, to call the organizational meeting, and to invite a group of people who had one common denominator—an interest in books, and a desire to help the Detroit Public Library. The invitation had been signed by Hal H. Smith, Mrs. Ernest Kanzler, Wendell Brown and George Pierrot.

Brown, presiding as temporary chairman, introduced the Library director, Ralph A. Ulveling, who explained the purpose of the proposed organization. It was twofold: to encourage public interest in and contributions to the Library's collection of rare books, manuscripts and other important literary material; and to provide funds from memberships, gifts and bequests for the purchase of such items. Another, implied purpose, was to create through the association of interested and influential citizens, an affiliated arm of the Library which could exert a strong public relations influence.

The idea of forming such an organization was well received. Brown produced previously prepared articles of incorporation of a non-profit organization to be known as Friends of the Detroit Public Library, Inc. They were approved and signed, bylaws were adopted, and a previously prepared slate of officers was presented. Those nominated had been approached beforehand and had agreed to serve. They were unanimously elected to serve through December 31, 1943. The president was Hal H. Smith; J. Shurly Horwitz was vice president; Mrs. James B. Angell, secretary; and Wendell Brown, treasurer. Besides the officers, the board of directors was made up of such well-known Detroiters as Harvey Campbell, vice president of the Board of Commerce; Allen B. Crow, president of the Economic Club of Detroit; William F. Lawler, business man and amateur historian, Lee A White, a newspaper official, and Ulveling.[1]

Despite the fact that the nation was at war when the Friends was organized it was significant that a group of substantial citizens and civic leaders could take the time from demanding affairs and devote attention to the Library. From the very outset, the Friends became an important force in the Detroit community, and assumed a role in relation to the Library for which there had been a long-felt need.

Unlike the Library systems of other cities, that of Detroit, with a few notable exceptions, never greatly benefited from trusts and endowments set up by private citizens. Wealthy Detroiters, for reasons best known to themselves, found other places and institutions where their names could be perpetuated and their generosity appreciated. In 1872, when preparations were being made to build the Centre Park library, subscriptions to a building fund were called for. None were forthcoming, and the appeal to the public, proving futile, was soon abandoned. The Library had to wait until 1903, nearly forty years after its establishment, before it enjoyed "the novel sensation of a money bequest—the first in its history." Miss Julia H. Williams * made provision in her will for a gift of $150 to be spent for books on music, drama and sculpture. Another $150 was left a few years later by Sarah Cochrane, former chief of the Catalog Department. But such bequests were infrequent.[2]

"Of all the institutions which have been aided by private benefactions," Ulveling stated in 1948, "probably not one serves so many individual persons or so broad a segment of society as does the Public Library." The Library also is a requisite of industry in a highly competitive industrial society, he continued.

> Despite such a wide service program, only infrequently has the Detroit Public Library been made the beneficiary of substantial financial gifts or bequests. The largest, $750,000, came from Andrew Carnegie in 1910, at which time he was engaged in his great philanthropic program of helping libraries throughout the country. Two years earlier, through a bequest of James E. Scripps, the Library acquired the fine building, which for many years housed the Scripps Branch Library. In 1921, Clarence M. Burton, some years after giving his valuable collection of books and manuscripts, set up a $50,000 endowment fund (now grown to $150,000) to aid the development of the Burton Historical Collection. A few years later, Mrs. Theodore A. McGraw, Jr. and Mrs. Clarence A. Lightner established a $20,000 endowment to honor Dr. Theodore A. McGraw and Dr. Theodore A. McGraw, Jr. In 1944, Hal H. Smith, first president of the Friends of the Detroit Public Library, Inc., bequeathed $5000 to that organization which he had enthusiastically helped to establish and later to guide. The most recent gift, received in 1948, is a $10,000 endowment fund from the estate of Mrs. Grace W. Biddle.[3] †

Mrs. Biddle's gift, Ulveling pointed out, was only the sixth of its kind received by the Library since the Civil War. The total value of these bequests, not including the Carnegie gift, amounted

---

* Julia H. Williams was a native of Detroit, born about 1883. She died in the spring of 1903 while visiting in New York. She was said to have been "devoted to the literature of art and drama, and was a frequent visitor to the Library."

† Other substantial gifts and bequests, some of which are mentioned in the text either in whole or in part, and their donors, included: Carl F. Clarke, $60,500; Dr. Arthur B. McGraw, $1000; Mrs. Arthur B. McGraw, $35,000; Grant H. Nablo, $5000; Joseph Henry Flavell, $326,000; Mrs. Lynn McNaughton, $3500.

to less than $100,000. This sum looked pale alongside the millions given to the Boston and New York public libraries, and other substantial money gifts to the Cleveland and Chicago libraries. These and other cities also had large endowed private libraries to supplement the book service provided by the public libraries, whereas in Detroit "the Public Library must alone carry the full responsibility for such services." [4]

One of the most unusual of the Library's legacies was that made by Edward E. MacCrone in 1961. An investment banker and an enthusiastic friend of the Library, MacCrone's will provided that a portion of his estate amounting to $400,000, be left in trust with the proceeds accumulating for a hundred years. At the end of that time, in the year 2061, the fund is to be divided into ten equal parts. One share, to be known as the "Ralph A. Ulveling Fund," is to be given to the Library Commission "as a tribute to his [Ulveling's] ability and wisdom in guiding the affairs of the Library." It has been estimated that the Library's share may be as much as $25,000,000.

While monetary gifts were hard to come by, donations of books, many of them valuable, were regularly given to the Library, and a good part of its collection, especially in the early days, was built up through the generosity of its friends, both in Detroit and elsewhere. Anticipating that it would be the recipient of books and documents of various kinds, one of the first things the original library committee did in 1865 was to recommend "that a printed form of acknowledgment of books donated be prepared to be signed by the chairman of the Library Committee and the librarian, and returned to the donors." [5] The first of these acknowledgments was sent out during 1866 after the Library had been in operation little more than a year. The first recorded donor was County Clerk James D. Weir who gave the Library twelve volumes, presumably official publications such as compiled laws. Others whose donations in that year were noted were Judge James V. Campbell, ten volumes, and Samuel Zug and Frederick Stearns, one book each. The biggest donation in 1866 was that made by Henry Ledyard who turned over to the Library 1081 volumes from the library of his father-in-law, Senator Lewis Cass, who died during that year. Cass possessed one of the largest early private libraries in Detroit. The bulk of it was included in the Ledyard gift. It was a valuable collection from a sentimental as well as a pecuniary standpoint, and increased the Public Library's total collection by about ten per cent. The Library Committee officially accepted the Cass donation "which we shall cherish as an excellent momento of that great statesman." [6]

From that time on, the Library collection was regularly augmented by an increasingly large number of donated books. So important were these acquisitions regarded that for many years each individual donation was listed in the annual reports. Each year there was to be found in the list of donors the names of some of Detroit's most distinguished men, such outstanding citizens as Senator Zachariah Chandler, John Owen, members of the Duffield, Woodbridge, Alpheus Williams and other leading families. Many book donations came also from outside the city. Justin Winsor, the Boston librarian, for years was a regular donor. Various universities, including Yale and Pennsylvania, sent their publications, as did major libraries such as those in Providence, St. Louis, San Francisco, and even some in foreign countries, particularly England.

In 1882 the collection was substantially increased by acquisition of the library of the Young Men's Society. Most of the Society's books were purchased, but "at very low rates," and it was noted that after the society, which was liquidating, had paid off its debts, it

> very generously gave us not only a large amount of books and documents remaining unsold, but also sold us at a nominal sum, which did not change the essential character of a gift, a large series of newspapers bound and unbound, and a number of portraits of historical value.[7]

Anticipation of its friends' generosity was part of the calculations of the Library as it built up its book collection, and from time to time the public was reminded that gifts were welcome. From the beginning, the Commission was interested in acquiring historical material, the nature of which precluded purchase with Library funds in most cases. The Commission stated in 1886:

It would be foreign to the purpose of the Commission to spend money, at least in considerable sums, for anything but what are strictly library purposes. But we are encouraged in the hope that this collection will become a most important one, and will be made by the action of private and associated donors.[8]

In acknowledging gifts in 1887, particularly a medical collection from Dr. James F. Noyes and public documents from the estates of John S. Newberry and former Governors Robert Mc-Clelland and John J. Bagley, the Commission observed that they "were exceedingly valuable, not alone intrinsically, but because they could not have been got through the channels of trade." [9]

Thus the Library fared very well over the years in accumulating not only large numbers of books and documents, but many very rare and unusual items which served the needs of scholars and heightened the Library's reputation as a research center. But while this type of material came in a steady stream and was gratefully received, the money benefactions were infrequent. This imposed a handicap upon the institution, making it difficult and usually impossible to purchase items of the sort which supplement special collections and add to a library's reputation as the repository for choice, unique and valuable materials.

It was that vacuum which the Friends of the Detroit Public Library, Inc. was created to fill. The idea of such an organization was not new. The first one of which there is a record was formed in Paris in 1913 to support the Bibliotheque Nationale. The pattern evolved quickly and spread to England and the United States, where Adam Strohm observed its usefulness and advocated a similar organization for Detroit in 1937. He stated in a communication to the Commission:

> In recent years some interesting successful movements have taken place in libraries, universities and art institutes, namely, the bringing into being of what in our case would be the "Founders or Friends of the Library." Detroit has not yet come to the front along those lines. If the precedent of other cities is of value, one of the first things to learn is that of being good mixers. Round tables are nowadays arranged for at annual library meetings with discussions of "Friends of the Library" groups. A new methodology for the establishing of fruitful public relations, a new etiquette for accepting and administering gifts is to be conceived. In formulating policies and setting up objectives this challenge confronts us:—Are we thereby making friends? [10]

Despite this obvious call for action, none was taken immediately, partly because it was felt by Library personnel that the movement should originate with and be sponsored by private interests and should not be regarded as an official branch or department of the Library. The proper time arrived in the early 1940's when income tax laws made contributions to nonprofit organizations a definite advantage, particularly to people of substantial means. Then too, in the period in which the Detroit Friends came into existence, there were several local book and rare item dealers with materials the library could not afford to purchase with its own fund. They were instrumental, up to a point, in interesting people as a group in acquiring some of this material to be donated to the Library.[11]

Naturally, the Library was delighted when the organization was formed, and the institution cooperated in every way to make it a success. Noting its formation, the Commission referred to it as an "important step." It was remarked soon after the Friends was organized:

> The purpose of this undertaking was to bring together people interested in fine books and, through the modest dues paid by all who wished to be identified with the effort, to purchase desirable source materials needed for the Library. Such encouraging success has been shown to date that it now seems likely that within a very few years the Friends will become a significant force in promoting Detroit's cultural growth.[12]

Tangible benefits were quickly evident. Within a year after its founding, the Friends presented their first gift, described as "a Latin Bible printed in Nuremberg by Anton Koberger, 1477,— A beautiful copy of an early printed Bible." It is one of the Library's rarest treasures.[13]

The Friends quickly became a prestige organization despite the fact that membership was open to anyone. Regular dues were nominal—three dollars a year, although there were various classes of membership. Life memberships were offered at $1000. There is also an Industrial Membership which enables the city's large business concerns to show their interest and give their support. Before very long the rolls contained several hundred names, and while some of the city's most distinguished people were on the roster, the general membership was drawn from all walks of life.

391

While the Friends remained independent from the Library's administration, it was so closely integrated with the institution that within a short time it was given office space in the Library. The Friends employed several devices to create interest and establish good public relations. Periodic meetings were held, open to the public, at which the attraction usually was a nationally recognized literary figure. In 1944 a Mark Twain exhibit was held, for which material was drawn from libraries and private collections all over the United States. A beautifully printed catalog of the exhibit was prepared, a scholarly work of superb typographical quality. This was the first of several such exhibits.* In 1945 publication of a quarterly bulletin was begun. Called *Among Friends* it attained wide circulation. It was suspended temporarily in 1953 and resumed in new format, but with the same title, in 1955.

The man who generated enthusiasm for the Friends and who proved to be its organizing genius was Hal Horace Smith, a successful corporation lawyer, whose avocation was book collecting. Born at Ionia, May 1, 1873, Smith attended the University of Michigan and was admitted to the practice of law in 1896. He moved to Detroit in 1905, and became a partner in the law firm of Beaumont, Smith & Harris. He was a director of the old Union Trust Company and several industrial firms, counsel for the Michigan Manufacturers Association and the Michigan Bankers Association, and drafted Michigan's Workmen's Compensation Act.

Outside of his business and professional activities, his chief interest was books. In his palatial Grosse Pointe home he assembled a fine private library which reflected his personal tastes. He was the author of a book, *On the Gathering of a Library,* a scholarly dissertation with wide appeal for bibliophiles. The moti-

---

* One of these exhibits nearly resulted in disaster in February, 1955. A display of the manuscript diary of Walt Whitman from March, 1876 to May 31, 1889, loaned by Charles E. Feinberg, was stolen from its showcase in the Main Library. The diary was insured in the amount of $20,000, a nominal sum for an item which was considered to be virtually priceless. The thief was not apprehended, and the insurance company settled for the full amount which was turned over to Feinberg by the Library Commission on September 7, 1955. On December 28, the diary was returned to the Library by mail and restored to its owner who, in turn, returned the insurance settlement.

vation which explains his deep interest in the Friends is found in an article he wrote for the quarterly publication of the Detroit Trust Company, in which he stated:

> A public library undoubtedly performs its most immediate service when it furnishes books for recreational reading and reference books which the student, whether in a manufacturing institution, chemical laboratory, bank or law office, finds it necessary to consult. But there is another and perhaps a broader service that it can perform—broader but of no less value than the other. That service is the stimulation of interest in literature, in books and in all that goes with them—their typography, the story of their making, their place in history and civilization. Everything about a book has its cultural value for they are the repositories of the culture of the centuries. Even to handle them stirs an inspiration for when one has once found any interest in books, he is invited, in fact he is almost driven, to travel down the road to increasing knowledge.[14]

Smith held the position of president of the Friends until his death, December 21, 1944. The Library mourned him, and his loss was felt throughout the community. The Detroit *Free Press* said of him: "He was one of the great builders of Detroit in the days of its formation as a metropolitan community." He remained a "friend" of the Library in death, for his will contained a bequest of $5000, the first substantial legacy to the Friends for the Library's ultimate benefit.

Another pillar of the Friends was Mabel L. Conat who served as its secretary for several years after a noteworthy career as a librarian. A native Detroiter, Miss Conat attended the University of Michigan and upon her graduation joined the Detroit Public Library staff in 1909. In 1911 she went to the University of Illinois where she remained four years, returning to Detroit as first assistant reference librarian in 1915. While a member of the Detroit staff, she also taught in library schools in New Jersey and Illinois. She became chief of the Reference Department, and after the reorganization of the 1940's in which she had an important hand, she was made director of Reference Services. Upon her retirement in 1950, she became secretary of the Friends, a post she occupied until her "second retirement" in 1963. She was succeeded in that position by Mrs. Evelyn Tintera, former executive secretary of the Michigan Library Association.[15]

One of the collecting fields upon which the Friends trained its sights was that of automotive history. No major library, Detroit's included, had much automotive material prior to World War II. It was desirable to build such a collection in Detroit, where much of the automobile industry was concentrated and where many of its founding fathers had lived or still lived. If there was to be an archival record of the industry, Detroit was the logical place for it, and the Detroit Public Library was the only possible repository. So the accumulation of such material became almost the number one project of the Friends, according to Miss Conat.[16] That is further borne out by a 1944 statement in the Commission proceedings:

> The librarian reported briefly on the broad plans by the Friends of the Detroit Public Library, Inc., for gathering through the leaders of the automotive industry and other interested persons, the complete records essential to a proper development of the Automotive History Collection now being established in the Library.[17]

The results were highly satisfactory and, through the efforts of the Friends, the Library was placed in a position of pre-eminence in the field of automotive history. Within a few years the Friends had purchased, in whole or in part, or had been responsible for the donation of some outstanding collections, including the Cave, Johnson and Dyke. The D. Cameron Peck Collection was purchased for $20,000. Of that amount $15,000 was given by the Automobile Manufacturers Association and the balance by the Friends. The Drusilla Farwell Foundation and the R. L. Polk Company, by persuasion of influential members of the Friends, presented the Bendix collection. These automotive materials, "when added to the extensive holdings previously amassed, makes this Library the outstanding research center in that broad subject field," became the Library's proud boast.[18]

The Friends' interest, however, was not restricted exclusively to the automobile. Every department of the Library benefited by donations, either from the organization or from individual members. Partly as a result of the accumulation of extremely valuable items, the Library was able to establish its Rare Book Room in 1948.

The Rare Book Room was an offshoot of the reorganization

plan of the 1940's and was under the supervision of the general Reference Department. Its need became apparent to Miss Conat when the number of rarities began to increase through the generosity of the Friends. Miss Conat realized that in addition to those gifts, the Library over the years had accumulated many books and documents, some of them priceless. These were scattered through the various departments; some were kept in locked cases, others were in the stacks. It was felt that measures should be taken to preserve these treasures. World War II taught that the possibility of bombings in a future conflict required extraordinary precautions. Colonel Edwin S. George, a Commission member, donated the furnishings for a special room, and Miss Conat caused the stacks to be combed and the rare items pulled out for deposit in the Rare Book Room. The room and the collection was placed in charge of Mrs. Frances Brewer. In 1958 the collection had grown to such proportions that the Rare Book Room was given divisional status, and a short time later its name was changed to Gifts and Rare Books Division.

In general, the Rare Book collection consists of books which support the collections of the special departments of the Main Library, but are too valuable or too frail to be shelved in the general stacks where they would be handled without special care. Special collections include examples of books gathered to show the history of printing and the art of the book.[19]

The rare quality of a book, according to Mrs. Brewer, is largely determined by supply and demand. In general a rare book is one worth more than $75, although age is also a factor. Again speaking generally, most books printed in America prior to 1800 and in Europe prior to 1700 are regarded as rare. The present collection is marked by selectivity, in that it has been accumulated piece by piece and is not the gift of one or two wealthy donors. In that respect, the Detroit collection is considered unique.

In 1964 the collection numbered about 30,000 items. Library officials shy away from placing a monetary estimate on the total value. The collection, they point out, has its intangible values as well. It is generally agreed that the most cherished treasure in the collection is the manuscript diary of George Washington which he kept from October 1789 to March 1790. This was given to the

395

Library in 1921 by the late Henry B. Joy, president of the Packard Motor Car Company.[20]

It would require a thick catalog to list and describe the other treasures of the Rare Book Room, but among them, to mention only a few, are an original and unpublished Mark Twain manuscript, a collection of letters bearing the autographs of all the presidents of the United States, several Lincoln letters, a Shakespeare second folio, and an outstanding collection of Bibles, including a leaf of the Gutenberg Bible printed at Mainz about 1450 A.D. The oldest complete book in the collection is a copy of Cicero's *De Officius,* published in 1466, and the oldest item is a manuscript of the Gospels, written in Armenian, dating from 1223 A.D.

The addition of the Rare Book collection added considerably to the Library's standing and prestige. It has been pointed out that rare materials are now available to scholars in Detroit, whereas up to a few years ago it was necessary for them to travel to New York, Washington or other cities to examine and use material of this nature.

It is true, of course, that the contents of the Rare Book Room as well as noteworthy collections in other departments are not exclusively the result of the activities and generosity of the Friends. But the organization's work has been outstandingly successful. During the first twenty years of its existence, it contributed $14,688 for memorial gifts; special contributions from individual members amounted to $42,600. Legacies totaled more than $70,000, and it was estimated that more than $110,000 was spent for books for the Library, while other books, donated by members had an approximate value of $90,000. Added to this, is the intangible worth of the Friends to the Library through a public relations program—a worth upon which no price tag can be placed.[21]

"Surely," the Commission acknowledged, "the City of Detroit has reason to be deeply grateful for these additions to the literary and historical resources of the Library for use by the community." [22]

CHAPTER 25

"LIKE A RIVER FLOWING"

THE SKY WAS BLUE and cloudless and it was unseasonably hot. By midafternoon on Sunday, June 23, 1963, many of the residential areas of Detroit had a deserted appearance. That was because more than 100,000 citizens, mostly Negroes, were downtown, taking part in a gigantic parade—the March to Freedom— demonstrating their insistence upon equal civil rights. Other thousands stood along the Woodward Avenue curbside watching the procession move from above Grand Circus Park past the City-County Building and turn onto Jefferson to Cobo Hall where an address was delivered by the Negro leader Dr. Martin Luther King, of Atlanta, Georgia.

The newspapers, in Detroit and across the nation, proclaimed the march as an epoch-making event. The attention it received almost banished from the papers the account of another historic occurrence. At exactly the same time that the March to Freedom was taking place, Detroit was dedicating its newest Main Library with appropriate ceremonies. This was the fourth time in just short of one hundred years that Detroiters had assembled for a

397

similar purpose. The first time was in 1865 when the first Library was opened in the Capitol High School. The second such occasion was in 1877 when the Centre Park Library, the first building devoted exclusively to library purposes was opened. The third time was in 1921 when the Main Library at Woodward and Kirby was dedicated.

The fourth building was actually an enlargement of the 1921 Library, an extension consisting of the addition of two wings, a long connecting concourse, and other facilities which, in effect, created an entirely new Main Library complex. About two hundred people assembled in the auditorium. They included Dr. Leon Fram, president of the Library Commission, Library Director Ralph A. Ulveling, Commissioner Harvey M. Merker, chairman of the building committee, and former Commissioner Henry Brennan who had given yeoman service as chairman of the building committee until his retirement from the Board in 1962. The dedicatory oration was delivered by Dr. Clarence B. Hilberry, president of Wayne State University, the Library's fast growing neighbor in the Cultural Center. If the event attracted less attention than the one taking place on lower Woodward Avenue, it was no less a milestone in the city's history and progress. For the dedication was an acknowledgment by the people of the enlarged role the Library was being called upon to play as a significant—and the only—major reference-research center in a vast metropolitan area. It was the climax of about twenty years of planning and striving.

But before the new Main Library's completion, there was another item of unfinished business of importance. That was the construction of a new service building, housing the work and maintenance shops and the bindery. It was a necessary part of the Library's expanding system.

When the 1921 Main Library was opened, rooms were provided in it for workshops and the bindery. But within four years, the latter was crowded out by demands for space for other essential Library activities. On May 5, 1925, the Commission approved a ten-year lease of bindery quarters in the City of Detroit's municipal garage on East Jefferson Avenue at Dubois Street.[1] There it remained (the lease was renewed) for thirty years in

398

rooms which soon became inadequate. It was the hope and ambition of the Commission that something better could be had, and in 1928 the Commission declared that it "feels justified in recommending that a suitable service building be erected on the old Main Library site, a recommendation that has received the hearty approval of representative downtown business interests." [2] But a depression and a World War made it impossible to carry out that plan, and a better use was found for the Centre Park property. Still, the need for a service building was regularly mentioned. Lack of funds, however, prevented anything being done until 1955 when the Commission's hand was more or less forced. Plans for Main Library reconstruction and additions made it urgent that the workshops be moved, and the bindery was evicted from the municipal garage because the city wanted the space for its own printing department. The bindery moved into rented quarters at 650 West Baltimore.[3]

At this time, the John C. Lodge and the Edsel Ford expressways were being completed, and the Michigan Highway Department had on its hands some surplus real estate which had been taken for right-of-way. This was put up for sale, including a parcel on Third at the intersection of the two expressways. The size of the lot was right and the location, only a few blocks from the Main Library, was ideal. Lengthy negotiations resulted in the sale of the land to the Library for $50,000 in 1958. A $500,000 bond issue was authorized, and a building was designed by the city engineer. A construction contract amounting to $379,034 was awarded Paul H. Johnson, Inc., in the late summer of 1958. Within a year, a simple, yet functional building was completed, and on September 27, 1959, it was officially placed in service.[4]

The overcrowding which forced the bindery out of the Main Library was felt in other parts of the building too. The bronze front doors had hardly been opened for the first time in 1921 when it became apparent that the place would not long be large enough. In 1924 Divie B. Duffield told his fellow commissioners "that because of the possible addition to the Main Library building within the next few years the availability of the premises for the placing of monuments is unavoidably speculative . . . no statues or monuments should be placed on the grounds at all." [5]

399

That statement was intended to discourage local organizations from turning the Library grounds into a statue orchard. Italians wanted a monument to Dante placed there; the St. Andrew's Society felt that the Library grounds would be the ideal place for a statue of Robert Burns. The Commission realized the danger that in accepting one or two such statues they would have to accept others. They finally settled on a Memorial Walk. Organizations were permitted to plant trees in honor of their heroes and heroines along one of the walks in the rear of the building. But the fact that the need for the grounds was used as an excuse indicated that the Commission recognized the necessity for ultimate expansion.

That the statue ban was more than a convenient excuse was soon proved. In 1926 the Commission approved a ten-year expansion program, one item of which called for additions to the Main building in the 1934–35 fiscal year at a cost of $1,536,000. About the same time, the Commission officially admitted that the Main building was fast becoming outgrown.[6] The 1925–26 annual report pointed out:

> The present Main Library building, originally designed for a city which MIGHT grow to a million population is now serving a city well beyond that mark. Before five years are passed we will be looking at the two million mark in population. Not to plan now to be ready then is, frankly, to be stupid. The concentration of homes near the Art Center, augmented by apartment buildings, already taxes the physical capacity of the Library. . . . Fortunately, we have available space to the north and to the south of the present building.[7]

Equally important, the report continued, Cass Gilbert, the architect, in designing the building, had done so with the thought that eventually it would have to be enlarged, and he had made some preliminary and informal sketches of wings which could be added on the north and south sides along the Woodward Avenue front. The drawings were kept in the Commission's files for future reference,[8] but ultimately they were discarded when new plans were adopted.

Meanwhile there was discussion of several ways by which the interior could be remodeled and more space obtained. But in the end these discussions invariably came back to Gilbert's original idea of putting on additions. Strohm declared in 1926:

400

Probably the most satisfactory relief in the situation would involve an enlargement of the building or the erection of the two wings planned for future expansion in our program for the Main Library. One of these buildings should at once be given over to an Historical Building or Hall of History.[9]

From that time, the need for relief was a recurring topic at Commission meetings. "The need of additions to the Main Library and to your annual appropriation for the book fund are of prime importance," the Common Council was told in 1929.[10] At that time it was pointed out that

the Main Library building has lived to the age where it is very conscious of its physical limitations. It is creaking in some corners from mere pressure and, like other things in Detroit, is afflicted with the traffic jam. Little can be done with the building itself that will give substantial relief. This will come only through the erection of one or both of the contemplated wings which are to flank the Main building. . . .[11]

This was the Commission's expression less than ten years after it had completed a new Main Library which, it was predicted in 1921, would adequately serve the city for at least fifty years!

In 1930 the depression was beginning to take hold, and the ten-year program of 1926 had to be revised. New estimates were made, and with more hope than assurance the Commission called for construction of one wing in 1934–35, and the second in 1939–40. There would be further revision before the first step could be taken.[12]

The depression of the 1930's effectively killed all possibility of expansion. Plans, however, were not abandoned; they were merely put on the shelf to await better times. Then, with the new demands imposed upon the Library by World War II, the necessity for more room became evident with nearly every day that passed. It was stated in 1943:

The future cannot be discussed without giving serious attention to the urgent need for expanding the Main Library accommodations as soon as funds and building conditions permit. Public service areas, preparations departments and the book stacks are all so overtaxed that normal functions must be planned and organized, not from the standpoint of their relationship to related units, but entirely from the viewpoint of fitting an activity into any area or even any two or

401

three widely separated areas that can be made available. In the book stacks repeated shifting of large book collections is necessary to take advantage of small spaces developed through the seasonal use of first one, then another type of book. The crippling of service which thus results is no longer reflected at the Main Library only, but, through a retarding of the necessary centralized processes, the entire system of branch libraries is affected. Correction of this condition should be given priority over all other items in the building program for the postwar years.[13]

The Library Commission did not wait for V-E Day or V-J Day to begin its postwar planning. Cass Gilbert died in 1934, but his son, Cass Gilbert, Jr., and Francis Keally were selected to continue his work. Both had been associated with him in designing and constructing the Main Library and were well qualified to carry on. The Commission committed itself to going ahead when, in 1944, it sought information from the Cass Gilbert firm about "any proposed plans which this firm has made." [14] That inquiry really marked the first positive step in the expansion program. The Gilbert and Keally commission dated from September 12, 1944, and with it went a word of caution.

> Because the existing unit has won widespread acclaim as an architectural achievement, one which reflects credit on the city, the greatest care will have to be exercised in planning the facade, that the completed structure may be as unified and perfect a composition as the original building.[15]

Conferences with the architects gave the Commission all the assurance that was needed. Preliminary sketches disclosed that Gilbert and Keally "have succeeded in developing a fine composite which, metaphorically, will be a unified symphony rather than many related parts of one whole." [16]

The plan followed that of the senior Gilbert's idea of extending the wings to the north and south, but his concept of placing them on the Woodward Avenue front were completely discarded. New drawings were presented with modification of the Cass Avenue front. These plans were approved in December, 1944. At that time, $40,000 was appropriated for the initial fees, and a firm of consulting engineers was authorized to begin some of the preliminary work. By 1946 matters had progressed to a point where

402

the Commission felt justified in applying to the Federal Works Agency for a grant of $118,750 for completing the plans. This grant later was not needed. All drawings and specifications were ready in 1949, but prior to that a contract was awarded for test borings.[17]

Between 1950 and 1958, effort was devoted principally to the completion of detailed plans and specifications. In the process there were major revisions which materially changed the original concept. Arrangements also had to be made for financing the work, no easy task because the postwar period was one of rapidly rising costs which found the city hard pressed for money. Yet the period was not an idle one. Progress was steady, although from the sidewalk it was not always discernible. In 1954 the Commission estimated that it would need $9,500,000 to complete the work and asked the Common Council to approve a bond issue of that amount.[18] A delay followed while the city examined its purse. Finally it was decided to do the work in stages, and bonds would be issued as the money was needed to complete each contract. The first series of bonds in the amount of $2,500,000 was authorized January 15, 1957, although not all of the bonds were immediately sold. Doing the work by stages was not the most economical method, but city authorities insisted it be done that way and the Commission had no choice but to acquiese. Mounting construction costs became alarming. The Commission explained:

> There has been a rise in building costs as shown in the well recognized *Engineering News-Record* building cost index from 1949 to 1958 of 45 and a fraction per cent. The increased cost of the additions as now designed is due primarily to such rise in building costs in the last nine years and not in any sense or degree to any rise in the ideas of the Commission members. If the building had proceeded in 1949 probably some other city building would have had to be deferred. Thus the increased costs of building would have been on such other deferred building and not on the Library. The Library should not be blamed because it was deferred and the increased costs are now on the Library. In the meantime, there have been developed methods of construction which are not as costly as the methods called for in the 1949 plans or as used in the existing Main Library. These less costly methods are being used and in this way the increase in cost is being held down as much as possible

403

consistent with maintaining the harmonious architectural appearance of the Main Library with the additions completed. The exterior walls of the additions instead of being built of thick marble blocks as is the Main Library itself, are to be built of thin marble slabs like the City-County Building, Veterans Building and other Civic Center construction.[19]

With these and other dollar saving modifications agreed upon; with the initial bond money available, and agreement with city authorities that the work would be spread over a five-year period, the light was green at last. On July 8, 1958, a contract for $1,089,000 for the excavation and foundation was awarded to the O. W. Burke Company. Shortly thereafter ground was broken.

Now signs of progress were visible, and Ulveling reported happily that construction, with its dirt, noise and confusion, with its rumble of steam shovels and bulldozers and the cacaphony of air hammers was "a good noise." [20] Early in 1959 the second stage contract was awarded for the concrete and structural frame, and there was a promise (which went awry by a few months) that all would be completed in 1962. Other contracts were let, and during 1960 the cornerstone was laid. It was reported in 1960:

> The rather slow progress in the construction of the building is due to financing schedules. Since contracts are let only as the money becomes available, the total job has had to be stretched out into five separate building contracts. This procedure necessarily increases the total cost and gives rise to a situation in which the funds available, although adequate for completing the building, will be insufficient for the interior fittings.[21]

The obvious solution was to solicit gifts to provide those things, such as an auditorium and other necessities which were regarded as requisite. A plan for soliciting private donations was outlined by Ulveling to the Commission, was given approval and put into effect with heartening results. Fifty-five thousand dollars of a larger bequest to the Friends of the Detroit Public Library, Inc., by Carl F. Clarke,* was donated to provide an auditorium seating 375. The Edwin S. George Foundation gave $30,000 to finish

---

* Carl F. Clarke (1894–1959) was for many years in the food brokerage business. He not only was a patron of the Detroit Public Library, but also of the Detroit Historical Society.

and furnish a smaller, multipurpose 125-seat auditorium and meeting room. Renville Wheat, secretary of the McGregor Fund, announced late in 1960 the gift of $50,000, of which $30,000 was for the Children's Room and the $20,000 balance for un-designated purposes. Mrs. Arthur B. McGraw gave $30,000 to furnish the Rare Book Room, and Commissioner Thomas Long made a $10,000 donation "to be used for some purpose in the furnishing, equipping or decorating of Main Library addition or alteration." Commissioner Lawrence Reynolds gave $5000, and $15,000 came from the Daughters of the American Revolution. And that was by no means all. Private industry helped too. The Ford Motor Company gave $100,000 for furnishings and equip-ment for the room set aside for the Technology and Science Department and Automotive History Collection. General Motors Corporation matched the Ford gift to set up a bibliographic center to provide research service to be established in the center of the main floor in the area connecting the old building and the new concourse. Chrysler Corporation contributed $25,000 for the Sociology and Economics Department. Not to be outdone by out-siders, the Library staff raised $8600 which was used to furnish the staff lounge and dining area.

One unique and valuable gift was a massive 16-by-40 foot mosaic mural set above the new Cass Avenue entrance. The mural, exhibiting five groups of allegorical figures, was given by the Abbey Fund which is administered by the National Academy of Design. The work was executed by Millard Sheets, of Clare-mont, California, who was selected from a field of nine artists who had been invited to compete by the Academy which paid the winner $33,400 for the design and installation. Eventually all of these things were completed and in place, and in the spring of 1963 the 1921 building, now called the Central Building, was closed to permit removal of books to the new rooms and stacks in the wings.[22]

All was in readiness for the June 23 dedication except for alterations and renovation, both interior and exterior, of Central Building. That work was still in progress during 1964.

Visitors to a series of open houses and receptions saw what might be claimed as the most modern and complete library structure in existence, one which quickly gained both national and international acclaim. As described by Ulveling,

> It is not intended primarily for the general nonspecialized reader, though service to those readers is of course available in the building. Rather, it is a reference-research library, completely departmentalized with enormous collections of highly specialized books, manuscripts, and maps assembled to serve the needs of people in industry, of scholars, and of laymen having specialized interests.[23]

Seeing the new Library for the first time, the observer is impressed by its immensity. The Central Hall, a huge building in its own right, has 180,000 square feet of floor space. The new sections added 240,000 square feet, providing a total of 420,000 square feet and more than doubling the original Library's size. The wings and other adjoining new areas consist of four floors. Two of these are stack levels below grade, and the long, open and unobstructed rows of stacks present a perspective that is almost awesome. Pages quickly discovered that they could best negotiate the vast distances on roller skates. On the first basement level are to be found the Friends Auditorium, the Explorers Room, the staff lounge and cafeteria, all tastefully and cheerfully decorated. All levels are served by automatic elevator.

Eventually, entrance will be available either from Woodward or Cass avenues. In the center, connected by a corridor running east and west through the entire building, will be the catalog room and bibliographic center. Adjoining on the north side will be General Information Service; on the south, the Map Room. History and Travel will occupy its former quarters in the Central Building, while opposite, in what was the Children's Room, will be the biography collection.

Entering the building from Cass Avenue, the visitor finds himself in the spacious concourse, lighted by continuous ceiling-length windows. A book return desk faces him at the right; at the left is the book charge desk, the check room, and a large room devoted to education film service. Proceeding along the concourse toward the south wing, one comes first to the Business and Finance Room. The first floor of the south wing proper is given to Sociology and Economics, and Philosophy, Religion and Educa-

406

tion. The second floor, reached by escalator, houses Technology and Science and Automotive History.

The extreme west end of the first floor of the north wing contains the Children's Room with its furniture scaled down to a size befitting its patrons. Adjoining is the Browsing Library, while the rest of the wing's first floor is occupied by the Burton Historical Collection. The second floor is taken up entirely by administration offices. The balcony of the concourse has the Rare Book Room and a row of soundproof study carrels for those doing research work. Fine Arts, Music and Performing Arts, and Language and Literature occupy their old locations on the third floor * of the Central Building, although with considerably enlarged facilities. Adam Strohm Hall, which started out in 1921 as the Main book delivery room, will be used as an exhibition gallery.†

All departments are served by the most modern devices for easy communication and fast delivery of books. There is a complete system of intercommunication, pneumatic tubes and conveyors. If the patron is overwhelmed by the magnitude of the building and its contents, he will find an illuminated directory board in the concourse, the gift of C. Allen Harlan. A push of a button will direct him to any one of two hundred listed locations.

The addition of the wings and the modernization of the Central Building represent the climax to a century of the Library's growth and development. Whereas the original Main Library provided— with considerable crowding—for a book capacity of about 1,000,000 volumes, the 1963 complex offers stack room and shelf space for 2,620,000. All of this was accomplished at a total cost, including remodeling, of $11,750,000, of which more than $500,000 was donated.

This, then, is the Detroit Public Library a century after its humble beginning in a small room in what was Michigan's first Capitol building. The hundred years since then have seen it grow into an institution serving not only America's fifth largest city, but

---

* Originally the second floor, this level became the third floor when the mezzanine was made into a floor by extensive remodeling.

† As this was written, plans were underway for a set of murals in Adam Strohm Hall, a gift of the Friends of the Detroit Public Library, in honor of Mr. and Mrs. Joseph Henry Flavell. John S. Coppin, a prominent Detroit artist, was commissioned to execute the murals.

also one of the great industrialized metropolitan centers of the world. From a collection of about five thousand volumes, it has grown into a system of twenty-seven neighborhood or community branches, a downtown library and, as the nucleus of the whole, the magnificent Main Library, devoted to fulfilling the reference-research needs of a highly complicated industrial society.

And what of the future? That can be assessed from its past. As human knowledge and experience increase, so it may confidently be predicted, will the Library grow, adding new specialized collections as the need for them arises. That it will tend to become the control point of a metropolitan area library system seems almost certain. In this role, it will only be carrying on in the tradition of public service to which its founders dedicated it in 1865. The spirit of the institution was caught by the artist Millard Sheets, who included these words in the mural over the Cass Avenue entrance:

> Like a river flowing through the ages uniting distant men, knowledge, and thought into a community of ideas of the world and of time is the accumulated record of mankind.

Those words are prophetic from the standpoint of the Library's mission and its destiny. For the history of the Detroit Public Library is more than a chronicle of the past. It is a promise of the future.

APPENDICES

APPENDIX A

1808 First suggestion on record for a public library in Detroit made by Father Gabriel Richard to the Governor and Judges. October 18.

1817 City Library Association incorporated. August 26.

1818 Detroit Mechanic's Society organized June 13. Its library established ca. 1860.

1833 Detroit Young Men's Society organized January 18. Acquired books of City Library Association.

1835 Michigan's first constitution drafted; contained clause providing for support of libraries by penal fines. May-June. Similar clauses in all subsequent Michigan constitutions.

1842 Special law required Board of Education to establish district library in Detroit.

1860 Supreme Court ordered penal fines credited to library fund; heretofore largely diverted to other public uses. May.

1861 Board of Education library committee drafted program for establishment of public library. Civil War caused delay.

1864 Library committee called for immediate establishment of public library. Henry Chaney sent East in April and August to purchase books with $7000 from library fund.

1865 Detroit Public Library opened in Capitol High School with Henry Chaney, principal, as librarian. March 25. Books circulated for first time May 2. Collection totalled 8864 volumes at end of year.
4700 borrowers' cards issued during Library's first year.

1866 Personal library of Lewis Cass presented to Library.

1867 German books purchased; beginning of foreign language collection.
Book collection reached 15,020 volumes.

1868 Library made depository for U.S. documents and Smithsonian Institution publications.

1871 Chaney became full-time librarian.
Addition to old Capitol building provided more space for library.
Periodical reading room opened.

1872 Centre Park acquired as site for new library. August 19.
Book circulation for year exceeded 100,000 volumes.

1873 Plans approved for Centre Park building. February 24.
Legislature authorized $150,000 building fund to be raised by taxation or bond issue. March 27.

1874 Common Council approved building fund of $125,000 to be raised by taxation over three-year period. April 27.

1875 Cornerstone of Centre Park Library laid. May 29.

1877 Centre Park Library dedicated with 5000 persons in attendance. January 22.

1878 Henry Chaney resigned April 11. Succeeded by Rev. Manasseh Hickey.

1880 Henry Gillman appointed librarian to succeed Hickey. April.
Library subscribed for first time to leading periodicals.
First card catalog compiled.
Library Commission created by Board of Education. December 28.

1881 Library Commission of seven members became governing

body of Library, replacing Board of Education's committee on library. January 29.

James V. Campbell elected first president of Library Commission. February 18.

State law permitted city to levy 1/5 mill on each $100 of assessed value for Library's support.

1882   Library acquired books of Young Men's Society library by purchase and donation. September 14.

1883   Competitive examinations given candidates for Library staff positions. ca. November 8.

1884   Work begun on 2-story addition to Centre Park building. June 9. Completed March 1, 1886.

1885   Henry M. Utley appointed librarian to succeed Gillman. August 1.

1886   Library acquired maps and documents of Michigan Historical Society. Also became custodian of collection of Detroit Scientific Association, including books of the Mechanics' Society Library.
Sunday service inaugurated. February 29.
Telephone installed in Library. ca. April.
Dewey decimal classification system adopted. October 7.

1887   Library lighted by electricity. July 1.
School libraries furnished by Public Library.

1890   General catalog and two supplements completed.
Book collection exceeded 100,000 volumes at end of year.

1891   Polish language books added to foreign collection.
Library cooperated with University of Michigan by providing supplemental reading material for extension courses.
Book withdrawals for year exceeded 250,000 volumes.
Michigan Library Association organized; Henry M. Utley elected first president.

1893   Commissioner Butzel advocated branches in neighborhood stores.

Collection of Detroit Scientific Association transferred to Art Museum. March 28.

Legislature passed enabling act to allow Library to raise funds to enlarge Centre building. June 1.

Reference reading room opened. ca. December 1.

1894　Minimum age for card holders reduced from 14 to 12 years. Resulted in increased juvenile patronage. November 8.

1895　Medical collection established when Detroit Medical and Library Association turned its books and pamphlets over to the Library. February 7.

1896　Mayor Pingree advocated opening two branches; one on east side, one on west side of city.

Children's reading room opened; beginning of Children's Department. May 28.

Books in Braille available to blind. December 3.

1897　Chauncey Hurlbut's will left money to the Water Board for development of Water Works Park. His personal library also willed to Water Board for use of public. Oval storage tank later developed into a branch library building which was maintained by the Water Board and operated by the Library Commission.

1898　Reserve postal plan first adopted. March 17.

Spanish-American War caused decrease in book circulation.

Cooperation between Library and public schools attracted international attention.

Circulation for year exceeded 1,000,000 mark.

1899　Commissioner Follin advocated making Library a county instead of city agency.

Alcove furnished with rugs and rocking chairs for exclusive use of women readers. May 18.

Special delivery service of books to readers' residences. ca. June 1.

Branch Department organized; Jessie C. Chase appointed superintendent. ca. July 1.

Library organized into six departments: cataloging, circulation, reference, branch, juvenile, periodical. October 19.

1900 First branch opened in Central High School, April 2. Branch 2 opened in Harris School, April 16; Branch 3 in Western High School, October 25.

Librarian instructed to procure all works not already in the Library relating to Michigan or printed or published in the state. April 19.

1901 Special meeting of Commission called to consider need for new main Library building. January 10.

Library Commission incorporated with power to own, purchase or condemn property. March.

Public given access to fiction alcoves. April 14.

Andrew Carnegie offered $750,000 to construct new main and branch buildings. City asked to submit question of issuing $500,000 of Library bonds for purpose of complying with Carnegie offer. June 20.

1902 City Savings Bank failure tied up entire library fund of $38,757. February 10.

Saturday afternoon story-hour for children begun. October 18.

Voters approved $500,000 Carnegie bond proposal, but city officials blocked issuance of the bonds. November 4.

1903 Commission voted to purchase sites for branches. January 3.

First branch opened in rented store building on Gratiot near McDougall. March 1.

1904 Contract with express company provided auto delivery service between Main Library and branches. April 21.

1905 Playground libraries established.

Law made minimum appropriation of 1/5 mill mandatory. March.

Library "factory stations" opened in industrial plants and settlement houses. First one opened in Burroughs Adding Machine Company factory. ca. November.

1906 Hoyt Henshaw Stevens library for sick children donated by Mr. and Mrs. F. W. Stevens. January 18.
First permanent branch building erected by Commission at Field and Agnes opened June 1.

1907 Voters rejected Carnegie gift offer, but approved $750,-000 Library bond issue. April 1.
Option taken on DAC property, Woodward near Forest, for new Main Library site. December.

1909 Mrs. F. W. Stevens donated Mary E. Brewer library for invalids. May 5.
Scripps branch at Grand River and Trumbull opened. Land and building donated by James E. Scripps and family. July 1.
Circulation of books through branches exceeded that at Main Library for first time.

1910 Carnegie offer accepted by Common Council. First Library bonds issued and sold for acquisition of branch sites. March 22.
Medical collection turned over to Wayne County Medical Society. August 24.
Commission is committed to Main Library site in what became the Cultural Center. Options on DAC property allowed to lapse. ca. December 20.

1911 Options sought for new Main Library site in Woodward-Cass-Kirby-Putnam block. May 3.
Adam Strohm appointed first assistant librarian. October 11.
Department of Blind opened at Scripps branch. November 9.
Order Department established. December 28.

1912 Non-residents granted right to withdraw books upon payment of $1 annual fee.
Rule requiring guarantor for card holders dropped except in case of children.
Open shelf room opened. April 17.
First parcel of property in new Main Library site acquired

by purchase. Condemnation proceedings on remainder started in 1913. June 9.

Henry M. Utley retired. November 1.

Proposed pension plan for Library employees drafted by Commissioner Osius. November 5.

Commission adopted policy of naming branches for commissioners and other prominent persons instead of designating them by number. December 17.

Lothrop branch, West Grand Boulevard at Warren, first to be completed under Carnegie program, opened December 12. Bowen branch, West Grand Boulevard at Vernor, opened December 28. Utley branch, Woodward at King, opened May 20, 1913.

1913   Adam Strohm appointed librarian. July 1.

Architectural contract for new Main Library awarded Cass Gilbert. December 22.

1913–   Library's fiscal year changed to July 1–June 30 to con-
14   form to that of city government.

1914   Extension Department became Stations Department. February 3.

Burton Historical Collection established by donation by Clarence M. Burton of his private library of local and regional history. March 16.

Children's Department reorganized under one head. Schools division created. May 5.

1915   New Main Library excavation contract awarded January 4. Ground broken January 12.

Structural steel contract let for new Main Library. May 13. Framework was up by end of year, after which work was suspended for three years. Delay due to World War I, financing difficulties, labor and transportation shortages.

Library acquired small truck, its first piece of automotive equipment. June 1.

Civics division established. Later became Sociology and Economics Department.

1915–   Library played important part in Americanization pro-
25   gram for benefit of city's foreign-born population.

1916 Delay in completing new Main Library became an issue in mayoralty campaign and in 1917 the subject of a grand jury investigation.
Art Museum branch opened October 3. Turned over to Arts Commission July 1, 1947.

1917 Death of Henry M. Utley. February 17.
United States enters World War I. Library called upon to furnish many new home front services. April 6.
Bernard Ginsburg branch opened; last branch built under Carnegie program. May 15.
Branch libraries closed mornings to conserve coal.
State legislature provided for establishment of county libraries.
Technology Department established. September.
Library Service, DPL publication, first issued. September 22.
Cornerstone of new Main Library laid. November 1.

1918 Branch opened in Board of Commerce office; origin of Business and Finance Department. January.
Detroit adopted new city charter. June 25.

1919 Question answering service by telephone inaugurated.
Centre Park suggested as site for joint branch library and Board of Education office building. December 16.

1920 Branch and Station Departments combined to form Extension Department. May 11.
Wayne County Library organized under supervision of Detroit Public Library. December 1.

1921 Diary of George Washington presented to Library by Henry B. Joy. January 4.
Main Library opened for public use. March 29. Formally dedicated. June 3.
Completion of new Main Library made possible establishment of Music and Drama, and Fine Arts departments.
C. M. Burton set up endowment fund for support of Burton Historical Collection. August 16.

State Law placed Library budget under supervision of mayor and Common Council.
Centre Park library became known as Downtown Annex.

1923 Wayne County Medical Society medical library transferred to Detroit College of Medicine building under supervision of Detroit Public Library. Became Medical Science Department. May 1.
Downtown Annex moved to old police headquarters at Randolph and Farmer, site of present Water Board building. November 15.

1924 Commercial branch moved from Board of Commerce to Downtown Annex. Became Business and Commerce division. January.
Milo M. Quaife, noted historian, appointed editor of Burton Historical Collection. April 1.

1925 Parent-Teachers room opened. Collection later became part of Schools Department.
Office of business manager created. July 1.

1926 Educational Director of Reading, and Readers' Adviser posts created. June 3.
Plans for joint Library-Board of Education building in Centre Park abandoned.

1927 Quarters rented in Barlum Tower for Downtown Annex. December 6.

1927– Home circulation for fiscal year was more than 5,000,000
28 books.

1928 Ralph A. Ulveling appointed Extension librarian. July 1.
Newspaper reading room opened in rented quarters at 130 Cadillac Square. October 23.

1929 Centre Park building ordered razed. November 19.

1930 Self-charging system for charging out books pioneered by Detroit Public Library.
Right to Centre Park transferred to Library by Board of Education. October 14.

1930– General period of economic depression. Library income
35 drastically reduced while service demands from unemployed result in increased patronage.

1931 Staff Association organized. May.
Factory stations discontinued.
Training class discontinued.

1932 New Downtown Library in Centre Park, built in 1931, opened for use. January 4.
25-cent registration fee charged adults. June 7.
Department of Blind transferred to Wayne County Library. July 1.
Death of C. M. Burton. October 23.
State adopted 15-mill tax limitation amendment to constitution; eventually resulted in curtailment of Library income. November 8.

1934 25-cent registration fee discontinued. March 15.
Library pioneers in new type of readers' advisory service.

1935– Library benefits from federal work relief programs.
36

1936 Library employees' credit union established.

1937 Henry Glover Stevens Memorial Library, covering field of social work, donated to Public Library. April 6.
Pension plan for Library employees adopted. June 8.
Staff Memorial and Fellowship Association incorporated. November 30.

1938 Library "goes on the air" with regular radio programs.
Technology Department moved into Farr building, Putnam at Cass. ca. February 15.
Library received first state aid grant. July 1. Aid program discontinued in 1939, but resumed in 1941–42 fiscal year and thereafter maintained regularly.

1940 Bookmobile service started. February 5.
Library observes its 75th anniversary. June 30.
Book collection exceeds 1,000,000 volumes. June 30.

1941 Adam Strohm retired as librarian. June 30. Succeeded by

Ralph A. Ulveling. Charles M. Mohrhardt made associate librarian.
United States enters World War II, December 7. For next four years the Library fulfilled significant home front role, particularly in field of technology reference service to local war industry.
Hurlbut branch in Water Works Park permanently closed when park was closed to public as war security measure. December 8.

1942   Library made depository for Library of Congress catalog. Library pioneered in development of Reader-Interest classification.
Friends of the Detroit Public Library, Inc. organized. September 24.

1943   United States troops quartered on Main Library grounds during race riots. June 20–30.
Wayne County Library cut ties with Detroit system and became independent agency. December 1.
Nucleus of E. Azalia Hackley Memorial Collection of Negro music, dance and drama presented to Library by Detroit Musicians Association. December 10.

1944   Automotive History Collection established. February 1.
Cass Gilbert, Jr. and Francis Keally named architects for Main Library addition. July 1.
Telephone reference desk set up in General Reference room.
Youth Service Division created for teenage readers.

1945   Municipal Reference Library opened. April 9.
Departmental reorganization started. Completed 1949.

1946   Library employees included in general city employees benefit program. June 4.
Army Map Service makes Library depository for 50,000 maps.

1947   Ceiling projectors made available for bedridden people. ca. March 18.

IBM machines installed for control of book circulation. ca. June 3.

Films and film strips made available by Library.

1948 General Information and Home Reading departments established.

Rare Book room dedicated. October 12.

1949 Medical Science Department turned over to Wayne State University College of Medicine. January 1.

Detroit voters adopt city charter amendment allowing supplementary appropriations over the 15-mill limit. April 4.

Contract with eight suburban libraries to furnish them with film service. June 21.

Joint Union Catalog discontinued. July 1.

As the result of departmental reorganization, Language and Literature, and History and Travel departments created.

1950 Benjamin Franklin branch opened; first functionally designed branch in which Detroit system pioneered. January 4.

Philosophy, Religion and Education Department established. March.

Special hospital service begun at Harper Hospital. November 1

1951 Florine Whitaker Richardson became first woman elected to Library Commission. March 20.

Death of Adam Strohm. October 30.

1952 John Crerar Library labor collection acquired.

1953 Automotive History Collection given divisional status. ca. September.

1955 Adam Strohm Hall dedicated. March 2.

Edgar DeWitt Jones collection of Lincolniana presented by C. Allen Harlan. June 7.

WTVS-Channel 56 educational television station dedicated. Library produces its first program. October 27.

1956 Cooperative arrangement with University of Michigan

School of Library Science for pre-professional training in Detroit. ca. September 18.

1957   Authorize first issue of Library bonds to finance new Main Library addition. January 15.
Detroit Public Library-Wayne State University library joint Acquisitions Committee organized.

1958   Contract for inter-library loan service with Oak Park. First such contractual arrangement with suburbs. ca. April 15.
Abraham Lincoln statue placed on north grounds of Downtown Library. April 16.
First contract awarded for new Main Library addition. July 8.

1959   New bindery and service building occupied at Edsel Ford and Third. September 27.
Commission proposed system of state reimbursement for metropolitan area reference service. October 20.

1962   Reciprocal experimental agreement between Detroit and three area libraries to honor borrowers' cards. January 1.
Library designated "fallout shelter" by Office of Civil Defense. September 18.

1963   Business and Finance Department moved from Downtown Library to Main Library.
Main Library wings and addition dedicated. June 23.
Farr building, Putnam at Cass, razed.

APPENDIX B

Henry Chaney	1865–1878
Manasseh Hickey	1878–1880
Henry Gillman	1880–1885
Henry Munson Utley	1885–1912
Adam J. Strohm	1912–1941
Ralph A. Ulveling	1941–

APPENDIX C

Sidney D. Miller	1865, 1869–70
Robert W. King	1865, 1872
Herman Kiefer	1865
William D. Wilkins	1866, 1871, 1873, 1875–76
George M. Rich	1866
Stephen B. McCracken	1866
David O. Farrand	1867, 1870
Ervin Palmer	1867
Andrew Stutee	1867
Charles K. Backus	1868–71
James A. Brown	1868–69
James M. Welch	1868
William Y. Rumney	1871–73
James W. Bartlett	1870
William Jennison	1872–73
James W. Romeyn	1874–75
John W. McGrath	1874
James J. Martin	1874, 1876

John W. Strong	1875
John T. Liggett	1875–76
Willard M. Lillibridge	1875
Henry F. Lyster	1876–77
Joseph Nicholson	1876
David J. Workum	1876
Robert E. Roberts	1877–79
William N. LaDue	1877
Charles A. Kent	1877–79
Andrew Borrowman	1877–78
Alfred Chesebrough	1878–80
John S. Schmittdiel	1878–79
Richard DoRan	1879
Joseph D. Sutton	1880
William A. Owen	1880
Theodore F. Kerr	1880
Overton L. Kinney	1880

APPENDIX D

James V. Campbell	1881–89
Alfred Chesebrough	1881–84
Herman Kiefer	1881–83
Alexander Lewis	1881–87
George V.N. Lothrop	1881–85
William D. Wilkins	1881–82
Levi L. Barbour	1882–89
Magnus Butzel	1883–1900
Herbert Bowen	1885–97, 1905–10
Joseph A. Marsh	1885–86
George S. Hosmer	1886–96
Richard Storrs Willis	1888–99
Henry A. Harmon	1889–98
Edwin F. Conely	1890–95
C. Henri Leonard	1896–1901
John S. Gray	1897–1902
John E. Clark	1898–1903
Maynard D. Follin	1899–1904
James E. Scripps	1900–05
George Osius	1900–12

427

Eugene A. Bresler	1902–07
Sidney T. Miller	1903–08
Divie B. Duffield	1904–15, 1920–35
Ralph Phelps, Jr.	1906–17
Hinton E. Spalding	1908–13
Bernard Ginsburg	1909–14
Clarence A. Black	1911–13
Paul R. Gray	1913–24
Charles R. Robertson	1914–28
Edward S. Piggins	1914–19
Johnston B. Kennedy	1915–26
Charles J. Thiry	1916–18
David E. Heineman	1918–20
John R. Russel	1918–20
Wilfred C. Leland	1919
John A. Russell	1920–25
Clarence A. Lightner	1920–29
John F. O'Hara	1925–30
Andrew P. Biddle	1926–44
Charles S. Kennedy	1926, 1933–45
Leo M. Franklin	1927–48
M. Hubert O'Brien	1929–43
Edwin S. George	1930–51
Daniel J. Healy	1931–33
Frank H. Alfred	1935–37
Edward J. Poselius	1938–46
Oscar C. Hull	1943–44
Lawrence Reynolds	1944–61
Thomas G. Long	1944–

Harvey M. Merker	1946–
Henry J. Brennan	1946–62
Henry Meyers	1948–52
Florine W. Richardson	1951–59
Leon Fram	1953–
Mildred M. Jeffrey	1959–
Lola Jeffries Hanavan	1961–
John Dancey	1962–

APPENDIX E

MEMBERS EX OFFICIO,
DETROIT LIBRARY COMMISSION, 1881–1965

Michael Firnane	1881–82
Carlos E. Warner	1882–83
Charles I. Walker	1883–85
George Gartner	1885–86
Henry A. Harmon	1886–87
William V. Moore	1887–89
William Voigt	1889–90
William Adair	1890–91, 1892–93
Benjamin R. Hoyt	1891–92
James W. Seely	1893–94
John E. Clark	1894–96
Caleb S. Pitkin	1896–97
Thomas G. Craig	1897–98
Thomas Henderson	1898–99
Horace G. Smith	1899–1900
Edward F. Marschner	1900–1902
Lumus C. Newton	1902–03
Gilbert P. Johnson	1903–04
Joseph Shivers	1904–05

Simpson C. Leonard	1905–07
Charles J. George	1907–09
Charles F. Kuhn	1909–10
Charles R. Robertson	1910–12
Hiram C. Goldberg	1912–13
Albert McMichael	1913–16
George W. Auch	1916–17
Samuel C. Mumford	1917–18, 1925–26
Andrew P. Biddle	1918–19
John S. Hall	1919–20
Joseph S. Stringham	1920–21
Edward D. Devine	1921–22
Frank H. Alfred	1922–23
Laura F. Osborn	1923–24, 1928–29, 1933–34, 1940–41, 1947–48, 1952–53
Allen Campbell	1924–25, 1926–27
John H. Webster	1927–28, 1935–36, 1941–42, 1948–49
Frank A. Gorman	1929–30, 1932–33, 1936–37, 1942–43
Burt R. Shurly	1930–31, 1937–38, 1943–44, 1949–50
A. Douglas Jamieson	1931–32, 1939–40, 1946–47, 1951–52
Angus McLean	1934–35
Oscar C. Hull	1938–39
Clark D. Brooks	1944–45, 1950–51
Howell Van Auken	1945–46
Jane H. Lovejoy	1953–54

Louise C. Grace	1954–55, 1959–60
William D. Merrifield	1956–57, 1962–63
Leonard Kasle	1957–58, 1963–64
Remus G. Robinson	1958–59
Gladys F. Canty	1960–61
Betty S. Becker	1955–56, 1961–62

APPENDIX F

* Mr. Bulkley died in June 1958.
(Note: Terms begin following annual meeting in May of each year.)

APPENDIX G

MAIN LIBRARY

Opened March 25, 1865, in the Detroit High School which was originally the State Capitol building at State and Griswold (Capitol Park). Moved January 22, 1877, into new building erected for Library purposes in Centre Park, Gratiot at Farmer. Present Main Library opened March 21, 1921, at Woodward and Kirby avenues. Enlarged portion opened June 23, 1963.

DOWNTOWN LIBRARY

The building was completed in 1931 and opened to the public January 4, 1932, on the site of the Centre Park main library which was torn down in 1929. Between 1929 and 1932 temporary quarters were occupied in the old police headquarters (site of the Water Board Building) and in the Barlum Tower (now Cadillac Tower).

SERVICE SHOPS

Maintenance departments were originally housed in the Centre Park building and after 1921 in the Main Library. Space for the bindery was provided in a room in the basement of the Centre

434

Park Library, and a bindery room was included in the 1921 Main Library. Need for space, however, made it necessary to provide outside quarters for the bindery, and from 1925 to 1955 it was housed in rented quarters in the municipal garage at East Jefferson and Dubois Street. In 1955 it was moved to rented quarters at 650 West Baltimore where it remained until 1958 when the Service Shops building, which includes maintenance departments and the bindery was opened in a building constructed for that purpose at 5828 Third Avenue.

BRANCHES

ART MUSEUM. Opened in the old Art Museum, East Jefferson at Hastings, October 1916. Quartered in the present Detroit Institute of Arts when that building was completed in 1927. Administration of the branch and its collection given to the Arts Commission, July 1, 1947.

BOARD OF COMMERCE. Opened in 1918 in the offices of the Detroit Board of Commerce. Moved in January 1924 to Downtown Library as part of the Business and Commerce Department.

HERBERT BOWEN. Originally designated Branch 3, it was opened in Western High School October 25, 1900. Moved to 464 Dix Avenue, February 1907. Moved to present building, West Grand Boulevard at West Vernor Highway December 28, 1912. Named for a member of the Library Commission.

MAGNUS BUTZEL. Originally designated Branch 10, it was opened in its present building at East Grand Boulevard at Harper Avenue, October 13, 1913. Named for a member of the Library Commission.

JAMES VALENTINE CAMPBELL. Originally Branch 8, it was opened in a rented store building at West End Avenue near West Jefferson, September 1, 1907. It was also known as the Delray branch and the West Fort Street branch. It was moved to 3327

West Jefferson, January 1, 1910, and to 1503 West Fort, September, 1913. The present building was occupied January 4, 1922, at West Fort Street and Rademacher Avenue. Named in honor of the first president of the Library Commission.

CHANDLER PARK. Opened March 23, 1957, in a building erected for that purpose at 12800 Harper Avenue. Named for the area of the city which the branch serves.

HENRY CHANEY. Opened June 30, 1955, in a building constructed for branch purposes at 16101 Grand River at Mansfield. Named in honor of Detroit Public Library's first librarian.

JESSIE C. CHASE. Opened July 24, 1952, in a building erected as a branch at 17731 West Seven Mile Road. Named in honor of Jessie Clara Chase, the Library's first superintendent of branches.

EDWIN F. CONELY. Opened as Branch 6 on October 1, 1908, at 1479 Michigan Avenue. Moved to its present building at 4600 Martin Avenue September 15, 1913. Named in honor of an early member of the Library Commission.

DIVIE B. DUFFIELD. Opened November 24, 1916, in a building erected by the Library Commission for branch purposes at 2507 West Grand Boulevard. Named for a member of the Library Commission.

THOMAS A. EDISON. Opened December 9, 1948, in rented quarters. Moved to its present permanent location, 18400 Joy Road on January 25, 1955. Named for the American scientist and inventor who, as a boy, was a patron of the Detroit Public Library.

BENJAMIN FRANKLIN. Opened January 23, 1929, as the Outer Drive branch, one block north of the present location at 13651 East McNichols Road. Closed temporarily in 1932, but reopened one month later with funds raised by residents of the neighborhood. Moved to present location January 24, 1950. This was the first of the Detroit Public Library's functionally-designed modern branches. It was named for the great American statesman, philosopher and man of letters.

BERNARD GINSBURG. Opened as Branch 11 in rented quarters at 540 Hastings Street, December 1913. Moved to a permanent building at 91 Brewster Street, between St. Antoine and Hastings, May 15, 1917. Because of declining patronage, this building was turned over to the Recreation Department in May 1927 and the branch was re-located in a rented store on Hastings. It remained there until November 1928 when the branch was closed permanently. Named for a member of the Library Commission.

JOHN S. GRAY. Opened as Branch 4 in temporary quarters at Field and Agnes, February 1, 1904. Removed to present location, 1117 Field, June 1, 1906. Named for a member of the Library Commission.

GEORGE S. HOSMER. Opened as Branch 2, April 16, 1900, in the Harris School, Pulford Avenue, then being used as a high school pending completion of Eastern High School. Moved to rented quarters on Gratiot near McDougall, January, 1903, and to a permanent branch building at Gratiot and Pulford, January 7, 1911. Closed May 30, 1932, the building being turned over to the Board of Health. Named for a well-known jurist and member of the Library Commission.

BELA HUBBARD. Opened February 15, 1951, in rented quarters on West McNichols at Southfield. Moved to present permanent library building, 12929 West McNichols, September 10, 1953. Bela Hubbard, for whom the branch was named was a geologist, explorer, writer, large landowner and Detroit civic leader.

CHAUNCEY HURLBUT. Opened as a deposit station in Water Works Park in 1900. Became a full branch, Number 7, in September 1905. Closed for reasons of national security during

World War I, and again for reasons of economy from 1932 to 1936. On December 8, 1941, the day after the attack on Pearl Harbor, the branch was again closed for security reasons. It was not reopened at the close of World War II. The branch was named for Chauncey Hurlbut, a president of the Water Board, who bequeathed funds for the improvement of Water Works Park and construction of a library building in the park.

THOMAS JEFFERSON. Opened in rented quarters on Warren Avenue, September 27, 1937, as the East Warren branch. Removed to present location, 12350 East Outer Drive, October 4, 1951, the first National Library Day. Named for the author of the Declaration of Independence and third President of the United States.

ELISABETH KNAPP. Opened October 3, 1950, at 13330 Conant near Davison. Named in honor of the Library's first supervisor of children's work and chief of the Children's Department.

ABRAHAM LINCOLN. Opened October 18, 1926, in rented quarters as the North Woodward branch on Woodward near Seven Mile Road. Later moved to Seven Mile and John R where it remained until October 29, 1951, when it was established in a permanent building at 1221 East Seven Mile Road. Named for the sixteenth President of the United States.

GEORGE V.N. LOTHROP. Opened as Branch 9, December 12, 1912, in a building erected for the purpose at West Grand Boulevard and Warren Avenue. Named in honor of George Van Ness Lothrop, member of the Library Commission and ambassador to Russia.

MARK TWAIN. Opened February 22, 1940, on the site of the former George Osius branch, 8500 Gratiot at Burns. Named in honor of the American author and humorist.

MEDICAL SCIENCE. Established in the Centre Park Library as the Medical Collection in 1895 when the Detroit Medical and Library Association turned its books over to the Detroit Public Library. In 1910, the collection was transferred as a permanent loan to the Wayne County Medical Society and housed in its headquarters at 33 High Street. On October 22, 1923, the collection was transferred to the Detroit College of Medicine and Surgery, 625 Mullett Street, where it was administered as a branch by the Detroit Public Library. On July 1, 1949, the entire collection was turned over to the Wayne State University College of Medicine.

MONNIER. Opened January 11, 1926, in a building formerly used as a school, and leased from the Board of Education until March 1, 1949, when the building was transferred to the Library Commission. It is located at 13600 Grand River at Schaefer Road. The branch takes its name from the Monnier School which was named after William A. Monnier, builder and land developer in northwest Detroit.

JOHN MONTEITH. Opened May 1, 1926, at Kercheval and Eastlawn. It was the first regional branch. Named in honor of the first president of the University of Michigan.

MUNICIPAL REFERENCE LIBRARY. Opened April 9, 1945, in the Water Board Building as a service intended primarily for the city's governmental offices. Moved in 1955 to its present location on the tenth floor of the City-County Building, 2 Woodward Avenue.

GEORGE OSIUS. Opened as Branch 12 in September, 1914, at Gratiot and Burns. Building demolished in 1939 because of widening of Gratiot Avenue. Replaced by the Mark Twain Branch, 8500 Gratiot. Named for a member of the Detroit Library Commission.

FRANCIS PARKMAN. Opened as the Oakman branch, November 1, 1922, in rented quarters on Woodrow Wilson. Moved to its present building at 1766 Oakman Boulevard near Linwood April 16, 1931. Named in honor of the American historian.

REDFORD. Opened November 23, 1926, at 21511 West Mc-Nichols at Grand River in a new building intended for the Redford village hall. The building was turned over to the Library Commission when Redford was annexed by the City of Detroit. It is named for the area it serves.

GABRIEL RICHARD. Opened February 5, 1923, in a building erected for the purpose at 9876 Grand River at Stoepel. It was named in honor of the pioneer rector of St. Anne's Roman Catholic Church, who was also one of Michigan's earliest educators, the first vice president of the University of Michigan, and the first bishop-designate of the Detroit diocese.

ROGER WILLIAMS. Originally designated the Brightmoor Branch, it was opened in February 1927, in rented quarters on Fenkell Avenue a block from its present location. It was closed because of the depression in 1932, and reopened as the Fenkell Avenue branch, October 7, 1937 in a former branch bank building at 20845 Fenkell near Burt Road. In October, 1941, the building was purchased by the Library Commission, and the branch was then given its present name in honor of the founder of Rhode Island and a pioneer advocate of religious liberty.

HENRY R. SCHOOLCRAFT. Opened in a building constructed for its use at Davison and Lumkin avenues, November 22, 1921. It was closed permanently October 23, 1947, and the building was sold to the Department of Parks and Recreation. The area is now served by the Elisabeth Knapp branch. The Schoolcraft branch was named for Henry Rowe Schoolcraft, pioneer explorer, scientist and authority on the Indians.

JAMES E. SCRIPPS. Opened March 1, 1904, as Branch 5 in a rented store at Grand River and Calumet. Moved July 3, 1909, to the former residence of George G. Booth, in Scripps Park which was donated to the city by the Scripps-Booth family. It was closed because of financial conditions June 30, 1932, but the children's room was reopened May 11, 1935. The premises were shared by the Wayne County Library from 1921 to 1959 when the building was vacated. The Scripps branch housed the Department of the Blind from 1910 to 1919, and again in 1932 when services for the blind were turned over to the Wayne County Library. The branch was named for the founder of the Detroit *News* who was also a member of the Library Commission.

SHERWOOD FOREST. Opened August 17, 1942, in rented quarters on Livernois Avenue. Moved to a temporary building on the present site at 7117 West Seven Mile Road in September 1945. A permanent building was opened February 20, 1951. Named for the area of the city which it serves which, in turn, was named for the English forest which was the legendary seat of operations of Robin Hood.

SPRINGWELLS AVENUE. Opened in rented quarters as a sub-branch on Springwells Avenue at Senator. Established as a regular branch July 1, 1929, and closed permanently because of the depression May 30, 1932.

HENRY M. UTLEY. Opened as Branch 1, April 2, 1900, in Central High School. Moved to rented store quarters at 1519 Woodward Avenue between West Grand Boulevard and Milwaukee Avenue, March, 1905. Moved to present building at 8726 Woodward at Alger, May 30, 1913. Named in honor of Henry Munson Utley, librarian from 1885 to 1912.

CHARLES IRISH WALKER. Opened November 30, 1921, at 10720 Mack Avenue at Montclair. Named in honor of Charles I. Walker, president of the Detroit Board of Education and ex officio member of the Library Commission.

LAURA INGALLS WILDER. Opened in rented quarters at 6815 East Seven Mile Road, May 12, 1949. Named for the noted American writer of children's stories of pioneer life.

441

NOTES

In the Notes the abbreviations used are DPL for Detroit Public Library and DBE for Detroit Board of Education.

Chapter 1

1. Detroit *Advertiser & Tribune,* March 24, 1865.
2. *Ibid.*
3. Detroit *Advertiser & Tribune* and Detroit *Free Press,* various issues, January–March 1865.
4. DPL, *A Brief Historical Summary* (Detroit, 1887), pp. 4–11.
5. Detroit *Free Press,* March 2, 1865.
6. Detroit *Advertiser & Tribune,* March 27, 1865.
7. *Annual Report, DBE, 1864,* Report of the Committee on Library, pp. 23–27.
8. *Ibid.* Also see *Annual Report, DBE, 1866.*
9. Farmer, Silas, *The History of Detroit and Michigan* (Detroit, 1884), pp. 474–75.
10. Catlin, George B., *The Story of Detroit* (Detroit, 1926), pp. 461–62.
11. Detroit *Free Press,* August 26, 1863.
12. Detroit *Free Press,* March 26, 1865.
13. Detroit *Advertiser & Tribune,* March 27, 1865.
14. *Annual Report, DBE, 1860,* Report of the Library Committee, pp. 103–5.
15. *Annual Report, DBE, 1863,* Report of the Committee on Library, pp. 3–9.
16. *Annual Report, DBE, 1865,* Report of the Committee on Library, p. 20.
17. *DPL, Annual Report, 1950–51,* p. 10. (Cited hereafter as *Annual Report*)
18. *Annual Report, DBE, 1865,* Report of the Committee on Library, p. 17.

Chapter 2

1. Woodford, Frank B., *Yankees in Wonderland* (Detroit, 1951), pp. 11–13.
2. Quaife, M. M. and Glazer, Sidney, *Michigan* (New York, 1948), pp. 149–50.
3. Smith, Alice Elizabeth, *James Duane Doty, Frontier Promoter* (Madison, 1954), p. 39.
4. Kirkland, Caroline Matilda, *A New Home or Life in the Clearings* (Introduction by John Nerber) (New York, 1953), pp. 5, 6.
5. De Tocqueville, Alexis, *Democracy in America* (2 vols.; Paris, 1838), (modern text New York, 1945), I, 316–17.
6. Woodford, Frank B., *Lewis Cass—The Last Jeffersonian* (New Brunswick, 1950), p. 161.
7. Woodford, Frank B., *Mr. Jefferson's Disciple—A Life of Justice Woodward* (East Lansing, 1953), pp. 145–64.
8. Woodford, *Lewis Cass,* p. 162; Cooley, Thomas McIntyre, *Michigan* (Boston, 1885), pp. 306–29.
9. De Tocqueville, *op. cit.,* II, 363.
10. J. D. Doty to H. R. Schoolcraft, Detroit, September 27, 1822, in *Territorial Papers of the United States,* ed. C. E. Carter, XII, 268.
11. Henry Whiting to H. R. Schoolcraft, Detroit, June 2, 1829, *Territorial Papers of the United States,* XII, 46.
12. M. L. Woolsey to H. R. Schoolcraft, Detroit, September 27, 1831, *Territorial Papers of the United States,* XII, 352.
13. Woodford, *Mr. Jefferson's Disciple,* p. 127.
14. Woodford, *Yankees in Wonderland,* p. 27.
15. Bald, F. Clever, *Detroit's First American Decade* (Ann Arbor, 1948), pp. 91–92.
16. Bidlack, Russell E., *The City Library of Detroit, 1817–1837* (Ann Arbor, 1955), p. 5.
17. *Annual Report, DBE, 1866,* Report of the Committee on Library, p. 16.
18. Gabriel Richard to Governor and Judges, Detroit, October 18, 1808, in Michigan State Archives, Lansing.
19. Bidlack, *op. cit.,* pp. 5–14.
20. *Ibid.,* pp. 26–29.
21. Farmer, *The History of Detroit. . . . ,* pp. 710–11.
22. *Ibid.,* p. 712.
23. Detroit *Advertiser & Tribune,* June 12, 1866.
24. *Annual Report, DBE, 1860,* Report of the Library Committee, p. 7.
25. *Annual Report, DBE, 1863,* Report of the Committee on Library, p. 20.
26. *Ibid.,* pp. 29–30.

27. Detroit *Free Press,* September 24, 1871.
28. *Annual Reports, 1882,* p. 120; *1886,* pp. 84–85.

Chapter 3

1. Cooley, *Michigan,* p. 211.
2. Fuller, George M. (ed.), *Historic Michigan* (n. p., 1924), I, 247.
3. Dorr, Harold M. (ed.), *The Michigan Constitutional Conventions of 1835–36* (Ann Arbor, 1940), p. 32.
4. Bald, F. Clever, *Michigan in Four Centuries* (New York, 1954), p. 196.
5. Cooley, *op. cit.,* p. 306.
6. Dorr, *op. cit.,* p. 17.
7. Cooley, *op. cit.,* p. 306.
8. Bald, *op. cit.,* p. 198.
9. Wing, Talcott, *History of Monroe County Michigan* (New York, 1890), pp. 136, 491.
10. Farmer, *The History of Detroit. . . . ,* p. 759. Lanman, Charles, *The Red Book of Michigan* (Detroit, 1871), p. 437. Monroe *Evening News,* December 12, 1958.
11. Dorr, *op. cit.,* p. 67.
12. *Ibid.,* p. 479.
13. *Ibid.,* p. 340.
14. State of New York, *Compiled Laws of 1825,* Ch. 203, Sec. 2.
15. State of Michigan, *Journal of the House of Representatives 1837,* Report of the Superintendent of Public Instruction, Document No. 7, p. 546.
16. "Historical Development of Public Libraries in Michigan," typescript in DPL, Librarian's Office Correspondence 1933, General Libraries folder, Box 16. See also Howland, Delores L., "History of the Township Library, 1835–50," (University of Michigan School of Library Science, n. d.), typescript furnished by Russell E. Bidlack, Department of Library Science, Ann Arbor, pp. 1–25.

Chapter 4

1. Farmer, *The History of Detroit. . . . ,* pp. 737–40.
2. Burton, Clarence M. (ed.), *The City of Detroit, Michigan* (4 vols.; Detroit–Chicago, 1922), I, 736–38.
3. *Acts of the Legislature of the State of Michigan Passed at the Annual Session of 1842* (Detroit, 1842).
4. Farmer, *op. cit.,* pp. 759–61.
5. *Annual Report, DBE, 1860,* Report of the Library Committee, p. 100.
6. *Annual Report, DBE, 1860,* Fines and Recognizances and Library Fund, pp. 34–35.

7. *Annual Report, DBE, 1855,* p. 30.
8. *Annual Report, DBE, 1860,* Report of the Library Committee, pp. 100–1.
9. *Ibid.,* p. 101.
10. *Ibid.,* p. 102.
11. *Annual Report, DBE, 1862,* Report of the Library Committee, pp. 30–32.
12. DPL, *A Brief Historical Summary,* pp. 10–11.
13. Detroit *Post,* December 24, 1867.
14. Detroit Common Council, *Journal 1866–1867,* p. 132.
15. Detroit *Advertiser & Tribune,* October 20, 1868.
16. *Annual Reports, DBE, 1868,* Report of the Committee on Library, p. 13; *1869,* p. 14.
17. Detroit Library Commission, *Proceedings,* November 21, 1895, p. 486. (Cited hereafter as *Proceedings,* with the date.)
18. *Proceedings,* September 16, 1897, pp. 2–9.
19. *Proceedings,* September 7, 1905, pp. 93–96.

Chapter 5

1. *Annual Report, DBE, 1865,* Report of the Committee on Library, p. 19.
2. *Annual Report, DBE, 1866,* Report of the Committee on Library, p. 14.
3. *Ibid.,* p. 15.
4. Detroit *Free Press,* March 17, 1866.
5. *Annual Report, DBE, 1868,* Report of the Committee on Library, p. 18.
6. Detroit *Post,* December 24, 1867. Detroit *Free Press,* June 10, 1871. *Annual Report, DBE, 1866,* p. 6.
7. *Annual Report, DBE, 1869,* Report of the Committee on Library, p. 16.
8. Detroit *Post,* December 24, 1867.
9. Detroit *Free Press,* September 25, 1868.
10. *Annual Report, DBE, 1869,* Report of the Committee on Library, p. 18.
11. Detroit *Free Press,* December 6, 1870.
12. Lodge, John C. and Quaife, M. M., *I Remember Detroit* (Detroit, 1949), p. 25.
13. *Annual Report, DBE, 1871,* Report of the Committee on Library, pp. 22–23.
14. Detroit *Daily Union,* May 15, 1869.
15. *Annual Report, DBE, 1870,* Report of the Committee on Library, p. 21.
16. Detroit *Free Press,* June 10, 1870.

445

17. Detroit *Free Press,* October 25, 1870.
18. *Annual Report, DBE, 1871,* Report of the Committee on Library, pp. 25–26.
19. Woodford, Frank B. and Hyma, Albert, *Gabriel Richard—Frontier Ambassador* (Detroit, 1958), p. 123.
20. Catlin, *The Story of Detroit,* p. 420.
21. Detroit Common Council, *Journal . . . 1872,* p. 75.
22. *Ibid.,* p. 115.
23. Detroit *Advertiser & Tribune,* April 17, 1872.
24. *Annual Report, DBE, 1872,* Report of the Committee on Library, p. 21.
25. Detroit *Advertiser & Tribune,* May 7, 1873.
26. Pope, Charles Henry (comp.), *The Cheney Genealogy* (Boston, 1897), pp. 316, 396. Also, *Michigan Pioneer and Historical Collections* (Lansing, 1886), VIII, 117–18.
27. *Annual Report, DBE, 1871,* Report of the Committee on Library, p. 23.
28. Detroit *Free Press,* September 17, 1871. Also, *Annual Report, DBE, 1877,* Report of Committee on Public Library, p. 70.
29. *Annual Report, DBE, 1866,* Report of the Committee on Library, p. 38.
30. Detroit *Free Press,* January 15, 1867.
31. *Sunday News-Tribune,* January 24, 1897.

Chapter 6

1. Detroit *Advertiser & Tribune,* May 8, 1873.
2. Detroit *Free Press,* April 26, 1874.
3. *Annual Report, DBE, 1872,* Report of the Committee on Library, p. 98.
4. Detroit *Free Press,* February 28, 1873.
5. *Ibid.*
6. *Annual Report, DBE, 1873,* Report of the Committee on Library, p. 20.
7. *Acts of the Legislature of the State of Michigan, Regular Session 1873* (Lansing, 1873), Act. No. 313, Sec. 12, Vol. III, 76.
8. Burton, (ed.), *The City of Detroit . . . . ,* I, 331–32.
9. *Annual Report, DBE, 1873,* Report of Committee on Library, p. 20.
10. Detroit *Free Press,* March 28, 1873.
11. Detroit *Free Press,* April 10, 1873.
12. *Annual Report, DBE, 1874,* Report of the Committee on Library, pp. 14–15.
13. *Ibid.,* pp. 16–17.
14. Detroit *Post,* August 25, 1874.

15. *Annual Report, DBE, 1875,* Report of the Committee on Library, p. 68.
16. Balch, George W., "A Paper on the Early History of the Detroit Public Library" (n.p., n.d.), copy attached to *Proceedings,* December 7, 1899.
17. Detroit *Free Press,* April 4, 1875.
18. Detroit *Free Press,* March 30, 1875.
19. Detroit *Free Press,* May 30, 1875.
20. Newspaper clipping, undated, unidentified, in DPL History Notebook, II, 1875–1900.
21. Detroit *Free Press,* January 23, 1877.
22. *Annual Report, DBE, 1877,* Report of the Committee on Library, p. 70.

Chapter 7

1. *Library Service,* III, No. 13 (February 15, 1920), 3.
2. *Proceedings,* July 21, 1887.
3. Detroit *Free Press,* January 21, 1877.
4. *Annual Report, DBE, 1877,* Report of the Committee on Public Library, p. 64.
5. *Proceedings,* November 20, 1890.
6. *Annual Report, DBE, 1877,* Report of the Committee on Public Library, p. 64.
7. *Proceedings,* February 12, 1891.
8. *Annual Report 1887,* p. 16.
9. *Proceedings,* December 14, 1882.
10. *Annual Report 1892,* p. 7.
11. *Annual Report 1893,* pp. 12–13.
12. *Annual Report 1895,* pp. 12–15.
13. *Proceedings,* April 4, 1900; January 10, 1901.
14. *Proceedings,* December 7, December 21, 1893.
15. *Annual Report 1884,* p. 149. *Proceedings,* May 18, 1899.
16. *Annual Report 1885,* p. 74.
17. *Annual Report 1882,* pp. 139–40.
18. *Annual Report 1898,* p. 13.
19. *Annual Report, DBE, 1863,* Report of the Committee on Library, p. 12.
20. *Proceedings,* October 7, 1886.
21. *Proceedings,* October 21, 1886.
22. *Proceedings,* November 18, December 2, 1886.
23. *Proceedings,* February 3, 1887.
24. *Proceedings,* June 20, 1885.
25. *Proceedings,* January 25, December 2, 1886.
26. *Proceedings,* February 3, 1887.

27. *Proceedings,* February 1, 1900.
28. *Annual Report 1942–43,* p. 8. *Main Library Tour Guide* (DPL, 1956), p. 17.
29. Ulveling, Ralph A., Staff Memo, September 24, 1936, DPL Librarian's Correspondence.
30. John Chancellor to Ulveling, Chicago, November 3, 1936, DPL Librarian's Correspondence.
31. Ruth Rutzen, interview with author, March 24, 1964.
32. *Annual Report 1949–50,* p. 9. S. Das Gupta, "American Libraries— Some Impressions," *Annals of Library Science,* III, No. 3 (September 1956), 97.

Chapter 8

1. *Annual Report, DBE, 1870,* Report of the Committee on Library, pp. 76–77.
2. Utley, Henry M., *Handbook of the Detroit Public Library* (Detroit, 1914), pp. 15–16.
3. Farmer, *The History of Detroit. . . . ,* p. 761.
4. *Post & Tribune,* December 28, 1880.
5. *Ibid.*
6. Utley, *op. cit.,* p. 16.
7. *Post & Tribune,* December 28, 1880.
8. Detroit *Free Press,* December 29, 1880.
9. *Post & Tribune,* January 11, 1881.
10. *Post & Tribune,* January 28, 1881.
11. *Post & Tribune,* January 30, 1881.
12. *Post & Tribune,* February 15, 1881.
13. Frederick M. Crunder to H. M. Utley, St. Louis, May 13, 1890, in Librarian's Office Correspondence, Libraries and Librarians to 1891 folder, Box 1.
14. Utley, *op. cit.,* p. 16.
15. *Annual Report 1881.*
16. *Ibid.*
17. Utley, *op. cit.,* p. 17.
18. *Annual Report, DBE, 1878,* Report of the Committee on Public Library, p. 61.
19. Detroit *Journal,* January 2, 1903. Detroit *Tribune,* May 15, 1898.
20. *Post & Tribune,* April 9, 1878.
21. *Post & Tribune,* April 10, 1878.
22. Detroit *Free Press,* April 10, 1878.
23. DPL, *A Brief Historical Summary,* p. 24.
24. *Annual Report, DBE, 1880,* Annual Report of the Committee on Public Library, p. 49.
25. *Annual Report 1881.*

26. Detroit *Free Press,* July 23, 1885. Detroit *Post,* July 23, 1885.
27. Detroit *News,* December 7, 1901.
28. *Ibid. Today,* December 12, 1901. Detroit *Free Press,* December 12, 1901.
29. Detroit *Tribune,* January 17, 1902.

Chapter 9

1. *Proceedings,* October 6, 1904.
2. *Proceedings,* November 3, 1904.
3. *Proceedings,* January 7, 1905.
4. Detroit *Tribune,* January 18, 1886.
5. Detroit *Tribune,* February 22, 1886.
6. Detroit *Tribune,* March 22, 1886.
7. Detroit *Free Press,* March 9, 1886.
8. Detroit *Tribune,* April 2, 1886.
9. *Annual Reports 1888,* p. 13; *1891,* p. 15.
10. *Annual Report 1877,* p. 53. *Proceedings,* February 18, 1880; May 5, 1887; March 15, 1888; April 5, 1900; June 27, 1901; September 8, 1909. Detroit *Free Press,* February 18, 1880; December 21, 1900.
11. *Annual Reports 1884,* p. 62; *1894,* p. 7. *Proceedings,* January 19, 1884; January 25, 1886; November 28, 1890; January 5, March 2, 1893; December 6, 1894; July 30, 1897. *Advertiser & Tribune,* June 5, 1877.
12. *Annual Report 1903,* p. 20. *Proceedings,* February 18, March 4, November 18, 1897; May 7, 1903.
13. *Annual Reports 1893,* pp. 7, 13; *1896,* p. 17. *Proceedings,* November 7, 1895; October 7, 1897; January 6, 1898.
14. *Annual Reports 1884,* p. 151; *1894,* p. 10. Librarian's Office Correspondence, L. E. Stearns to Utley, Madison, Wis., May 9, 1901, Libraries and Librarians folder, 1899, Box 1; Louis K. Gibbs to Bernard Ginsburg, March 8, 1918, Adam Strohm to Gibbs, March 16, 1918, Complaints folder, Box 2.
15. Detroit *Free Press,* May 19, 1895.
16. Detroit *Free Press,* May 8, 1898.
17. Detroit *News-Tribune,* September 4, 1898.
18. *Annual Report 1902,* p. 15.
19. John S. Gray to Utley, Los Angeles, March 16, 1902, Librarian's Office Correspondence, Commission folder, Box 1.
20. *Annual Report 1902,* p. 15.
21. *Ibid. Proceedings,* March 20, 1902.

Chapter 10

1. *Proceedings,* July 6, 1893.
2. *Annual Report 1893,* p. 7.

3. *Sunday News-Tribune,* January 21, 1894.
4. *Annual Report 1896,* p. 15.
5. *Proceedings,* July 18, 1901. *Annual Report 1901,* p. 32.
6. *Proceedings,* March 3, 1898; November 16, 1899; March 15, 1900. *Annual Report 1899,* p. 9. R. Morrison to Utley, April 18, 1900, DPL Correspondence, Extension folder, Box 1.
7. *Annual Reports 1897,* p. 12; *1902,* p. 18; *1905,* p. 17; *1941–42,* p. 7. *Proceedings,* December 21, 1899.
8. *Proceedings,* October 19, 1899.
9. *Proceedings,* January 20, 1900.
10. *Proceedings,* March 15, 1900.
11. *Annual Report 1899,* p. 5.
12. *Annual Report 1902,* p. 19.
13. *Annual Report 1903,* p. 14.
14. *Annual Report 1902,* p. 20.
15. *Proceedings,* January 3, 1903. Utley to Bothrop & Duffield Land Co. Ltd., January 7, 1903, DPL Correspondence Sites folder, Box 1.
16. *Proceedings,* January 14, February 4, 1904.
17. *Proceedings,* February 18, March 4, 1897.
18. *Proceedings,* May 4, June 1, 1899. *Annual Report 1899,* p. 7.
19. *Proceedings,* July 18, 1901. *Annual Report 1901,* p. 32.
20. *Proceedings,* March 5, 1903.
21. *Proceedings,* October 1, December 17, 1903. *Annual Report 1903,* p. 19.
22. *Proceedings,* December 17, 1903.
23. *Annual Report 1909,* p. 36.
24. *Proceedings,* April 18, 1907.
25. *Annual Report 1908,* p. 15.
26. *Proceedings,* January 17, October 10, October 24, November 21, 1901.
27. *Annual Report 1905,* pp. 37–50.
28. *Proceedings,* December 6, 1906. *Annual Report 1906,* p. 14.
29. *Proceedings,* November 22, 1905. *Annual Reports 1908,* p. 15; *1909,* p. 16.
30. *Proceedings,* January 18, 1906.
31. *Annual Report 1909,* p. 10.
32. Aniela Poray to Commission, June 3, 1914, DPL Correspondence, Stations folder, Box 3.
33. Adam Strohm to W. H. Loveling, February 26, 1914, DPL Correspondence, Stations folder, Box 3.
34. *Annual Report 1909,* p. 9.

Chapter 11

1. Reynolds, Robert L., "The Works Are Not Worth One Drop of Human Blood," *American Heritage,* August 1960, pp. 108–9.

2. Hendrick, Burton J., *Miscellaneous Writings of Andrew Carnegie* (Garden City, N. Y., 1933), II, 206.
3. *Ibid.*, p. 210.
4. Koch, Theodore Wesley, *A Book of Carnegie Libraries* (White Plains, N. Y., 1917), pp. 7, 8.
5. *Annual Report 1901*, p. 14.
6. Detroit *Free Press*, July 2, 1901.
7. Detroit *Journal*, February 8, 1901.
8. *Ibid.*
9. C. Henri Leonard Scrapbook, Burton Historical Collection, DPL.
10. *Annual Report 1901*, p. 16.
11. Detroit *Free Press*, July 2, 1901.
12. *Annual Report 1901*, p. 16.
13. Leonard Scrapbook.
14. Detroit *Free Press*, July 2, 1901.
15. Leonard Scrapbook.
16. *Ibid.*
17. DPL Correspondence, Carnegie Corporation 1901–1920 folder, Box 29.
18. *Ibid.*
19. *Proceedings*, July 9, 1901.
20. Detroit *Journal*, July 1, 1901.
21. Detroit *Free Press*, July 3, 1901.
22. Detroit *Free Press*, July 3, July 10, 1901. Detroit *Journal*, July 3, August 15, 1901. Detroit *Tribune*, July 31, 1901.
23. Detroit *Journal*, July 13, July 15, 1901.
24. Brown Craigie to Carnegie, December 5, 1901, Carnegie Corporation microfilm records, DPL Correspondence.
25. *Proceedings*, November 30, December 5, December 12, 1901.
26. Detroit *Journal*, August 15, 1901. *Today*, December 27, 1901.
27. *Proceedings*, November 6, December 23, 1902. *Annual Report 1902*, p. 8. Detroit *Journal*, December 23, 1902. Detroit *Free Press*, December 24, 1902.
28. Sidney T. Miller to Carnegie, May 4, 1903, and James Bertram to Miller, March 23, 1903, Carnegie Corporation microfilms.
29. Miller to Carnegie, May 4, 1903, Carnegie Corporation microfilms.
30. *Proceedings*, April 7, 1904.
31. Carnegie to St. Andrew's Society, June 6, 1904, Carnegie Corporation microfilms.
32. *Proceedings*, March 21, April 18, June 6, 1907.
33. *Proceedings*, January 5, February 7, 1910.
34. Charles Sawyer to Bertram, March 23, 1910, Carnegie Corporation microfilms.
35. *Proceedings*, April 6, 1910.
36. Sawyer to Bertram, April 14, 1910, Carnegie Corporation microfilms.

"Library Bonds Issued by City of Detroit," record furnished by Debt Administration Division, City Controller, October 4, 1963.

Chapter 12

1. *Proceedings,* May 4, May 18, June 8, June 22, 1910.
2. *Proceedings,* November 5, 1912.
3. *Annual Reports 1910,* p. 6; *1914–15,* p. 6.
4. Hill, Frank Pierce, *James Bertram* (New York, 1936), p. 58.
5. *Proceedings,* July 20, 1910.
6. *Annual Report 1911,* p. 20.
7. Bertram to Brett, February 5, February 20, 1915, Carnegie Corporation microfilms.
8. *Proceedings,* March 22, 1911.
9. William T. Dust to Strohm, November 5, 1913, DPL Correspondence, Duffield Branch folder, Box 2.
10. *Annual Report 1916–17,* p. 7.
11. Strohm to Lester, May 5, 1937, Carnegie Corporation microfilms. Lester to Strohm, May 12, 1937, DPL Correspondence, Carnegie Corporation folder, Box 20.
12. *Annual Report 1922–23,* p. 9.
13. *Proceedings,* September 1, 1953.
14. *Annual Report 1924–25,* p. 7.
15. *Ibid.,* p. 12.
16. *Library Service,* III, No. 16 (April 1, 1920).
17. *Library Service* (supplement), III, No. 16 (April 1, 1920).
18. *Proceedings,* March 5, 1957.
19. Ulveling, Ralph A., "Administration of Branch Systems," in *Current Issues in Library Administration,* Carleton B. Joeckel (ed.) (Chicago, 1939), pp. 152–53.
20. *Annual Report 1945–46,* p. 6.
21. Ulveling, "Administration of Branch Systems," p. 160.
22. *Annual Reports 1936–37,* p. 5; *1942–43,* p. 10.
23. *Annual Reports 1944–45,* p. 12; *1946–47,* p. 2.
24. *Annual Reports 1949–50,* p. 3; *1954–55,* p. 1; *1956–57,* p. 3.
25. *Proceedings,* September 17, 1957.
26. *Annual Report 1925–26,* p. 4. Strohm to Detroit *Free Press,* January 16, 1925, DPL Correspondence, Newspaper file, Box 7.
27. *Proceedings,* October 7, 1947. *Annual Report 1946–47,* pp. 2, 9.
28. *Annual Report 1954–55,* p. 1.

Chapter 13

1. *Annual Reports 1886,* p. 79; *1890,* p. 13; *1898,* p. 7; *1900,* p. 18; *1901,* p. 10. *Proceedings,* January 3, 1901.

2. *Annual Report 1903*, pp. 8, 9. *Proceedings*, January 15, 1903.
3. *Annual Report 1904*, p. 9.
4. *Annual Report 1908*, p. 8.
5. Detroit *Journal*, December 24, 1900.
6. *Annual Report 1901*, p. 12.
7. Detroit *News*, July 9, 1901.
8. *Annual Report 1902*, p. 10.
9. *Proceedings*, November 6, December 23, 1902; January 3, 1903.
10. *Proceedings*, January 15, 1901.
11. Burton, (ed.), *The City of Detroit.* . . . , I, 847. DPL Correspondence, Bond Issue folder, Box 29.
12. *Proceedings*, June 22, 1910.
13. *Proceedings*, October 7, 1910; May 3, 1911. Records, Real Estate Division, Corporation Counsel, City of Detroit.
14. William C. Weber to Andrew Carnegie, March 3, 1911, Carnegie Corporation microfilms. Strohm to Charles Moore, November 30, 1914, DPL Correspondence, Museum of Arts folder, Box 1.
15. *Annual Report 1914–15*, p. 7.
16. Report of Special Committee on Site for Main Library Building (c. 1911), DPL Correspondence, Minutes of Meeting in Connection with Site and Building folder, Box 30.
17. *Proceedings*, November 11, 1912.
18. Records of Real Estate Division, Corporation Counsel, City of Detroit. Supplemental data furnished by Wayne County Tract Index Department.
19. *Proceedings*, September 13, October 11, 1912. *Annual Report 1912*, p. 17. *Library Journal*, January 1913.
20. *Proceedings*, June 4, December 22, 1913; January 4, 1915.
21. *Proceedings*, April 20, December 13, 1915.
22. Bertram to Strohm, July 22, 1915, DPL Correspondence, Carnegie Fund folder 1901–1920, Box 29.
23. *Annual Report 1914–15*, pp. 9, 10.
24. Detroit *Journal*, September 22, 1916.
25. Detroit *Journal*, September 23, 1916.
26. *Annual Report 1914–15*, pp. 13, 14.
27. *Proceedings*, April 5, May 1, November 2, December 18, 1917. Bertram to Strohm, November 23, 1917, Carnegie Corporation microfilms.
28. *Proceedings*, March 17, May 1, November 2, 1917.
29. *Proceedings*, November 6, 1917.
30. *Proceedings*, May 25, September 16, 1915; November 2, 1916; October 22, 1918.
31. DPL Correspondence, New Main Library Inquiries, Suggestions folder, Box 32; Tunnel Under Woodward folder, Box 33. *Proceedings*, March 2, 1920.

32. *Proceedings,* November 5, 1918; July 25, January 7, September 16, November 18, 1919; January 20, November 23, November 24, 1920. DPL Correspondence, Ralph Stone to Strohm, November 10, 1919, New Main Library General folder, Box 32.
33. *Proceedings,* December 14, 1920.
34. *Proceedings,* February 14, March 1, April 19, June 7, 1921. DPL Correspondence 1921, Dedication New Main folder, Box 5.
35. For a complete description of the Main Library of 1921, including illustrations and floor plans, see *Library Service* (Special Number), V, No. 15 (June 15, 1922).

Chapter 14

1. *Annual Report 1896,* p. 10.
2. Detroit *Free Press,* December 13, 1868.
3. *Annual Report 1881,* p. 116.
4. *Annual Report 1884,* p. 147.
5. *Annual Report 1894,* p. 10.
6. *Proceedings,* November 8, 1894; February 23, 1895.
7. Detroit *Free Press,* May 19, 1895.
8. *Annual Report 1896,* p. 10.
9. Detroit *News,* November 13, 1937. *Proceedings,* March 17, 1931.
10. *Annual Report 1896,* p. 11.
11. Detroit *Tribune,* September 6, 1896.
12. *Annual Reports 1901,* p. 34; *1903,* p. 17; *1908,* p. 17. *Proceedings,* January 7, 1897.
13. *Proceedings,* January 14, 1904.
14. *Annual Reports 1902,* p. 21; *1904,* p. 12; *1905,* p. 17. *Proceedings,* October 18, 1902; February 4, 1904.
15. *Proceedings,* January 14, 1904.
16. *Annual Report 1909,* p. 6.
17. *Annual Report 1910,* p. 12.
18. Detroit *Times,* April 10, 1931. *Proceedings,* May 5, 1914.
19. *Annual Reports 1913–14,* p. 17; *1915–16,* p. 10.
20. *Annual Report 1916–17,* p. 16.
21. *Annual Report 1922–23,* p. 10.
22. Detroit *Free Press,* April 26, 1874; June 10, 1877.
23. *Proceedings,* July 13, 1882; December 6, 1888. *Annual Report 1887,* p. 11.
24. *Annual Report 1888,* p. 6.
25. *Proceedings,* September 19, 1889. *Annual Reports 1888,* p. 15; *1889,* p. 6; *1890,* p. 11.
26. *Annual Reports 1890,* pp. 11, 12; *1891,* pp. 6, 13; *1892,* p. 19.
27. *Annual Reports 1900,* p. 14; *1902,* p. 18; *1910,* p. 32; *1912,* p. 33.
28. *Annual Report 1896,* pp. 14–15.

29. *Proceedings,* September 17, 1896.
30. *Proceedings,* October 6, 1914. *Annual Report 1924–25,* p. 13.
31. *Proceedings,* January 18, 1906; January 3, 1907.
32. *Library Service,* X, No. 2 (November 15, 1926), 13.
33. *Annual Report 1944–45,* p. 8.
34. *Annual Reports 1891,* p. 5.
35. *Annual Reports 1925–26,* p. 13; *1930–31,* p. 6.
36. *Annual Report 1957–58,* p. 3.
37. *Annual Report 1918–19,* p. 9.

Chapter 15

1. *Annual Report 1887,* p. 8.
2. *Annual Report 1892,* p. 8.
3. *Annual Reports 1920–21,* p. 5; *1921–22,* p. 4.
4. *Annual Report 1925–26,* p. 7.
5. *Post-War Standards for Public Libraries* (Chicago, 1943), p. 20.
6. Ulveling, Ralph A., "The Years Ahead," in *Annual Report 1942–43,* pp. 5–6.
7. Malone, Richard, "The Public Library and Mass Media," in *Annual Report 1950–51,* pp. 26–27.
8. *Annual Report 1890,* p. 8.
9. *Proceedings,* September 4, 1890; March 3, 1886.
10. *Proceedings,* April 15, 1886.
11. *Annual Report 1904,* p. 7.
12. *Annual Report 1942–43,* p. 7.
13. DPL Correspondence, Estimates folder, Box 1.
14. *Annual Report 1929–30,* p. 6.
15. *Annual Report 1939–40,* p. 9.
16. *Annual Report 1960–61,* p. 8.
17. *Annual Report 1882,* p. 139.
18. *Annual Report 1952–53,* p. 5.
19. Detroit *Journal,* January 1, 1898.
20. *Annual Report 1923–24,* p. 5.
21. *Annual Report 1926–27,* p. 5.
22. *Annual Reports 1946–47,* p. 9; *1949–50,* p. 10.
23. *Annual Report 1892,* p. 15.
24. DPL Correspondence, Librarian's Correspondence file 1920–21, Books folder, Box 14.
25. *Annual Report 1928–29,* p. 12.
26. *Annual Report 1950–51,* pp. 18–23.
27. Butzel to Utley, February 21, 1895, DPL Correspondence, Commission folder, Box 1.
28. *Proceedings,* January 12, 1882.
29. Detroit *Free Press,* June 10, 1877.

30. *Annual Report 1884*, pp. 146–47.
31. *Ibid.*, p. 145.
32. *Annual Report 1923–24*, p. 21.
33. *Proceedings*, December 3, 1896; April 4, 1901. *Annual Reports 1903*, p. 16; *1925–26*, p. 10.
34. *Annual Reports 1912*, p. 10; *1915–16*, p. 5; *1919–20*, p. 3.
35. *Annual Reports 1904*, p. 14; *1915–16*, p. 13; *1922–23*, p. 17; *1927–28*, p. 13. *Library Service*, XVI, No. 3 (Spring 1939), 5.
36. *Library Service*, XVI, No. 1 (Autumn 1938), 8.
37. Chancellor, John M., "Is Detroit Again Pointing the Way?" *Bulletin of the American Library Association*, XXVIII, No. 5 (May 1934), pp. 232, 274.
38. *Proceedings*, June 6, 1889; December 3, December 17, 1896. *Annual Reports 1896*, pp. 5, 17; *1897*, p. 5.
39. *Library Service*, III, No. 3 (October 1, 1919), 4; IV, No. 10 (January 1, 1921), p. 3. *Annual Report 1928–29*, p. 10.
40. *Annual Report 1950–51*, pp. 35, 36.
41. *Proceedings*, May 5, 1909.
42. *Library Service* (supplement) IV, No. 11 (January 15, 1921), 4. *Annual Reports 1944–45*, p. 10; *1949–50*, p. 10.
43. *Proceedings*, September 9, 1947. *Annual Report 1946–47*, p. 10.
44. Ogburn, William F., quoted in *Current Issues in Library Administration* (Chicago, 1938), p. 137.

Chapter 16

1. *Proceedings*, February 7, 1895.
2. DPL Correspondence, Newspaper folder, Box 5.
3. *Ibid.*
4. DPL Correspondence, Books folder, 1938–39, Box 22.
5. DPL Correspondence, Newspaper folder, 1922–23, Box 6.
6. Act 38, Public Acts of 1931.
7. Detroit *Free Press*, May 18, 1944.
8. *PM*, June 2, 1944.
9. This statement and the following account of what was said at the meeting are included in "Transcript of Opinions Expressed at a Special Meeting of the Detroit Library Commission, May 23, 1944," mimeograph, 18 pp., copy in Home Reading Services, DPL.
10. Staff Memo: Branch Librarians and Department Heads, from Charles M. Mohrhardt, associate librarian, May 24, 1944, in *Strange Fruit* folder, DPL Correspondence.
11. Detroit *Free Press*, May 28, 1944.
12. Ulveling to Byron C. Hopkins, June 5, 1944, in *Strange Fruit* folder, DPL Correspondence.
13. Quoted in Detroit *News*, April 25, 1954.

14. A complete transcript of testimony and opinions in People *vs* Butler is in the DPL (R 810.93 ZG 875B9).
15. *Annual Report 1956–57*, p. 4.

Chapter 17

1. Detroit *Free Press,* June 17, June 20, 1914. See also DPL Correspondence, Miscellaneous, Scrapbook Clippings folder, Box 33, and Strohm folder, Box 3. Also *Detroit Saturday Night,* June 27, 1914.
2. DPL Correspondence 1936–37, Books folder, Box 20.
3. "Adam Strohm—A Memorial, December 1951," in Burton Historical Collection, Strohm reading room file.
4. Hazel B. Timmerman to Strohm, May 14, 1928, in DPL Correspondence, Extension Dept. folder, Box 13.
5. *Proceedings,* October 8, 1885.
6. Detroit *Tribune,* September 6, 1901.
7. *Annual Report 1908,* p. 19.
8. Strohm to George N. Fuller, July 3, 1920, in DPL Correspondence 1919–20, F Miscellaneous folder, Box 17.
9. *Annual Report 1947–48,* p. 6.
10. *Proceedings,* November 2, 1954.
11. *Annual Report 1946–47,* p. 7.
12. *Annual Report 1935–36,* p. 6.
13. *Annual Report 1937–38,* p. 6.
14. *Annual Report 1944–45,* p. 13.
15. *Proceedings,* October 5, 1954.
16. *Annual Report 1905,* p. 9.
17. *Annual Report 1883,* p. 48.
18. *Annual Report 1897,* pp. 7–8.
19. Duffield to Smith, July 20, 1913, in DPL Correspondence, Civil Service folder, Box 2. For prior correspondence on this matter see *Proceedings,* June 13, 1913.
20. Duffield to Strohm, February 3, 1922, DPL Correspondence 1922–23, Detroit Library Commission folder, Box 6.
21. *Proceedings,* September 17, 1940; January 7, 1941.
22. *Proceedings,* September 20, 1960.
23. *Proceedings,* June 19, 1903; November 11, 1909; January 1, March 2, 1910. *Annual Reports 1911,* p. 17; *1918–19,* p. 6.
24. *Proceedings,* January 5, 1937.
25. *Proceedings,* September 18, 1956.
26. *Proceedings,* March 8, 1927; November 29, 1955; November 21, 1961. *Annual Reports 1942–43,* p. 10; *1955–56,* p. 2.
27. *Proceedings,* July 1, 1884.
28. *Annual Report 1911,* p. 7. See also various items in DPL Correspondence, Pension System folder, Box 2.

29. *Annual Reports 1913–14,* p. 6; *1924–25,* p. 4; *1926–27,* p. 3; *1936–37,* p. 3. *Proceedings,* April 21, 1925; July 7, 1936; June 8, 1937.
30. *Proceedings,* March 1, 1938. *Annual Report 1937–38,* p. 4.
31. *Proceedings,* May 2, 1946.
32. *Annual Report 1945–46,* p. 5. *Proceedings,* February 5, 1957.

Chapter 18

1. Farmer, *The History of Detroit. . . . ,* p. 714.
2. *Proceedings,* July 11, 1885; February 13, 1886. *Annual Report 1885,* p. 66. "Agreement between Detroit Scientific Association and Detroit Public Library, July 24, 1885," in Burton Historical Collection.
3. Detroit *Free Press,* February 18, 1888.
4. *Proceedings,* February 18, March 4, March 18, 1886; March 3, 1892. *Annual Report 1886,* pp. 78, 83–84.
5. *Proceedings,* March 3, May 12, September 3, November 11, 1892; January 5, March 23, April 20, 1893. *Annual Reports 1892,* p. 6; *1893,* p. 6.
6. *Proceedings,* February 7, 1895. *Annual Report 1895,* p. 15.
7. *Proceedings,* January 9, February 6, June 4, August 20, 1896; December 13, 1900.
8. *Proceedings,* March 18, 1897.
9. *Proceedings,* January 21, 1897.
10. *Proceedings,* March 3, 1898; December 20, 1900. *Annual Reports 1900,* p. 16; *1901,* p. 36.
11. *Proceedings,* July 20, August 24, 1910. *Annual Report 1910,* p. 6.
12. *Proceedings,* February 2, March 1, 1921; December 5, 1922; May 1, 1923. *Annual Reports 1923–24,* p. 20; *1925–26,* p. 24.
13. *Annual Report 1925–26,* p. 24. DPL Correspondence 1926–27, Medical Science Dept. folder, Box 11.
14. Biddle, Andrew P., "From the Library Committee," *Detroit Medical News,* XXXII, No. 17 (December 23, 1940), 5.
15. *Proceedings,* January 8, 1935; January 19, November 2, 1937. *Annual Report 1947–48,* p. 4.
16. *Proceedings,* June 17, 1947; January 20, 1948; January 4, 1949; February 2, 1954. *Annual Report 1946–47,* p. 11.
17. *Proceedings,* January 13, 1883; March 4, 1886; February 2, 1887. *Annual Reports 1885,* p. 185; *1887,* p. 12; *1891,* p. 18.
18. Farmer, *The History of Detroit. . . . ,* pp. 696–70. *Proceedings,* March 19, 1900.
19. *Proceedings,* January 7, 1914.
20. Detroit *Free Press,* November 18, 1911.
21. *Annual Report 1913–14,* p. 19.
22. *Proceedings,* March 16, 1914.

23. DPL Correspondence, Burton Historical Collection folder, Box 2. *Annual Report 1913–14,* pp. 9, 19.
24. DPL Correspondence, Strohm to Public Lighting Commission, January 18, 1915, Burton Historical Collection folder, Box 2. Detroit *Free Press,* September 21, 1915.
25. Strohm to Burton, May 19, 1915, DPL Correspondence, Clarence M. Burton folder, Box 2.
26. *Proceedings,* July 13, 1926.
27. Burton, Patricia Owens, *Clarence M. Burton, Detroit's Historian* (Detroit, 1953), p. 76.
28. *Annual Report 1924–25,* p. 17.
29. *Proceedings,* January 4, 1927; October 16, 1929.
30. *Annual Reports 1920–21,* p. 4; *1958–59,* p. 2. *Proceedings,* May 23, 1950.
31. Krum to Strohm, December 11, 1914, DPL Correspondence, Burton Historical Collection folder, Box 2.
32. *Proceedings,* November 1, 1921.
33. *Annual Report 1943–44,* p. 9.

Chapter 19

1. Detroit *Tribune,* August 4, 1899.
2. *Annual Report 1940–41,* p. 7.
3. DPL Correspondence 1924–25, Business Manager folder, Box 8. *Proceedings,* October 27, 1925.
4. *Proceedings,* September 10, 1946. *Annual Report 1945–46,* p. 7.
5. *Annual Report 1947–48,* p. 3.
6. *Annual Report 1949–50,* p. 8.
7. Organization Chart, DPL, January 25, 1962.
8. *Annual Report 1892,* pp. 9, 17.
9. *Proceedings,* January 16, 1908.
10. DPL Correspondence 1924–25, Commission folder, Box 8.
11. *Annual Report 1943–44,* pp. 6–7.
12. "DPL Branch Library Program Survey 1957," compiled by Community and Group Services.
13. King, Kenneth E., "Community and Group Services," *Among Friends,* Winter 1957–58.
14. *The Michigan Librarian,* XXIX, No. 4 (December 1963), 7.
15. *Annual Report, DBE, 1875,* Report of the Committee on Library, p. 76.
16. *Annual Report 1883,* p. 47.
17. *Annual Report 1884,* p. 148.
18. *Ibid.,* p. 135.
19. *Proceedings,* December 7, 1893. *Annual Report 1893,* p. 11.
20. *Annual Report 1896,* p. 10.

21. *Annual Report 1902,* p. 17.
22. *Annual Report 1915–16,* p. 8.
23. *Annual Report 1943–44,* p. 6.
24. *Annual Report 1921–22,* p. 5.
25. Harris, Katherine G., "Metropolitan Reference Services: Patterns, Problems, Solutions," *Library Journal,* LXXXVIII, No. 8 (April 15, 1963), 1606.
26. *Ibid.,* 1607.
27. *Proceedings,* October 20, 1959.

Chapter 20

1. *Proceedings,* September 24, 1891.
2. *Annual Report 1891,* p. 12.
3. *Library Service,* II, No. 19 (June 1, 1919), pp. 2, 3.
4. Lovett, William P., *Detroit Governs Itself* (Boston, 1930), pp. 20–21.
5. See Isabel Weadock to Strohm, April 7, 1917, in DPL Correspondence 1916–18, Museum of Art folder 1916–18. Miss Weadock wrote: "It must make you feel that all your struggle for Detroit has not been in vain."
6. *Annual Report 1915–16,* p. 14.
7. *Library Service,* I, No. 4 (November 3, 1917), 2.
8. *Annual Report 1918–19,* p. 8.
9. *Library Service,* II, No. 11 (February 1, 1919), 3.
10. *Annual Report 1928–29,* p. 5.
11. Norton, William J., "Henry Glover Stevens, an Address Delivered January 6, 1939," (DPL, 1939). Detroit *Free Press,* February 13, 1934. *Annual Report 1937–38,* p. 3.
12. Sisson, Helen, "The Labor Collection of the Detroit Public Library," *Among Friends,* Summer 1961.
13. Strohm to City Clerk Richard Lindsay, November 20, 1918, DPL Correspondence 1916–18, City Clerk folder.
14. *Annual Report 1945–46,* p. 7.
15. *Proceedings,* April 17, 1945.
16. *Proceedings,* October 19, 1948; November 20, 1951.
17. DPL, *A Brief Historical Summary,* p. 14.
18. *Annual Report 1883,* p. 47.
19. *Annual Report 1884,* p. 135.
20. *Annual Report 1906,* p. 9. *Proceedings,* April 2, April 16, 1908.
21. *Annual Report 1915–16;* p. 9.
22. DPL Correspondence 1916–18, Strohm to M. McAllister, June 9, 1917, F Miscellaneous folder; Technology Department file. *Proceedings,* May 1, 1917.

23. *Library Service,* Vol. I, No. 6, December 1, 1917; pp. 1, 2.
24. *Annual Report 1917–18;* p. 6.
25. *Library Service,* Vol. II, No. 2, September 15, 1918; p. 4.
26. *Library Service,* Vol. III, No. 14, March 1, 1920; p. 1.
27. *Annual Report 1922–23;* p. 5.
28. DPL Correspondence 1932–33, memo Technology Department to Librarian, July 13, 1932, Technology Department folder, Box 17.
29. *Annual Report 1928–29;* p. 13.
30. Interview with Robert Runser, January 16, 1964.
31. *Annual Report 1958–59;* p. 5.
32. Runser interview, *supra.*
33. Bradley, James J.: "The Automotive History Collection," in *Among Friends,* Summer 1959.
34. *Proceedings,* February 1, 1944.
35. *Proceedings,* May 5, 1944.

Chapter 21

1. *Proceedings,* January 6, 1898.
2. *Annual Report 1898,* p. 5.
3. *Proceedings,* September 21, 1899.
4. *Annual Report 1914–15,* pp. 11–12.
5. *Annual Report 1915–16,* p. 6.
6. *Proceedings,* April 3, 1917.
7. *Proceedings,* April 5, 1917. Strohm to Col. Carl Reichmann, March 16, 1918, DPL Correspondence 1916–18, Books folder, Box 7.
8. *Proceedings,* November 12, 1917; March 5, June 4, 1918.
9. *Annual Report 1917–18,* p. 5.
10. DPL Correspondence, American Library Association 1917–18 folder, Box 8. *Annual Report 1916–17,* p. 11. *Proceedings,* August 7, 1917.
11. *Proceedings,* January 18, October 22, 1918.
12. *Annual Report 1917–18,* p. 6.
13. *Annual Report 1916–17,* pp. 11–13.
14. *Ibid.,* p. 18.
15. *Annual Report 1918–19,* p. 6.
16. D. Ashley Hooker, quarterly report Technology Department, October 1–December 31, 1918, DPL Correspondence, 1916–18, Technology folder, Box 9. *Annual Report 1918–19,* p. 8.
17. Grace A. England to Strohm, August 20, 1915, DPL Correspondence, Municipal and Social Service Division folder, Box 2; Strohm to Thomas F. Farrell, February 11, 1916, Inquiries folder, Box 2.
18. *Library Service,* L, No. 15 (April 15, 1918), 2.
19. DPL Correspondence 1916–18, Americanization Committee folder, Box 2.

20. *Annual Report 1923–24,* p. 19.
21. *Annual Report 1941–42,* p. 1.
22. *Proceedings,* November 5, 1940.
23. *Annual Report 1941–42,* pp. 3–7. American Library Association, "Libraries and the War," (n.p., 1942).
24. *Annual Report 1945–46,* p. 8.
25. See various contemporary Detroit newspaper accounts, June 21–27, 1943; New York *Times,* June 28, 1943. Also World War II Records Division, National Archives and Records Service, Washington.
26. "The Events of the Week of June 20th," (DPL, June 24, 1943).
27. Ulveling, Ralph A., "From Rioting to Reading—A Case Study," *Bulletin of the American Library Association,* XXXVII, No. 8 (September 1943), pp. 255–57.
28. Ulveling, Ralph A., "The Public Library in the Large Community," in *The Library in the Community,* Leon Carnovsky and Lowell Martin, eds. (Chicago, 1944), pp. 23–27.
29. *Annual Report 1944–45,* pp. 6–7.
30. Ulveling, Ralph A., "Areas of Service to War-Affected Populations," *Bulletin of the American Library Association,* XXXVIII, No. 4 (April 1944), pp. 132–34.
31. *Proceedings,* September 4, 1951; September 18, 1962.

Chapter 22

1. Proposed chapter in report for Carnegie Corporation (ca. 1933), typescript in Burton Historical Collection. (Hereafter referred to as Carnegie Report.)
2. Carnegie Report, p. 2.
3. *Annual Report 1929–30,* p. 14.
4. *Annual Report 1931–32,* p. 10.
5. Carnegie Report, p. 10.
6. *Annual Report 1931–32,* p. 3.
7. *Proceedings,* December 19, 1930.
8. Mayor Frank Murphy to Dr. Andrew P. Biddle, August 22, 1931, in Burton Historical Collection.
9. Carnegie Report, p. 3.
10. *Proceedings,* May 6, 1930. *Annual Report 1930–31,* p. 5.
11. *Annual Report 1931–32,* p. 9. Carnegie Report, p. 4.
12. Strohm to Biddle, July 18, 1932, DPL Correspondence 1932–33, Registration Charge folder, Box 16. *Proceedings,* March 15, 1934.
13. *Annual Report 1931–32,* pp. 6, 8.
14. Carnegie Report, p. 6.
15. *Ibid.*
16. *Annual Report 1936–37,* p. 12.
17. *Annual Report 1935–36,* pp. 3, 5.

18. *Annual Report 1916–17*, p. 6.
19. *Proceedings,* January 21, 1919.
20. *Proceedings,* February 4, 1919; August 17, October 8, 1920. *Annual Reports 1919–20,* p. 2; *1925–26,* p. 4.
21. *Proceedings,* September 12, 1922; September 18, November 20, 1923. *Annual Report 1921–22,* p. 5.
22. *Proceedings,* January 14, January 18, May 3, June 7, September 7, October 10, October 18, October 23, December 6, 1927.
23. *Proceedings,* June 18, November 19, 1929. *Annual Report 1928–29,* p. 4.
24. *Proceedings,* September 15, 1930.
25. *Proceedings,* October 14, 1930.
26. *Annual Report 1929–30,* p. 3.
27. *Proceedings,* March 3, 17, 1931. *Annual Report 1930–31,* p. 4. DPL Correspondence 1932–33, Downtown Library folder, Box 17.

Chapter 23

1. *Annual Report 1899,* p. 11.
2. *Annual Report 1904,* p. 8.
3. *Proceedings,* October 8, 1920.
4. *Proceedings,* November 9, December 21, 1920. Additional data furnished by Walter Kaiser, Wayne County librarian, from Wayne County Library records.
5. "Wayne County Library," a typescript history of the Wayne County Library system (ca. 1935), Wayne County Library, Wayne, Mich.
6. *Proceedings,* December 15, 1959.
7. *42nd Annual Report, 1962,* Wayne County Library System.
8. *Annual Report 1942–43,* p. 3. For material on the Wayne County Library see DPL Correspondence 1919–20, County Libraries folder; also 1921, Wayne County Library Service folder.
9. *Annual Report 1959–60,* p. 2.
10. Detroit *Free Press,* June 12, 1877.
11. *Annual Report 1905,* p. 13.
12. *Annual Report 1939–40,* p. 8.
13. DPL Correspondence, War Defense Area folder, Box 23.
14. *Proceedings,* June 21, 1949. *Annual Report 1949–50,* p. 11.
15. *Proceedings,* April 15, 1958; October 10, December 12, 1961. *Detroit Legal News,* May 23, 1963.
16. *Annual Report 1955–56,* p. 2.
17. *Proceedings,* October 20, 1959.
18. Harris, "Metropolitan Reference Services. . . ," *Library Journal,* LXXXVIII, No. 8, 1608.
19. *Annual Reports 1937–38,* p. 4; *1939–40,* p. 4.

20. For annual State grants see records of the Budget Bureau, City of Detroit, and annual reports, DPL.
21. *Annual Report 1944–45*, p. 2.
22. *Proceedings,* June 29, 1948; January 18, March 1, 1949. *Annual Report 1948–49*, pp. 3, 9.

Chapter 24

1. Minutes of meeting September 24, 1942, records of Friends of the Detroit Public Library, Inc.
2. *Annual Report 1903*, p. 3. *Proceedings,* November 6, 1917.
3. *Annual Report 1947–48*, pp. 7–8.
4. *Annual Report 1943–44*, p. 6.
5. *Annual Report, DBE, 1865*, Report of the Committee on Library, p. 20.
6. *Annual Report, DBE, 1866*, Report of the Committee on Library, pp. 6, 15.
7. DPL, *A Brief Historical Summary*, p. 40.
8. *Annual Report 1886*, p. 78.
9. *Annual Report 1887*, p. 12.
10. Strohm to Commission, May 10, 1937, in DPL Correspondence 1936–37, Commission folder, Box 20.
11. Interview with Mabel L. Conat, January 23, 1963.
12. *Annual Report 1942–43*, p. 8.
13. *Ibid.*, p. 18.
14. Smith, Hal H., "Making Friends for Books," *DTC* [Detroit Trust Company] *Quarterly,* Autumn 1943.
15. *Among Friends,* No. 31, Summer 1963.
16. Conat interview, January 23, 1963.
17. *Proceedings,* April 18, 1944.
18. *Annual Report 1952–53*, p. 3. *Proceedings,* January 8, 1946.
19. Interview with Frances Brewer, January 20, 1963.
20. *Library Service,* V, No. 6 (December 15, 1921), 1.
21. "Friends for Twenty Years 1942–1962," (Friends of the Detroit Public Library, Inc., October 16, 1962).
22. *Annual Report 1944–45*, p. 23.

Chapter 25

1. *Proceedings,* May 5, 1925.
2. *Annual Report 1927–28*, p. 3.
3. *Proceedings,* February 15, May 3, 1955. *Annual Report 1956–57*, pp. 2, 3.
4. *Proceedings,* February 18, August 13, 1958; September 1, 1959.
5. *Proceedings,* January 8, 1924.

6. *Proceedings,* December 23, 1926.
7. *Annual Report 1925–26,* p. 3.
8. A picture of the enlargement of the Library with the wings, proposed by Cass Gilbert, was shown in the 1942–43 annual report.
9. *Annual Report 1925–26,* p. 10.
10. *Annual Report 1928–29,* p. 3.
11. *Ibid.,* p. 7.
12. *Annual Report 1929–30,* p. 4.
13. *Annual Report 1942–43,* pp. 8–9.
14. *Proceedings,* May 16, 1944.
15. *Annual Report 1942–43,* p. 9.
16. *Annual Report 1943–44,* p. 13.
17. *Proceedings,* December 17, 1944; February 18, 1947; September 14, 1948. *Annual Report 1948–49,* p. 1.
18. *Proceedings,* February 2, 1954.
19. *Annual Report 1956–57,* p. 2.
20. *Annual Report 1957–58,* p. 1.
21. *Annual Report 1959–60,* p. 1.
22. Detroit *Free Press,* June 23, 1963.
23. Ulveling, Ralph A., "Detroit Doubles into Three," *Library Journal,* December 1, 1963, p. 4531.

INDEX

469

483